# THE
# EVANGELICALS

# THE EVANGELICALS

## A Historical, Thematic, and Biographical Guide

ROBERT H. KRAPOHL
AND
CHARLES H. LIPPY

**Greenwood Press**
Westport, Connecticut • London

**Library of Congress Cataloging-in-Publication Data**

Krapohl, Robert H.
    The evangelicals : a historical, thematic, and biographical guide
    /  Robert H. Krapohl and Charles H. Lippy.
      p.  cm.
    Includes bibliographical references and index.
    ISBN 0–313–30103–4 (alk. paper)
    1. Evangelical work—United States—History.   I. Lippy, Charles
H.  II. Title.
  BV3773.K73    1999
  280'.4'0973—DC21     98–30499

British Library Cataloguing in Publication Data is available.

Library of Congress Catalog Card Number: 98–30499
ISBN: 0–313–30103–4

First published in 1999

Greenwood Press, 88 Post Road West, Westport, CT 06881
An imprint of Greenwood Publishing Group, Inc.

Printed in the United States of America

The paper used in this book complies with the
Permanent Paper Standard issued by the National
Information Standards Organization (Z39.48–1984).

10 9 8 7 6 5 4 3 2 1

# Contents

**PART II:   Themes and Issues in Modern American
  Evangelicalism**

**PART III:   A Biographical Dictionary of Modern American
  Evangelical Leaders**

# Preface

When many Americans think of their religious identities, particularly if they come from within the Christian tradition, they look to a denominational heritage—the Baptists, the Methodists, the Catholics, or any one of countless others. Greenwood Press has recognized that way of looking at religion in American culture through its series on Denominations in America. Yet more and more Americans also think of themselves in terms that cut across denominational boundaries or elude them altogether. Such is the case with evangelicals, who are found in almost all the traditional denominations, dominating some and remaining a vital minority in others.

We believe that examination of those religious styles and identities that defy denominational limits is as important as looking at denominations and groups if one is to have a solid understanding of the contours of American religious life. Hence we have adapted the model of the Denominations in America series to scrutinize the people, institutions, and religious culture of modern American evangelicalism. We divide our book into three sections. The first will look at the history of modern American evangelicalism, after wrestling with issues of describing and defining this vital, but sometimes elusive, movement. Although American evangelicalism has a rich history in the United States, as discussed in chapter 2, we focus on the period from after the Civil War to the close of the twentieth century and call it "modern." We found that telling the story of modern American evangelicals chronologically sometimes obscured vital thematic developments or long-term issues that cried out for fuller treatment. Hence in the second section, our major alteration of the format that characterizes the Denominations in America series, we look at selected themes and issues, ranging from evangelical piety and worship to the interplay of evangelical currents with popular culture. The third section, like the Denominations series, provides biographical vignettes of nearly sixty-five individuals whose work was critical to the shaping of American evangelicalism in the late nineteenth and twentieth centuries. In the narrative sections, we have not included detailed documentation about the life or work of any individuals whose biography is profiled in the last part. Rather, an asterisk before a name indicates that a profile of that individual appears in the last section. There, following the brief summary of an individual's life and evaluation of the contribution made to evangelical developments, works by the person profiled appear under the letter ''A'' while other biographical profiles and secondary works about the subject appear under the letter ''B.''

At the end of both Part I and Part II is a bibliography of materials pertinent to that section. It does not include every work cited, but highlights only those sources pertaining to modern American evangelicalism. As well, works about specific figures profiled in Part III are included only in the bibliographical citations following the individual profiles, not in the bibliographies for the other sections.

Had other scholars tackled this project, they would no doubt have selected different individuals to profile and different themes to address in the second section of the book. We are keenly aware, for example, that the more strident fundamentalist wing of the evangelical heritage, particularly those who are popularly known as ''separatist fundamentalists,'' appear here to receive short shrift. When we outlined the material for this book, we knew that some colleagues were at that time considering a companion book that would deal only with the fundamentalist wing of evangelicalism. After we learned that a companion volume was not to be forthcoming at the same time, we pondered whether we could expand our effort to embrace more of the fundamentalist story and its leaders. All too quickly we realized that to do so responsibly would require a book too large to be useful. Hence, as with any scholarly endeavor, we recognize the subjective element in material we chose to include and the material that we had to omit, often reluctantly.

Even before we had met in person, we agreed to embark on this project together. Lippy sought out Krapohl as a collaborator after reading and editing Krapohl's piece on the *Christian Advocate* that Krapohl wrote for another Greenwood book, *Popular Religious Magazines of the United States*, which Lippy edited with Mark Fackler. Because one of us (Lippy) is a professor of religious studies and one (Krapohl) a reference librarian, we chose to divide writing assignments rather than working together on each chapter or biographical profile. But each of us carefully read, critiqued, and reviewed again the work of the other. Lippy bears primary responsibility for chapters 2, 3, 5, 6, 7, 8, 10, 12, 13, 14, and 15; Krapohl bears primary responsibility for chapters 1, 4, 9, and 11 and all the biographical entries.

Coordinating the writing was something of a challenge, particularly because Krapohl was living in Texas and Lippy in Tennessee during most of the four years we labored together. Because each of us worked somewhat independently of the other, we offer individual acknowledgments.

Robert H. Krapohl
Charles H. Lippy

Special thanks go to Mardelle Brown of Back to the Bible Ministries, Jamie Puckett and Dan Stuck of Josh McDowell Ministries, Bob Shuster of the Billy Graham Center, and Keith Wells of Trinity International University for providing information about the lives of several subjects of the biographical profiles. Colleagues in the Social Science and Humanities Department of the Baylor University Library, while sometimes perplexed by the time I spent on this book, were unfailingly supportive. They include Bill Hair, Lynn Ball, Pat Bibb, Phil Jones, John Mosley, Janet Sheets, Ethel Walton, and my dean, Avery Sharp. I could not have completed my work without the assistance of the Interlibrary Loan department.

My teaching colleagues at Baylor, Jim Barcus, Mike Beaty, Barry Hankins, and Bill Pitts, willingly offered their expertise, as did my fellow scholar-librarian, John Gresham of Franciscan University. My sincere thanks also go to my collaborator, Chuck Lippy. When Chuck approached me about this project, I jumped at the chance to work with such an esteemed historian of American religion. I have little doubt that Chuck has often wondered what he got himself into when he took me on as a writing partner. Almost always supportive, Chuck has not hesitated to go to the whip on a couple of occasions in order to move his novice and recalcitrant collaborator. For his patience, encouragement, editorial wisdom, and friendship, I am grateful beyond words. From the joy and the ordeal of this project, I have learned some lasting lessons from the master, Professor Lippy.

Authors often become unrecognizable beasts who were once known as spouses and parents. Because of the dislocations that this project caused my family, I offer my greatest love and appreciation to my wife Laura, daughters Ashley and Bethany, and son Benjamin.

—Robert H. Krapohl

Were I to list all those whom I wrote, telephoned, or sent an e-mail asking for help in tracking down a source or verifying a citation, I would need many pages. Those are always the unsung heroes and heroines whose help makes any book possible. To all those who assisted me in such endeavors, I offer my gratitude. My own understanding of evangelicalism, its richness and its burdens, has been stimulated by countless conversations with other historians of American religion. I have benefited especially from insights I gained in the writings of and conversations with Wayne Flynt, Nancy Hardesty, David E. Harrell Jr., Merrill Hawkins, and Bill J. Leonard.

As has been the case for several years, I have made use of the wealth of resources available through the Woodruff Library and Pitts Theological Library at Emory University. I am appreciative as well of the Interlibrary Loan staff of the Lupton Library at the University of Tennessee at Chattanooga for tracking down so many items for me.

My colleagues in the Department of Philosophy and Religion at the University of Tennessee at Chattanooga are always collegial and understanding; it is a joy to work with them. I am particularly grateful to my department head, Herbert Burhenn, and dean, Tim Summerlin, for released time in the spring of 1997. A semester freed from classroom responsibilities allowed me the large blocks of time needed to write my portions of this book.

It has been a particular joy to work with Rob Krapohl. I have learned much from his meticulous scholarship, sensitivity to nuance in writing, and the deft way he applies a critical eye to the very religious style that nurtures him.

—Charles H. Lippy

# Abbreviations

| | |
|---|---|
| ABMU | American Baptist Missionary Union |
| ACCC | American Council of Christian Churches |
| BBU | Baptist Bible Union |
| BIOLA | Bible Institute of Los Angeles |
| BGEA | Billy Graham Evangelistic Association |
| CAM | Central American Mission |
| CBA | Christian Booksellers Association |
| CBC | Columbia Bible College |
| CBN | Christian Broadcasting Network |
| CIM | China Inland Mission |
| CMA | Christian and Missionary Alliance |
| COGICS | Church of God in Christ Singers |
| CURE | Christians United for Reformation |
| ERA | Equal Rights Amendment |
| ETS | Evangelical Theological Society |
| FCA | Fellowship of Christian Athletes |
| FGBMFI | Full Gospel Business Men's Fellowship International |
| GBA | Gospel Broadcasting Association |

| | |
|---|---|
| ICBI | International Council for Biblical Inerrancy |
| ICCC | International Council of Christian Churches |
| ICFG | International Church of the Foursquare Gospel |
| ISCC | International Council of Churches |
| ITC | Interdenominational Theological Center |
| IVCF | InterVarsity Christian Fellowship |
| KJV | King James Version |
| NAE | National Association of Evangelicals |
| NBEA | National Black Evangelical Association |
| NRB | National Religious Broadcasters |
| OPC | Orthodox Presbyterian Church |
| ORU | Oral Roberts University |
| PFM | Prison Fellowship Ministries |
| SBC | Southern Baptist Convention |
| SBL | Society for Biblical Literature |
| SCLC | Southern Christian Leadership Conference |
| SVM | Student Volunteer Movement |
| TEAM | The Evangelical Alliance Mission |
| WCFA | World's Christian Fundamentals Association |
| WCTU | Women's Christian Temperance Union |
| YFC | Youth for Christ |
| YMCA | Young Men's Christian Association |
| YWAM | Youth With a Mission |
| YWCA | Young Women's Christian Association |

# Part I
# A History of Modern American Evangelicalism

# 1
# Describing American Evangelicalism

How should one define an "evangelical"? In the more than twenty years since this term burst into public consciousness with the 1976 U.S. presidential campaign of *Jimmy Carter, little of the confusion surrounding it has cleared. Although students of American religious history know that evangelicals were "there all the time," popular attention in Carter's campaign made the group seem like a *de novo* creation of the news media. Confusion surrounding the definition is understandable. Even so-called experts have a difficult time keeping the players straight. Witness the response of Foy Valentine, former head of the Southern Baptist Convention's Christian Life Commission, when asked if his Baptists were evangelicals:

Southern Baptists are *not* evangelicals. They want to claim us because we are big and successful and growing every year. But we have our own traditions, our own hymns, and more students in our seminaries than they have in all theirs put together. We don't share politics or their fussy fundamentalism and we don't want to get involved in their theological witch-hunts.[1]

Valentine's statement concatenated "evangelical" with "fundamentalist" in a most inaccurate way. Unfortunately, this misrepresentation was complicated further three years later when the media began to confuse American Protestant fundamentalism with the Muslim Shi'ite ideology of the Ayatollah Khomeini.[2] Additionally, Valentine's unequivocal assertion that Southern Baptists were not evangelicals surprised many observers of evangelicalism, not to mention a few Southern Baptists.

This, however, gets back to the definitional difficulty facing us, for as George Barna said in 1992, "almost nobody—including the people you might classify as evangelicals on the basis of their beliefs and practices—knows what the term 'evangelical' means.''[3] Like many terms, evangelicalism carries a good deal of historical baggage. Circumstances over time have dictated its usage (or non-usage) by various groups in American history. As succeeding chapters unfold the history of American evangelicalism, a clearer definition will emerge.

Before proceeding to that history, it is legitimate to raise the issue of relevance. Why should we be concerned with the question of who or what an evangelical is? In late twentieth-century America, ''religion increasingly is considered more a matter of private or subjective feeling than of shared meaning.''[4] Is it really significant if I know what you believe religiously as long as I respect your legal right to hold your own opinions? This extreme privatization of religion is not only misplaced, but erroneous, for people cannot keep deeply held religious beliefs exclusively to themselves. As belief contributes to social identity and determines conduct, our religion—that which is of ultimate significance to us—inevitably impinges on others.[5] So, if we can argue that evangelicalism is, at least partly, a public display of religion, then we need to be familiar with its belief structure.

Another reason why an understanding of evangelicalism is important is the prominent role that it has played in American religious history. Robert T. Handy, for example, claimed that the evangelical denominations were dominant in American history, particularly in the nineteenth century.[6] In the last fifteen years or so, that role has been increasingly highlighted in a myriad of books, surveys, and articles. While Martin Marty could lament in 1982 about the ''paucity of good research'' on evangelicalism,[7] just thirteen years later, Stephen Graham could stand amazed at the ''extraordinary amount of attention'' this ''industry in itself'' had received since 1980.[8] Leading the way in this literary barrage is a group of self-consciously evangelical historians who have produced a series of carefully researched, yet highly readable, monographs and essays. Dubbed by some the ''evangelical mafia'' because of their common professional interests and their close personal friendships, this group has been led by Nathan O. Hatch and *George M. Marsden of the University of Notre Dame and Mark A. Noll of Wheaton College.[9] Their consistent goal over the past two decades has been to underscore the significant role of evangelicalism throughout U.S. history.[10]

An understanding of evangelicalism is also important because of the sheer number of people who identify with the subculture.[11] In a Gallup Poll taken from 11–14 May 1995, 39 percent of those surveyed considered themselves ''evangelical Christians.''[12] If this poll has any validity, and its findings are consistent with other surveys, then we are speaking of approximately 98 million Americans who would fit into this category.[13] Statistics are deceiving, and it is exceedingly difficult to establish a set of ''evangelical criteria'' that satisfy all interested parties. However, no matter what data one uses, American evangelicals are not an inconsequential group.

The briefest survey of evangelicalism makes plain the difficulty implicit in every attempt to define the term. To this end, Derek Tidball likens the defining process to gripping a bar of wet soap.[14] Randall Balmer, on the other hand, strives for an elusive *via media* between "an extended technical treatment" and "the kind of dismissive description suggested by [U.S. Supreme Court Justice] Potter Stewart's attempt to define pornography a few years back: 'I can't define it . . . but I know it when I see it.' '"[15] Many students of evangelicalism share the frustration evinced by Tidball and Balmer. However, for the past quarter of a century or so, observers have brought both normative and historical approaches to their analyses of evangelicalism, with one or the other tending to dominate. Neither approach exists in isolation from the other; both continue to inform modern historiographical disputes over the origins and present identity of evangelicalism.[16]

Those interested in establishing norms as benchmarks of evangelicalism tend to emphasize the beliefs and practices of the movement. In this context, "norm" should be understood as "a standard or rule regulating behavior in a social setting."[17] For observers outside the movement who profess disinterested, scientific interest in evangelicalism, this "normative and prescriptive" approach means a stress on statistics, polling data, and case studies.[18] For scholars within the evangelical orbit, the normative approach brings great emphasis upon beliefs as theological convictions. Typically, the normative analysis begins by noting and enumerating the beliefs and practices of self-proclaimed evangelicals. Next, these points are used to form a generic definition of evangelicalism. Finally, this generic and provisional definition becomes an archetype to measure the "evangelical-ness" of other religious groups.

Examples of evangelical norms created from polling data are legion. As mentioned, Gallup equates evangelicals with those who have had a "born-again" or salvation experience. By implication, this is considered to be the *sine qua non* of evangelicalism.[19] Barna, in his 1992 study, found that evangelicals: (1) said the Bible is very important to them; (2) strongly agree that the Bible is the written Word of God and totally accurate in all it teaches; (3) believe that God is the all-powerful, all-knowing, perfect creator of the universe who rules the world today; (4) believe that people's prayers have the power to change their circumstances; (5) consider themselves Christians; (6) read the Bible at least once a week, outside of church; (7) shared their religious beliefs with someone who had different beliefs within the last month; (8) have made a personal commitment to Jesus Christ that is still important in their lives today; and (9) believe that when they die they will go to heaven because they have confessed their sins and have accepted Christ as their savior.[20] One quickly gets a sense of just how complicated this approach can get, when one realizes that Robert Webber identified fourteen "subcultural evangelical groups" in his 1978 book.[21]

Whose beliefs and practices will be normative for evangelicalism as a whole? There has been a good deal of conflict in recent evangelical historiography over this issue. Disinterested or scientific observers must also contend with problems inherent in compiling polling data. What questions will be asked of which groups? Can meaningful categories be formulated by data that often contain more than a fair amount of variation and nuance among the range of comparable answers? Can issues of religious conviction be isolated empirically from environmental factors like geography, social and economic status, education levels, familial dynamics, and other matters, all of which complicate the process in an exponential fashion? More fundamentally, can religious conviction be adequately conveyed through a rigid scientific methodology? Postmodernists would ask if such a purported methodology is even posssible.

Difficulties inherent in the normative approach can be further illustrated by the many scholarly attempts to define evangelicalism by delineating a core set of theological convictions. Although examples are legion, a few must suffice. John Gerstner is typical of those who define contemporary evangelicalism with a Christological focus that dwells on the unique being and mission of the God-man, Jesus. For Gerstner, the uniqueness of Jesus is conveyed through an emphasis on five important beliefs: (1) the efficacy of miracles, (2) the virgin birth, (3) the substitutionary atonement, (4) bodily resurrection of Christ, and (5) the verbal inspiration of the Scriptures. Actually, Gerstner's "new" evangelicalism (that which has developed since World War II) is, at its core, the old fundamentalism of the earlier twentieth century with a more culturally interactive facelift.[22]

William W. Wells cites three specific characteristics of evangelicals, configured around the axis of belief and practice: (1) belief in the unique divine inspiration, entire trustworthiness and authority of the Bible; (2) belief and personal appropriation by faith alone of God's promise that he will forgive, redeem, justify, and accept evangelicals into a personal relationship with himself on the basis of the life, death, and resurrection of Jesus; and (3) commitment to the pursuit of a holy life and to the disciplines seen as necessary for spiritual growth (e.g., prayer, Bible study, Christian fellowship, and evangelism).[23]

James Davison Hunter identifies evangelicals "by their adherence to: (1) the belief that the Bible is the inerrant Word of God; (2) the belief in the divinity of Christ; and (3) the belief in the efficacy of Christ's life, death, and physical resurrection for the salvation of the human soul."[24] In a lengthy elaboration reflecting his sociological training, however, Hunter proceeds to analyze evangelicalism further in a "social-scientific sense." Using Max Weber's typology of ascetic Protestantism, Hunter finds four traditions within American evangelicalism: the Baptist, the Holiness-Pentecostal, the Anabaptist, and the Reformational-Confessional. Each of the four traditions brings its own distinctive emphases and ancilliary doctrines to the evangelical subculture.[25] Ronald Nash, on the other hand, distinguishes "an essential core of beliefs that includes the deity of Christ, the virgin birth, the incarnation, the substitutionary atonement, the bodily resurrection of Christ, and Christ's literal return to earth at the end of the age." In addition to this Christological emphasis, Nash notes fundamental beliefs about the Bible: that it is "the Word of God and is normative for Christian belief and practice."[26]

In recent years, those with a normative bent reached a broad consensus around a set of convictions offered by British scholar David Bebbington. In *Evangelicalism in Modern Britain: A History from the 1730s to the 1980s*, Bebbington characterizes English evangelicals of the eighteenth century as holding to: (1) Conversionism, the belief that lives need to be changed; (2) Activism, the expression of the gospel of Christ in effort; (3) Biblicism, a particular regard for the Bible; and (4) Crucicentrism, a stress on the sacrifice of Christ on the cross.[27] Although Bebbington was examining evangelical history in a non-American setting, theologians and other historians saw a definitional virtue in his categories that were at the same time sweeping yet succinct. The widespread application of Bebbington's categories to the American scene has been promoted in large part through the efforts of Mark Noll and Derek Tidball, who called Bebbington's definition "as near to a consensus as we might ever expect to reach."[28]

The other major emphasis in evangelical studies has been predominantly historical. Into this camp falls the "evangelical mafia" (Marsden, Noll, and Hatch along with their many associates). Noll has called his own approach "descriptive [and] historical," rather than prescriptive and normative.[29] Kenneth Collins evaluated this historical approach, somewhat erroneously, as the activity of those who "merely record as an item of historical fact and interest the self-claim of [the evangelical] theologians." Such an endeavor, says Collins, "implies no endorsement of such claims."[30] A better way of characterizing the historical approach of evangelical scholars like Marsden, Noll, and Hatch is, in the words of Leonard I. Sweet, "observer-participant," in that they are "historians with a calling."[31] As Noll puts it, his historical scholarship is motivated by the conviction "that the object of research is also a definitive revelation from God."[32] For an evangelical Christian, this belief will inalterably influence the way one approaches the object.

If there is a fault line in modern American evangelicalism, it lies squarely between the imposing tectonic plates of the Calvinistic and Arminian traditions. The major historiographical debate concerning the origin and contemporary identity of evangelicalism follows the contours of this age-old divide. Douglas Sweeney calls the Calvinistic/Reformed view "the predominant model" in evangelical historiography. Basically, it issues from a host of evangelical theologians and historians who count themselves among the religious and intellectual heirs of John Calvin. Sweeney singles out Marsden and Noll, along with Joel Carpenter, Donald Bloesch, and Bernard Ramm as the most prominent representatives of this school.[33] Others, like Perry Miller, Sydney Ahlstrom, Shelton Smith, Robert Handy, Lefferts Loetscher, William McLoughlin, and Ernest Sandeen, if not personally aligned with the Calvinistic/Reformed tradition, had their historical scholarship influenced by this paradigm. The Calvinistic/Reformed view owes its prominence to its long history in America (dating back to the Puritans), its eloquent spokespeople, and its "insider" or "establishment" status.[34] Its contemporary incarnation can be summarized as follows: (1) It emphasizes ideas and theological propositions. (2) It tends to view the rise of "neo-Evangelicalism" in the 1940s and 1950s as a dissenting movement that originated in predominantly Reformed American fundamentalism (especially, the conservative and confessional Old School Presbyterianism of Princeton Seminary). Hence, neoevangelical leaders like *Harold John Ockenga and *Carl F. H. Henry were primarily interested in "reforming" fundamentalism, the religious subculture in which they grew up in during the 1920s and 1930s. (3) Enamored with the epistemology popularized at the end of the nineteenth century by the Dutch Reformed theologian-statesman Abraham Kuyper, the Calvinistic/Reformed perspective promotes a world-view that emphasizes the transformation of contemporary secular culture in an explictly Christian fashion. In a sense, the Reformed approach wishes to restore contemporary American evangelicalism to the position of religious, intellectual, and social prominence it enjoyed during the antebellum years of the previous century.[35]

This dominant view of the development of contemporary American evangelicalism approximates in remarkable fashion Richard Quebedeaux's category of "Establishment Evangelicalism" in his book *The Young Evangelicals*. Influenced by the Calvinistic/Reformed paradigm, Quebedeaux accurately describes the contemporary subculture of establishment evangelicals: its conservative theology and its openness to religious dialogue and interaction with the larger society (for redemptive purposes). He also presciently locates its organizational structure as transdenominational, with its epicenter of power and influence in the upper Midwest, particularly in the fifty-mile radius around Chicago, which includes Wheaton College (Wheaton, Illinois), Trinity College and Trinity Evangelical Divinity School (Deerfield, Illinois), and InterVarsity Press (Downers Grove, Illinois).[36]

Increasingly in evangelical circles, there is growing dissent from the Calvinistic/Reformed historiographical interpretation. Although the viewpoint is persuasive, even elegant at times, it simply does not adequately explain the incredible breadth and diversity of the evangelical subculture, a diversity characterized at different times as a "mosaic," a "kaleidoscope," or, most recently, a "network of networks."[37] Accordingly, a chorus of scholars, primarily, although not exclusively, in the theological lineage of John Wesley, have attacked against the " 'Presbyterianization' of 'evangelicalism' and 'evangelical' historiography."[38] For the past several decades, the most vociferous and widely published representatives of the Arminian/Wesleyan/Holiness view have been Timothy L. Smith and Donald Dayton.[39]

Smith first challenged the Calvinistic/Reformed historiographical paradigm in 1957 with his *Revivalism and Social Reform*.[40] Explanations for revivalism, commonly defined as the "major American religious phenomenon . . . whereby a speaker attempts to bring people to a conversion experience," are crucial in any serious definition of evangelicalism.[41] According to Kathryn Long, Smith's work was a "revisionist history" and the key aspect of his methodology was "his redefinition of revivalism as a synonym for Wesleyan Arminianism. Since all revivalism was by definition Arminian, [even] revivalistic Calvinists were little more than Wesleyans in disguise."[42] The monograph was a *tour de force*, breaking the interpretive stranglehold that Reformed historians of evangelicalism had on the movement. Scholars now had to come to grips with the influence of Methodism and other Wesleyan movements on the larger span of American history. The fact that for many years Smith represented a ''voice crying in the wilderness'' is a testimony to the entrenchment of the Reformed view of evangelical history.

In the past two decades, the most strident advocate of the Arminian/Wesleyan/ Holiness view has been Donald Dayton, professor of theology and ethics at Northern Baptist Theological Seminary. Dayton's first major foray into the historiographical spotlight came with his ten-part series published from June–July 1974 through May 1975 in the *Post-American* (now *Sojourners*) magazine. The series, later published in book form, bore the significant title, ''Recovering a Heritage.''[43] Dayton's overriding academic imperative is to ''recover'' the ''lost history'' of American evangelicalism, specifically, to highlight the oft-ignored roots of modern evangelicalism in the Methodist denominations of the early nineteenth century and the Wesleyan-oriented Holiness and Pentecostal groups (e.g., Churches of the Nazarene, Assemblies of God, Churches of God in Christ) of the late nineteenth and early twentieth centuries. In Dayton's understanding, the Arminian/Wesleyan/Holiness view of evangelicalism is essentially a reaction to the Calvinistic/Reformed perspective. While he acknowledges that the Reformed view of American evangelical history has been the dominant one, he also asserts: (1) This is a distortion of the historical record, given the size and influence of Methodism for the period stretching from approximately 1820 to World War I. (2) What is commonly called ''neoevangelicalism'' in the post– World War II era may be understood as the fragmentation of Methodism and the rise of various Holiness, Pentecostal, and charismatic groups as well as the ''reforming'' of Old School Presbyterianism. (3) It is a distortion to regard the development of fundamentalism and neoevangelicalism principally as a conservative religious reaction to modernism.[44] (4) The Calvinistic/Reformed perspective fails to see (or admit) that the true ''engine'' of antebellum evangelicalism in the nineteenth century was Wesleyan Methodism and, secondarily, the revivalist-oriented, new school Presbyterianism of Charles G. Finney, which borrowed liberally from Wesleyan theology and practice. If anything, old school Presbyterianism was a socially conserving force, not an instrument for social reform (especially in the American South). (5) The notion of ''cycles of revivalism and reform,'' first suggested by Congregationalists in the eighteenth century and popularized recently in William McLoughlin's *Revivals, Awakenings, and Reform*, is a fiction of the Reformed perspective.[45] Revivalism has ebbed and flowed continuously throughout American evangelical history, primarily through those groups associated with Wesley. (6) Finally, if this Arminian/Wesleyan/Holiness perspective is valid, then modern American Protestantism can be seen, in large part, as the evolution of evangelical groups from ''sectarian mentality'' into a more ''churchly style.'' Dayton calls this the *embourgeoisment* of evangelicalism.[46]

Dayton's points are well taken and argued with passion. Even those who generally support a Reformed perspective admit that the contributions of the Methodists and their associates have received short shrift in evangelical history.[47] Because of this, American evangelicalism has been defined almost exclusively in Reformed terms. To state his case more resoundingly, Dayton has used Marsden as a foil. The two have debated either in print or in a scholarly forum at least three separate times.[48] Reading Dayton's criticisms, one gets the sense that his salient points are muted by his tendency to focus on Marsden as the personification of everything he finds objectionable in "the presbyterian paradigm.[49] Like the "religious outsiders" whose role in American evangelicalism he purports to defend, Dayton has taken on the *persona* of "scholarly outsider" in contrast to Marsden's establishment figure as "the doyen of 'evangelical studies' in our time."[50]

A reliable definition of American evangelicalism must derive from a synthetic approach that draws from both the Reformed and the Wesleyan perspectives. As Douglas Sweeney claims, "both . . . approaches to neo-evangelical historiography are helpful as far as they go. However, neither approach *by itself* has yet provided a complete portrayal of the movement" (emphasis added).[51] Sweeney goes on to add, "When used in tandem, the Reformed and Holiness approaches to neo-evangelical historiography can complement each other's research and shed light on what Dayton calls 'the strange schizophrenia' of contemporary evangelicalism."[52] As Carpenter affirms, "The moral of the story, then, is that we who study evangelicals have much to learn from each other, much to add to the whole picture. The learning, I am convinced, will come through sharing the stories we have found and seeing how they impinge on and synchronize with each other. This will be more productive than presuming to see it all, and to see it better, with only one set of lenses or another."[53] Even Marsden admits, "If instead of insisting that we must have opposing paradigms we read the data through the simpler lens of recognizing that there are multidimensional and mutually porous evangelical movements, it seems to me we would be proceeding more constructively."[54] American evangelicalism is a far too diverse and complicated phenomenon to fit neatly into any one interpretive grid or paradigm.

Now we can construct a working description of American evangelicalism. It may be characterized as:

1. Complex, dynamic, and protean. The complexity of the movement defies analogy: mosaic, kaleidoscope, network of networks—no one adjective suffices.

2. Transdenominational in nature. There are evangelicals in every Protestant denomination (Calvinist/Reformed; Wesleyan/Holiness/Pentecostal; Baptist; Anabaptist; Lutheran) and even some within the American Roman Catholic Church.[55]

3. Normatively described. The norms vary according to the commentator, ranging from Gallup's simple criterion of "born-again" to Webber's "major emphases" that divide American evangelicalism into at least fourteen groups. Finding a panoramic com-

pactness in Bebbington's categories, this study will opt for his norms of conversionism, activism, biblicism, and crucicentricism.

4. Historically described. American evangelicalism grew out of currents stretching back
   to the Protestant Reformation. It possesses direct British antecedents standing in the
   theological and ecclesiastical lines of the Puritans, British dissenters (Separatists, Presbyterians, and Baptists), Wesleyans, and Calvinistic Anglicans like George Whitefield.
   Yet beginning in the mid–eighteenth century, these varied formative influences began
   to synthesize and metamorphosize into a uniquely American strain of religion. Although evangelicals organized around a core set of theological norms (which largely
   differed along the Calvinistic/Arminian divide) and emphasized individual conversion
   and group revivalism, there was an immense variety in evangelical expression from
   the beginning.

5. Symbiotically linked to the larger American culture. Before the Civil War, the theological and moral agenda of the Calvinistic/Reformed strain of evangelicalism (''Pres-
   bygationalism'') dominated American culture. With the rise of modernism and the
   religious pluralization of the late nineteenth century, evangelicals, as a group, were
   increasingly pushed to the cultural periphery. For most of this century, evangelicalism
   has looked more and more like a subculture. Even on this point, there is great variety,
   with some evangelicals strongly accommodating of the larger secular, or nonreligious,
   culture and others, at the opposite fringe (e.g., the fundamentalists), fiercely opposi-
   tional to the culture.

6. Identified either ''intentionally'' or ''unintentionally.'' This category relates to the
   degree that certain groups identify themselves as evangelicals. ''Intentional evangelicals'' are those who consider evangelicalism to be their primary category of religious
   identification. Marsden also calls these people ''card carrying evangelicals.''[56] Although a relatively small group in numerical terms, intentional evangelicals are the
   gatekeepers of the American evangelical subculture, controlling its primary educational, publishing, and parachurch institutions. ''Unintentional evangelicals,'' on the
   other hand, are much less self-conscious about their association with American evangelicalism. Unintentional evangelicals may meet the normative theological and be-
   haviorial criteria for being ''evangelical-like'' while not even considering themselves
   evangelicals. Three good examples of unintentional evangelicals in contemporary
   America are Southern Baptists, Pentecostals, and Mennonites. Almost all Southern
   Baptists are evangelicals in the normative sense. However, until recently, because of
   their regional identity and strong denominational exclusivism, few Southern Baptists
   thought of themselves as part of the evangelical subculture.[57] Most modern Pentecostals, in the early period of their movement, saw themselves as part of a unique, new
   dispensation in God's economy: the ''latter rain.'' This made Pentecostalism radically
   separate from all existing religious structures, including evangelicalism.[58] Finally,
   there are the Mennonites, an Anabaptist group ''always within the evangelical Christian tradition,'' yet representing ''a distinct hermeneutical community'' from it.[59] Only
   at the end of the century when denominationalism was eroding and some believed
   the greatest foe to religious faith to be militant secularism, did many intentional and
   unintentional evangelicals reexamine their own history and their relationship to a
   dynamic religious subculture. Only now are scholars taking seriously a diverse movement that has left an indelible mark on the whole of American religion.

## NOTES

1. Kenneth L. Woodward et al., "Born Again!" *Newsweek* (25 October 1976): 76.

2. A good discussion of the relative ignorance displayed by the secular media toward religious issues is Wesley G. Pippert, "Worldly Reporters and Born-Again Believers: How Each Perceives the Other," in *American Evangelicals and the Mass Media*, edited by Quentin J. Schultze (Grand Rapids, Mich.: Eerdmans, 1990), pp. 275–82. The suggestion that late twentieth-century American fundamentalism and the Shi'ite ideology of Khomeini were cut from the same fabric was made by groups like Norman Lear's People for the American Way. See Beth Spring, "Norman Lear's Lobbying Style Troubles Some Supporters," *Christianity Today* 26 (12 November 1982): 78–80.

3. George Barna, *The Barna Report 1992–93* (Ventura, Calif.: Regal Books, 1992), p. 81.

4. James A. Beckford, "New Religions," in *Encyclopedia of Religion*, 16 vols., edited by Mircea Eliade (New York: Macmillan, 1987), 10:390.

5. Following Emile Durkheim, several modern scholars note: "The most 'elementary' or fundamental forms of religion focus on the idea of society. The essence of religion is found in the way(s) it enables persons to identify with the values associated with a particular group." Lawrence S. Cunningham et al., *The Sacred Quest: An Invitation to the Study of Religion* (New York: Macmillan, 1991), p. 17. Referring to the American situation since World War II, Robert Wuthnow adds, "To assert that religion is formally in the private sector is, however, not meant to imply that it has been thoroughly 'privatized,' that is, become an example of atomized, consumption-oriented civil privatism." See Wuthnow, *The Struggle for America's Soul: Evangelicals, Liberals, and Secularism* (Grand Rapids, Mich.: Eerdmans, 1989), p. 107.

6. Robert T. Handy, *A Christian America: Protestant Hopes and Historical Realities* (New York: Oxford University Press, 1971). Handy asserted this thesis much more explicitly on p. ix of the revised edition (1984) of this work.

7. Martin E. Marty, "The Editor's Bookshelf: American Religious History," *Journal of Religion* 62 (1982): 102, as noted in D. G. Hart, "Introduction," in *Reckoning with the Past: Historical Essays on American Evangelicalism from the Institute for the Study of American Evangelicals*, edited by D. G. Hart (Grand Rapids, Mich.: Baker, 1995), p. 13.

8. Stephen R. Graham, "Selected Publications in the History of American Christianity, 1980–1994," *Covenant Quarterly* 53:1 (February 1995): 38.

9. The appellation "evangelical mafia" comes from James Turner in his "Foreword" to Hart, ed., *Reckoning with the Past*, p. 7. To date, the best examination is Maxie B. Burch, *The Evangelical Historians: The Historiography of George Marsden, Nathan Hatch, and Mark Noll* (Lanham, Md.: University Press of America, 1996).

10. Collectively, Hatch, Marsden, and Noll wrote, edited, or co-edited twenty-one books between 1980 and 1997. Most prominent are George M. Marsden, *Fundamentalism and American Culture: The Shaping of Twentieth-Century Evangelicalism, 1870–1925* (New York: Oxford University Press, 1980); Mark A. Noll, *Between Faith and Criticism: Evangelicals, Scholarship, and the Bible in America* (New York: Harper and Row, 1986); Nathan O. Hatch, *The Democratization of American Christianity* (New Haven: Yale University Press, 1989); Mark A. Noll, *A History of Christianity in the United States and Canada* (Grand Rapids, Mich.: Eerdmans, 1992); George M. Marsden, *The Soul of*

*the American University: From Protestant Establishment to Established Nonbelief* (New York: Oxford University Press, 1994); Mark A. Noll, *The Scandal of the Evangelical Mind* (Grand Rapids, Mich.: Eerdmans, 1994); and George M. Marsden, *The Outrageous Idea of Christian Scholarship* (New York: Oxford University Press, 1997).

11. A "subculture" may be defined as "a group or class of lesser importance or size sharing specific beliefs, interests, or values which may be at variance with those of the general culture of which it forms part" (*Oxford English Dictionary*, 2d ed., vol. 17 [Oxford: Clarendon Press, 1989], s.v. "subculture"). For American evangelicalism as a "subculture," consult Patricia Klein et al., *Growing Up Born Again: A Whimsical Look at the Blessings and Tribulations of Growing Up Born Again* (Old Tappan, N.J.: Fleming H. Revell, 1987); see also Randall Balmer, *Mine Eyes Have Seen the Glory: A Journey into the Evangelical Subculture in America* (New York: Oxford University Press, 1989), particularly Balmer's autobiographical prologue, pp. 3–11.

12. George Gallup Jr., *The Gallup Poll: Public Opinion, 1995* (Wilmington, Del.: Scholarly Resources, 1996), p. 232. The question asked was: "Would you describe yourself as a 'born-again' or evangelical Christian, or not?" Besides the 39 percent that answered affirmatively, 53 percent said no, while 8 percent had no opinion.

13. Barna puts the figure at 40 percent in his 1992–93 report. His criteria for "evangelical" were similar to the Gallup survey. Specifically, the Barna parameters were personal commitment to Jesus Christ and belief in an eternal afterlife in heaven because one has confessed his/her sins and accepted Christ as Savior. *Barna Report 1992–93*, p. 78.

14. Derek J. Tidball, *Who Are the Evangelicals? Tracing the Roots of the Modern Movements* (London: Marshall Pickering, 1994), p. 12.

15. Balmer, *Mine Eyes Have Seen the Glory*, p. ix.

16. The best essay on the historiography of American evangelicalism, although dated, is Leonard I. Sweet, "The Evangelical Tradition in America," in *The Evangelical Tradition in America*, edited by Leonard I. Sweet (Macon, Ga.: Mercer University Press, 1984), pp. 1–86. See also Sweet's "Wise as Serpents, Innocent as Doves: The New Evangelical Historiography," *Journal of the American Academy of Religion* 56:3 (1988): 397–416. A rather short update on the subject is John Fea, "American Fundamentalism and Neo-Evangelicalism: A Bibliographic Survey," *Evangelical Journal* 11 (Spring 1993): 21–30. Although he does not deal with the evangelical historians directly, Henry Warner Bowden examines many of the preliminary methodological considerations in "The Historiography of American Religion," in *Encyclopedia of the American Religious Experience*, 3 vols., edited by Charles H. Lippy and Peter W. Williams (New York: Scribners, 1988), 1: 3–16 and idem, *Church History in an Age of Uncertainty: Historiographical Patterns in the United States, 1906–1990* (Carbondale, Ill.: Southern Illinois University Press, 1991).

17. David Jary and Julia Jary, *The HarperCollins Dictionary of Sociology* (New York: HarperPerennial, 1991), s.v. "norm."

18. This would be the approach of a social scientist. One also sees it in the works of "professing" sociologists like Wuthnow's *Struggle for America's Soul* and Nancy Tatom Ammerman's *Bible Believers: Fundamentalists in the Modern World* (New Brunswick, N.J.: Rutgers University Press, 1987).

19. Alister McGrath notes that after years of attempting to define evangelicalism in a precise fashion, the Gallup organization "gave up the battle" in 1986, settling for the born-again identification. Alister McGrath, *Evangelicalism and the Future of Christianity* (Downers Grove, Ill.: InterVarsity, 1995), p. 53.

20. *Barna Report 1992–93*, p. 81.

21. Robert E. Webber, *Common Roots: A Call to Evangelical Maturity* (Grand Rapids, Mich.: Zondervan, 1978), p. 32.

22. John H. Gerstner, "Theological Boundaries: The Reformed Perspective," in *The Evangelicals: What They Believe, Who They Are, Where They Are Changing*, edited by David F. Wells and John D. Woodbridge, rev. ed. (Nashville: Abingdon, 1975), pp. 32–33.

23. William W. Wells, *Welcome to the Family: An Introduction to Evangelical Christianity* (Downers Grove, Ill.: InterVarsity, 1979), pp. 10–11.

24. James Davison Hunter, *American Evangelicalism: Conservative Religion and the Quandary of Modernity* (New Brunswick, N.J.: Rutgers University Press, 1983), p. 7.

25. Ibid., pp. 7–9.

26. Ronald H. Nash, *Evangelicals in America: Who They Are, What They Believe* (Nashville: Abingdon, 1987), p. 26.

27. David Bebbington, *Evangelicalism in Modern Britain: A History from the 1730s to the 1980s* (Grand Rapids: Mich.: Baker, 1992), pp. 2–17.

28. Noll, *Scandal of the Evangelical Mind*, p. 8; Tidball, *Who Are the Evangelicals?*, p. 4.

29. Noll, *Between Faith and Criticism*, p. 1.

30. Kenneth J. Collins, "Children of Neglect: American Methodist Evangelicals," *Christian Scholar's Review* 20:1 (September 1990): 11. Collins suggests that Marsden, Noll, and Hatch have a level of detachment from their subjects that they do not claim for themselves. In a significant but rarely quoted essay from 1981, Noll said that "the claim that we gain historical knowledge only through detached, verifiable and utterly objective inquiry must be rejected as a blundering, insensitive mistake." Three years later, Marsden stated, "Based on a synthesis of ideas from [Carl] Becker and Cornelius Van Til, I have argued that the very facts of history differ for the Christian and the non-Christian historian. There is, in this sense, nothing like objective history." Although less explicit, Hatch has consistently championed what he calls "Christian thinking" in as secular an arena as the research university. See Mark Noll, "Scientific History in America: A Centennial Observation from a Christian Point of View," *Fides et Historia* 14:1 (Fall-Winter 1981): 27; George Marsden, "Common Sense and the Spiritual Vision of History," in *History and Historical Understanding*, edited by C. T. McIntire and Ronald A. Wells (Grand Rapids, Mich.: Eerdmans, 1984), p. 57; and Nathan O. Hatch, "Evangelical Colleges and the Challenge of Christian Thinking," in *Making Higher Education Christian: The History and Mission of Evangelical Colleges in America*, edited by Joel A. Carpenter and Kenneth W. Shipps (Grand Rapids, Mich.: Eerdmans, 1987), pp. 155–71. In a wry and insightful essay, Leonard Sweet called the historical approach of Noll, Marsden, Hatch et al., the "observer-participant" perspective; see Sweet, "Wise as Serpents, Innocent as Doves," pp. 398–99.

31. Sweet, "Wise as Serpents," p. 403.

32. Noll, *Between Faith and Criticism*, p. 7.

33. Douglas A. Sweeney, "The Essential Evangelicalism Dialectic: The Historiography of the Early Evangelical Movement and the Observer-Participant Dilemma," *Church History* 60:1 (March 1991): 71.

34. Collins, "Children of Neglect," p. 7.

35. Ibid., pp. 7–10. See also Sweeney, "Evangelicalism Dialectic," pp. 71–74, and Sweet, "Wise as Serpents," pp. 399–401. Marsden sets out the Kuyperian viewpoint in

George M. Marsden, "The Collapse of American Evangelical Academia," in *Faith and Rationality: Reason and Belief in God*, edited by Alvin Plantinga and Nicholas Wolterstorff (Notre Dame, Ind.: University of Notre Dame Press, 1983), pp. 219–64.

36. Richard Quebedeaux, *The Young Evangelicals: Revolution in Orthodoxy* (New York: Harper and Row, 1974), pp. 28–33.

37. "Mosaic" and "kaleidoscope" are suggested by Timothy L. Smith in "The Evangelical Kaleidoscope and the Call to Christian Unity," *Christian Scholar's Review* 15:2 (1986): 128. Mark Noll offers the "network of networks" analogy (particularly apt in the age of the Internet). The quote is from David van Biema, "In the Name of the Father," *Time* 147:20 (13 May 1996): 75.

38. Donald W. Dayton, "Another Layer of the Onion, Or Opening the Ecumenical Door to Let the Riffraff In," *Ecumenical Review* 40:1 (January 1988): 100.

39. Sweeney, "Evangelicalism Dialectic," p. 73.

40. Timothy L. Smith, *Revivalism and Social Reform: American Protestantism on the Eve of the Civil War* (reprint, Baltimore: The Johns Hopkins University Press, 1980; originally issued as *Revivalism and Social Reform in Mid-Nineteenth-Century America* [New York: Abingdon, 1957]).

41. Edward L. Queen II, Stephen R. Prothero, and Gardiner H. Shattuck Jr., *Encyclopedia of American Religious History*, 2 vols. (New York: Facts On File, 1996), s.v. "revivalism." Leonard I. Sweet, "Nineteenth-Century Evangelicalism," in *Encyclopedia of the American Religious Experience*, 2:886, has called revivalism "the main ritual of evangelical Protestantism" and evangelicalism's "chief instrument of evangelism."

42. Kathryn Long, "The Power of Interpretation: The Revival of 1857–58 and the Historiography of Revivalism in America," *Religion and American Culture* 4:1 (Winter 1994): 91.

43. Donald W. Dayton, *Discovering an Evangelical Heritage* (1976; reprint with a new preface, Peabody, Mass.: Hendrickson, 1988).

44. Another term difficult to define with epistemological precision, modernism is the perception that history is characterized by constant change. Over time, individuals, cultures, and even species inevitably change as they interact with their environments. Hence the very idea of "truth" is changeable, as it is shaped by inexorable and impersonal historical forces. The standard treatment remains William R. Hutchison, *The Modernist Impulse in American Protestantism* (Cambridge, Mass.: Harvard University Press, 1976), especially pp. 41–75, which nicely ties modernism to nineteenth-century evangelicalism.

45. William G. McLoughlin, *Revivals, Awakenings, and Reform: An Essay on Religion and Social Change in America, 1607–1977*, Chicago History of American Religion Series, edited by Martin E. Marty (Chicago: University of Chicago Press, 1978).

46. Dayton's argument appears in its fullest form in his "Yet Another Layer of the Onion." In response to Marsden's *Reforming Fundamentalism*, Dayton outlined specific modifications and elaborations of his argument in " 'The Search for the Historical Evangelicalism': George Marsden's History of Fuller Seminary as a Case Study," *Christian Scholar's Review* 23:1 (September 1993): 12–33. The *embourgeoisment* idea is very similar to a thesis advanced in Roger Finke and Rodney Stark, "How the Upstart Sects Won America: 1776–1850," *Journal for the Scientific Study of Religion* 28:1 (March 1989): 27–44.

47. Joel A. Carpenter, "The Scope of American Evangelicalism: Some Comments on the Dayton-Marsden Exchange," *Christian Scholar's Review* 23:1 (September 1993): 55, notes that Dayton's "efforts—along with those of Timothy Smith—to recover a broader

and deeper field of vision have had a good effect on the contemporary historiography of evangelicalism.'' Also, Marsden, in the same journal, adds: ''Donald Dayton has rendered an invaluable service for the study of American evangelicalism through his studies of the holiness and pentecostal sides of those traditions. Those studies can indeed cast some light on our understanding of the more Reformed parts of the heritage'' (p. 40). Perhaps most significantly, Hatch, in his presidential address to the American Society of Church History, noted: ''The most basic features of the Methodist terrain remain unknown and unexplored and there is no graduate center that has taken up the challenge of using Methodist sources to shed light on broad historical questions'' (this address was published as ''The Puzzle of Methodism,'' *Church History* 63:2 (June 1994): 175–89; quote from p. 177.). More than the other significant Reformed-oriented historians, Hatch has appeared sympathetic to some of Dayton's major points; see his *Democratization of American Christianity*.

48. *Christian Scholar's Review* 7:2–3 (1977): 203–11; a symposium at the national meeting of the American Academy of Religion (1988); and in *Christian Scholar's Review* 23:1 (September 1993): 12–40, 62–71.

49. In ''Scope of American Evangelicalism,'' Joel Carpenter calls Dayton's theological agenda ''combative.'' He claims that Dayton has a ''grudge'' against neoevangelicals and wonders why Dayton continues ''to press the attack.'' The discussion with Dayton is a ''historiographical argument.''

50. The term ''religious outsiders'' is taken from R. Laurence Moore, *Religious Outsiders and the Making of Americans* (New York: Oxford University Press, 1986). The Dayton quote is from Dayton, ''Search for the Historical Evangelicalism,'' p. 22.

51. Sweeney, ''Evangelicalism Dialectic,'' p. 76.

52. Ibid., p. 80.

53. Carpenter, ''Scope of American Evangelicalism,'' p. 61.

54. George Marsden, ''Response to Don Dayton,'' *Christian Scholar's Review* 23:1 (September 1993): 40.

55. Barna puts the figure at 22 percent of all American Catholics. *Barna Report 1992–93*, p. 80. Lyman A. Kellstedt and John C. Green, ''The Mismeasure of Evangelicals,'' *Books and Culture* 2:1 (January/February 1996): 15, say 23 percent. An analysis of this phenomenon may be found in *Evangelicals and Catholics: Toward A Common Mission Together*, edited by Charles Colson and Richard John Neuhaus (Dallas: Word, 1995).

56. George M. Marsden, ''Contemporary American Evangelicalism,'' in *Southern Baptists and American Evangelicals: The Conversation Continues*, edited by David S. Dockery (Nashville: Broadman and Holman, 1993), p. 30.

57. James Leo Garrett Jr., E. Glenn Hinson, and James E. Tull, *Are Southern Baptists ''Evangelicals''?* (Macon, Ga.: Mercer University Press, 1983), and the essays in Dockery, ed., *Southern Baptists and American Evangelicals*.

58. Donald W. Dayton, *Theological Roots of Pentecostalism* (Peabody, Mass.: Hendrickson, 1987), pp. 22–28.

59. C. Norman Kraus, ''Evangelicalism: A Mennonite Critique,'' in *The Variety of American Evangelicalism*, edited by Donald W. Dayton and Robert K. Johnston (Knoxville: University of Tennessee Press, 1991), pp. 184–203.

# 2
# Planting Evangelicalism in the United States

When *Newsweek* proclaimed 1976 the "year of the evangelical," for many it was as if a sleeping giant had suddenly awakened.[1] After all, Douglas Frank had claimed that American evangelicals entered the twentieth century "less than conquerors."[2] Popularly confused, if not equated, with fundamentalism, evangelicalism seemed to have shared the ignominy that consigned fundamentalism to the fringes of religious life after the furor over evolution in the 1920s.[3] Yet as Joel Carpenter and others have shown, both fundamentalism and evangelicalism thrived as religious subcultures, developing supportive networks to sustain their respective visions and institutions to strengthen their foundations.[4] It was as if evangelicalism were awaiting a *kairos*, an appointed time, when it would reemerge as not only a vital, but perhaps even dominant force in American religious life. As the twenty-first century dawns, American evangelicals rehearse a distinguished history, for the contemporary resurgence of an evangelical spirit in American Protestantism has roots in the religious life of the first Europeans who peopled what became the United States as well as in antebellum religious currents. Every emphasis on inner experience of the saving presence and power of God in Christ buttressed the evangelical spirit.

Evangelicalism traces strands of its heritage to Martin Luther and the Reformation.[5] Luther's insistence that an experience of faith, of trust in the righteousness of God, was central to salvation generated an enduring sense that personal experience was the *sine qua non* of authentic Christianity. The more pietistic Reformation elements planted a biblical consciousness on the Protestant mind and a yearning for practical, godly living that resound within American evangelicalism.[6] But more direct roots of modern evangelicalism are found in the religious life of those who came to America's shores. For example, the Puritans looked to some inner experience to signal that God had chosen them to be among the elect.[7] Mere attendance on the means of grace, such as attending worship as required by law or praying and studying the Scriptures in the home, did not mark one as regenerate. Individuals had to testify to a distinct work of grace before being admitted to the church covenant. The centrality of personal experience, sometimes marked by affective or emotional expression, was one characteristic of the Great Awakening, the sporadic series of revivals of the late 1730s and 1740s. Through the powerful oratory of preachers such as Jonathan Edwards, George Whitefield, Gilbert Tennant, and Samuel Davies, the Awakening made personal, inner experience of the work of God in Christ basic to American Protestantism. The early Puritans were heavily influenced by the Calvinist heritage that placed great importance on the idea of election or predestination. Although they talked about conversion, they did not mean that persons chose to accept God's work of grace in their lives, an idea associated with Arminianism. Rather, they believed that God did the choosing, that humans were basically passive agents who contributed nothing to their own salvation. But the importance attached to personal experience of conversion meant that the Arminian understanding gradually undermined the Calvinist basis for much American Protestant thought. If each individual should have some inner experience, then each must be actively involved in the process of salvation, not just a passive bystander.

In the last third of the eighteenth century, the evangelical style bolstered by Arminian tendencies received a boost as Methodism gained a foothold in North America. John Wesley, founder of the Methodist strain of Christianity, was unabashedly Arminian in his understanding of religious experience, and Methodism's reliance on itinerants who criss-crossed large areas to preach to ordinary folk helped implant in American Protestantism the notion of individual choice in matters of salvation. Baptists also gained influence in the years following the Awakening in part because they, too, saw individual experience as paramount. In the first half of the nineteenth century, Methodists and Baptists more deeply imprinted the evangelical strain on the nation's religious life when they became the largest among American Protestant denominational families. The Awakening era also brought the first sustained efforts among Euro-Americans to evangelize African American slaves, with evangelically oriented Presbyterians, Methodists, and Baptists at the forefront.[8] Emphasis on personal experience over doctrine and openness to more enthusiastic expressions of religious feeling appealed to African Americans more than other approaches. One result was the emergence of an evangelical ethos among Christian slaves that resonated with African religiosity. The ''invisible institution'' vital to slave religion, the manifestation of religious feeling and hopes for freedom in spirituals, and the call-response style distinctive to African American public prayer and preaching reflect this fusion of evangelical ways with the African heritage.

Forces identified with the Awakening mixed with the contagious civic enthusiasm surrounding the era of independence to add a millennialist dimension to American evangelicalism. Early Puritan immigrants, for example, gave their millennialist overtones because they believed that their recovery of true Christianity heralded what was to come when Christ returned to earth in triumph. Awakening preacher Jonathan Edwards took this view one step further, for he believed that the religious revival of his age signaled that Christ's millennial reign would begin in America. "[W]hat we now see in America, and especially in New England, may prove the dawn of that glorious day," wrote Edwards.[9] Even those whose thinking was more political and cast more in the rationalist language of the Enlightenment saw the democratic surge emerging from the independence of the United States in millennialist terms.[10] What this millennialist dimension added to Protestant evangelicalism was a social vision, a conviction not only that individual Americans would experience salvation, but also that the social order itself could be transformed into a Christian culture as individuals were converted. When the social order was fully transformed, American culture would indeed be heaven on earth.

Revivals of a different sort and having somewhat different antecedents helped stamp an evangelical style on the frontier areas of the South and Old Southwest early in the nineteenth century. During the eighteenth century, Separate Baptists and Scotch-Irish migrating down the eastern slopes of the Appalachians cemented an evangelical presence on parts of the Old South, and those who crossed over the mountains helped plant an evangelical style there.[11] But the even greater isolation of the frontier made some features of the transplanted traditions especially relevant. For example, the Scotch-Irish had in their religious background sacramental meetings that brought folk from around the countryside together to fellowship and mark their being at peace with God and each other through celebration of the Lord's Supper.[12] On the old frontier, the heritage of the sacramental meeting was one root of the camp meetings that shaped much of Southern evangelical life. The greater dispersion of the population and the desire to gather folk together when preachers were in an area were contributing factors. Although the first camp meeting is lost to history, since the Cane Ridge (Kentucky) meeting in 1801 camp meetings have sustained an evangelical ethos, especially in Southern Protestantism. Settlers from miles around converged, bringing provisions to last a week or two until a sacramental service brought the meeting to a close. During meeting time, often several preachers would set up stands and proclaim messages that frequently reflected different denominational nuances. The excitement of being together joined with the contagion generated by powerful preaching to produce a season of spiritual ecstasy. Highly intense, emotion-laden conversions became the order of the day. Methodist itinerant Peter Cartwright offered potent descriptions of those seized by the jerking exercise while sensing the power of God within.[13] Shattering traditional gender roles, women exhorted through prayer; those under conviction of sin and eager for salvation gathered in a closed-off area, a pen, to await the Spirit's movement. After camp meetings became annual events, organizations formed to plan the gatherings, thus ensuring that the meetings would to impress the evangelical mood on American Protestantism. For thousands, the inner experience of conversion not only brought eternal salvation but served as a badge of trustworthiness and responsible citizenship here and now.

The camp meeting brought another enduring dimension of evangelicalism to the fore: the passion for living out biblical precepts. In the early nineteenth century associated with figures such as Barton Stone, who arranged the Cane Ridge camp meeting, and Alexander Campbell, this effort to replicate New Testament patterns and practices bears the label of Restorationism. It developed in part because of the evangelical commitment to Scripture, which led to the conviction that Christians could and should recapture in their lives and in their Christianity exactly what was common to believers of the apostolic age. Another consequence of this mode of evangelicalism is a willingness to transcend denominational lines, but only with those who share what is thought to be authentic Christianity; ironically, the Restorationist impulse gave birth to its own denominations in the Disciples of Christ, the Churches of Christ, and the Latter-day Saints, or Mormons. As well, millennialism underlies Restorationism in the expectation that the eschatological age would commence once the replication of New Testament patterns was complete.

The evangelical temperament animated by the camp meeting and Restorationism echoed in the revivals most often linked to Charles Grandison Finney in the northern urban areas.[14] Dubbed "new measures" because Finney adapted camp meeting techniques to an urban setting, these revivals, when linked with those on the frontier, generated what some label the Second Great Awakening. Finney, for example, called penitents forward to an "anxious bench" much as those under conviction had gathered in the pen in front of the camp meeting preacher's stand. He organized prayer meetings for women and broke with social convention in allowing women to pray in public at his meetings under certain circumstances. Finney's work was initially centered in the rapidly expanding area of New York State along the Erie Canal where the fires of revivalism became so common that the region became known as the "burned-over district." As elsewhere, the evangelically inclined denominations that emphasized inner religious experience and personal piety reaped the greatest numerical results from the years of recurring revivals launched by Finney.

An added feature was a potent social vision that accompanied new measures revivalism. Finney and other like-minded Protestants became convinced that through cooperative endeavor, they could transform the social order. Groups such as the American Bible Society, the American Tract Society, the American Antislavery Society, and others targeted specific social issues and needs and sought to remedy problems largely through an individualistic approach. These and other "voluntary societies," largely propelled by women although control remained in male hands, crossed denominational lines.[15] The hope was that as the evangelical message transformed people, the way they carried themselves in society in living Christian values would in turn redirect the social order. It motivated what historian Robert T. Handy has called the "Protestant Quest for a Christian America."[16] In the 1830s, the hopes for molding an evangelical culture received a major boost in the movement for public or common schools. Already evangelical church folk and denominations had begun establishing colleges and seminaries; church-related colleges, although not always associated with evangelical denominations, would remain a fixture of American higher education for generations. The public schools, then confined primarily to more urban areas of the North and Midwest, almost at once became institutions for planting an evangelical view of the world on the mind of the nation's children. Curricular materials simply assumed a Protestant evangelical consciousness. The values implicit in the most widely used primers for teaching reading, for example, echoed what was preached in the churches.[17] Little wonder that those who did not find absolute truth in the evangelical way would look for alternatives, such as parish or parochial schools, where they could fuse different religious and social values. Public schools retained a Protestant character well into the twentieth century, and its eventual erosion prompted evangelicals not only to establish their own ''Christian'' schools but also frequently to seek to control local public schools in order to restore an ethos reflecting an evangelical understanding of the world.[18] The vision of social transformation also provided the impetus for supporting missions overseas.[19] A Christian America would not only be an example of the ideal civilization, the ''city on a hill'' of Puritan John Winthrop's seventeenth-century vision.[20] It would also be the catalyst for Protestant Christianity's fulfilling the New Testament mandate to ''go . . . and make disciples of all nations'' (Matthew 28:19). The earliest missionary societies crossed denominational boundaries in membership and support, but by the mid–nineteenth century virtually every Protestant denomination in the United States had its own missionary agencies, usually one directed to domestic or home missions and the other to foreign missions. The missionary enterprise also extended to Native Americans, both as an antidote to and an arm of U.S. Indian policy.[21]

The hunger to create an evangelical Christian culture and to carry that evangelical culture to all nations was fueled by more than a commitment to live out one understanding of the gospel. Countervailing forces threatened the dominance of the unofficial evangelical religious establishment in antebellum America; most of these became more significant in postbellum American life. Perhaps the greatest threat came from the increasing numbers of persons outside the evangelical Protestant fold. Their presence fostered the conviction there was an urgent need to protect a pure culture from contamination and to bring those outside the evangelical circle inside. In other words, missions were required at home as well as abroad. Some of these alternatives had roots in American religious life as deep as those of evangelical Protestantism. Puritan New England, for example, not only nurtured a religion of personal experience informed by Calvinism, but also gave birth to that rational expression of religion known as Unitarianism. For Unitarians, who came to dominate parts of New England for a time, authentic religion was much more a matter of the head than of the heart, of intellectual understanding than affective experience. The emphasis on an inner experience of conversion appeared to many Unitarians and kindred spirits as sheer emotionalism run amok.

Destined quickly to surpass Unitarians in numerical importance were immigrants who were Christians, but of a Roman Catholic persuasion. From the 1830s on in antebellum America, the bulk of Roman Catholic immigrants came from Ireland, although thousands claimed areas of Germany as their place of origin. In late twentieth-century America, there is a kind of rapprochement between many Protestant evangelicals and Roman Catholics because their convictions on social issues such as abortion are similar. In pre–Civil War society, there were virtually no points of concord. Evangelicals tended to regard Catholics as superstitious folk who could not be trusted because of their devotion to a foreign prince, the pope. Some, such as Lyman Beecher, suspected a Catholic plot to overthrow the American democratic government by encouraging Catholics to settle in the western regions and use them as a power base for revolution.[22] Others saw Catholic worship and devotion, from the mystery of the Latin Mass to private saying of the Rosary, as fraught with heresy. Roman Catholicism became the largest single religious communion in the nation by 1850, spurring evangelicals to step up efforts to give society a Christian cast and to convert all nations to their way of being Christian and being civilized. The unfortunate result was a strident anti-Catholicism; one well-known example is the burning of the Ursuline Convent just outside Boston in Charlestown, Massachusetts, in 1836.

In some areas, Jewish immigrants challenged the primacy of evangelical Protestantism. In antebellum America, the Jewish population was concentrated in coastal cities; Charleston, South Carolina, boasted the largest Jewish population of any U.S. city in the early nineteenth century. Because Jews were not Christians at all, their presence thwarted the evangelical hope for a Christian culture molded around Protestant ideals. But because evangelical Protestants took the Scriptures seriously, they saw Christianity in a symbiotic relationship with the Hebrew religious tradition that shaped both Christianity and Judaism. Hence Jews could not easily be dismissed. This ambivalence came into sharper focus in the decades surrounding the turn of the twentieth century when immigration from central and eastern Europe swelled the ranks of the nation's Jewish population and brought antisemitic tendencies to the fore.

Evangelicalism also played into the way yet other Americans developed alternatives that also seemed dangerous to the Protestant hegemony on the surface. The 1830s and 1840s especially brought religious experimentation, much of it originating in the "burned-over district" of New York. In the heart of the region, Joseph Smith attracted a following that coalesced into the Mormons, or Latter-day Saints. Not too far from the Hill Cumorah, where Smith had his visionary experience of finding golden plates containing the text of the Book of Mormon, John Humphrey Noyes organized his communitarian enterprise at Oneida, which endured until 1881. In western New York, the rappings the Fox sisters claimed to have heard gave a boost to Spiritualism in American religious life. Then, too, it was in the "burned-over district" that William Miller began proclaiming that Christ would soon return to earth. Miller fixed various dates first in 1843 and then in 1844 for Christ's Second Advent, but when his predictions seemed to fail, most of his adventist followers returned to other denominations. Some, however, turned the "great disappointment" into a rallying cry for a fresh religious alternative; Ellen G. White, for example, drew on the millennialist impulse to fashion her own teachings into the basic beliefs of the Seventh-Day Adventists. These and others exemplify the religious implications of what historian Alice Felt Tyler more than half a century ago called "freedom's ferment."[23]

In time, many firmly in the evangelical fold began to yearn for deeper personal experience. This yearning gained expression in various ways, but nearly all concerned the pursuit of holiness or sanctification. Theologically, sanctification was central to early Methodist teaching that made the quest for spiritual perfection, entire sanctification, the goal of the religious life after an initial experience of the heart brought justification. Interest in some second experience of grace or even some gradual growth in piety that brought perfection or holiness was not limited to the heirs of John Wesley. Charles Grandison Finney and Asa Mahan, Finney's associate at Oberlin College, both began to view perfection as the logical outgrowth of the work of grace in the lives of the converted. Perfection for them, as for those of a Methodist ilk, did not mean that persons would never make mistakes, but that individuals would in time see their own will so conforming to the will of God that sin would no longer taint their actions. John Humphrey Noyes and the Oneida community latched on to the expectation that this sort of perfection was attainable; they claimed that through their living the principles of New Testament Christianity by sharing all things in common, they already experienced the kind of life that marked the heavenly realm. Hence, they were popularly called the Oneida Perfectionists. The most enduring expression of this passion for holiness centered around the Methodist laywoman Phoebe Palmer.[24] Palmer became so intent on seeking a "second blessing" after an experience of justification, a life of total holiness, that she organized prayer meetings in her New York City home. Her Tuesday Afternoon Meeting for the Promotion of Holiness became the nucleus of a national evangelical revival in the late 1850s. The idea of gathering for prayer spread rapidly among businessmen and others who organized their own meetings to seek the second blessing.[25] Some camp meetings became centers of holiness activity. Although the Civil War shattered the pace of the holiness revival, the hope for attaining sanctification endured, in part because in 1867 the National Camp Meeting Association for the Promotion of Holiness was organized. Holiness was in many ways a logical concomitant to evangelical social reform endeavors that cultivated a Protestant Christian culture in the United States. It was also a logical response to the diversity of religious expression that was gaining ground, as Roman Catholic and Jewish immigration continued apace and as others formed alternatives such as Mormonism or Spiritualism. The Holiness movement was a revival in the literal sense of that term, a breathing of life into something thought headed for extinction, the evangelical style within American Protestantism. Holiness was destined to be a major force within evangelical Protestantism for decades to come, although the division that nearly destroyed the nation in midcentury muted its impact for a time.

Even as Holiness gained a hearing and many evangelicals struggled to ensure that American society would remain a Protestant Christian culture, forces that ultimately brought on the Civil War were also at work. Historians still debate whether the war between the states was inevitable. Arguments range from highlighting economic differences between a rapidly industrializing North and a South dependent on an outmoded slave labor system to ones emphasizing the chasm between those who found slavery morally repugnant and those who accepted slavery as a necessary evil or even a positive good in a moral society. Evangelicals took all positions. There is an additional religious dimension to the national schism. Clarence Goen forcefully reminded us that the evangelical experience of conversion and the understanding of the world that accompanied it created powerful affective ties stretching across regional as well as denominational lines.[26] When the largest evangelical denominations, the Methodists and the Baptists, formed regional institutions because of disagreements over slavery (Methodists in 1844 and Baptists in 1845), those affective ties were broken. Goen argued persuasively that the broken religious ties not only paved the way for the political division that came with the organization of the Confederate States of America, but made that division inevitable. Once the unofficial evangelical consensus that had buttressed a culture fell apart, war became the only means of determining which evangelical understanding of the world would prevail. When the war ended, evangelical forces would face fresh challenges, and a modern American evangelicalism would emerge as a central feature of the American religious landscape.

## NOTES

1. Kenneth L. Woodward et al., "Born Again!" *Newsweek* 90 (25 October 1976): 68–76.

2. Douglas W. Frank, *Less Than Conquerors: How Evangelicalism Entered the Twentieth Century* (Grand Rapids, Mich.: Eerdmans, 1986).

3. Among the earliest to dismiss evangelicalism was the acerbic H. L. Mencken, who in his *Prejudices: Fourth Series* (New York: Knopf, 1924), called its belief structures a "childish theology" worthy of appropriation only by "gaping primates in the upland valleys" of the nation.

4. Joel A. Carpenter develops these ideas in the following works: "Fundamentalist Institutions and the Growth of Evangelical Protestantism, 1929–1942," *Church History* 49 (1980): 62–75; idem, "The Fundamentalist Leaven and the Rise of an Evangelical United Front," in *The Evangelical Tradition in America*, edited by Leonard I. Sweet (Macon, Ga.: Mercer University Press, 1984), pp. 257–88; idem, "Revive Us Again: Alienation, Hope, and the Resurgence of Fundamentalism, 1930–1950," in *Transforming*

*Faith: The Sacred and Secular in Modern American History*, edited by M. L. Bradbury and James B. Gilbert (Westport, Conn.: Greenwood, 1989), pp. 105–25; and idem, *Revive Us Again: The Reawakening of American Fundamentalism* (New York: Oxford University Press, 1997).

5. On connections between the Lutheran tradition and the evangelical heritage, see Mark Ellingsen, "Lutheranism," in *The Variety of American Evangelicalism*, edited by Donald W. Dayton and Robert J. Johnston (Knoxville: University of Tennessee Press, 1991), pp. 222–44.

6. See C. John Weborg, "Pietism: Theological Service of Living Toward God," in ibid., pp. 161–83. See also F. Ernest Stoeffler, *The Rise of Evangelical Pietism* (Leiden: E. J. Brill, 1971).

7. See Sydney E. Ahlstrom, "From Puritanism to Evangelicalism: A Critical Perspective," in *The Evangelicals: What They Believe, Who They Are, Where They Are Changing*, edited by David F. Wells and John D. Woodbridge (Nashville: Abingdon, 1975), pp. 269–89.

8. On the similarity between the African and evangelical Protestant world views and the compatibility in the style of religiosity fostered by each, see Robert M. Calhoon, "The African Heritage, Slavery, and Evangelicalism," *Fides et Historia* 21 (June 1989): 61–66.

9. Jonathan Edwards, "Some Thoughts Concerning the Present Revival of Religion in New-England" (1742) in *The Great Awakening*, edited by Clarence C. Goen, *Works of Jonathan Edwards*, vol. 4 (New Haven: Yale University Press, 1972), 358.

10. See Nathan O. Hatch, *The Democratization of American Christianity* (New Haven, Conn.: Yale University Press, 1989); idem, "Millennialism and Popular Religion in the Early Republic," in *The Evangelical Tradition in America*, edited by Leonard I. Sweet (Macon, Ga.: Mercer University Press, 1984), pp. 113–47; and idem, *Sacred Cause of Liberty: Republican Thought and the Millennium in Revolutionary New England* (New Haven, Conn.: Yale University Press, 1977).

11. On the penetration of Baptists and the Scotch-Irish into Southern and Appalachian cultures, see Rhys M. Isaac, *The Transformation of Virginia, 1740–1790* (Chapel Hill: University of North Carolina Press, 1982); Richard R. Beeman, *The Evolution of the Southern Backcountry: A Case Study of Lunenburg County, Virginia, 1746–1832* (Philadelphia: University of Pennsylvania Press, 1984); and Deborah Vansau McCauley, *Appalachian Mountain Religion: A History* (Urbana: University of Illinois Press, 1995), chaps. 9 and 10.

12. Among the better studies of the camp meeting are: John G. Boles, *The Great Revival, 1787–1805: The Origins of the Southern Evangelical Mind* (Lexington: University Press of Kentucky, 1972); Dickson D. Bruce, *And They All Sang Hallelujah: Plain-Folk Camp-Meeting Religion, 1800–1845* (Knoxville: University of Tennessee Press, 1974); and Paul K. Conkin, *Cane Ridge: America's Pentecost* (Madison: University of Wisconsin Press, 1990). For the connection to Scotch-Irish sacramentalism, see Leigh Eric Schmidt, *Holy Fairs: Scottish Communions and American Revivals in the Early Modern Period* (Princeton, N.J.: Princeton University Press, 1989).

13. Peter Cartwright, *Autobiography of Peter Cartwright* (1856), excerpted in *The American Evangelicals, 1800–1900*, edited by William G. McLoughlin (New York: Harper and Row, 1968), p. 49.

14. Literature on Finney is growing. More recent studies include Charles E. Hambrick-Stowe, *Charles G. Finney and the Spirit of American Evangelicalism* (Grand Rapids,

Mich.: Eerdmans, 1996); Kevin Hardman, *Charles Grandison Finney, 1792–1875: Revivalist and Reformer* (Syracuse, N.Y.: Syracuse University Press, 1987); and Lewis A. Drummond, *Charles Grandison Finney and the Birth of Modern Evangelism* (London: Hodder and Stoughton, 1983).

15. Most of the relevant features of the "benevolent empire" of social reform societies may be understood through consulting Clifford S. Griffin, *Their Brothers' Keepers: Moral Stewardship in the United States, 1800–1865* (New Brunswick, N.J.: Rutgers University Press, 1960); John W. Kuykendall, *"Southern Enterprize": The Work of National Evangelical Societies in the Antebellum South* (Westport, Conn.: Greenwood, 1982); and Timothy L. Smith, *Revivalism and Social Reform: American Protestantism on the Eve of the Civil War* (reprint, Baltimore: The Johns Hopkins University Press, 1980; originally issued as *Revivalism and Social Reform in Mid-Nineteenth-Century America* [New York: Abingdon, 1957]).

16. Robert T. Handy, "The Protestant Quest for a Christian America, 1830–1930," *Church History* 22:1 (March 1952): 8–20. Handy expanded his thesis in *A Christian America: Protestant Hopes and Historical Realities*, 2nd ed. (New York: Oxford University Press, 1984). See also Ernest Lee Tuveson, *Redeemer Nation: The Idea of America's Millennial Role* (Chicago: University of Chicago Press, 1968).

17. On the popular "eclectic readers" first drafted by William Holmes McGuffey, see John H. Westerhoff, *McGuffey and His Readers: Piety, Morality, and Education in Nineteenth Century America* (Nashville: Abingdon, 1978), and Richard D. Mosier, *Making the American Mind: Social and Moral Issues in the McGuffey Readers* (New York: King's Crown Press, 1947).

18. While the "Christian school" movement will be discussed in detail later, helpful background may be found in Melinda Bollar Wagner, *God's Schools: Choice and Compromise in American Society* (New Brunswick, N.J.: Rutgers University Press, 1990), and Paul F. Parsons, *Inside America's Christian Schools* (Macon, Ga.: Mercer University Press, 1987).

19. See Patricia R. Hill, "The Missionary Enterprise," in *Encyclopedia of the American Religious Experience*, 3 vols., edited by Charles H. Lippy and Peter W. Williams (New York: Scribners, 1988), 3:1681–96; William R. Hutchison, *Errand to the World: American Protestant Thought and Foreign Missions* (Chicago: University of Chicago Press, 1987); and Clifton Jackson Phillips, *Protestant America and the Pagan World* (Cambridge, Mass.: Harvard University Press for the Harvard University East Asian Research Center, 1969).

20. The famous metaphor is found in John Winthrop's "A Model of Christian Charity," excerpted in *The American Puritans: Their Prose and Poetry*, edited by Perry Miller (Garden City, N.Y.: Doubleday, 1956), pp. 78–84.

21. The best studies are Henry Warner Bowden, *American Indians and Christian Missions: Studies in Cultural Conflict* (Chicago: University of Chicago Press, 1981), and Robert F. Berkhofer Jr., *Salvation and the Savage: An Analysis of Protestant Missions and American Indian Response, 1787–1862*, rev. ed. (New York: Atheneum, 1972).

22. Lyman Beecher, *A Plea for the West* (1835; reprint, New York: Arno, 1977).

23. Alice Felt Tyler, *Freedom's Ferment: Phases of American Social History from the Colonial Period to the Outbreak of the Civil War* (Minneapolis: University of Minnesota Press, 1944).

24. For Palmer, see Charles E. White, *The Beauty of Holiness: Phoebe Palmer as Theologian, Revivalist, Feminist, and Humanitarian* (Grand Rapids, Mich.: Zondervan

[Francis Asbury Press], 1986), and Harold E. Raser, *Phoebe Palmer: Her Life and Thought* (Lewiston, N.Y.: Edwin Mellen, 1987).

25. Mark A. Noll, *A History of Christianity in the United States and Canada* (Grand Rapids, Mich.: Eerdmans, 1992), pp. 287–88, calls attention to the businessmen's revival.

26. Clarence C. Goen, *Broken Churches, Broken Nation: Denominational Schisms and the Coming of the Civil War* (Macon, Ga.: Mercer University Press, 1985). See also Richard Carwardine, *Evangelicals and Politics in Antebellum America* (New Haven, Conn.: Yale University Press, 1993).

# 3
# Evangelicalism in Victorian America

American evangelicalism in the decades between the close of the Civil War and the nation's entry into the First World War reflected currents shaping the larger society, even as it shaped how millions viewed that society and participated in it. Some changes were primarily intellectual: the use of critical method in analyzing biblical texts, serious interest in religions outside the Judeo-Christian orbit, and development of evolutionary theories. Early work in these areas was concentrated in German universities where a growing number of American scholars pursued advanced study. In turn, these scholars incorporated critical method, comparative religion, and evolutionary theory into developing postbaccalaureate curricula in American universities. They reached ordinary folk indirectly at first; preachers, evangelists, and other religious leaders who either espoused the new ideas or were terrified by them served as conduits mediating them to the masses. In some cases, their import did not become clear until the fundamentalist-modernist controversy of the 1920s.

Use of critical method to study Scripture involved asking questions of authorship and audience, time and place of writing, literary form and genre, and similar issues. Biblical criticism meant sustained, careful analysis of texts, not to tear them to shreds, but to understand their meaning. In other words, scholars began to look at the Bible and other sacred texts the same way they looked at any literature. For German academicians such as Johann Gottfried Eichhorn, Wilhelm Leberecht de Wette, Julius Wellhausen, and Ferdinand Christian Baur critical method was central. What were the results? As scholars scrutinized the Pentateuch, for example, they revived centuries-old questions about Mosaic authorship; they argued that some texts belonged in the genre of myth, not history. Some set out to find the historical Jesus, convinced this figure differed from the Christ of faith. None desired to undermine doctrine, but others feared that critical method would destroy orthodox Christianity. For them, if the Bible were not historically accurate in every detail and claim, the foundation of faith disappeared and belief in the inspiration of Scripture evaporated. Hence, there were efforts to contain, if not quash, it. One involved heresy charges brought in 1893 against Charles Augustus Briggs, professor of Hebrew Bible at New York's Union Theological Seminary. Stripped of his ordination by Presbyterian authorities for asserting that Adam and Eve were not necessarily historical figures, Briggs retained his professorship because the seminary severed its Presbyterian ties rather than dismiss him. For staunch evangelicals, biblical criticism quickly transformed belief in the inspiration of the Bible into belief in the inerrancy of Scripture.

Related fears centered on comparative religion, which owed its genesis in part to Christian missionaries who encountered Hindus, Buddhists, Taoists, and others as they ministered in foreign lands. Although many missionaries were aghast at indigenous religious and cultural styles, some realized communicating their message required understanding local customs. Much information about non-Western religions appeared in articles and letters written by missionaries that were published in periodicals sponsored by mission boards and agencies. Some missionaries who became sensitive to the religiosity around them recognized that, like Christianity, other religions dealt with questions of personal identity, meaning in life, the problem of evil, and hope for some sort of afterlife. The next step was to compare how different religions wrestled with these common issues. The field of comparative religion, now commonly called the history of religions, was born. Many evangelicals feared that relativism or essentialism, the idea that at base all religions were the same and equally valid, would result. They believed comparative religion undermined Christianity's claims to absolute, final truth.

For many years, evangelicals saw science as an ally because the Scottish Common Sense philosophy undergirding evangelical theology had corollaries in Baconian approaches to science. Both saw truth as straightforward and self-evident, known by intuition or inductive reasoning (common sense). Even Scripture was scientific because its truth became self-evident when texts were examined properly. Many evangelicals still relied on Common Sense Realism and Baconian science when evolutionary theory and a different understanding of scientific method became attractive. In the popular mind, evolution remains associated with Charles Darwin, who advanced his ideas in *The Origin of Species* (1859) and *The Descent of Man* (1871).[1] Darwin built on hypotheses promulgated by others, such as British geologists James Hutton and Charles Lyell who believed that geological shifts resulted not from catastrophic, cataclysmic changes, but from a steady process that brought gradual transformation. Darwin extended this idea to animal (and thus human) development in the theory of natural selection. His views were not immediately accepted by American academics. Harvard's Asa Gray became an early supporter, but saw nothing incompatible between Darwin's understanding and traditional Christian affirmation of

divine creation. Others believed evolutionary theory discredited the biblical creation narratives, if not the existence of God. At the time, these issues troubled
primarily evangelical theologians; by the second decade of the twentieth century
they had an impact on the evangelical masses.[2]

Evangelicals in Victorian America likewise had also to contend with social
and cultural shifts so interconnected that it is impossible to discuss them independently. The industrialization that began to refashion American economic life
during the era of the Second Great Awakening moved at a frantic pace as the
century drew to a close. Thousands left farms and villages for cities, hoping to
improve and secure their economic lot. The 1920 census revealed that more than
half the U.S. population lived in urban areas. The nation had shifted from a
rural to an urban base. The decades between the Civil War and World War I
also mark the heaviest immigration to the United States. Because the overwhelming majority came from southern, central, and eastern Europe, they
brought greater ethnic diversity than existed when northern and western European ethnic styles dominated. Most were Roman Catholic, Orthodox, or Jewish.
The presence of millions of non-Protestants, not just nonevangelicals, altered
the religious landscape permanently, challenging and ultimately destroying visions for an evangelical culture. Immigration, urbanization, and industrialization
spawned a host of new cultural situations. Poor and unsafe working conditions
generated labor unrest and contributed to the formation of labor unions. The
millions pouring into the cities confronted inadequate housing and poor sanitation facilities that created the slum or ghetto. Schools were unprepared to deal
with thousands of new students who could not speak English. By the century's
end, African Americans began arriving in northern cities in larger numbers,
adding another layer to the mix. Then, too, the nation was moving westward.
By 1890, the frontier of myth vanished as the population filled in the gaps from
coast to coast. At the same time, some regions began to develop distinctive
identities, sometimes because of relative isolation (Appalachia) and sometimes
because of historical circumstances (the Old South). The United States in 1920
was a very different place than the United States of the antebellum period when
evangelical hopes ran high.

One evangelical response to this new world was to continue the urban revival
so successful in the ministry of Charles Grandison Finney. The premier figure
was *Dwight Lyman Moody. Like Finney before him and *Billy Sunday after,
Moody had not intended a religious vocation and received no formal theological
education. Rather, just before the Civil War, Moody began volunteer work in
Chicago's slums, inviting persons to church, organizing Sunday school classes,
and informally testifying to the gospel of personal salvation. Moody was successful in business as a shoe salesman and in ministry as an evangelist. That
success allowed him to bridge the antebellum evangelical world with the industrial, business-based world of the later nineteenth century. Moody's message
was the evangelical call for individual conversion, coupled with an individualistic approach in dealing with social issues. For him and others of his ilk, society

would be reformed—and the evangelical vision of a Christian society attained—only when individuals were converted. The structures of society would remain tainted by sin, but that blemish could be transcended by the piety of the saved. Moody also added pieces to the emerging mosaic of modern revivalism. His background in sales gave him a penchant for organization. As Stuart Henry has noted, Moody's "revivals were organized to the last detail."[3] Revivalism became a business befitting the age. Moody also recognized the power of music and was among the first to employ a full-time musician, Ira D. Sankey, who sang and composed gospel songs that became favorites of the masses who flocked to the tabernacles built just for Moody's meetings. Moody, like Finney, also ventured into education, founding both the Northfield schools in his native Massachusetts and what is now the Moody Bible Institute, to train persons for evangelical religious work. In time, the Moody Bible Institute became the center of a large-scale evangelical operation that included a publishing arm and a radio station.

Moody's approach echoed in cities across the nation. As a former employee, Moody was an ardent supporter of the YMCA, founded in part to provide housing in a wholesome (evangelical) environment for young men seeking employment in the nation's cities. The YWCA served a similar function for women, albeit with more rules and regulations for residents in order to protect them from the evils of the city.[4] Bible study groups, special interest classes, and athletic activities were regular parts of the Y program. The assumption was that young evangelicals who moved to the cities would yield to temptation unless ensconced in an evangelical milieu. Historians have also called attention to the ways in which Holiness congregations in the cities attracted rural migrants, sometimes, as in the case of the Church of the Nazarene, becoming new denominations as a result.[5]

City missions or rescue missions, some still in operation, ministered to those who yielded to temptation.[6] The designation "rescue mission" betrays the rationale that guided them. The homeless and the indigent, the drunkard and the one who had lost all to gambling or some other social evil, could receive a bed for the night and some food for the price of listening to an evangelical message with a call for conversion. For thousands, it was a small price to pay, and for the newly saved, conversion provided an entree into social respectability. The Salvation Army devoted itself to this style of ministry, becoming a denomination in the process.[7] Akin to the rescue mission was the settlement house; Chicago's Hull House, founded by Jane Addams, is among the more well known.[8] Settlement houses tried to alleviate the worst of slum living conditions by providing recreational programs for children, classes in domestic affairs for women, and numerous related activities. The "institutional church" in a sense combined the traditional church with the settlement house; it generally contained a gymnasium and other recreational facilities, classrooms where everything from cooking and sewing to industrial arts might be taught, and a sanctuary for worship.[9] Some settlement houses extended their services to immigrants, but many served primarily those of Euro-American stock for whom urban life brought economic distress, not economic success. Institutional churches in ethnic neighborhoods often contained rooms where newly arrived immigrants found temporary housing. African Americans faced the same kinds of social dislocation, but the prevalence of racism in the North meant that they were excluded from these evangelical social service agencies as frequently as they were welcomed by them.

Other evangelical responses to the changing culture of the late nineteenth century cast a wider net. A good example is the Evangelical Alliance, particularly the work and writings of Congregationalist Josiah Strong, its long-time executive secretary.[10] Strong brought a sociological perspective to his interpretation of challenges to the evangelical vision in *Our Country*, his most well-known work.[11] Convinced that individual salvation offered the only alternative to both personal damnation and the collapse of American society, Strong called for efforts to convert immigrants to Protestantism through city mission work and the institutional church, and other cooperative ventures. In retrospect, Strong comes across as a racist, anti-Catholic imperialist because for him becoming an evangelical Protestant was a prerequisite to becoming a good citizen. But to label him as such is to do him a disservice. Strong was simply convinced that the benefits of technology as represented by industrialization and urbanization strengthened the mandate to mold American society into the kingdom of God on earth. Doing so, however, involved turning everyone into an evangelical Protestant.[12]

Some endeavors to mold the larger society according to evangelical mores echoed the antebellum zeal for social reform. One example is the Women's Christian Temperance Union (WCTU), founded in 1873 by *Frances Willard, who later became an advocate of both woman's suffrage and the ordination of women. The WCTU became not only the largest women's organization of its day, but a major voice for social reform.[13] With the Anti-Saloon League, begun in 1893, the WCTU led the movement that brought the national experiment with Prohibition after World War I. It also saw itself as protecting the American family from destruction because of alcoholism. Although moderate consumption of alcoholic beverages was frequently part of immigrants' cultures of origin, evangelicals emphasized its connections to urban poverty and slum life. Even though the WCTU and the Anti-Saloon League in time called for the government to enact and enforce Prohibition, their thrust was primarily individualistic. That is, individuals were urged one by one to sign pledges promising to abstain from alcoholic beverages.

Many influenced by modernist theology also had an interest in social reform, although their approach called for change in the structures of society as well as conversion of individuals. Here Protestant advocates of the Social Gospel such as Walter Rauschenbusch and Washington Gladden and Roman Catholic thinkers such as John A. Ryan are representative. Rauschenbusch, for example, was convinced that as long as sin marked social structures, individuals would never be in an environment conducive to conversion and a life of piety. Most evangelicals, however, were reluctant to endorse the scale of social change that Rauschenbusch saw as essential to bring the reign of God to its culmination in American society. In the South, where evangelicals tried to keep religious institutions from meddling with social structures, the more radical Social Gospel gained infrequent hearing. As Charles Reagan Wilson deftly argued, later nineteenth-century Southern evangelical preachers helped create a mythic, idealized past where virtue and piety reigned supreme—a Southern civil religion of the Lost Cause—more than they wrestled with the social problems that came with Reconstruction.[14] But women and denominational women's organizations were more likely to see the social implications of faith; they founded settlement houses in the region's industrializing cities and took the lead in the anti-lynching movement.[15]

Change came to family life as well. In the antebellum agrarian context, place of work and place of residence were likely the same; in the city, the husband/father often worked outside the home in a factory or other industry, bringing home wages to support the family. As a result, the home became the sphere of women, contributing to what Ann Douglas termed the "feminization of American culture."[16] Religious nurture of children and family became the responsibility of women, and the Victorian home became an extension of the church, functionally replacing the church as the locus of religiosity.[17] The number of women who claimed church membership continued to exceed the number of men. Although professional ministry generally remained closed to women, some evangelically inclined denominations relied on women to staff settlement houses, city missions, and institutional churches, and lead religious education activities.[18] Among Methodists, such women were known as deaconesses. Men in turn found social and religious outlets in fraternal organizations such as the Masons or the Odd Fellows.[19] Fraternal organizations and lodges were not new, but in the half century after the Civil War, membership in them reached its peak. With rituals full of religious language and imagery, much of it feminine, lodges became surrogate religious institutions, a "men's sphere" to counterbalance the home as "women's sphere." Evangelicals were frequently wary of such organizations, but generally powerless to stop individuals from joining them. One historian suggested that all major U.S. cities had more lodges than churches at the beginning of the twentieth century.[20] The evangelically oriented *Christian Cynosure*, founded in 1868 as the periodical of the National Christian Association Opposed to Secret Societies, trumpeted the evils of lodge membership; much of its material came from Jonathan Blanchard, who served as president of both Knox College and the Illinois Institute, forerunner of Wheaton College.[21]

Camp meeting grounds also underwent transformation. Many became extensions of the Victorian home, as wives and children frequently moved to permanent or semipermanent dwellings on the grounds for the summer season, joined by their husbands on weekends.[22] The Holiness ethos pervaded many long-established meetings, shifting the emphasis from conversion to attaining sanctification. The focus of the camp meeting gradually moved in a different direction. Camp grounds located in rural areas or along the seaboard became refuges from the threats of the cities. Those attending meetings were hardly heathen; most were nurtured in the churches. Camp meeting chroniclers reported ever fewer conversions, but more edifying gatherings.[23] Some camp meetings reflected ways evangelicals responded to perceived threats to the authority of Scripture. In 1876, several individuals, many of Presbyterian affiliation, organized what became known as the Niagara Bible Conference.[24] The emphasis was almost exclusively on eschatological prophecy, especially prominent in the books of Daniel and Revelation. Two years later, the first International Prophecy Conference was held. The Niagara conferences also spawned many local or regional annual variants, some in large cities; international ones convened about once a decade. Both fizzled, as did the camp meetings more generally, with the outbreak of World War I.

The approach to Scripture undergirding the prophetic conferences represents an enduring intellectual response of evangelicalism to modernist thought. Emerging first in Britain among the Plymouth Brethren led by John Nelson Darby, who in later life spent considerable time in the United States, these hermeneutical principles derived from a system called premillennial dispensationalism.[25] Behind premillennial dispensationalism lie two key assumptions. The first is the conviction that the divine creation of the world occurred in 4004 B.C.E. The other is that the Bible is a reliable, totally accurate, scientific account of human history and a guide to what will transpire when history draws to a close with Christ's physical Second Coming. According to Darby, history from creation to Second Coming is divided into blocks of time called dispensations. In each dispensation, the Divine will was revealed to humanity in a way appropriate to the times. Each time, humanity failed to follow God's way, making a new dispensation necessary. Since in the Book of Revelation and other ancient literature seven symbolized completeness or perfection, Darby insisted that there would be seven dispensations. The present is the sixth, the "church age," that is moving quickly toward judgment because both church and its Christian civilization have failed. Premillennial dispensationalism represents a curious blend of optimism and pessimism. The pessimism comes because the faithful fail to meet God's tests. The world becomes a grim arena; all human society is fraught with evil. Dispensationalists therefore evince little interest in social reform and much more in rescuing individuals from evil to spare them judgment. The optimistic strand reflects what will transpire at history's close. The millennial age, inaugurated when Christ returns as political ruler of the earth for one thousand years (the millennium), succeeds the church age. Then comes the final conflict between good and evil, the last judgment, and finally the dawn of a new creation. The study Bible published in 1909 bearing the name of Bible conference stalwart *C. I. Scofield impressed the dispensationalist scheme on the evangelical mind. Called "the most influential single publication in millenarian and Fundamentalist historiography"[26] and with total sales near the 12 million mark by the end of the century, the *Scofield Reference Bible* used an elaborate scheme of cross-references to fit all Scripture into the dispensationalist framework. Scofield worked with the King James Version; when that version was modernized, editors produced an updated *Scofield Reference Bible* in 1967. Premillennial dispensationalism also became fixed in some evangelical circles through church workers who studied at Moody Bible Institute and similar schools and then carried this ideology to congregations where they worked.

Another evangelical response to modern thought was the "higher life" or "victorious life" thinking that initially developed in Holiness circles around Keswick in England's Lake District. At first, this stance appears to echo the Wesleyan Holiness movement in its concern for the higher life lived in the presence of the Holy Spirit, but its advocates came more from evangelically inclined churches in the Reformed tradition.[27] "Higher life" preachers such as Presbyterian *J. Wilbur Chapman and Congregationalist *Reuben A. Torrey promoted a deep personal experience following conversion that drew individuals to a higher plane, until spiritual power infused all of life. Other connections to Holiness came when some "higher life" proponents, many familiar to the Bible conference/camp meeting circuit, made the epitome of personal religious experience the surrendering of all to Jesus. In return, one received victory over all evil in one's own life. *Charles G. Trumbull, for example, promoted "victorious life" teaching through the *Sunday School Times* that he edited. It gained other institutional expression when *Robert C. McQuilkin Jr., a friend of Trumbull, founded Columbia Bible College in South Carolina in 1923.[28] "Victorious life" perspectives, current in many evangelical circles today, shared with premillennial dispensationalism the conviction that everyday society was a realm of evil. As in earlier evangelicalism, in "higher life" or "victorious life" thought those experiencing salvation somehow transcend the empirical realm, becoming removed from or victorious over its vicissitudes. Individual, not social, experience remained primary, and the urbanizing, industrializing world could be understood, if not dismissed, because it was "other" than the realm of pure spirituality.

Also related to this later Holiness is the modern Pentecostal movement, with origins in revivals at Los Angeles's Azusa Street Mission in Los Angeles in 1906, although surviving evidence documents Pentecostal expression in African American congregations near Durham, North Carolina, in the 1880s.[29] The Azusa Street revivals, which attracted national attention, were led by *William J. Seymour, an African American Holiness preacher. Under Seymour's preaching, glossolalia, or speaking in tongues, became a regular feature at Azusa Street Mission services.[30] One of Seymour's mentors was *Charles Fox Parham, a one-time Methodist Holiness preacher whose ministry centered in Topeka, Kansas, and then in Houston, Texas. In Parham's thinking, the connection of Pentecostalism to an evangelical approach to Scripture is apparent. Parham and students at a school affiliated with his church studied the New Testament accounts of Pentecost and of charismatic gifts, becoming convinced that Scripture literally promised verification or authentication of sanctification in spiritual gifts or a baptism of the Holy Spirit. Speaking in tongues was the most common, but the gift of healing, more prominent later, was not uncommon.

A similar understanding of other passages of Scripture, especially the sixteenth chapter of Mark, turned some Pentecostal expression in different directions, primarily in Appalachia. In Mark 16, signs of authentic faith include not only speaking in tongues and the ability to heal, but handling serpents and drinking toxic substances. Sometime around 1910 (the precise date is unknown), George Went Hensley initiated the practice of handling poisonous snakes and drinking strychnine as part of worship.[31] Hensley was briefly associated with a new Pentecostal denomination, the Church of God (Cleveland, Tennessee), and the Chattanooga area became the early center of serpent handling. Hensley's travels took him throughout Appalachia, and serpent handling spread because of his work. Never attracting large numbers of adherents, serpent handling took hold in evangelical congregations scattered through West Virginia, Kentucky, the Carolinas, eastern Tennessee, northwest Georgia, and northeast Alabama.

The most sophisticated evangelical theological response to modernism was the Princeton theology, so called because its most articulate advocates were professors at Princeton Theological Seminary, a Presbyterian institution.[32] Among them over a few generations were Archibald Alexander, *Charles Hodge, Archibald Alexander Hodge, and *Benjamin Breckinridge Warfield. Committed to the Reformed theological heritage, informed philosophically by Scottish Common Sense Realism, and accepting the inductive methods of Baconian science, the Princeton theologians reacted especially against modernism's presumed assault on the reliability of Scripture. For them, finding different strands of writing in the Pentateuch or classifying some biblical literature as myth meant that Scripture was unreliable or false. Common Sense Realism required them to affirm all Scripture as historically and scientifically true. In time, evangelicals who spoke of biblical "inerrancy" found their theoretical basis in the Princeton theology. So, too, did those who attacked theories of evolution as standing in contradiction to the Genesis accounts of creation.

Princeton voices, especially that of Warfield, joined with those of some dispensationalists in articulating reservations about some of the evangelical styles that were current. The Holiness belief that sanctification was attainable here and now, along with the higher life or victorious life teaching that total surrender resulted in triumph over all sin came under particular attack. To those informed by the Reformed tradition's appreciation of the depth of human depravity, these approaches minimized the ower of sin in human life, if they did not virtually deny its presence among the sanctified who had moved to a higher spiritual plane. There was also concern about the authenticity of charismatic gifts. Princeton theologians and dispensationalists alike tended to argue that manifestation of charismatic gifts was restricted to the apostolic age; contemporary expressions were therefore delusions.

In the twentieth century, these various theological strands interconnected and

sometimes blended in a variety of ways. Some configurations yielded Fundamentalism; others, a conservative, orthodox stance that provided a constant
counter to liberal theological currents. Yet others sustained a bewildering array
of Pentecostal expressions. All suggest that evangelicalism responded creatively
to the challenges of the later nineteenth century. As evangelicals built networks
through camp meetings and conferences, revival meetings such Moody's, periodicals trumpeting everything from premillennial dispensationalism to the gifts
of the Spirit, and institutions such as Wheaton College, Moody Bible Institute,
and Columbia Bible College, they laid strong foundations for the future. But
internal disagreements among evangelicals, especially over sanctification, holiness, higher life and victorious life teaching, and charismatic gifts indicated that
evangelicals were not fashioned from a single mold.

## NOTES

1. Both are available in a combined modern edition: Charles Darwin, *The Origin of
Species and The Descent of Man* (New York: Random House, 1977).

2. See James R. Moore, *The Post-Darwinian Controversies: A Study of the Protestant Struggle to Come to Terms with Darwin in Great Britain and America, 1870–1900*
(Cambridge, Eng.: Cambridge University Press, 1979), and David N. Livingstone, *Darwin's Forgotten Defenders: The Encounter between Evangelical Theology and Evolutionary Thought* (Grand Rapids, Mich.: Eerdmans, 1987).

3. Stuart C. Henry, "Revivalism," in *Encyclopedia of the American Religious Experience*, 3 vols., edited by Charles H. Lippy and Peter W. Williams (New York: Scribners, 1988), 2:808.

4. On the YMCA, see the relevant chapters of C. Howard Hopkins, *History of the
Y.M.C.A. in North America* (New York: Association, 1951). A recently reprinted early
history of the YWCA is Elizabeth Wilson, *Fifty Years of Association Work Among Young
Women, 1866–1916* (New York: National Board of the Young Women's Christian Association of the United States of America, 1916; reprint, New York and London: Garland,
1987).

5. Timothy L. Smith, *Called Unto Holiness: The Story of the Nazarenes, the For-
mative Years* (Kansas City, MO.: Nazarene Publishing House, 1962), argues that the
Church of the Nazarene emerged as a creative response to urban conditions; Robert L.
Cross, ed., *The Church and the City* (Indianapolis: Bobbs-Merrill, 1967), claims that the
Nazarenes represent more the transplanting of a rural religious style into the city.

6. See especially Carroll Smith-Rosenberg, *Religion and the Rise of the American
City: The New York City Mission Movement, 1812–1870* (Ithaca, N.Y.: Cornell University Press, 1971).

7. See Edward H. McKinley, *Marching to Glory: The History of the Salvation Army
in the United States, 1880–1992*, 2nd ed. (Grand Rapids, Mich.: Eerdmans, 1995). For
the British beginnings of the Army, see Norman H. Murdoch, *Origins of the Salvation
Army* (Knoxville: University of Tennessee Press, 1994).

8. See Norris Magnuson, *Salvation in the Slums: Evangelical Social Work, 1865–
1920* (Metuchen, N.J.: Scarecrow, 1977). Magnuson also discusses city missions and
rescue missions.

9. A good contemporary description of the institutional church is found in Charles Stelzle, *Christianity's Storm Centre: A Study of the Modern City* (New York: Fleming H. Revell, 1907), pp. 163–91. Stelzle was a Presbyterian minister who served as superintendent of the northern Presbyterian Department of Church and Labor when it was set up in 1903.

10. See Philip D. Jordan, *The Evangelical Alliance for the United States of America, 1847–1900: Ecumenism, Identity, and the Religion of the Republic* (Lewiston, N.Y.: Edwin Mellen, 1983).

11. Josiah Strong, *Our Country*, edited by Jurgen Herbst (Cambridge, Mass.: Belknap Press of Harvard University Press, 1963). See also Strong, *The Challenge of the City* (New York: Missionary Education Movement, 1907).

12. A nearly contemporaneous study of efforts to convert Catholic immigrants is Theodore Abel, *Protestant Missions to Catholic Immigrants* (New York: Institute of Social and Religous Research, 1933).

13. Several of Willard's most important writings are collected in Carolyn DeSwarte Gifford, ed., *The Ideal of "The New Woman" According to the Women's Christian Temperance Union* (New York and London: Garland, 1987). Also see Frances Willard, *Women in the Pulpit* (Chicago: Women's Christian Temperance Publishing Association, 1889), reprinted in *The Defense of Women's Rights to Ordination in the Methodist Episcopal Church*, edited by Carolyn DeSwarte Gifford (New York and London: Garland, 1987).

14. Charles Reagan Wilson, *Baptized in Blood: The Civil Religion of the Lost Cause, 1865–1920* (Athens: University of Georgia Press, 1980).

15. See John P. McDowell, *The Social Gospel in the South: The Woman's Home Mission Movement in the Methodist Episcopal Church, South, 1886–1939* (Baton Rouge: Louisiana State University Press, 1982).

16. Ann Douglas, *The Feminization of American Culture* (New York: Knopf, 1978).

17. See especially Colleen McDannell, *The Christian Home in Victorian America, 1840–1900* (Bloomington: Indiana University Press, 1986).

18. A provocative contemporary account is Annie Turner Wittenmeyer, *Women's Work for Jesus* (New York: Nelson and Phillips, 1873; reprint, New York: Garland, 1987).

19. See Mark C. Carnes, *Secret Ritual and Manhood in Victorian America* (New Haven, Conn.: Yale University Press, 1989).

20. Fergus MacDonald, *The Catholic Church and the Secret Societies in the United States*, edited by Thomas J. McMahon, United States Catholic Historical Society Monograph Series 22 (New York: United States Catholic Historical Society, 1946), p. 100.

21. See *A Brief History of the National Christian Association* (Chicago: Ezra A. Cook, 1875); Robert Wayne Smith, "A Study of the Speaking in the Anti-Secrecy Movement, 1862–1882, with Special Reference to the National Christian Association" (Ph.D. diss., State University of Iowa, 1956); Clarence N. Roberts, "The Crusade Against Secret Societies and the National Christian Association," *Journal of the Illinois State Historical Society* 64 (Winter 1971): 382–400; and Richard S. Taylor, "Christian Cynosure," in *Popular Religious Magazines of the United States*, edited by P. Mark Fackler and Charles H. Lippy (Westport, Conn.: Greenwood, 1995), pp. 115–20.

22. See Ellen Weiss, *City in the Woods: The Life and Design of an American Camp Meeting on Martha's Vineyard* (New York: Oxford University Press, 1987).

23. See Charles H. Lippy, "The Camp Meeting in Transition: The Character and Legacy of the Late Nineteenth Century," *Methodist History* 34:1 (October 1995): 3–17.

24. There is good discussion of the Niagara Bible Conferences in Ernest R. Sandeen, *The Roots of Fundamentalism: British and American Millenarianism, 1800–1930* (Chicago: University of Chicago Press, 1970).

25. See Paul S. Boyer, *When Time Shall Be No More: Prophecy Belief in Modern American Culture* (Cambridge, Mass.: Belknap Press of Harvard University, 1992), and Timothy P. Weber, *Living in the Shadow of the Second Coming: American Premillennialism, 1875–1982*, enl. ed. (1979; reprint, Chicago: University of Chicago Press, 1987). See also Clarence B. Bass, *Backgrounds to Dispensationalism* (Grand Rapids, Mich.: Eerdmans, 1960).

26. Sandeen, *Roots of Fundamentalism*, p. 222.

27. Grant Wacker, "The Holy Spirit and the Spirit of the Age in American Protestantism, 1880–1920," *Journal of American History* 72 (1985): 45–62, and Douglas W. Frank, *Less than Conquerors: How Evangelicals Entered the Twentieth Century* (Grand Rapids, Mich.: Eerdmans, 1986), chap. 4, provide good introductions to "higher life" and "victorious life" thinking.

28. See Bruce L. Shelley, "Sources of Pietistic Fundamentalism," *Fides et Historia* 5 (Spring 1973): 68–78.

29. For insightful studies of modern Pentecostalism, see Robert Mapes Anderson, *Vision of the Disinherited: The Making of American Pentecostalism* (New York: Oxford University Press, 1979); Nils Bloch-Hoell, *The Pentecostal Movement* (London: Allen and Unwin, 1964); W. J. Hollenweger, *The Pentecostals: The Charismatic Movement in the Churches* (Minneapolis: Augsburg, 1969), Vinson Synan, *The Holiness-Pentecostal Movement in the United States* (Grand Rapids, Mich.: Eerdmans, 1971); and Grant Wacker, "Pentecostalism," in *Encyclopedia of the American Religious Experience*, 2: 933–45.

30. A good contemporary account of glossolalia is F. G. Henke, "The Gift of Tongues and Related Phenomena at the Present Day," *American Journal of Theology* 13 (1909): 196–201. See also Felicitas D. Goodman, *Speaking in Tongues: A Cross-Cultural Study of Glossolalia* (Chicago: University of Chicago Press, 1972), and John P. Kildahl, *The Psychology of Speaking in Tongues* (New York: Harper & Row, 1972).

31. The best recent study is David Kimbrough, *Taking Up Serpents: Snake Handlers of Eastern Kentucky* (Chapel Hill: University of North Carolina Press, 1995).

32. See Mark A. Noll, ed., *The Princeton Theology, 1812–1921* (Grand Rapids, Mich.: Baker, 1983), and W. Andrew Hoffecker, *Piety and the Princeton Theologians: Archibald Alexander, Charles Hodge, and Benjamin Warfield* (Grand Rapids, Mich.: Baker Book House, 1981).

# 4
# The Fundamentalist-Modernist Controversy

From the 1880s on, the primary obstacle to the optimistic evangelical vision of "a Christian America" was labeled variously as "modernism" or "liberalism." In a theological context at the turn of the century, modernism generally meant: (1) the conscious, intended adaptation of religious ideas to modern culture, (2) the idea that God is immanent in human cultural development and revealed through it, and (3) the belief that human society is moving toward realization of the Kingdom of God.[1] To accommodate the prevailing empirical epistemology, modernists conceived hermeneutical techniques for interpreting biblical texts that shifted from the literalist to the allegorical, mythical, and symbolic.[2]

Evangelicals increasingly despaired over the corrosive effects of such a modernist approach upon traditional biblical concepts of the person and character of Christ, the special divine creation of humanity, providence, and the absolute uniqueness of Christianity as the one faith by which all must be saved. To most evangelicals, these were foundational verities upon which their lives and destinies rested. However, as the pace of modernism accelerated in the psychic dislocation of World War I, the conservative evangelical subculture was forced into a decidedly defensive stance by the 1920s. When last ditch efforts to hold the line on the teaching of evolution in the public schools and attempts to control denominations like the Northern Baptists and Presbyterians were routed, the cultural marginalization of American evangelicalism was complete.

Although the Holiness and Pentecostal movements of the late nineteenth and early twentieth centuries can be seen as conservative, evangelical responses to the modernist trends of America culture, the most characteristic reaction is popularly known as "fundamentalism." Holiness and Pentecostal adherents were often an ethnically diverse lot who eschewed theology in favor of emotional religion and lived on the sociological periphery of America. Those who became known as fundamentalists usually were from the groups that comprised the "evangelical empire" of the nineteenth century: Presbyterians, Baptists, and Congregationalists. The first fundamentalists tended to be well-educated, urban dwellers, whose serious concern for theological formulation brought them into direct and unavoidable conflict with modernism.[3] These fundamentalists felt threatened by a changing America because they understood all too well what was at stake.

In the transitional period between the Civil War and World War I, few modernists within American evangelicalism wanted to discard the traditional faith altogether. Kenneth Cauthen makes a helpful distinction between what he calls "evangelical liberalism" and "modernistic liberalism." Evangelical liberals "were those determined to maintain the historical continuity of the Christian doctrinal and ecclesiastical tradition, except insofar as modern circumstances required adjustment or change." To these individuals, the Bible remained extremely important, although not in a literalistic sense, because it focused the Christian on Christ who remained the exemplary human example. Modernistic liberals, on the other hand, "approached religion as a human phenomenon, the Bible as one great religious document among others, and the Christian faith as one major religio-ethical tradition among others."[4] Modernistic liberals were the radical fringe among the nontraditionalists of American evangelicalism. Evangelical liberals, more numerous and clearly gaining in influence by the end of the nineteenth century, still shared enough of traditional evangelicalism's reverence for Christ and the Bible to seem part of the fold and an alarming threat only to those factions of evangelicalism, like Old School Presbyterianism, that demanded a very high degree of divine inspiration in their hermeneutical approach to biblical texts. Thus, during the transitional period from 1865 to 1910, a more benign form of modernism, as typified by the evangelical liberals, had ample opportunity to grow almost imperceptably within the bosom of American evangelicalism before it confronted widespread resistance from those who might be called fundamentalists.

Beyond a general opposition to the modernistic impulse, what did early fundamentalists believe? By 1910, a consensus emerged around the "five fundamentals" of the faith adopted by the General Assembly of the (Northern) Presbyterian Church. These beliefs, which were not to be compromised in any way, were: the inerrancy of Scripture, the virgin birth of Christ, his vicarious atonement, his bodily resurrection, and the historicity of Christ's biblically recorded miracles.[5] The key statement, since the other four issued from it, concerned the inerrancy of Scripture. Based on inductive Baconian scientific approach and Scottish Common Sense Realism, the doctrine of inerrancy was championed by Princeton theologians *Benjamin Breckinridge Warfield and *J. Gresham Machen. To prove the Bible was in error, said Warfield, the biblical critic would have to produce error in the "original autographs" (the original texts untainted by copying and transmission), a feat that was plainly impossible since those texts no longer existed. In addition, Warfield noted that a perceived error in the Bible could result from a faulty intepretation on the part of the critic or to errors introduced by copyists that were not present in the original auto-graphs.[6] Inerrancy became the linchpin in the developing fundamentalist defense of traditional Christianity. To yield on inerrancy meant to surrender the other key fundamentals concerning the person and work of Christ. This "Manichean" view that permitted no middle ground for compromise explains the ferocity that fundamentalists exhibited in their increasingly open battles with modernists after World War I.[7]

Besides the "five fundamentals," premillennial dispensationalism was a key belief common to many fundamentalists that tended to galvanize them during the first two decades of the twentieth century. Particularly important in the fun-damentalist conflict with modernism was the dispensationalist conviction that the institutional Christian church had apostasized and fallen into ruin. This per-ception provided fundamentalists with a pessimistic world-view and also the conviction that modernism in the Church was a satanic threat to traditional Christianity to be resisted at any cost.[8]

Fundamentalism spread rapidly throughout American evangelicalism both by way of the Holiness and higher life movements and through the many Bible and prophecy conferences sponsored by dispensationalists. The Niagara Bible Conference of 1876 was followed by the International Prophecy Conference of 1878 and further conferences in Chicago (1886), Allegheny, Pennsylvania (1895), Boston (1901), Chicago (1914), Philadelphia (1918), and New York City (1918). These conferences, assiduously publicized by dispensational journals like Arno C. Gaebelein's *Our Hope*, helped create a ready-made network of contacts for the fundamentalists.[9]

The movement was also led informally by several pastor-evangelists who gave it shape and direction. The pattern was set by *Dwight L. Moody, who "while remaining on the best of terms with denominations . . . spurned denominational affiliations and built his own evangelistic empire, free from ecclesiastical con-trol."[10] For Moody that empire included not only his Chicago pulpit, but also Moody Bible Institute, his Northfield Conferences in Massachusetts, and his influential advocacy of the Keswick movement, biblical infallibility, and pre-millennialism. The last two points were particularly important for Moody's role as a "progenitor of fundamentalism."[11]

Moody became an archetype for fundamentalist leadership. However, his con-cern that all else be secondary to his essential work as a revivalist set him apart from those who attempted to follow him. Moody's associates, *J. Wilbur Chap-man, A. C. Dixon, *A. J. Gordon, and *Reuben A. Torrey, were not able to follow the moderation of their mentor as successfully in more radical times. All were dynamic evangelists, fervent advocates of the higher life movement, and avid students of biblical prophecy.[12] Gordon died in 1895 and Chapman in 1918, but Dixon and Torrey moved resolutely in the direction of fundamentalism as the postwar era began.

This decidedly conservative move can be seen in two major initiatives: the publication of *The Fundamentals* and the creation of the World's Christian Fundamentals Association (WCFA). Both Dixon and Torrey served as editors of *The Fundamentals*, a series of twelve paperback volumes published between 1910 and 1915 and bankrolled by a wealthy southern California oil millionaire, Lyman Stewart. With about 3 million volumes distributed free to all interested Christian denominational workers and educators in the English-speaking world, *The Fundamentals* became a symbolic point of reference in identifying a "fundamentalist movement" by the start of World War I. In terms of substance, the essays, written by a host of conservative Protestants, lack the stridency one might expect. Major fundamentalist concerns like Darwinism, dispensationalism, and premillennialism were scarcely broached. Yet taken as a whole, *The Fundamentals* summarize the antimodernist world-view of their authors quite comprehensively.[13]

The other major fundamentalist initiative launched by Dixon and Torrey was the establishment of the WCFA in 1919. With the crucial assistance of William B. Riley, the pastor of First Baptist Church of Minneapolis, a man whom Ferenc Szasz has called "the organizing genius of American Fundamentalism," Dixon and Torrey intended the WCFA to be the major interdenominational force in the American fundamentalist movement after the Great War. The specific objectives of the WCFA were to organize conferences and Bible institutes around the country to rally conservative evangelicals against the threat of theological modernism.[14]

Although the efforts of Dixon, Torrey, and Riley were crucial in giving direction to fundamentalism, in the popular imagination the evangelist who best personified the militancy of the movement was *Billy Sunday. The most successful evangelist of his era, Sunday was outspokenly critical of modernism although he cared little for the complexities of theology. During World War I, Sunday was unapologetically patriotic, thereby giving focus to a particular wartime preoccupation of fundamentalism: the German menace. Yet for all his visibility, Sunday remained an outsider and took no active leadership in the fundamentalist movement, although many observers habitually linked him with it.[15]

America's entry into the Great War in 1917 deeply intensified emotions on both sides of the modernist-fundamentalist divide. Modernists, taking their cue from President Woodrow Wilson, saw the war effort as part of their ongoing crusade to realize the Kingdom of God—the brotherhood of man under the Fatherhood of God. Cooperation among Christians of all stripes and the leveling of theological barriers essential to the modernist credo raised expectations that Protestants could unite after the war to finish the reform efforts of the Social Gospel movement and initiate an era of peace and prosperity. Out of this spirit came the Interchurch World Movement, which was viewed as a religious arm of the League of Nations. Anticipation was high that the temperance effort would finally result in legally mandated Prohibition. In addition, many evangelicals of a more liberal bent actively planned for the institutional union of many Protestant denominations.[16]

If modernists were almost euphoric about the possibilities after World War I, the growing fundamentalist faction within American evangelicalism was falling into a morbid state of gloom over national and world events. Dispensational premillennialism gave fundamentalists a template through which to measure the affairs of the world. Their universal conclusion was that the world was galloping toward Armageddon; more and more Americans were forsaking God at the risk of divine judgment; and the institutional church, hijacked by theological modernists, was ruined. Conservative evangelicals, also caught up in the crusade mentality of the times, looked for a chief bogey man and found it in the higher criticism of the modernists that undermined the traditional force of Bible-based evangelicalism. Dispensationalists believed it was a confirmation of their reading of biblical prophecy that the ''Beast'' of the book of Revelation—whom many took to be Germany during World War I—was also the birthplace of the nefarious higher critical theories.[17]

A growing preoccupation with the evils of higher criticism led fundamentalists during the war era and in the 1920s to focus their fury on the University of Chicago. Founded in 1893, supported by Baptist John D. Rockefeller and led by William Rainey Harper, the Divinity School at Chicago quickly became the leading center for theological modernism, particularly within the Northern Baptist denomination. Harper, although thoroughly devoted to the Bible, was an unabashed modernist in his interpretive approach, and he recruited religious scholars like Shailer Mathews, George B. Foster, Gerald Birney Smith, and Shirley Jackson Case, who shared his convictions. During the war and particularly after it, the most consistent modernist rejoinder to the growing fundamentalist cacaphony came from the halls of the University of Chicago Divinity School.[18]

When World War I ended in November 1918, America's crusading zeal was fully engaged. With the overthrow of the Kaiser, much of that zeal was transferred to Bolshevism. In an oft-repeated pattern, dispensationalists sought and found a new scenario for the end times with the coming to power in Russia of Lenin and his ''godless Communists.'' Here was a new group that could stand in for the antichrist in the final days before Christ's return.[19] The fact that some in the growing American labor movement had displayed socialist proclivities that mirrored the rise of Bolshevism abroad led to the ''Red Scare'' at home of 1919–20. Revivalists like Sunday and other fundamentalists contributed to a growing sense of postwar hysteria with their continuous trumpeting of the evils of communism.

The Red Scare was an appropriate introduction to the 1920s, a time when America seemed to be pulled in opposing directions at the same time. On the one hand, many seemed eager to cast aside the old nineteenth-century moralism that had largely been built on evangelicalism. Disillusioned with national crusades and wearied by the deprivation of war, these individuals wanted to concentrate on personal fulfillment and to enjoy the technological and scientific fruits of America's growing consumer economy. On the other hand, there were traditionalists who viewed the postwar situation with alarm. The old moralistic and agrarian America of the previous century was being replaced by something unknown and ominous. Particularly for fundamentalist evangelicals, a profound fear of social change, mingled with patriotic zeal and reinforced by a pessimistic view of history, led to the conviction that modernism was an implacable foe that must be stopped at all costs.

For American fundamentalists, the primary areas of concern were the perceived modernist "takeover" of various denominations and the loss of control over their public schools evidenced by the teaching of evolution.[20] At the heart of the denominational battles was Harry Emerson Fosdick, a popular preacher who pastored in the two evangelical denominations most affected by the modernist-fundamentalist debates of the 1920: the Northern Presbyterians and the Northern Baptists. Fosdick, on 21 May 1922, fired the shot that brought the theological debates within evangelicalism into the public domain with his famous sermon, "Shall the Fundamentalists Win?" Delivered from the pulpit of the First Presbyterian Church of New York City, the sermon was a reasoned defense of key assumptions of theological modernism, an indictment of fundamentalism, and a plea for tolerance within the church. In the inflamed climate of the early 1920s, the response of fundamentalists was predictable and shrill. Conservative Presbyterians quickly took to the ramparts. Fosdick was answered by "Shall Unbelief Win?" a pungent sermon by Clarence E. Macartney, pastor of Arch Street Presbyterian Church in Philadelphia.[21] By 1923, J. Gresham Machen published his highly influential book, *Christianity and Liberalism*, which, with an eye toward Fosdick and his ilk, contrasted "true Christianity" with "Liberalism." With this work, Machen came to the fore as the intellectual leader of the fundamentalist movement.[22]

Through the revivals of Sunday, the mobilizing efforts of fundamentalist organizations like the WCFA and the Baptist Bible Union (BBU), formed by Riley, T. T. Shields of Toronto, and J. Frank Norris of Fort Worth in 1923, and the cogently argued works of conservative scholars like Machen, it seemed to many that the fundamentalists were winning in early 1923.[23] In retrospect, however, it is apparent that the ground beneath them was beginning to collapse. By the early 1920s, significant segments of America had departed too far from the traditional evangelicalism of the previous century. Particularly among the burgeoning opinion makers of modern America, the university educated and the new professional classes, the theology of the fundamentalists was increasingly viewed as quaint and anachronistic at best and shrill and divisive at worst. In the battle for control of the American public square, fundamentalists were doomed to defeat at the very time they seemed on the verge of triumph.[24]

The road to defeat was a long one, but the signposts could be seen by the Northern Presbyterian Assembly of 1923. They were unmistakable by the time the road reached Dayton, Tennessee, in mid-1925. The figure spanning these points was William Jennings Bryan, three-time candidate for president, secretary of state in the Wilson administration, and outspoken advocate for rural America. As a Presbyterian layperson, Bryan had taken up the cause of fundamentalism by 1916. With other conservative evangelicals, he was convinced that evolution was the key plank in the modernist agenda that threatened traditional Christianity and, hence, the moral rectitude of America.[25] With the same flamboyance he brought to politics, Bryan took up the crusade against evolution. By 1923, Bryan was the symbolic leader of the fundamentalist cause, and his strident stand against the teaching of evolution only increased his visibility. It made a great deal of sense, then, for conservatives within the Northern Presbyterian church to run Bryan for the crucial position of moderator of the 1923 Presbyterian General Assembly. In this contest, Bradley Longfield says, "the choice was clear cut. On one side stood Bryan who for over two years had been castigating colleges that wrecked the faith of students by teaching Darwinism as a fact. On the other side stood [Charles] Wishart, president of the College of Wooster, a Presbyterian school that unapologetically taught evolution as part of the science curriculum."[26] Although Bryan appeared to be the clear leader, it was Wishart who narrowly won when two other candidates dropped out in the third round of voting.[27]

Bryan and his fundamentalist allies quickly shifted their focus to the teaching of evolution and the disciplining of Fosdick. At that point the situation became increasingly complicated. With regard to Darwinism, there were many conservatives within the Presbyterian Church, including Machen, who were sympathetic toward some forms of "Christian or theistic evolution."[28] Hence, Bryan's efforts to commit his church to an absolute ban on the teaching of evolution were severely undercut. When the situation moved to the Fosdick case, the liberal New York Presbytery counterattacked with a vengeance. Led by Henry Sloane Coffin, the liberals not only exonerated Fosdick of any wrong doing, but conceived and propagated the "Auburn Affirmation," which argued for doctrinal diversity and toleration with the Northern Presbyterian Church. Although fundamentalist Charles Macartney won the position of moderator at the 1924 General Assembly, the conservatives failed to press their advantage, as Fosdick was not disciplined or the Auburn Affirmation censured.[29] The dénouement of the conflict came in 1925. In order to forstall schism within the Northern Presbyterian camp, the 1925 General Assembly appointed a special commission to steer a middle course between the fundamentalists and the modernists. In actuality, the commission's report opted for toleration of diversity over the strict enforcement of orthodoxy favored by fundamentalists.[30] This was an ominous development for conservatives and a clear indication that modernists were now in ascendency.

The reason for the change in fortunes between modernists and fundamentalists can be traced to the events in Dayton, Tennessee, during the summer of 1925. The Scopes trial that pitted Bryan against Clarence Darrow over the teaching of evolution in the public schools of Tennessee had disastrous consequences for the image of fundamentalism. Although Bryan succeeded in winning the conviction of biology teacher John Scopes, the victory was strictly Pyrrhic. The trial assumed almost epic proportions with a climactic cross-examination of Bryan, the warhorse of fundamentalism, by modernist champion Darrow. Exulting over the conviction of Scopes, Bryan died five days after the trial, never realizing that his devastatingly poor performance on the witness stand had confirmed all the worst stereotypes of fundamentalists as uneducated, unthinking, and reactionary. A genuine media event covered via telephone and telegraph by 150 reporters, the Scopes trial established an image that American fundamentalists would not easily shake.[31] Especially significant were the reports of H. L. Mencken, irascible reporter and wit of the *Baltimore Evening Sun*, who characterized fundamentalists as "uneducated *homo boobiens*."[32]

With Bryan's passing, Machen became the most visible of the fundamentalists. Yet, Machen found himself increasingly under attack on his own turf. A reorganization of Princeton Seminary by its president, J. Ross Stevenson, put greater emphasis on "practical ministry" than had the Old School theology. Suspicious of Stevenson, Machen viewed this as a turn in a more liberal direction. In addition, the General Assembly of 1926 delayed the confirmation of Machen's appointment as professor of apologetics and ethics. These changes so undermined Machen's position that he left Princeton. In 1929, with such students as *Harold John Ockenga and Carl McIntire in tow, Machen moved to Philadelphia where he established Westminster Theological Seminary.[33] Although Machen remained a prominent figure in the fundamentalist movement until his death in 1937, his realm of influence was rapidly shrinking.

By the end of the 1920s, fundamentalism was in full retreat across the span of American evangelicalism. Because of their strong creedal tradition, structured form of government, and cast of assertive personalities, Northern Presbyterians illustrated the fundamentalist-modernist struggle most vividly in the twenties. But they were not the only evangelical group to wrestle with the issue. Northern Baptists, the Disciples of Christ, Seventh-Day Adventists, Pentecostals, Church(es) of the Nazarene, and various independent sects all suffered theological convulsions. Other denominations, like the regionally based Southern Baptists and Missouri Synod Lutherans, would reap the bitter fruit of the controversy at a later date.[34]

However, fundamentalists did not go the way of the dinosaur. Increasingly forced out of mainstream American culture, they directed their energies inwardly and created a robust subculture of churches, colleges, Bible institutes, parachurch organizations, and publishing houses. A particularly important enclave of conservative evangelicalism coalesced around the Dutch Calvinist emigrants of Michigan. Many of these settlers were followers of Abraham Kuyper, the Dutch statesman and theologian of the late nineteenth century. Basing his "neo-Calvinism" on philosophical Idealism and a radical Augustinian psychology, Kuyper avoided the rationalistic pitfalls that dogged the Scottish Common Sense approach of the Princetonians like Warfield and Machen.[35] By the late twentieth century, the Kuyperian approach was finding favor with a growing band of American evangelicals, including, in varying ways, historians such as *George Marsden and Mark Noll.

None of this promise was obvious at the end of the twenties. As far as most thinking, college-educated Americans were concerned, the fundamentalists were passing away, an inevitable casualty of modern, freethinking, progressive America. Yet, through colleges like Wheaton and Calvin, publishers like *Fleming H. Revell Jr., and the "Netherlands Quartet" of Grand Rapids (Eerdmans, Zondervan, Kregel, and Baker),[36] scores of churches, and hundreds of little-known pastors and evangelists, the still-sizable segment of conservative evangelicals persevered through the Great Depression and World War II, to reemerge at a more propitious time.

## NOTES

1. William R. Hutchison, *The Modernist Impulse in American Protestantism* (Cambridge, Mass.: Harvard University Press, 1976), p. 2.

2. Ferenc Morton Szasz, *The Divided Mind of Protestant America, 1880–1930* (University: University of Alabama Press, 1982), pp. 1–41. See also see George M. Marsden, *Understanding Fundamentalism and Evangelicalism* (Grand Rapids, Mich.: Eerdmans, 1991), pp. 9–61, and idem, *Fundamentalism and American Culture: The Shaping of Twentieth-Century Evangelicalism, 1870–1925* (New York: Oxford University Press, 1980), pp. 11–39.

3. The standard treatment remains Marsden's *Fundamentalism and American Culture*. Helpful in understanding fundamentalism's theological foundations is Ernest R. Sandeen, *The Roots of Fundamentalism: British and American Millenarianism, 1800–1930* (Chicago: University of Chicago Press, 1970).

4. Kenneth Cauthen, *The Impact of American Religious Liberalism* (New York: Harper & Row, 1962), pp. 26–30.

5. Edwin S. Gaustad, *A Religious History of America*, rev. ed. (San Francisco: Harper & Row, 1990), pp. 257–58.

6. Two works of Warfield are significant on this issue: "Inspiration" (with A. A. Hodge; 1881) and "The Inerrancy of the Original Autographs" (1893). Both essays are included in *The Princeton Theology, 1812–1921*, edited by Mark A. Noll (Grand Rapids, Mich.: Baker, 1983), pp. 218–32, 268–74.

7. Richard Hofstadter, *Anti-Intellectualism in American Life* (New York: Vintage, 1962), p. 135. Marsden adapts this to his discussion in *Fundamentalism and American Culture*, pp. 210–11.

8. Paul S. Boyer, *When Time Shall Be No More: Prophecy Belief in Modern American Culture* (Cambridge, Mass.: Belknap Press of Harvard University Press, 1992), pp. 92–97.

9. Timothy P. Weber, *Living in the Shadow of the Second Coming: American Premillennialism, 1875–1982*, enl. ed. (1979; reprint Chicago: University of Chicago Press, 1987), pp. 28–29. See also David A. Rausch, *Arno C. Gaebelein, 1861–1945: Irenic Fundamentalist and Scholar* (Lewiston, N.Y.: Edwin Mellen, 1983).

10. Marsden, *Understanding Fundamentalism and Evangelicalism*, p. 23.

11. Ibid., p. 33.

12. There is a dearth of scholarly work on the important associates of Moody. See Donald L. Martin, "The Thought of Amzi Clarence Dixon" (Ph.D. diss., Baylor University, 1989), and the profiles of Chapman, Gordon, and Torrey in the final section above.

13. George W. Dollar, *A History of Fundamentalism in America* (Greenville, S.C.: Bob Jones University Press, 1973), p. 175. See also Marsden, *Fundamentalism and American Culture*, pp. 118–23.

14. Szasz, *The Divided Mind of Protestant America*, pp. 92–97. The best examination is William Vance Trollinger Jr., *God's Empire: William Bell Riley and Midwestern Fundamentalism* (Madison: University of Wisconsin Press, 1990).

15. Lyle W. Dorsett, *Billy Sunday and the Redemption of Urban America* (Grand Rapids, Mich.: Eerdmans, 1991), pp. 85–114.

16. See Eldon G. Ernst, *Moment of Truth for Protestant America: Interchurch Campaigns Following World War One* (Missoula, Mont.: Scholars Press, 1974).

17. Boyer, *When Time Shall Be No More*, pp. 104–5. See also Robert Fuller, *Naming the Antichrist: The History of an American Obsession* (New York: Oxford University Press, 1995), pp. 130–33.

18. George M. Marsden, *The Soul of the American University: From Protestant Establishment to Established Nonbelief* (New York: Oxford University Press, 1994), pp. 239–50. For background on the religious motivation of Harper, see Conrad Cherry, *Hurrying Toward Zion: Universities, Divinity Schools, and American Protestantism* (Bloomington: Indiana University Press, 1995).

19. Boyer, *When Time Shall Be No More*, pp. 156–57; Fuller, *Naming the Antichrist*, pp. 154–56.

20. Szasz, *The Divided Mind of Protestant America*, p. 92.

21. Bradley J. Longfield, *The Presbyterian Controversy: Fundamentalists, Modernists, and Moderates* (New York: Oxford University Press, 1991), pp. 9–11. See also George M. Marsden, *Religion and American Culture* (San Diego: Harcourt Brace Jovanovich, 1990), pp. 181–83.

22. See Marsden, *Fundamentalism and American Culture*, pp. 174–75.

23. Dollar, *A History of Fundamentalism in America*, p. 105. Although he made common cause with the fundamentalists over the issue of modernism, Machen "did not like being called a fundamentalist," eschewing the emotionalism he viewed as endemic in the movement. See Marsden, *Understanding Fundamentalism and Evangelicalism*, p. 182.

24. Martin E. Marty, *Modern American Religion*, vol. 2, *The Noise of Conflict, 1919–1941* (Chicago: University of Chicago Press, 1991), pp. 198–205.

25. Lawrence W. Levine, *Defender of the Faith. William Jennings Bryan: The Last Decade, 1915–1925* (New York: Oxford University Press, 1965), pp. 272–81.

26. Longfield, *The Presbyterian Controversy*, p. 72.

27. Ibid., p. 73.

28. David N. Livingstone, *Darwin's Forgotten Defenders: The Encounter Between Evangelical Theology and Evolutionary Thought* (Grand Rapids, Mich.: Eerdmans, 1987), pp. 164–65.

29. Marty, *Modern American Religion*, pp. 183–84. See also Longfield, *The Presbyterian Controversy*, pp. 77–79, 100–103.

30. Longfield, *The Presbyterian Controversy*, pp. 147–53.

31. The text of the Scopes trial is in *The World's Most Famous Court Trial: Tennessee Evolution Case* (Cincinnati: National Book Company, 1925). Still fascinating and lively is Ray Ginger, *Six Days or Forever? Tennessee v. John Thomas Scopes* (Boston: Beacon, 1958). See also Arthur G. Hays, "The Scopes Trial," in *Evolution and Religion: The Conflict Between Science and Theology in Modern America*, edited by Gail Kennedy (Boston: D.C. Heath, 1957), pp. 35–36.

32. H. L. Mencken, "Fundamentalism: Divine and Secular," in *The Bathtub Hoax and Other Blasts and Bravos from the Chicago Tribune*, edited by Robert McHugh (New York: Knopf, 1958), p. 122. Interestingly, Mencken had a good deal of respect for Sunday and Machen. See D. G. Hart, "A Connoisseur of 'Rabble-Rousing,' 'Human Folly,' and 'Theological Pathology': H. L. Mencken on American Presbyterians," *American Presbyterians* 66:3 (Fall 1988): 199.

33. D. G. Hart, *Defending the Faith: J. Gresham Machen and the Crisis of Conservative Presbyterianism in America* (Baltimore: The Johns Hopkins University Press, 1994), pp. 20–29. See also Marsden, *Understanding Fundamentalism and Evangelicalism*, pp. 182–84.

34. Szasz, *The Divided Mind of Protestant America*, pp. 100–106.

35. James D. Bratt, *Dutch Calvinism in Modern America: A History of a Conservative Subculture* (Grand Rapids, Mich.: Eerdmans, 1984), pp. 14–33.

36. John Tebbel, *A History of Book Publishing in the United States*, Vol. 1, *The Expansion of an Industry, 1865–1919* (New York: Bowker, 1975), pp. 359–60, and Vol. 4, *The Great Change, 1940–1980* (New York: Bowker, 1981), pp. 605–607.

# 5
# The Emergence of Moderate Evangelicalism

For many, the controversies of the twenties consigned evangelicals and their fundamentalist cousins to the margins of American religious life. That view is naive at best, for the decades after the Scopes trial and the fundamentalist-modernist controversy were times of transition for all American Protestantism. Nonfundamentalists retained control of denominational structures, but an evangelical presence remained strong at the grass roots, among groups connected to the Holiness and Pentecostal movements, in the South and Midwest, and within scores of independent congregations. As well, networks based on educational institutions, publishing houses, mass circulation periodicals, and the like strengthened links among evangelicals. At the same time, social and cultural currents that had an impact on the whole of American religion also affected evangelicals. The thirties brought the Great Depression and the concomitant restructuring of American economic life. That era was also a time of a religious depression, as historian Robert Handy reminded us.[1] As the nation moved from the Depression into the Second World War, public issues dwarfed the significant transformations giving evangelical Protestantism renewed strength.

Within the fundamentalist-evangelical orbit, one sign of a new direction at first seems a step backward. Among those who felt the greatest defeat in the controversies of the twenties came a trend toward separatism. Dispensational premillennialism supported such moves. In the dispensation of the church age (the present), Christendom itself would be apostate. Churches and denominations could thus be labeled as evil; separating from them was one way to remain pure. Separatism easily obscured the strength of the fundamentalist-evangelical presence. Those who refused to deal with the oldline religious groups and their leaders could be dismissed as insignificant. Separatists actually freed other evangelicals, called by some "progressive evangelicals" or "positive fundamentalists,'' to move in fresh directions.[2] One example of the separatist impulse must suffice: the ministry of Carl McIntire.[3] A Presbyterian, McIntire in 1927 entered Princeton Theological Seminary where he studied with *J. Gresham Machen, one of most articulate voices for fundamentalism. When Machen left Princeton in 1929 to help found Westminster Theological Seminary, McIntire continued his studies at the new school. Although Machen and McIntire cooperated a few years later in establishing a new denomination, the Presbyterian Church in America, McIntire quickly found even Machen suspect since Machen remained in contact with with former colleagues in the Presbyterian Church U.S.A. and other denominations. In 1937, one year after the Presbyterian Church in America formed, it divided into McIntire's Bible Presbyterian Church and the Orthodox Presbyterian Church, made up of Machen's supporters. McIntire's separatism ultimately led him to reject even the designation ''fundamentalist.'' In his first book, *Twentieth Century Reformation*, he argued that using the term implies that there might be some other kind of authentic Christian, a position he totally rejected.[4] Based in Collingswood, New Jersey, McIntire built a small separatist empire, with a seminary, a radio station frequently in trouble with the Federal Communications Commission, and a publishing arm. In 1941, he spearheaded the formation of the American Council of Christian Churches to counter the Federal Council of Churches that he thought liberal and apostate. Similar separatist organizations followed. Among religious leaders, the separatist Bob Jones Sr., and his son and grandson bearing that name, were McIntire's most prominent allies. All of them insisted on rigorous autonomy for their congregations and religious enterprises. The Jones family, for example, left the southern Methodist church because they thought it too liberal, settling into an independent congregation linked to others only through the American Council of Christian Churches and personal associations of pastors, many educated at Bob Jones University.[5]

Evangelicals not of separatist persuasion or rigidly fundamentalist in theology began to look in other directions. Illustrative is *Charles E. Fuller, whose training at the Bible Institute of Los Angeles (BIOLA) put him firmly in the dispensational premillennialist camp. Early in his career as an itinerant evangelist, Fuller recognized the power of radio as an evangelistic tool, and in 1933, he abandoned pastoral ministry to form the Gospel Broadcasting Association to oversee his radio and evangelistic labors. Four years later, he moved to the Mutual Broadcasting Network, where his was among the first paid religious programs. By 1942, more than 450 stations carried his ''Old Fashioned Revival Hour,'' which garnered one of the largest audiences of any radio show, religious or otherwise. A larger vision pushed Fuller to reach out, perhaps reluctantly, to a broader evangelical base than his premillennial dispensationalist training would have indicated. In 1942 Fuller organized a foundation to finance education of missionaries that in 1947 became Fuller Theological Seminary.[6] He persuaded *Harold John Ockenga, evangelical pastor of Boston's Park Street Church, to head the school. Ockenga drew a faculty with impressive academic credentials because he believed it both desirable and possible to have an evangelical school as credible and respected as the denominational seminaries and independent institutions such as Union Theological Seminary (New York) and Yale Divinity School. Fuller was taken aback by the direction the institution bearing his father's name had taken. But because he also believed that controversy hindered proclamation of the gospel, he was loath to respond to fundamentalist criticisms of the seminary, even when he shared them. As well, his son Daniel had received a broader education, studying not only at Princeton Seminary but also at Basel, Switzerland (with Karl Barth). Although a committed evangelical, Daniel Fuller valued a more centrist approach that informed his own work at Fuller Seminary. As a result, Fuller Seminary became bridge between a narrow fundamentalism and a more moderate evangelicalism.

Three other organizations from the 1940s reveal how nonseparatist evangelicals built strong networks transcending denominational lines: the National Association of Evangelicals (1942), the National Religious Broadcasters (1944), and Youth for Christ, International (1944/45). Charles E. Fuller and Harold Ockenga worked with J. Elwyn Wright, who had earlier spearheaded formation of the evangelical New England Fellowship to give birth to the National Association of Evangelicals (NAE).[7] Ockenga served as the first president. The NAE was not designed to be a superchurch or the basis for a new denomination, but to promote evangelism, while avoiding the divisiveness that dominated fundamentalist cooperative endeavors.[8] NAE's constituency included some of the smaller Holiness and Pentecostal denominations that rejected separatist fundamentalism, groups that combined an ethnic base with orthodox theology (such as the Evangelical Free Church), independent fundamentalist congregations alienated by Carl McIntire and his American Council of Christian Churches, and individuals still active in oldline denominations. This diversity made the NAE representative of the directions moderate evangelicalism moved to gain an identity distinct from fundamentalism.

The National Religious Broadcasters (NRB) from its inception maintained close associations with the NAE.[9] One issue in the background was how to allocate radio time for religious broadcasts. When the nation's first radio station, Pittsburgh's KDKA, began operating in November 1920, no governmental guidelines regulated the industry. Virtually anyone could set up a radio station, and many evangelical preachers and congregations did so. In 1927, the Federal Radio Commission, predecessor of the Federal Communications Commission, set technical standards and assigned frequencies mandated by the government, moves that reduced considerably the number of stations competing for the airways. Most religious stations folded; the Moody Bible Institute's WMBI is a notable exception. As radio networks emerged, they allocated free broadcast time for religious programs as a public service. In most cases, networks and stations turned to denominations belonging to the Federal Council of Churches for programming, thereby excluding most evangelical groups along with Roman Catholic, Jewish, and other non-Christian voices. The well-known *National Ra-*

*dio Pulpit* that debuted on NBC in 1926 is a good example. The alternative was to purchase air time, often at rates few congregations could afford. Charles Fuller's radio ministry began that way, as did evangelical Missouri Synod Lutheran *Walter A. Maier's *The Lutheran Hour*, a mainstay of early religious radio.[10] Often given unpopular times and put together by amateurs, most evangelical programs through the 1930s are distinguished only by their poor technical quality. The founding of the NRB reversed that situation. Establishing a code of ethics to assure professional integrity, the NRB sponsored workshops to boost quality, offered publications full of advice, recognized achievement through an awards program, and set guidelines for technical quality. Consequently, by the 1950s evangelical broadcasting became recognized for its superior technical quality. Yet most who followed Fuller and Maier had to raise funds both to produce their programs and to purchase air time. The evangelical commitment to use new media such as radio and to purchase time when access was denied carried over into the television age.

Youth for Christ, International (YFC) came into existence because evangelicals wanted a dynamic ministry with teenagers whose childhoods were shaped by World War II.[11] At its inception in 1944, YFC had a separatist tinge; those attending meetings were urged to shun popular amusements and leisure activities, and YFC gatherings held on Saturday evenings competed with high school dances and the like. What brought YFC to national attention were rallies, held in large stadiums, that drew thousands. But the primary emphases of YFC's early ministry were high school Bible study clubs, a magazine called *Campus Life* that became increasingly sophisticated technically, and evangelistic outreach to inner city youth. Each joined calls for conversion to programs designed to protect the converted from contamination by the larger society.

Like other organizations that ignored denominational boundaries, YFC presaged the "parachurch" movements of a later age. Although most youth it reached were connected with evangelically oriented congregations, YFC embraced all who came. So, too, did similar ministries to college students, such as InterVarsity Christian Fellowship whose work on American campuses began in 1940. In time a multitude of evangelical parachurch groups offered their fare to different segments of the population. As early as 1937, Charles E. Fuller had helped start the Christian Business Men's Committee International. In 1951 *Demos Shakarian organized a more Pentecostally inclined group, the Full Gospel Business Men's Fellowship International (FGBMFI).[12] Like the Christian Business Men's Committee groups, FGBMFI targeted primarily white middle-class males with careers in business and the professions. Most of these parachurch endeavors, including Youth for Christ, reached almost exclusively a white clientele. Virtually all assumed as well that husbands/fathers worked outside the home and provided full support for their families, women were full-time homemakers and housewives, and children were reared in homes where both parents lived and were married to their original spouses.

This transdenominational milieu also nurtured one destined to epitomize later twentieth-century evangelicalism, *Billy Graham, for one of Graham's first positions was as a staff evangelist for Youth for Christ. His fame and influence, however, came as an itinerant evangelist in the mold of *Dwight Lyman Moody and *Billy Sunday. The time with Youth for Christ and a short pastorate in Chicago at a church that sponsored a weekly radio program set the stage for Graham's later success as a revivalist and master of the media. His Los Angeles crusade in 1949 gave him a national reputation; he gained international stature, as had Moody, with a successful London crusade five years later. By then, Graham already had his weekly "Hour of Decision" radio broadcast; his Billy Graham Evangelistic Association began to produce high quality religious films in 1951. The following year, Graham started his daily "My Answer" newspaper column. By the time of his widely publicized New York City crusade in 1957, Graham had become a symbol of American evangelicalism. Graham's early sermons and published writings echo the fundamentalism of his early training. Adept at articulating the inchoate fears and hopes of postwar America, Graham painted a picture of a world and a society overrun by evil. Communism, juvenile delinquency, and the Cold War became signs of the imminence of Christ's premillennial return. Time was short. The only hope for the nation and individuals was an inner experience of Christ. Conversion became almost a panacea for all personal and social problems. What gave Graham's message added force was his holding the Bible aloft and punctuating his rhetoric with exclamations of "The Bible says. . . ." The symbolism was clear: This was not the Bible of higher criticism, but a Bible containing the very words of God. Although Graham's sharp apocalypticism and easy identification of evil became muted and nuanced in time, the basic evangelical message of sin and salvation remained.

Early on Graham also distanced himself from separatist fundamentalists who equated most Christians, whether from the oldline Protestant denominations or the Roman Catholic tradition, with the powers of evil. Committed to proclaiming the gospel, Graham invited support from pastors and leaders, Protestant and Catholic, wherever he conducted a crusade. This cooperative spirit reaped him the condemnation of Bob Jones and other separatist fundamentalists who believed that Graham compromised the pure gospel. From the other end of the spectrum came criticism that Graham's approach was too simplistic. Critics of various theological stripes questioned Graham's ready association with political leaders; they believed that such association could be construed as endorsement of particular policies and politicians, as indeed it sometimes was.[13] Graham and other evangelicals also mingled with the business and political elite at prayer breakfasts that were common in the public piety of the first postwar decades. Despite criticism, Graham remained convinced of the need for a strong, centrist evangelical voice and for an articulate statement of orthodox theology. In 1955, aided by his more fundamentalist-inclined father-in-law, L. Nelson Bell, and Fuller Seminary professor Wilbur M. Smith, Graham helped lay the foundations for *Christianity Today*, with its evangelical political commentary and analysis of current religious issues. Sent free for a time to all Protestant clergy in the nation, *Christianity Today* became a respected herald for moderate evangelical orthodoxy after it debuted on 15 October 1956. Graham and his associates were fortunate in securing *Carl F. H. Henry, a well-respected evangelical theologian, as first editor.[14]

By the fifties evangelicals were again claiming their rightful place on the American religious landscape, but this neoevangelicalism faced many challenges. Most dealt with social issues that were especially problematic given evangelicalism's tendency to cast social issues in personal rather than corporate terms. One set came from the civil rights movement that paralleled Graham's rise in influence and had its own deep roots in an evangelical ethos. But the evangelicalism buttressing the civil rights movement emerged from the African American experience rather than a white, Anglo understanding. As Billy Graham symbolized white neoevangelicalism, so *Martin Luther King Jr., a Baptist pastor, symbolized the evangelicalism that cradled the civil rights movement. From the Montgomery, Alabama, bus boycott that began in December 1955 until his assassination in Memphis, Tennessee, in April 1968, King drew on Scripture and the lexicon of evangelicalism to shape his message of passive resistance to racism and of hope for an inclusive society where all God's children lived harmoniously as equals. In a sense, King and his associates insisted that the nation as a corporate entity should undergo conversion; it needed to repent of these sins of racism and discrimination and seek a new life based on the moral and ethical teachings of Christ. Only then would peace prevail in individual and national life. Where this vision parted company with white evangelicalism was in its insistence that public policy had moral implications and that governmental power should spur social change grounded in moral values. King and his Southern Christian Leadership Conference called for legislation to ensure voting rights, expand employment and educational opportunities, end inhuman living conditions in urban ghettos, and integrate all public institutions and services. They supported their political goals with biblical statements about justice and righteousness. As with Billy Graham, but from a different vantage point, only what the Bible said mattered, and like Graham, King embraced religious leaders from many traditions who shared the vision of a just and righteous society.

On the heels of the civil rights movement came the women's movement and a host of other "liberation" movements. For many, the sixties brought social revolution, as assumptions undergirding American life since the Victorian era— from racial stereotypes to gender roles—came under scrutiny and often were jettisoned. To some extent, the women's movement threatened to undermine evangelical self-understanding more than the movement toward racial equality.[15] For evangelicals, the Victorian home and the role of woman as wife and mother remained the ideal. She was responsible for religious nurture since her sensibilities were thought to be more receptive to the evangelical style. By the 1950s, this image ceased to mesh with social reality. The wartime economy had drawn millions of women into the labor force; although some welcomed the postwar return to the role of housewife and homemaker, many continued to work outside the home. Advancing educational opportunities brought more women into professional careers. The rise in the divorce rate, mistakenly attributed by some evangelicals to women abandoning their proper gender roles, required more women to support themselves and often their children as well. No religious communion could ignore these challenges, but for evangelicals the struggle was especially difficult. One symbolic issue was the ordination of women to professional ministry.[16] By the later twentieth century, most evangelical churches abandoned strict adherence to the biblical admonition for women to cover their heads when at worship, but many clung to the proscription against women teaching men, a mainstay in the argument against the ordination of women. Pentecostals, who were more likely to accept women preachers, still expected them to be subordinate to their husbands.[17] In the wake of calls for justice and equality in the civil rights movement, evangelical women could not be silenced by evangelical men claiming a higher authority.

Three signs of the new position of evangelical women were the launching in 1973 of *Daughters of Sarah*, an evangelical feminist periodical that remained a powerful voice until its demise in 1996;[18] the founding in 1974 of the Evangelical Women's Caucus (now the Evangelical and Ecumenical Women's Caucus), intent on addressing women's issues from a perspective both Christian and feminist;[19] and the publication in 1974 of *All We're Meant to Be: Biblical Feminism for Today* by Letha Scanzoni and Nancy Hardesty.[20] The fundamentalist periodical *Eternity* called *All We're Meant to Be* the most important religious book of the year.[21] All three challenged the traditional interpretation of Scripture that sustained a male-dominated status quo. *Daughters of Sarah* frequently contained thoughtful but revolutionary articles on biblical texts designed to rescue them from misinterpretation by a patriarchal Christianity that relegated women to second-class status. Reaction to evangelical feminism was swift in coming, but diverse in expression. Some evangelical churches gradually, if reluctantly, began to ordain women and restudy sacred writ. Others believed that the women's movement undermined the authority of Scripture in a more insidious way than higher criticism a century earlier. That these challenges came from within the evangelical ranks made them more dangerous. One response was to launch periodicals pitched to evangelical women who resisted Christian feminism. An example is *Today's Christian Woman*, founded in 1978 and now under the aegis of *Christianity Today*.[22] But these periodicals have a female readership that has jettisoned Victorian gender roles. Similar concerns have surrounded Ralph Blair and Evangelicals Concerned, the group he founded that insists that homosexuality is not a sin and that homosexuals can be evangelical Christians.[23] The real issue is the challenges to traditional biblical interpretation and authority, not sexuality.

Another set of challenges also had roots in the immediate postwar years. In 1954, following the collapse of French colonial control and the creation of North and South Vietnam on the Indo-Chinese peninsula, the United States sent military and civilian advisers to the area. Within a few years, war erupted, miring the nation in controversy until the last American troops withdrew in 1973. Before the debates over U.S. involvement in Vietnam divided Americans, evangelicals generally identified the American position on global matters with the cause of God. After all, since communism was "godless," democracy as epitomized by the United States must represent God's way. The controversy over Vietnam shattered that simplistic assumption and divided evangelicals as it did virtually every religious group and tradition. One path to understanding this challenge is to follow the group of students from Trinity Evangelical Divinity School (near Chicago in Deerfield, Illinois) who around 1970 joined protests against the United States's Vietnam policy. In 1971, seven of them produced the first issue of the *Post-American* (*Sojourners* since 1975), a magazine intended to arouse social conscience of evangelicals.[24] From the outset, the magazine and the Peoples' Christian Coalition, the community that emerged around it, revolved around *Jim Wallis, who was committed to social change and convinced that all churches had sold out to American culture, forfeiting the radical critique of culture basic to biblical Christianity. Moving to Washington in 1975, the Sojourners community symbolizes an evangelicalism willing to tackle social issues, including feminism, homosexuality, and abortion, and not dismiss them as irrelevant or as signs of evil in the world. Some have criticized Wallis, the Sojourners community, and other "young evangelicals"[25] for lagging behind society in wrestling with such issues, but they illustrate growing diversity within evangelical circles. No longer is there a single evangelical voice on any social issue. Nor can evangelicals retreat into rescuing individuals from a sinful society without simultaneously struggling to reform society.

This diversity and the threats it posed to a coherent evangelical world-view also came to *Christianity Today*. Editor Carl Henry personally doubted the wisdom of urging evangelical support for the Vietnam War; glimmers of his questioning crept into his editorial writing, usually in the guise of efforts to engage culture from an evangelical perspective. Consequently, some of the more politically conservative forces behind the magazine grew disenchanted with Henry. Others lumped Henry with those evangelicals who affirmed biblical authority, but refused to make the doctrine of inerrancy an essential of authentic evangelicalism. As a result, *Harold Lindsell replaced Henry as editor in 1968, although the precise reasons for Henry's leaving remain speculative. Lindsell represents another strand within the evangelical spectrum, one insistent on maintaining boundaries for acceptable belief and practice, but avoiding fundamentalism's separatism. Lindsell firmly believed that the challenges of the fifties and sixties, especially evangelical feminism, fractured the biblical authority supporting evangelicalism. Less in *Christianity Today* during his editorship and more in his own publications, Lindsell attacked the secularism that he believed had invaded evangelical churches. Characteristic are his *The Battle for the Bible* and its sequel, *The Bible in the Balance*.[26] For Lindsell, the changes of the latter part of the twentieth century brought war between truth and falsehood. As an intellectual who found evangelicalism's foundations crumbling, he wanted to protect truth from contamination, much like early fundamentalists, rather than examine cultural issues from an evangelical standpoint. Tim LaHaye sounded a more simplistic alarm, but one reaching the evangelical masses, in a cognate book, *The Battle for the Mind.*[27]

Some denominations also believed evangelicalism in danger. The evangelically inclined Lutheran Church-Missouri Synod reacted to perceived liberalism and secularism by purging from its Concordia Theological Seminary faculty those thought to question biblical inerrancy.[28] Those resisting split off and formed a small denomination that merged into the Evangelical Lutheran Church in America. By the mid–1970s, the Southern Baptist Convention became a hotbed of controversy, as biblical inerrantists wrestled control of the denominational bureaucracy from moderates. Moderates have formed seminaries and other institutional apparatus, but (by 1998) not a separate denomination.[29] Outside the denominations, perhaps the shrillest voice of doom was that of *Hal Lindsey, who reached the masses with his *The Late Great Planet Earth*, appearing in 1970.[30] Although not always employing a premillennial dispensationalist vocabulary, Lindsey painted an apocalyptic picture of current events since the establishment of an independent Israel. The message is familiar to evangelical understanding: The world is rushing toward the final confrontation between good and evil, with humanity's only hope being conversion. The same perspective shaped Lindsey's analysis of American culture in *Satan Is Alive and Well on Planet Earth*, in which the prevalence of recreational drug use, behavioristic psychology, and even glossolalia signalled Satan's presence.[31]

By the mid–1970s, evangelicalism was again central to the story of American religious life, even if evangelicals were mired in controversy over setting boundaries for acceptable belief or criticized for trumpeting sensationalist apocalyptic portrayals of contemporary culture. So commonplace were evangelical assumptions that religious and secular press alike proclaimed 1976 the "Year of the Evangelical," and presidential candidate *Jimmy Carter referred to being a "born again" Christian without having to explain the term.

## NOTES

1. Robert T. Handy, "The American Religious Depression, 1925–1935," *Church History* 29 (1960): 2–16.

2. George Marsden uses both designations in his incisive essay, "Unity and Diversity in the Evangelical Resurgence," in *Altered Landscapes: Christianity in America, 1935–1985*, edited by David W. Lotz, Donald W. Shriver, and John F. Wilson (Grand Rapids, Mich.: Eerdmans, 1989), pp. 61–76, revised and expanded as "Evangelicalism since 1930: Unity and Diversity," in Marsden, *Understanding Fundamentalism and Evangelicalism* (Grand Rapids, Mich.: Eerdmans, 1991), pp. 62–82. On the emergence of a more moderate evangelicalism in the post–World War II years, see Martin E. Marty, *Modern American Religion*, vol. 3, *Under God, Indivisible: 1941–1960* (Chicago: University of Chicago Press, 1996), chap. 25.

3. There is a paucity of secondary literature on McIntire. The following are helpful: Shelley Baranowski, "Carl McIntire," in *Twentieth-Century Shapers of American Popular Religion*, edited by Charles H. Lippy (Westport, Conn.: Greenwood, 1989), pp. 256–63; Gary K. Clabaugh, *Thunder on the Right: The Protestant Fundamentalists* (Chicago: Nelson-Hall, 1974), pp. 69–97; George W. Dollar, *A History of Fundamentalism in America* (Greenville, S.C.: Bob Jones University Press, 1973), pp. 237–40; Ralph Lord Roy, *Apostles of Discord: A Study of Organized Bigotry and Disruption on the Fringes of Protestantism* (Boston: Beacon, 1953); and Jutta Reich, *Amerikanischer Fundamentalismus: Geschichte und Erscheinung der Bewegung um Carl McIntire*, 2nd ed. (Heildesheim, Germany: H. A. Gerstenberg, 1972).

4. Carl McIntire, *Twentieth Century Reformation* (Collingswood, N.J.: Christian Beacon Press, 1944).

5. There is a dearth of analytical studies of the three Bob Joneses. Highly biased is R. K. Johnson, *Builder of Bridges* (Murphreesboro, Tenn.: Sword of the Lord, 1969), that deals primarily with Bob Jones Sr., and Bob Jones Jr. The most balanced brief appraisal is Edward L. Queen II, "Bob Jones, Sr., Jr., and III," in *Twentieth-Century Shapers of American Popular Religion*, pp. 196–202.

6. Essential for understanding the place of Fuller Seminary is George M. Marsden, *Reforming Fundamentalism: Fuller Seminary and the New Evangelicalism* (Grand Rapids, Mich.: Eerdmans, 1987).

7. James DeForest Murch has written two studies, now dated, that are helpful in understanding the early years of the NAE: *Cooperation Without Compromise* (Grand Rapids, Mich.: Eerdmans, 1956), and *Protestant Revolt* (Arlington, Va.: Crestwood Books, 1967). The second half of Bruce L. Shelley, *Evangelicalism in America* (Grand Rapids, Mich.: Eerdmans, 1967), also examines the work of the NAE. The formation of the NAE in discussed in Joel Carpenter, "From Fundamentalism to the New Evangelical Coalition," in *Evangelicalism and Modern America*, edited by George M. Marsden (Grand Rapids, Mich.: Eerdmans, 1984), esp. pp. 13–14, and idem, "The Fundamentalist Leaven and the Rise of an Evangelical United Front," in *The Evangelical Tradition in America*, edited by Leonard I. Sweet (Macon, Ga.: Mercer University Press, 1984), pp. 257–88. Important primary sources are found in Joel A. Carpenter, ed., *A New Evangelical Coalition: Early Documents of the National Association of Evangelicals* (New York: Garland, 1988).

8. George H. Williams and Rodney L. Petersen, "Evangelicals: Society, the State, the Nation (1925–75)," in *The Evangelicals: What They Believe, Who They Are, Where They Are Changing*, edited by David F. Wells and John D. Woodbridge (Nashville, Tenn.: Abingdon, 1975), pp. 221–22, give three other reasons for the founding of the NAE: distrust of both the American Council of Christian Churches (too fundamentalist) and the Federal Council of Churches (too liberal), a desire to have a theologically conservative influence in the political arena, and a concomitant desire to counter what was perceived to be a strong Roman Catholic influence on government at the state and federal levels.

9. The formation of the NRB is discussed briefly in Ben Armstrong, *The Electric Church* (Nashville, Tenn.: Thomas Nelson, 1979), pp. 48–52. Armstrong became the executive director of NRB in 1978. Much helpful information, as well as the most thorough discussion of the primary issues that made formation of the NRB plausible, is found in Lowell Sperry Saunders, "The National Religious Broadcasters and the Availability of Commercial Radio Time" (Ph.D. diss., University of Illinois, 1968). Also see

Joel A. Carpenter, "From Fundamentalism to the New Evangelical Coalition," in *Evangelicalism and Modern America*, p. 12.

10. On this era, see Dennis N. Voskuil, "The Power of the Air: Evangelicals and the Rise of Religious Broadcasting," in *American Evangelicals and the Mass Media*, edited by Quentin J. Schultze (Grand Rapids, Mich.: Academie Books of Zondervan, 1990), pp. 69–95.

11. On YFC, see Richard Quebedeaux, *The Worldly Evangelicals* (San Francisco: Harper & Row, 1978), pp. 103–104, and Joel A. Carpenter, *Revive Us Again: The Reawakening of American Fundamentalism* (New York: Oxford University Press, 1997), pp. 161–76. Also see James Hefley, *God Goes to High School* (Waco, Tex.: Word, 1970). Materials by early YFC leaders such as Mel Larson, Forrest Forbes, Torrey Johnson, and Robert Cook are collected in Joel A. Carpenter, ed., *The Youth for Christ Movement and Its Pioneers* (New York: Garland, 1988). See also Carpenter, "From Fundamentalism to the New Evangelical Coalition," pp. 14–15.

12. There are only a few scattered works discussing these groups, and most are written from an uncritical, "insider" perspective. See, for example, David R. Enlow, *Men Aflame: The Story of Christian Business Men's Committee International* (Grand Rapids, Mich.: Zondervan, 1962); Brian Bird, "The Legacy of Demos Shakarian," *Charisma* 11 (June 1986): 20–25; idem, "FGBMFI: Facing Frustrations and the Future," *Charisma* 11 (June 1986): 25–26, 28; Demos Shakarian, "FGBMFI Struggles Toward the Future," *Charisma* 13 (March 1988): 24. On InterVarsity Christian Fellowship, see Richard Quebedeaux, *The Young Evangelicals: Revolution in Orthodoxy* (New York: Harper & Row, 1974), pp. 90–94, and Douglas Johnson, ed., *A Brief History of the International Fellowship of Evangelical Students* (London: InterVarsity, 1964).

13. Some of this criticism informs, for example, Marshall W. Frady, *Billy Graham: A Parable of American Righteousness* (Boston: Little, Brown, 1979). See also the classic critique in Reinhold Niebuhr, "Liberalism, Individualism, and Billy Graham," *Christian Century* 73 (1956): 640–42. Mark Silk looks at this criticism in "The Rise of the 'New Evangelicalism': Shock and Adjustment," in *Between the Times: The Travail of the Protestant Establishment in America, 1900–1960*, edited by William R. Hutchison (Cambridge, Eng.: Cambridge University Press, 1989).

14. On *Christianity Today*, see John G. Merritt, "Christianity Today," in *Religious Periodicals of the United States: Academic and Scholarly*, edited by Charles H. Lippy (Westport, Conn.: Greenwood, 1986), pp. 134–40; Douglas A. Sweeney, "Christianity Today," in *Popular Religious Magazines of the United States*, edited by P. Mark Fackler and Charles H. Lippy (Westport, Conn.: Greenwood, 1995), pp. 144–51; and Daryl A. Porter, "*Christianity Today*: Its History and Development" (Th.M. thesis, Dallas Theological Seminary, 1978). See also the reminiscences in Carl F. H. Henry, *Confessions of a Theologian: An Autobiography* (Waco, Tex.: Word, 1986).

15. For a more in-depth appraisal, see Margaret L. Bendroth, "The Search for 'Women's Role' in American Evangelicalism, 1930–1980," in *Evangelicalism and Modern America*, pp. 122–34.

16. The historical background and contemporary issues are explored in Barbara Brown Zikmund, "Women and Ordination," in *In Our Own Voices: Four Centuries of American Women's Religious Writing*, edited by Rosemary Radford Ruether and Rosemary Skinner Keller (San Francisco: HarperSanFrancisco, 1995), pp. 291–340.

17. See Elaine Lawless, *God's Peculiar People: Women's Voices and Folk Tradition in a Pentecostal Church* (Lexington: University of Kentucky Press, 1988), and idem,

*Handmaidens of the Lord: Pentecostal Women Preachers and Traditional Religion* (Philadelphia: University of Pennsylvania Press, 1988).

18. See Joseph B. Modica, "Daughters of Sarah," in *Popular Religious Magazines of the United States*, pp. 202–206.

19. The Evangelical and Ecumenical Women's Caucus deserves serious study; to date, a few conference papers have been presented, but they are in some cases inaccurate historically or so biased in perspective as to lack value.

20. See Letha Dawson Scanzoni and Nancy A. Hardesty, *All We're Meant to Be: Biblical Feminism for Today*, 3rd ed. (Grand Rapids, Mich.: Eerdmans, 1992). Both Scanzoni and Hardesty have been active in the Evangelical Women's Caucus as well.

21. See the discussion in David Harrington Watt, *A Transforming Faith: Explorations of Twentieth-Century American Evangelicalism* (New Brunswick, N.J.: Rutgers University Press, 1991), chaps. 5 and 6, and in Bendroth, "Women's Role," p. 133.

22. Glenn Arnold, "Today's Christian Woman," in *Popular Religious Magazines of the United States*, pp. 463–65.

23. See Quebedeaux, *Worldly Evangelicals*, pp. 128–31. See also Ralph Blair, "An Evangelical Look at Homosexuality" (New York: Homosexual Community Counseling Center, 1972), and Randy Frame, "The Evangelical Closet," *Christianity Today* 34 (5 November 1990): 56–57.

24. See Mark G. Toulouse, "Sojourners," in *Popular Religious Magazines of the United States*, pp. 444–51. See also Boyd T. Reese Jr., "Resistance and Hope: The Interplay of Theological Synthesis, Biblical Interpretation, Political Analysis, and Praxis in the Christian Radicalism of 'Sojourners' Magazine" (Ph.D. diss., Temple University, 1991). Two works by Sojourners founder Jim Wallis are helpful: *Revive Us Again: A Sojourners Story* (Nashville: Abingdon, 1983), and *The Soul of Politics: A Practical and Prophetic Vision for Change* (New York: New Press, 1994), reissued as *The Soul of Politics: Beyond Religious Right and Secular Left* (San Diego: Harcourt Brace, 1995).

25. See Richard Quebedeaux, *Young Evangelicals*, pp. 118–23.

26. Harold Lindsell, *The Battle for the Bible* (Grand Rapids, Mich.: Zondervan, 1976), and idem, *The Bible in the Balance* (Grand Rapids, Mich.: Zondervan, 1979).

27. Tim LaHaye, *The Battle for the Mind* (Old Tappan, N.J.: Revell, 1980).

28. See Frederick W. Danker, assisted by Jan Schambach, *No Room in the Brotherhood: The Preus-Otter Purge of Missouri* (St. Louis, Mo.: Clayton Publishing House, 1977); Laurie Ann Schultz Hayes, "The Rhetoric of Controversy in the Lutheran Church-Missouri Synod with Particular Emphasis on the Years 1969–1976" (Ph.D. diss., University of Wisconsin at Madison, 1980); and John H. Tietjen, *Memoirs in Exile: Confessional Hope and Institutional Conflict* (Minneapolis: Fortress, 1990). On internal efforts to recover, see Waldo J. Werning, *Making the Missouri Synod Functional Again* (Fort Wayne, Ind.: Biblical Renewal Publications, 1992).

29. See David T. Morgan, *The New Crusades, The New Holy Land: Conflict in the Southern Baptist Convention, 1969–1991* (Tuscaloosa: University of Alabama Press, 1996); Nancy Tatom Ammerman, *Baptist Battles: Social Change and Religious Conflict in the Southern Baptist Convention* (New Brunswick, N.J.: Rutgers University Press, 1990); and Bill J. Leonard, *God's Last and Only Hope: The Fragmentation of the Southern Baptist Convention* (Grand Rapids, Mich.: Eerdmans, 1990).

30. Hal Lindsey, with C. C. Carlson, *The Late Great Planet Earth* (Grand Rapids, Mich.: Zondervan, 1970).

31. Hal Lindsey, with C. C. Carlson, *Satan Is Alive and Well on Planet Earth* (Grand

Rapids, Mich.: Zondervan, 1972). See Martin L. Jeschke, "Pop Eschatology: Hal Lindsey and Evangelical Theology," in *Evangelicalism and Anabaptism*, edited by C. Norman Kraus (Scottsdale, Pa.: Herald Press, 1979), and Dale Moody, "The Eschatology of Hal Lindsey," *Review and Expositor* 72 (Summer 1975): 271–78. Paul Boyer discusses Lindsey in his *When Time Shall Be No More: Prophecy Belief in American Culture* (Cambridge, Mass.: Belknap Press of Harvard University Press, 1992). See also Robert Fuller, *Naming the Antichrist: The History of an American Obsession* (New York: Oxford University Press, 1995).

# 6
# Evangelicalism's Pentecostal Dimension: The Healing and Charismatic Revivals

Moderate evangelicals and strident fundamentalists represented only two strands along the spectrum. A rather different expression of revivalism with a different set of prominent figures in the 1940s interacted more directly with Pentecostalism and emphasized first the gift of healing and then other spiritual gifts, especially glossolalia, or speaking in tongues.[1] The Pentecostal flavor of the healing and charismatic revivals is so strong that some would see them as phenomena distinct from evangelicalism. Yet they held much in common with more centrist evangelical approaches. Both, for example, appreciated inner, often intense, personal experience of God. The primary distinction was that moderate evangelicals, such as *Billy Graham, highlighted the initial experience of conversion or entry into the life of faith, while the more Pentecostally inclined accentuated a subsequent ecstatic experience confirming the presence of the Holy Spirit. At first such ecstatic experience usually involved receiving physical healing, but then more often glossolalia or a combination of spiritual gifts. The greater appeal of the healing and charismatic revivals to those already converted, not nonbelievers, may explain why William G. McLoughlin wrote a cogent and compelling history of American revivals and religious awakenings without even mentioning the healing and charismatic presence.[2] Leaders of the healing and the charismatic revivals believed in the authority of Scripture, but the nuanced emphasis differed. For moderate evangelicals, sacred writ provided believers with a guide for daily life, a framework to interpret and explain all human experience. Pentecostals and charismatics thought Scripture testified to the power of God available to believers in miraculous ways here and now.

In the 1940s and 1950s, eschatological undercurrents helped sustain both, although neither moved toward premillennial dispensationalism. In the wake of World War II, the Korean Conflict, and then the Cold War, moderate evangelicals like Graham communicated a sense of urgency. The specter of "the bomb" brought images of Armageddon alive; to survive, cried evangelicals, Americans needed to reaffirm their religious roots. Evangelical Protestantism and American nationalism went hand-in-hand. A different eschatological expectation buttressed those in the Pentecostal and then charismatic orbits. Here, the outpouring of spiritual gifts such as healing and speaking in tongues harkened the impending eschaton. In the last days such spiritual gifts would appear. In the early healing and charismatic revivals, passages in the Old Testament book of Joel that pre-millennial dispensationalists thought pointed to Christ's Second Coming, informed this eschatology:

Be glad, then, ye children of Zion, and rejoice in the Lord your God: for he hath given you the former rain moderately, and he will cause to come down for you the rain, the former rain, and the latter rain the first month. And the floors shall be full of wheat, and the fats shall overflow with wine and oil. And I will restore to you the years that the locust hath eaten, the cankerworm, and the caterpillar, and the palmerworm, my great army which I sent among you. And ye shall eat and be satisfied, and praise the name of the Lord your God, that hath dealt wondrously with you: and my people shall never be ashamed. And ye shall know that I am in the midst of Israel, and that I am the Lord your God and none else: and my people shall never be ashamed. And it shall come to pass afterward, that I will pour out my spirit upon all flesh; and your sons and your daughters shall prophesy, and your old men shall dream dreams, and your young men shall see visions: And also upon the servants and upon the handmaids in those days will I pour out my spirit. And I will shew wonders in the heavens and in the earth, blood, and fire, and pillars of smoke. The sun shall be turned into darkness, and the moon into blood, before the great and the terrible day of the Lord come. And it shall come to pass, that whosoever shall call on the name of the Lord shall be delivered: for in mount Zion and in Jerusalem shall be deliverance, as the Lord hath said, and in the remnant whom the Lord shall call. (Joel 2:23–32, KJV)

The "latter rain" was a sign of the end with its pouring out of the Spirit, generally through the laying on of hands, and the promise of deliverance. Some thus talked about a "latter rain" movement and/or "deliverance" revivals. But just as the eschatological edge to moderate evangelicalism became muted with time, so did the eschatological dimension of the healing and charismatic revivals. The evangelists and their followers became an ongoing dimension of American religious life, not a temporary aberration.

Connections between healing and Christian faith have a long history apart from connections to evangelicalism and Pentecostalism. The New Testament urges prayers for the sick and reports miraculous healings by Jesus; the apostle Paul mentions the gift of healing, and the letter of James calls for anointing the sick as well, noting that the "prayer of faith will save the sick" (James 5:14–15). Then, too, in the ministry of the flamboyant *Aimee Semple McPherson, who claimed to have had an ankle healed by faith before she began her evangelistic career, there was precedent for including in revivals opportunities for those desiring healing to offer themselves for special prayer. In the immediate postwar years, the healing revivals are inextricably linked to the labors of individual evangelists such as *Oral Roberts, *William M. Branham, A. A. Allen, and *Kathryn Kuhlman.

Branham began his career as an independent Baptist evangelist in 1933 when he conducted his first tent revival, a common practice among early healers that helped revivals preserve something of a rural flavor. In 1946, Branham had a vision and realized the Spirit now gave him healing power, and when a girl for whom he prayed recovered from near death, he made prayers for the sick central to his revivals. Historians generally mark this turn in Branham's ministry as inaugurating the modern healing revival. Branham became the first healer to conduct campaigns in Europe, where thousands flocked to his rallies. But when charismatic renewal came to American Christianity in the late 1950s and the tone of the healing revival began to shift, Branham himself began to change, but in rather different directions. Branham held occasional healing revivals until his death in 1965, but more of his energy went into promoting controversial doctrines. For example, he advocated the doctrine of the "serpent's seed," which posited that because Eve presumably engaged in sexual intercourse with the serpent in Eden, some humans are descended from the "serpent's seed" and thus foreordained to life in hell. By the time Branham began to emphasize such seemingly aberrant beliefs, Oral Roberts had already eclipsed him as the premier faith healer.

Unlike Branham, Granville Oral Roberts was nurtured in Pentecostal religion. Although he believed he had been healed of both tuberculosis and stammering speech at a tent revival in Ada, Oklahoma, in 1935, Roberts did not immediately become a faith healer, but as an ordained Pentecostal-Holiness minister, he assisted his father at revivals, published his first books, conducted his own revivals, and then served several pastorates. What ultimately propelled Roberts to become a full-time healing evangelist were an unexpected healing at a service he was conducting while a pastor in Toccoa, Georgia, and then a conviction that he was taught incorrect biblical doctrine when he became a part-time student at Phillips University in 1947. Roberts followed the formula of the Pentecostal itinerant evangelist, holding services in tents erected for the occasion; at one point, Roberts's "tent cathedral" could accommodate 12,500 people. Sometimes dismissed as a fraud and showman, Roberts boosted the healing revival's credibility both in evangelical circles and within the established Protestant denominations. He did so in part because he drew on the same kinds of resources that had fashioned a tight network among evangelicals: a regular radio program, a television series followed by occasional prime time variety shows, a monthly magazine (originally called *Healing Waters*, but renamed *Abundant Life*), a newspaper column, and numerous books that bore Roberts's name as author.

Roberts moved easily in ecumenical circles, supporting formation of the Full Gospel Business Men's Fellowship International as a nondenominational Pentecostal-styled prayer fellowship, and he eagerly accepted Billy Graham's invitation to participate in the World Congress on Evangelism that Graham organized in Berlin in 1966. Roberts's leaving the Pentecostal-Holiness church to join a United Methodist congregation in Tulsa in 1968 signalled his success in giving the healing revival plausibility. At the same time, Roberts organized numerous structures to ensure transmission of his personal style of Pentecostal evangelicalism to future generations. The most important was the formation in Tulsa of Oral Roberts University, which opened in 1965, quickly achieved academic accreditation, and added numerous graduate professional schools to its campus. Roberts's interest in healing led to building the "City of Faith" hospital and medical research center located next to the university. Roberts occasionally stunned followers when he reported unusual ecstatic experiences, such as a conversation with a 900-foot tall Jesus or claims that God would take him "home" unless vast sums were raised to support his medical research center and hospital. Thus, as Roberts entered his twilight years, he remained both highly regarded and yet suspect as at the outset of his ministry.

A. A. (Asa Alonso) Allen (1911–70), more personally controversial than Branham or Roberts, was for some time the "boldest of the bold" among faith healers, renowned especially for his ability to cast out demons.[3] Allen came from a troubled background; a confirmed alcoholic by the time he was twenty-one, he also served a short jail sentence for theft prior to his conversion at a Methodist church where glossolalia was practiced. Allen became an Assemblies of God pastor in 1936, but was drawn to the orbit of the itinerant healing evangelists, particularly after attending an Oral Roberts revival in 1949. The next year he launched his own healing ministry, and in 1951 he purchased the requisite tent for his rallies. When he began a radio program, "The Allen Revival Hour" in 1953 and *Miracle Magazine* the following year, he was already a major player in the healing revival. Allen remained more suspect than Branham, Roberts, or most of the other healing evangelists because his reports of success seem exaggerated. They include claims of having restored the dead to life and having "miracle oil" gush from the hands and heads of persons attending one revival gathering. Critics always challenged the authenticity of claims to healing, believing that many who were healed faked their ailments or were "plants" placed in audiences. Some pondered whether many of the medical problems were psychosomatic in character. Allen's sensational claims bruised the credibility of many healers, who distanced themselves from his work. Indicative of Allen's shifting fortunes is the extent and character of coverage *Voice of Healing*, a magazine that functioned as a cross-denominational glue holding the fragile movement together, gave to his revivals. Allen's early labors received extensive, favorable coverage; later the magazine scarcely mentioned his work. *Miracle Magazine*, however, continued to report sensational cures and healings.

Ongoing rumors of Allen's excessive drinking, reinforced when he was arrested for drunken driving during a revival in Knoxville, Tennessee, in 1955, compounded the problem. He became a *persona non grata* among the Assemblies of God, which revoked his ministerial credentials. Undaunted, Allen began his own Miracle Revival Fellowship the next year in Dallas, moving it to southeastern Arizona in 1958 when he opened his Miracle Revival Training Center on some 4,000 acres called Miracle Valley. There he had his headquarters and church, wrote books, conducted a radio and television ministry, and administered his training school for preachers until his death from sclerosis of the liver in 1970. Even his final years were not without controversy. His 1967 divorce reopened questions about his integrity and leadership, and his 1970 announcement of plans for a rally in the largest revival tent ever erected echoed the sensationalism of former years.

Perhaps the most modest of the deliverance evangelists is one who unintentionally became a bridge to the charismatic movement, Kathryn Kuhlman, to whom Oral Roberts University awarded its first honorary doctorate. Kuhlman began her evangelistic career at age sixteen, when she travelled with the Parrott Tent Revival. Five years later she struck out on her own, settling in Denver, Colorado, in 1933. During her ministry at the Denver Revival Tabernacle, she married another evangelist once he divorced his first wife. Gossip surrounding the marriage followed when she returned to itinerant evangelism, even in Los Angeles where she arrived in 1944. While despairing about her situation, Kuhlman had a direct encounter with the Holy Spirit. She and her husband parted company, and Kuhlman struck out again on her own. When a woman with a tumor claimed healing during a Kuhlman revival near Pittsburgh in February 1946, attendance at her services mushroomed, and lines began to form at the close of services as people sought prayers for healing. Perplexed at receiving the gift of healing, Kuhlman slipped into a healing service in Pittsburgh and was appalled by the frenzy and by the revivalist's crediting success to his own healing power and failure to lack of faith on the part of the sick. Kuhlman resisted designation as a faith healer. "I have no healing virtue," she commented in an interview. "I have no healing power. I have never healed anyone. I am absolutely dependent upon the power of the Holy Spirit."[4] Her understanding echoed the Keswick Holiness tradition's belief that the Spirit endows with power for service, not powers that are personal possessions. Consequently, Kuhlman called her meetings "miracle services" in which she would pray for the healing of particular disorders in specified parts of the auditorium. From Pittsburgh, where she had her headquarters, she launched a radio ministry. A television ministry began later in Los Angeles, where Kuhlman started monthly services in 1965. Her first book, *I Believe in Miracles* (1962), became a best seller.[5]

What makes Kuhlman a bridge to the charismatic revival are the ecstatic experiences that came to many of those for whom Kuhlman prayed. Kuhlman referred to their "going under the power" of the Holy Spirit; the more common phrase has them "slain in the Spirit." When the charismatic revival flourished in the 1960s, Kuhlman seemed an ally because of these spectacular occurrences. Yet often Kuhlman remained outside the inner circle of the healing revival, shunned by Pentecostals willing to accept a woman preacher, but not one who married a divorced man. Those convinced that glossolalia was the most authentic witness of the presence of the Spirit recoiled because Kuhlman never recounted having such an experience herself. She always insisted that the new birth in conversion was the greatest miracle, not healing or glossolalia.

Most of the healing evangelists were not as notorious as Allen, as well known as Branham and Roberts, or as dramatic in style as Kuhlman. Many who proclaimed that they had the gift of healing worked the rural tent revival circuit, where they, too, were subject to ridicule and reaped criticism at the hands of detractors. "Fake healers" was one epithet hurled at them.[6] The "Elmer Gantry" image persistently dogged healing evangelists because of skepticism about their claims to supernatural power; occasionally law enforcement agents tried to investigate, but usually they dealt with complaints about excessive noise generated by the exuberant meetings. Other evangelicals viewed healers as seekers after self-glorification. Often negative stories in newspapers served simply to make healing revivals more popular, even if folks came only for the expected spectacle. Public perception had most healers at some point engaging in financial improprieties; the Internal Revenue Service investigated both the famous and the lesser known. Several healers followed the example of Oral Roberts and Billy Graham in setting up nonprofit evangelistic organizations to avoid suspicion of financial improprieties.

By the 1950s, other charismatic expressions began to eclipse faith healing among those seeking signs of the power of the Holy Spirit. Although the neo-charismatic surge had deeper roots,[7] most historians mark the birth of the contemporary movement in rector Dennis Bennett's April 1960 announcement at St. Mark's Episcopal Church in Van Nuys, California, that he had received the baptism of the Holy Spirit and spoken in tongues for at least a year. National media picked up on the ensuing controversy, bringing an awareness of charismatic phenomena to millions. Although Bennett resigned as rector the day of his dramatic announcement, Jean Stone, who attended his former parish, soon launched a monthly called *Trinity*. *Trinity* and *Full Gospel Business Men's Voice* became important vehicles connecting those eager to experience spiritual gifts.

Unlike charismatic expression that emerged from the Azusa Street revivals over half a century earlier, this one spread among mainline denominations. Individual pastors, small groups within local churches, and sometimes entire congregations among Episcopalians, Baptists, Lutherans, Methodists, Presbyterians, and even Mennonites were swept into the charismatic orbit. Few wanted to start new congregations or denominations; most believed the baptism of the Holy Spirit signalled renewal within Christianity as a whole. Such became evident when charismatic renewal spread to the Roman Catholic church in the United States, primarily first among laity excited about the prospects of church renewal unleashed by Vatican II. Many were clustered around Duquesne University (Pittsburgh) and Notre Dame University (South Bend, Indiana). In 1962, when Yale University students active in InterVarsity Christian Fellowship received the gift of tongues, the penetration of the charismatic movement into every level of

American Christian life was obvious. While charismatic renewal thus became a pan-Christian phenomenon, it made deeper initial inroads among the more liturgical denominations (Catholic, Episcopal, Lutheran). For Catholic charismatics, a degree of coherence came to the movement in 1967 with the formation in Ann Arbor, Michigan, of the Word of God community. In turn, it became the center for organizing conferences, bringing together leaders of other charismatic communities, and providing regular communication among Catholics who received the baptism of the Holy Spirit.

Soon Spirit-baptized evangelists led charismatic conferences and rallies across the country. Within Protestant denominations, fellowships or unofficial agencies emerged to link the charismatically inclined together. At the same time, however, countless independent charismatic congregations formed, some because mainline churches recoiled at the thought of charismatics in their midst. Many of these developed ties through the charismatic National Leadership Conference, founded in 1979, and other groups such as People of Destiny International and the Fellowship of Covenant Ministers and Conferences. The latter built on the work of Christian Growth Ministries, originally called the Holy Spirit Teaching Mission. Based in Fort Lauderdale, Florida, it organized many conferences, particularly targeting pastors attracted by the possibilities for church growth and expanded evangelism that charismatic renewal offered. As well, many independent ministries took on a more charismatic flavor; the charismatic dimension of Kathryn Kuhlman's services has already been noted. Many charismatically inclined evangelists became suspicious of the motivation of groups like Christian Growth Ministries. At one point, the Full Gospel Business Men's Fellowship International banned speakers from Christian Growth Ministries from its meetings.

Perhaps what cemented the place of the charismatic style in American religion was the rapid growth of the "electronic church" or "televangelism." Many of the most popular television preachers (such as Jim Bakker, Jimmy Swaggart, Kenneth Copeland, Kenneth Hagin, and *Pat Robertson) were Pentecostals or charismatics who spoke the language of Spirit-filled Christianity, even if their programs rarely, if ever, showed actual experiences of healing or glossolalia. By the end of the century, it was not unusual, even in traditional services, to see persons lifting their hands toward heaven while praying or singing, a commonplace practice among many Pentecostals and charismatics. As well, like others, healing and charismatic evangelicals formed networks of institutions and agencies that ignored denominational boundaries. Oral Roberts University represents one such endeavor; Pat Robertson's Regent University is another. The Franciscan University of Steubenville (Ohio), not far from Kathryn Kuhlman's Pittsburgh, has become an educational center for Catholic charismatics. For nearly two decades, the major link among faith healers was *Voice of Healing* magazine, founded and edited by Gordon Lindsay from 1948 until 1967 (when it became *Christ for the Nations*), which started to publicize William Branham's healing revivals. It listed and reported on numerous revivals conducted by other healers, many of whom became part of the *Voice of Healing* fellowship. One measure of the acceptability of an evangelist to other healers is whether campaigns conducted by the revivalist are promoted and reported in the magazine. By 1958, the focus of *Voice of Healing* shifted to international evangelism, but always with an emphasis on divine healing as the primary means of propagating the Gospel. A host of periodicals also link charismatics; among them are *New Wine, Our Life Together, Logos*, and *Manna*. Earlier evangelicals formed publishing houses to supply books and other literature reflecting their understanding of the Christian faith; charismatics have followed in their footsteps. Logos International, founded in Plainfield, New Jersey, in 1971, has become a major charismatic publishing house. Evangelical houses such as Fleming H. Revell and the Roman Catholic Paulist Press recognized the market for charismatic literature and offered a line of relevant titles.

Another mechanism linking those in the healing-charismatic orbit is the parachurch or nondenominational extra-ecclesiastical group. The most conspicuous examples are the Full Gospel Business Men's Fellowship International (FGBMFI), already mentioned in passing, and a cognate organization for women, Women's Aglow Fellowship. FGBMFI was the brainchild of Demos Shakarian, who desired to bring men together to share their faith and who remained president until 1988 when the continuing effects of a stroke left him unable to continue. Oral Roberts spoke at the first meeting in 1951 in Los Angeles. Chapters were then organized in other cities, tied together by the monthly *Full Gospel Business Men's Voice*. By the mid–1960s, there were more than 300 chapters; by 1988, there were more than 3,000 spread over nearly 90 nations.[8] Men testify to personal faith; meetings have reported healings, glossolalia, and deliverance from demons. Usually held in restaurants or hotels, often over breakfast or lunch, FGBMFI sessions still include prayers for healing and divine intervention in daily life. Some clergy critics claim that FGBMFI usurps local congregational loyalty for members; others are wary of its continuing ecumenical character.

Women's Aglow Fellowship has worked similarly since its founding in 1967 as the Full Gospel Women's Fellowship by persons connected with FGBMFI and charismatic Episcopal rector Dennis Bennett's church in Seattle.[9] Also often using the format of a meal, usually lunch (though some chapters offer evening meetings to accommodate women who work outside the home), followed by an inspirational talk and testimonies of members, Women's Aglow now counts more than 1,300 local units and draws women from a wide variety of denominational backgrounds. Although charismatic healing was initially a primary focus of Women's Aglow, its local units now serve more as support groups for evangelical and charismatic women, particularly for those going through times of personal crisis. In one sense, providing emotional healing and wholeness rather than physical healing and wholeness has become the *raison d'être* for the association. The more parachurch structures that allowed Pentecosals and charismatics to bond with one another, the more the place of these expressions of evangelicalism became a fixture of American religious life.

## NOTES

1. Scholarly analysis of neo-Pentecostalism and the healing revivals is increasing. See David E. Harrell Jr., *All Things Are Possible: The Healing and Charismatic Revivals in Modern America* (Bloomington: Indiana University Press, 1975). Other general studies that discuss Branham and the revivals include Steve Durasoff, *Bright Winds of the Spirit: Pentecostalism Today* (Englewood Cliffs, N.J.: Prentice-Hall, 1972); Nils Bloch-Hoell, *The Pentecostal Movement* (London: Allen and Unwin, 1964); Walter J. Hollenweger, *The Pentecostals: The Charismatic Movement In the Church* (Minneapolis: Augsburg, 1969), and Paul G. Chappell, "The Divine Healing Movement in America" (Ph.D. diss., Drew University, 1983). Chappell also provides a good, very brief overview in "Healing Movements," in *Dictionary of Pentecostal and Charismatic Movements*, edited by Stanley M. Burgess and Gary B. McGee (Grand Rapids, Mich.: Regency/Zondervan, 1988): 363–74. Both the healing and the charismatic revivals are discussed in Richard M. Riss, *A Story of Twentieth-Century Revival Movements in North America* (Peabody, Mass.: Hendrickson, 1988).

2. William G. McLoughlin, *Revivals, Awakenings, and Reform: An Essay on Religion and Social Change in America, 1607–1977*, Chicago History of American Religion Series, edited by Martin E. Marty (Chicago: University of Chicago Press, 1978).

3. Harrell, *All Things Are Possible*, p. 68. Allen wrote something of an autobiography with Walter Wagner: *Born to Lose, Bound to Win* (Garden City, N.Y.: Doubleday, 1970). From Allen's inner circle came Don Stewart with Walter Wagner, *The Man from Miracle Valley* (Long Beach, Calif.: Great Horizons, 1971). Stewart was Allen's long-time associate and successor. There are no full-length critical studies of Allen's life and ministry, but see James Morris, *The Preachers* (New York: St. Martin's, 1973), pp. 1–53.

4. "Healing in the Spirit," *Christianity Today* (20 July 1973): 4–10. The quote is found on p. 5.

5. Kathryn Kuhlman, *I Believe in Miracles* (Englewood Cliffs, N.J.: Prentice-Hall, 1962).

6. Harrell, *All Things Are Possible*, p. 100.

7. Harrell offers solid analysis of the early years of the charismatic movement in the second half of *All Things Are Possible*. There is an enormous literature examining charismatic renewal in both Protestant and Catholic circles. See, for example, Peter G. Hocken, "Charismatic Movement," *Dictionary of Pentecostal and Charismatic Movements*, pp. 130–60; Richard Quebedeaux, "Conservative and Charismatic Developments of the Later Twentieth Century," in *Encyclopedia of the American Religious Experience*, 3 vols., edited by Charles H. Lippy and Peter W. Williams (New York: Scribners, 1988), 2:963–76; idem, *The New Charismatics: The Origins, Development, and Significance of Neo-Pentecostalism* (Garden City, N.Y.: Doubleday, 1976); idem, *The New Charismatics II: How a Christian Renewal Movement Became a Part of the American Religious Mainstream* (San Francisco: Harper & Row, 1983); Arthur Bittlinger, ed., *The Church Is Charismatic* (Geneva: World Council of Churches, 1981); Peter Hocken, *One Lord, One Spirit, One Body* (Gaithersburg, Md.: Word Among Us, 1987); Rene Laurentin, *Catholic*

*Pentecostalism*, trans. by Matthew J. O'Connell (Garden City, N.Y.: Doubleday, 1977); Killian McDonnell, *Charismatic Renewal in the Churches* (New York: Seabury, 1976); Edward D. O'Connor, *The Pentecostal Movement and the Catholic Church* (Notre Dame, Ind.: Ave Maria Press, 1971); Kevin and Dorothy Ranaghan, *Catholic Pentecostals* (New York: Paulist, 1969); idem, *As the Spirit Leads Us* (New York: Paulist, 1971); John Sherrill, *They Speak with Other Tongues* (New York: Pyramid Books, 1964); Vinson Synan, *The Twentieth-Century Pentecostal Explosion: The Exciting Growth of the Pentecostal and Charismatic Renewal Movements* (Altamonte Springs, Fla.: Creation House, 1987); and idem, *In the Latter Days: The Outpouring of the Holy Spirit in the Twentieth Century* (Ann Arbor, Mich.: Servant Books, 1984).

8. The only monograph on FGBMFI, not well known or widely circulated, is Vinson Synan, *Under His Banner: History of Full Gospel Business Men's Fellowship International* (Costa Mesa, Calif.: Gift Publications, 1992). See also Durasoff, *Bright Winds*, pp. 145–56; Quebedeaux, *New Charismatics*, pp. 99–102; and William C. Armstrong, "Demos Shakarian: A Man and His Message," *Logos Journal* (Sept.-Oct. 1971): 13–14. From the inside, see Brian Bird, "FGBMFI: Facing Frustrations and the Future," *Charisma* 11 (June 1986): 25–26, 28; idem, "The Legacy of Demos Shakarian," *Charisma* 11 (June 1986): 20–25; and Demos Shakarian, "FGBMFI Struggles Toward the Future," *Charisma* 13 (March 1988): 24.

9. The most comprehensive study of Women's Aglow Fellowship is Ruth Marie Griffith, "A Network of Praying Women: The Formation of Religious Identity in Women's Aglow Fellowship" (Ph.D. diss., Harvard University, 1995); the first chapter provides discussion of both the religious and cultural context for and the history of Women's Aglow. Also see Susan M. Setta, "Healing in Suburbia: The Women's Aglow Fellowship," *Journal of Religious Studies* 12:2 (1986): 46–56.

# 7
# Evangelicalism Comes into Its Own

By the late 1970s, evangelicalism penetrated every facet of American Protestant life. With heroes such as *Billy Graham consistently named to "most admired" lists, growing acceptance of Pentecostal and charismatic expression, and one who drew on the evangelical lexicon to describe his personal religious experience elected to the presidency in 1976, it seemed as if an evangelical explosion fueled American religious life. In the last quarter of the twentieth century, that explosion manifested itself in many ways. Four angles of vision help bring that explosion into focus: the transformation of religious television and radio; expressions of evangelicalism in the megachurch and the parachurch movement; the presence of evangelical caucuses or kindred groups within oldline denominations; and how evangelicals translated their religious style into political action.

One marker of the explosion of an evangelical presence in television, radio, and other communications media is the career of *Marion Gordon (Pat) Robertson, whose 1-kilowatt UHF Virginia television station developed into the Christian Broadcasting Network (CBN) and brought Robertson such renown that he sought the Republican presidential nomination in 1988. A dramatic, unexpected conversion in 1956 drew Robertson from legal and business interests to theological study and pastoral work as an associate to Harald Bredesen, a prominent charismatic. Ordained as a Southern Baptist in 1961, the year CBN began broadcasting, Robertson was adept at blending entertainment with religious proclamation and evangelically informed social and political commentary in ways that exploited the possibilities of television.[1] His "700 Club" moved to syndicated format in 1972, reaching more than 7 million American homes within a decade and a half. By the 1990s, Robertson controlled cable television's Family Channel and was also CEO of International Family Entertainment, owner of MTM productions and the Ice Capades, among other ventures. Robertson continued the evangelical technique of developing educational institutions to train students to perpetuate his vision of truth when he started CBN University (now Regent University).

In 1965 Robertson brought Jim Bakker (1940- ) and his then-wife Tammy Faye (1942- ) to CBN to host a children's show and then the "700 Club" program.[2] Eight years later, the Bakkers ventured out on their own, launching their wildly popular "PTL Club" program on the Trinity Broadcasting Network, which they helped start. Like the "700 Club," the "PTL CLub" followed the format of the talk show/news show, punctuated with emotional appeals by the Bakkers for financial support for various PTL enterprises. A favorite was Heritage Village U.S.A., a hotel, resort, theme park, and religious complex in South Carolina, just over the border from Charlotte, North Carolina. Affiliated with the Assemblies of God, the Bakkers became almost synonymous with the electric church until 1987, when their empire crumbled amid charges of tax evasion, diversion of funds, a sex scandal involving Jim Bakker, and Tammy Bakker's receiving treatment for drug dependency.[3]

Another televangelism star operated out of Louisiana. Jimmy Swaggart (1935- ), musician and cousin of Jerry Lee Lewis, enjoyed a radio program airing on more than 500 stations when he shifted his focus to television in 1973 and to the varied ministries of his Family Worship Center in Baton Rouge.[4] Master of gesture and dramatic orator, Swaggart held television audiences spellbound. But his messages sometimes echoed earlier separatist evangelicalism in attacks on Roman Catholicism, American cultural values, and even his own Assemblies of God Pentecostalism. As he became more controversial, he, too, fell into disgrace; in 1988 he lost his clergy credentials after admitting involvement with a prostitute.

Countless others attempted television ministries without attaining the popularity Robertson, Swaggart, and the Bakkers garnered. Earlier styles of evangelical programs with origins in programs of the 1950s were still found, although with less frequency. Local stations telecast worship services of area churches, some evangelical and some mainstream. Some celebrity preachers opted for more traditional kinds of religious programs. Among them were Robert Schuller, a Reformed Church in America clergyman who broadcast "Hour of Power" services from his Crystal Cathedral in Garden Grove, California,[5] and *Jerry Falwell, pastor of the independent Thomas Road Baptist Church in Lynchburg, Virginia, who named his televised services the "Old-Time Gospel Hour" after *Charles E. Fuller's radio broadcast, the "Old Fashioned Revival Hour."

Televangelism stirred many of the controversies surrounding evangelical forays into radio a generation or two earlier.[6] Many argued that the evangelists' persistent pleas for financial support drained resources from local congregations. Some believed that evangelical television lured people away from churches on Sunday mornings. The theologically inclined worried about the individualistic nature of televangelism and its failure to foster a sense of community, despite linking people through programs like Robertson's "faith partners" or official magazines of a particular ministry. Others fretted about the shallowness of the theology undergirding most television preaching; although informed by evangelical or even Pentecostal perspectives, it appeared overly simplistic on the television screen.[7] Numerous studies of evangelical television's audience challenged some of these assumptions, while raising other issues. Scholars repeatedly demonstrated that televangelists consistently overestimated the number of regular viewers, sometimes by several million. Even so, a 1984 study showed that around 13 million people (approximately 6 percent of the television audience) regularly watched religious television.[8] Other studies showed that a Southern white female church member and financial contributor over age fifty was the "typical" viewer. In other words, televangelism did not compete with churches for adherents or financial support. Evangelicals who argued that television brought converts to the faith found little evidence to support their claim. The criticism most easily sustained concerned misuse of financial contributions, particularly when the lavish lifestyles of many prominent religious television personalities became common knowledge; in several cases the Internal Revenue Service began investigations. The disintegration of the ministries of the Bakkers and Swaggart in the late 1980s tarnished the popularity of most evangelists with regular shows, but had its major impact in the decrease of financial support for televangelism and its related enterprises. Those trumpeting the demise of religious television, however, were sorely mistaken. The rapid expansion of cable television in the 1980s and 1990s and the presumed success of televangelism prodded oldline denominations to join forces to produce highly professional programs under the rubric "Catch the Spirit." The nation's largest Protestant denomination, the Southern Baptist Convention (with its strong evangelical ties), pondered launching its own cable network. By century's end, the number of religious (primarily evangelical) programs, channels, and cable options proliferated, even if the size of the viewing audience had leveled off.

At the same time, evangelical radio was enjoying both a metamorphosis and a boom. Although in a region such as Appalachia much broadcasting still originated with local Pentecostal preachers and singers,[9] the popularity of talk radio, the availability of syndicated evangelical programs (such as James Dobson's "Focus on the Family," Larry Burkett's Christian financial program, and Elisabeth Elliott's meditative reflections targeted to evangelical women), and the emergence of "contemporary Christian music" regenerated religious radio in the 1980s and 1990s.[10] Evangelical stations grew in number, some linked together through Christian (evangelical) networks. The unaware listener casually scanning from station to station could scarcely tell the difference between one broadcasting the latest rock music and one airing contemporary Christian music. As generations before them, evangelicals at century's end took full advantage of advances in communications technology.[11]

Some impetus for the transformation in popular evangelical music came from evangelical youth who embraced features of the counterculture flourishing in the late 1960s and 1970s. In the early 1970s, evangelicals concerned about losing adolescents and young adults to the hippie subculture, with its presumed mixture of rock music, drug use, sexual license, long hair, and social protest, broke with the informal tradition that evangelicals eschewed the ways of the world. As one sympathetic study put it, "Why should the devil have all the good music?"[12] The Jesus Movement, along with Jesus music, Jesus rallies, and other pop apparatus, was born.[13] Evangelical Christian young men donned blue jeans, wore their hair long, and joined mod Christian young women to clap to the rhythm of Gospel rock and pack football stadiums and parks where they sang lively praise songs and heard evangelical preaching. By avoiding traditional religious buildings for rallies, the movement echoed the revivalist heritage; by opting for arenas and other outdoor areas associated with sports, it presaged the Promise Keepers movement promoting male spirituality in the 1990s. The Jesus Movement not only nurtured contemporary Christian music, but in its insistence on informality in worship nudged "contemporary Christian worship" into being. It also reflected evangelicalism's emphasis on feeling over doctrine in religious experience. Rallies and songs produced an emotional "high" better than the illegal drugs used by youthful contemporaries. "Jesus freaks" also had periodicals, such as the *Hollywood Free Paper* and *Right On!*, that interacted with the counterculture. The popularity among Jesus people of *Hal Lindsey's bestselling *The Late Great Planet Earth* added an eschatological excitement to the larger movement. Controversy surrounded the Jesus Movement, however. Some of its personalities who attracted publicity appeared to exercise dangerous control over the lives and minds of followers. Particularly suspect were David Berg and his Children of God group and Tony and Sue Alamo with their Christian Foundation. Critics who feared anything unfamiliar lumped such groups with more exotic specimens such as the Hare Krisha movement and talked about a "cult" scare (although few defined precisely what constituted a cult) within the evangelical orbit. By the 1980s, when American culture as a whole turned in more conservative directions, the Jesus Movement also faded as a distinct phenomenon.

Many Jesus People were among the earliest born of the post-World War II "baby boomer" generation, the largest swelling of the native born population in the nation's history. More people came to maturity and moved into middle age in the 1980s and 1990s than ever before, on the whole better educated and used to a higher standard of living than earlier generations. At the same time, from the 1960s on, the oldline denominations charted declines in membership; growth among more evangelical groups, especially of a Pentecostal or charismatic bent, and among independent congregations offset some of the drop, but concern mounted that the boomer generation was lost to organized religion. Sociologists knew that Americans tended to withdraw from active religious involvement as adolescents and young adults and then return as they reached middle age, sought religious nurture for their children, and settled into maturity. The fear in the 1980s and 1990s was that the baby boomer generation would not follow the pattern. A team led by Robert Bellah sounded an alarm in *Habits of the Heart*.[14] Informants revealed little sense of enduring commitment to religious institutions and a very privatized spirituality. Boomers seemed to jettison traditional religion, although few abandoned some understanding of moral and ethical behavior.[15] Other studies indicated that more conservative religious groups fare better than more liberal ones.[16] In this context, conservative meant more than orthodox practice; it also involved a sense of certainty when it came to right and wrong, appropriate and inappropriate behavior, true or false belief.[17] Some questioned whether there was enduring commitment from boomers attracted to more conservative churches. Sociologist Nancy Tatom Ammerman, for example, characterized the religion of the boomers as "Golden Rule Christianity" or a basic moral sense unencumbered by traditional religious trappings.[18]

Some evangelical leaders sought to respond to the spiritual yearnings of the boomers and of "Generation X" that followed them through the multifaceted ministries of the megachurch.[19] There is no standard definition of megachurch; one rule of thumb is that the megachurch attracts at least 10,000 people to weekend services. Generally megachurches drew on contemporary Christian music and worship formats, held informal services at other than the traditional Sunday morning time (although there would be a service then), emphasized dynamic preaching that stressed practical application of principles to daily life, and offered subsidiary programs ranging from aerobics and exercise classes, self-help groups of all sorts (often following the twelve-step approach developed by Alcoholics Anonymous), and sports teams to Bible study classes to attract the interest and meet the perceived needs of boomers as religious seekers.[20] Although some megachurches have affiliation with oldline denominations, many are independent.

Perhaps the most well known is Willow Creek Community Church in the upscale Chicago suburb of South Barrington, Illinois.[21] Drawing an overwhelmingly white, well-educated, upwardly mobile, generally professional and white collar, and at least upper middle class constituency, Willow Creek began in 1973 as a youth ministry called Son City, spearheaded by Reformed Church in America clergyman *Bill Hybels. When the group expanded to more than 1,000 in a year, Hybels started to meet in Chicago's Willow Creek Theater. Hybels today is the senior minister of Willow Creek, now on a large campus devoid of overt religious symbols. It attracts more than 15,000 to its Saturday evening and Sunday services, most of whom are not formal members. The church's objective is not to add members to the rolls, but to draw persons into the more than 400 small groups it offers. The loyalty that individuals develop toward Willow Creek stems from the community they sense among the small group(s) in which they participate, not from the experience of worshiping with thousands in an auditorium with state-of-the-art sound and video equipment. Willow Creek's statement of faith is solidly evangelical, if not fundamentalist, but few who attend may be familiar with it. Like evangelical ministries of earlier days, Willow Creek offers seminars and training programs for clergy and staff from other churches, many from oldline denominations, and the growing network of "Willow Creek churches," like those identified with Calvary Chapel and the Vineyard Fellowship, has characteristics of a denomination in the making.

For evangelicals who measure success by numbers, megachurches like Willow Creek stand as examples of what churches should be doing. This is so, too, with parachurch movements such as Promise Keepers, a pan-denominational, multiracial ministry promoting male spirituality begun by former University of Colorado football coach Bill McCartney in 1990.[22] The initial idea was to urge men to bond together to recommit themselves to promises they had made to God, their wives, their children, and their fellow human beings—particularly those of other races. Promise Keepers' format appeals to stereotypical American males: rallies held in football stadiums where those attending could shout cheers for Jesus while waiting to hear inspirational speakers, but all in the company of other men. Attendance at the nearly two dozen rallies held in 1996 totalled more than 1.5 million men. The Promise Keepers organization helps organize local affiliates, conducts training programs for clergy on how to minister effectively to men, and produces literature promoting its ideals.[23] A periodical, *New Man*, debuted in 1994.

Yet another signal of evangelicalism's strength is the presence of evangelical or conservative caucuses within the oldline denominations. One example is the Good News movement that developed within the United Methodist Church, using resources of evangelical Asbury Theological Seminary. Good News emerged in part as a response to the membership decline of the United Methodist Church, which lost more than 2 million members since 1960, despite the merger with a smaller denomination in 1968. Good News believed that Methodists had lost their zeal for winning souls, and hopes to recover that commitment to evangelism. A cognate group, the Confessing Movement, was formed by theologically conservative United Methodists in 1996 and marshaled sufficient financial resources to have a paid staff by 1997. The Confessing Movement focuses on doctrine and its implications for practice. It began in part because of controversy over denominational reports on human sexuality and debates over the ordination of homosexuals. Firmly opposed to that idea, the Confessing Movement wants to guarantee that denominational programs and publications measure up to its doctrinal standards, based on John Wesley's theology. Evangelicals within the United Methodist church have also formed an alternative missions vehicle, the Mission Society for United Methodists. None of these is an official church agency, but all signal the strength of the evangelical impulse within the nation's second largest Protestant denomination.[24] Parallel groups have arisen in virtually all of the oldline denominations for the same reasons. Presbyterians, for example, have Presbyterians United for Biblical Concerns, Presbyterians for Democracy and Religious Freedom, the Covenant Fellowship of Presbyterians, and the Presbyterian Lay Committee. Episcopalians have the Fellowship of Witness, while the National Evangelistic Association of the Christian Church and the

Conference on Spiritual Renewal nudge the Disciples of Christ to recall evangelical concerns. A cognate group within the United Church of Christ is the Biblical Witness Fellowship.

Perhaps the most public way in which evangelicals demonstrated that their brand of Christian expression had come to maturity came in active engagement in politics in the last third of the twentieth century. Evangelicals, especially fundamentalists or separatists, long had a healthy disdain for the social order as an arena where sin would always prevail. Social and political issues were matters of "the world," while evangelicals were concerned primarily with personal salvation. As early as the late 1940s, however, evangelical theologian *Carl F. H. Henry challenged fellow believers to abandon their apparent lack of social concern, which he attributed to the enduring influence of separatist fundamentalism.[25] Conventional wisdom recognized that evangelicals, even those heeding Henry's call, tended to be conservative in their politics and suspicious of movements for social change. This quiet, if not quiescent, conservatism began to awaken as evangelicals felt that the values they presumed informed public policy had receded.

In 1966, the Congress on the Church's Worldwide Mission at Wheaton College called Christian social action essential to global evangelization; three years later a prominent speaker at the United States Congress on Evangelism, Leighton Ford, brother-in-law of Billy Graham, insisted that evangelical Christians must make social action a central testimony to their personal faith. Ford and Henry both signed the Declaration of Evangelical Social Concern prepared by an ad hoc group meeting in Chicago in November 1973; many often call it the "Chicago Declaration." From that gathering at the Wabash YMCA came the impetus for forming Evangelicals for Social Action and the Evangelical Women's Caucus. With added ferment from groups such as the People's Christian Coalition, the nucleus of the Sojourners Community, all these reveal a passion brewing to translate evangelical convictions into concrete social and political action.

More public expressions of evangelical social concern received validation when the born-again *Jimmy Carter became president of the United States in 1977. But many evangelicals still feared that Supreme Court decisions regarding abortion and prayer and Bible reading in the public schools, along with the civil rights movement and subsequent calls for women's rights and gay rights, destroyed the unofficial alliance between evangelical faith and public values. The year of Carter's election, Jerry Falwell organized several mass rallies under the banner of "I Love America." In 1979, building on the momentum the rallies generated, he organized a political organization, Moral Majority,[26] the name reminiscent of the "silent majority" of Richard Nixon's rhetoric a decade earlier. With Moral Majority, Falwell sought to develop a network of followers to bring about desired changes in public policy by influencing legislation from the local to the national levels, registering voters sympathetic to its aims, and supporting election of candidates who reflected his views. What motivated Falwell to start Moral Majority in 1979, in addition to dissatisfaction with prevailing practices regarding abortion and religion in public schools, were the social movement influenced by feminism and the call for homosexual rights. For Moral Majority, women's liberation and gay rights signalled the demise of the nuclear family and the morality basic to American life.[27] It thus campaigned to defeat ratification of the Equal Rights Amendment. Related to its idealization of traditional women's roles was the antiabortion or "pro-life" position that Falwell brought into nearly every address. He also linked gay rights to the presumed growth of pornography. As well, Moral Majority condemned heavy regulation of the private Christian schools springing up as alternatives to public schools. It wanted to be "tough on crime," endorsing the death penalty and antidrug laws. It exalted capitalism and free enterprise, while criticizing most welfare programs. At times, Moral Majority rhetoric approached a conspiracy theory: evil forces out to destroy all Americans held dear lurked around every corner. Moral Majority became identified with the conservative wing of the Republican Party, particularly when Jimmy Carter failed to embrace Falwell's political agenda.[28] Carter's ambivalence toward his positions may have prompted Falwell to organize Moral Majority. In the 1980 presidential election, Moral Majority supported Ronald Reagan, not Carter. Falwell basked in the publicity Moral Majority reaped after the election, although by the time Reagan came into office, analysts of the "new religious political right" were already debating whether its presence would endure.[29]

Moral Majority was one of many evangelical and/or fundamentalist groups rushing into the political arena. The National Conservative Political Action Committee, Christian Voice, the National Pro-Life Political Action Committee, Concerned Women for America, and the Roundtable all burst on the scene in the 1980s. The program of these groups, all overwhelmingly Protestant in their constituencies, received endorsement from one prominent Catholic, Phyllis Schlafly, an attorney by profession and an outspoken political conservative. This political activity added a new dimension to evangelicalism: It became a multifaceted political force in Washington. Using the latest communications technology, groups maintained vast mailing lists, communicated almost instantly with millions, and made extravagant claims about the number of their committed supporters. While Moral Majority claimed a membership of millions, many were only names on a mailing list. Nevertheless, by 1988 Moral Majority underwrote a budget of over $8 million. In response to this conservative political presence, television mogul Norman Lear started People for the American Way, concerned that Falwell and his compatriots violated the cherished American principle of separation of church and state in principle, if not in fact.

Perhaps because Moral Majority failed to get its national platform enacted (except for defeating the Equal Rights Amendment), perhaps because Falwell the evangelist believed political activity sapped his ability to win souls for Christ, or perhaps because he became disillusioned with prominent evangelicals when he briefly guided the enterprises of Jim Bakker after Bakker's downfall, Falwell in 1986 stepped down as president of Moral Majority; in August 1989, he dissolved the organization, claiming that it had achieved its aim of assuring a voice for the "religious right" in American political life. Falwell did not abandon political interests altogether, however. In February 1997, he organized and moderated a "National Pastors' Policy Briefing" that drew nearly 500 evangelical pastors and their spouses to Washington. Falwell urged them to lift the political consciousness of their church members, bemoaning the fact that nearly 40 percent of evangelicals voted to reelect President Bill Clinton.

In 1988, the year before Falwell disbanded Moral Majority, Pat Robertson aggressively, but unsuccessfully, sought the Republican presidential nomination, enjoying considerable support among more charismatically inclined evangelicals. Instead of fading into the political background, he established another evangelical political outfit, the Christian Coalition.[30] Robertson tapped Ralph Reed to direct the organization while Reed was finishing a doctorate in history at Emory University in Georgia. By 1994, Reed claimed, the group had more than a million and a half members and had added members at the rate of more than 8,000 per week since the inauguration of Bill Clinton as president.[31] The Coalition's newsletter, *Christian American*, goes to an even larger mailing list. By 1996, the organization's annual budget surpassed $20 million. Christian Coalition worked at national, state, and local levels. Coalition members learned grassroots politics, gaining control of local school boards, city and county councils, and local and state Republican Party machinery. Some evangelicals objected to "voter guides" that Coalition members placed on windshields of cars in church parking lots prior to elections, and endorsement of candidates brought challenges over the group's tax-exempt status.[32] News media reported on "stealth candidates," realtively unknown persons in political races regarded as long-shots who refrained from mentioning their Christian Coalition connections until the conclusion of their (often successful) political campaigns. Nationally, when Republicans gained control of both houses of Congress in the 1994 elections, Ralph Reed and the Christian Coalition took some credit for the victory. Reed also endorsed the "Contract with America" set forth by Newt Gingrich, the first Republican Speaker of the House in forty years. The Coalition followed with its "Contract with the American Family," expecting the Republican Congress to enact legislation reflecting its agenda.[33] In this regard, the platform earlier set forth by Moral Majority endures, for the Christian Coalition is adamantly anti-abortion (pro-life), resolutely opposed to initiatives intended to guarantee equal rights for homosexuals, and eager to find ways to reinstate prayer and Bible reading in public schools.

Politically reinvigorated evangelicals made some unlikely allies. Although many evangelicals harbored negative views of the Roman Catholic Church, leaders established working relationships with Catholics who opposed abortion and who saw the Coalition's support for Christian schools as buttressing traditional Catholic positions regarding parochial schools. Some Catholics joined the Christian Coalition, although the membership reported by the organization has always been inflated. Others joined a parallel organization, Catholic Alliance, an adjunct to the Christian Coalition. However they might concur with the Christian Coalition's antiabortion stand, some Catholic prelates were aghast at this sort of association.[34]

At the same time, the Coalition reaped continuing criticism that it was anti-Semitic, a charge also leveled against Pat Robertson. Reed and other Coalition voices acknowledged that racism once infected the outfit as they sought to woo African American voters away from supporting Bill Clinton's reelection in 1996. Among politically active evangelicals, Reed received criticism for being too pragmatic and therefore too willing to compromise; for some, protecting the purity of evangelical religious truth required protecting the purity of a political position or social policy. Reed left the Coalition in 1997 to pursue a career as a political consultant.

Many other groups with specific social or political agendas also have evangelical connections. The American Family Association, based in Tupelo, Mississippi, is one. Led since its founding by Donald Wildmon, an ordained United Methodist, the American Family Association first directed its attention to perceived expressions of immorality on television programs. Wildmon urged followers to boycott businesses that sponsored objectionable programs. By the late 1990s, the American Family Association added its voice to those opposing gay rights or extending certain benefits, such as employer-sponsored health insurance coverage, to same-gender domestic partners. Some groups are more regionally oriented. The Traditional Values Coalition, for example, has concentrated its efforts in the western states, although it maintains an active Washington lobbyist and a network of more than 30,000 churches nationally. California fundamentalist preacher Lou Sheldon serves as its head, while his daughter Andrea oversees lobbying efforts.

Not all politically inclined evangelicals were drawn to the likes of Moral Majority or the Christian Coalition. In 1996 Jim Wallis, leader of the Sojourners community, spearheaded the formation of Call to Renewal, a political and social action group intended as a distinct alternative to groups on the political right. Call for Renewal is also concerned about social trends, including the breakdown of the traditional family and apparent erosion of "family values." It refuses, however, to target feminists and homosexuals as those responsible for the problem. On issues relating to feminist concerns, the Evangelical Women's Caucus and Evangelicals Concerned also represented distinct alternatives to positions taken by Falwell, Robertson, Reed, and their compatriots.

As evangelicalism came to maturity, it moved more securely into the public arena. Although individual evangelicals had long been socially involved, by the later twentieth century several organizations formed to channel the political and social interests of evangelicals into concrete action. While many of them, particularly those attracting the most media coverage, were identified with conservative political positions and personnel, others were not. If evangelicalism embraced a range of religious expressions that moved from the moderate conservatism of Billy Graham to rigid separatist fundamentalism, it also embraced a range of political expressions. Critics who pronounced the evangelical political presence dead every time a favorite candidate lost or a policy was rejected were misguided in their appraisal of evangelicalism's political strength. But those attributing the surge of conservatism in American political life to evangelical forces were likewise overly simplistic. Precisely how to translate evangelical faith into political action remains a challenge as American evangelicals enter the twenty-first century.

## NOTES

1. The literature on televangelism and the electronic church is voluminous. Many of the most significant monographs and articles published prior to 1995 are noted in Charles H. Lippy, *Modern American Popular Religion: A Critical Assessment and Annotated Bibliography* (Westport, Conn.: Greenwood, 1996), chap. 5. The bibliographic notes in Erling Jorstad, *Popular Religion in America: The Evangelical Voice* (Westport, Conn.: Greenwood, 1993), chap. 5 ("Popular Religion and the Transformation of Television"), are also very helpful. A useful reference tool, with more than 400 alphabetical entries, is Hal Erickson, *Religious Radio and Television in the United States, 1921–1991: The Programs and Personalities* (Jefferson, N.C.: McFarland, 1992). In addition, see Janice Peck, *The Gods of Televangelism: The Crisis of Meaning and the Appeal of Religious Television* (Cresskill, N.J.: Hampton, 1993); Steve Bruce, *Pray TV: Televangelism in America* (New York: Routledge, 1990); and Bobby C. Alexander, *Televangelism Reconsidered: Ritual in the Search for Human Community*, American Academy of Religion Studies in Religion No. 68 (Atlanta: Scholars Press, 1994). For a brief, but provocative appraisal, see Jeffrey K. Hadden, "The Rise and Fall of American Televangelism," in *Religion in the Nineties*, Annals of the American Academy of Political and Social Science 527, edited by Wade Clark Roof (Newbury Park, Calif.: Sage Periodicals, 1993), pp. 113–30.

2. Joe E. Barnhart with Steven Winzenburg, *Jim and Tammy: Charismatic Intrigue Inside PTL* (Buffalo: Prometheus Books, 1988), is one of the few full-length studies of the Bakkers. Also see Russell Watson et al., "Holy War: Heaven Can Wait," *Newsweek* 109 (8 June 1987): 58–62.

3. For years, the *Charlotte Observer* had monitored the financial maneuvering of Bakker and his associates. Some feel that the newspaper was critical in the downfall of the Bakkers. See the study by *Charlotte Observer* writer Charles E. Shepard, *Forgiven: The Rise and Fall of Jim Bakker and the PTL Ministry* (New York: Atlantic Monthly Press, 1989).

4. By 1987, Jimmy Swaggart Ministries in Baton Rouge had published nearly forty books giving Swaggart as author. There is little solid secondary literature apart from stories in the popular press. See, for example, Edith L. Blumhofer, "Divided Pentecostals: Bakker vs. Swaggart," *Christian Century* 103 (6 May 1987): 430–31; Martin E. Marty, "Onward, Christian Shoulders," *Christian Century* 103:38 (10 December 1986): 1135; and two pieces of Kenneth L. Woodward: "King of Honky-Tonk Heaven," *Newsweek* 101 (30 May 1983): 89ff., and idem, "Swaggart's One-Edged Sword," *Newsweek* 102 (9 January 1984): 65. Robert Paul Lamb, "Jimmy Swaggart's Ministry," *Charisma* 3 (March 1977): 17–20, is an early, uncritical exposition.

5. Schuller stands in the tradition of *Norman Vincent Peale: Both are affiliated with

the Reformed Church in America and both espouse a theology that blends pop psychology with religious tenets, positive thinking for Peale and possibility thinking for Schuller. See Dennis Voskuil, *Mountains into Goldmines: Robert Schuller and the Gospel of Success* (Grand Rapids, Mich.: Eerdmans, 1983). See also Michael Nason and Donna Nason, *Robert Schuller: The Inside Story* (Waco, Tex.: Word, 1983).

6. A good summary is found in William Martin, "Mass Communications," in *Encyclopedia of the American Religious Experience*, edited by Charles H. Lippy and Peter W. Williams (New York: Scribners, 1988), 3: 1711–26. See also Robert Abelman and Stewart Hoover, eds., *Religious Television: Controversies and Conclusions* (Norwood, N.J.: Ablex Corp., 1990), and titles in n.1 above.

7. See the scathing critique from a separatist fundamentalist perspective in Michael Horton, *The Agony of Deceit: What Some TV Preachers Are Teaching* (Chicago: Moody, 1990).

8. See Martin, "Mass Communications," pp. 1719–20.

9. See Howard Dorgan, *The Airwaves of Zion: Radio and Religion in Appalachia* (Knoxville: University of Tennessee Press, 1993).

10. See Jorstad, *Popular Religion in America* chap. 6.

11. For a broader bibliographical perspective, see Elmer J. O'Brien, "American Christianity and the History of Communication: A Bibliographic Probe," in *Communication and Change in American Religious History*, edited by Leonard I. Sweet (Grand Rapids, Mich.: Eerdmans, 1993), pp. 452–79.

12. Paul Baker, *Why Should the Devil Have All the Good Music?* (Waco, Tex.: Word, 1979).

13. Most studies of the Jesus Movement are contemporary with the phenomenon itself. See, for example, Robert S. Ellwood, *One Way: The Jesus Movement and Its Meaning* (Englewood Cliffs, N.J.: Prentice-Hall, 1973); Lowell D. Streiker, *The Jesus Trip: Advent of the Jesus Freaks* (Nashville: Abingdon, 1971); and Ronald M. Enroth, Edward Ericson Jr., and C. Breckinridge Peters, *The Jesus People: Old-Time Religion in the Age of Aquarius* (Grand Rapids, Mich.: Eerdmans, 1972).

14. Robert Bellah, Richard Madsen, William M. Sullivan, Ann Swidler, and Steven M. Tipton, *Habits of the Heart: Individualism and Commitment in American Life* (Berkeley: University of California Press, 1985).

15. On the religion of the boomer generation, see Wade Clark Roof, *A Generation of Seekers: The Spiritual Journeys of the Baby Boom Generation* (San Francisco: HarperSanFrancisco, 1994), and Benton Johnson, Donald A. Luidens, and Dean R. Hoge, *Vanishing Boundaries: The Religion of Mainline Protestant Baby Boomers* (Louisville, Ky.: Westminster/John Knox, 1994). The latter focuses on baby boomers who were reared in Presbyterian churches.

16. See especially Dean M. Kelley, *Why Conservative Churches Are Growing*, rev. ed. (New York: Harper & Row, 1977), and Dean R. Hoge and David A. Roozen, eds., *Understanding Church Growth and Decline, 1950–1979* (New York: Pilgrim Press, 1979).

17. See Kathleen C. Boone, *The Bible Tells Them So: The Discourse of Protestant Fundamentalism* (Albany: State University of New York Press, 1989).

18. Nancy Tatom Ammerman, "Golden Rule Christianity: Lived Religion in the American Mainstream," in *Lived Religion in America: Toward a Theory of Practice*, edited by David D. Hall (Princeton, N.J.: Princeton University Press, 1997), pp. 196–216.

An abbreviated version appeared in the January 1997 issue of *Congregations*, the journal of the Alban Institute.

19. See Tom Raabe, *The Ultimate Church: An Irreverent Look at Church Growth, Megachurches, and Ecclesiastical "Show-Biz"* (Grand Rapids, Mich.: Zondervan, 1991), and Charles Truehart, "Welcome to the Next Church," *Atlantic Monthly* 277 (August 1996): 37–58. Megachurches and other contemporary evangelical styles are deftly explored in Randall Balmer, *Mine Eyes Have Seen the Glory: A Journey into the Evangelical Subculture in America* (New York: Oxford University Press, 1989).

20. On the significance of the small group in the contemporary American religion, see Robert Wuthnow, ed., *"I Come Away Stronger": How Small Groups Are Shaping American Religion* (Grand Rapids, Mich.: Eerdmans, 1994). The importance of the small group as an accompaniment to the increasing privatization of religion in American culture is also discussed in Wade Clark Roof and William McKinney, *American Mainline Religion: Its Changing Shape and Future* (New Brunswick, N.J.: Rutgers University Press, 1994).

21. See Gregory Allen Pritchard, "The Strategy of Willow Creek Community Church: A Study in the Sociology of Religion" (Ph.D. diss., Northwestern University, 1994), published in revised form as *Willow Creek Seeker Services: Evaluating a New Way of Doing Church* (Grand Rapids, Mich.: Baker, 1996); and Kimon Howland Sargeant, "Faith and Fulfillment: Willow Creek and the Future of Evangelicalism" (Ph.D. diss., University of Virginia, 1996). See also David S. Luecke, "Is Willow Creek the Way of the Future?" *Christian Century* 114:16 (14 May 1997): 479ff.; Michael Lewis, "God Is in the Packaging: To Sell Bottled Water, or Eternal Life, Just Know the Customers and Meet Their Needs. Amen," *New York Times Magazine* (21 July 1996): 14ff.; and Trueheart, "Welcome to the Next Church." Also instructive is Sabrina Tingley, "Willow Creek Community Church and Holy Covenant United Methodist Church: A Comparison," *Chicago Theological Seminary Register* 76:3 (Fall 1996): 2–11. For an "insider" perspective, see Lynne Hybels and Bill Hybels, *Rediscovering Church: The Story and Vision of Willow Creek Community Church* (Grand Rapids, Mich.: Zondervan, 1995), and Lee Strobel, *Inside the Mind of Unchurched Harry and Mary: How to Reach Friends and Family Who Avoid God and the Church* (Grand Rapids, Mich.: Zondervan, 1993). On the methods of Willow Creek and other megachurches, see George G. Hunter III, *Church for the Unchurched* (Nashville: Abingdon, 1996).

22. For an insider perspective, see John Trent et al., *Go the Distance: The Making of a Promise Keeper* (Colorado Springs, Colo.: Focus on the Family Publishing, 1996). See also "The Promise of a Promise Keeper," *Good News* (September-October 1995): 12–17. For analysis, see Mary Stewart Van Leeuwen, "Servanthood or Soft Patriarchy? A Christian Feminist Looks at the Promise Keepers Movement," *Journal of Men's Studies* 5:3 (February 1997): 233–61. More in the format of the expose is Donna Minkowitz, "In the Name of the Father," *Ms.* 6:3 (November-December 1995): 64–71. Also see Jeff Wagenheim, "Among the Promise Keepers," *Utne Reader* No. 73 (January-February 1996): 74–77; Edward Gilbreath, "Manhood's Great Awakening," *Christianity Today* 39:2 (6 February 1995): 20–28; and Joseph Shapiro, "Heavenly Promises," *U.S. News & World Report* 119:13 (2 October 1995): 68–70.

23. Much of the Promise Keepers literature is printed by evangelical James Dobson's Focus on the Family publishing arm.

24. These groups form the basis for Ted W. Jennings, "The 'Houston Declaration' Is Heretical," *Christian Century* 105 (20 April 1988): 399–401; Randy Frame, "United

Methodists Bury Theological Pluralism,'' *Christianity Today* 32 (17 June 1988): 60ff.; ''UMC Evangelicals Dissent,'' *Christian Century* 109 (5–12 February 1992): 120; ''United Methodists Form Confessing Movement,'' *Christian Century* 112 (7 June 1995): 600–601; John Zipperer, ''United Methodists: Confessing Movement Grows amid Doctrinal Disputes,'' *Christianity Today* 39 (2 October 1995): 105; and '' 'Confessing' Statement Termed Divisive,'' *Christian Century* 113 (3 April 1996): 365.

25. This was a major thrust of his *The Uneasy Conscience of Modern Fundamentalism* (Grand Rapids, Mich.: Eerdmans, 1947).

26. Literature on the Moral Majority and cognate political organizations that draw heavily on support from the so-called ''religious right'' is voluminous. In addition to the titles identified in Lippy, *Modern American Popular Religion*, chap. 4, see William C. Martin, *With God on Our Side: The Rise of the Religious Right in America* (New York: Bantam Books, 1996). The PBS documentary series of the same title is also helpful. Other recent studies that give an overview of conservative and fundamentalist involvement in politics include Albert J. Menendez, *Evangelicals at the Ballot Box* (Buffalo: Prometheus Books, 1996); Randall Frame and Alan Tharpe, *How Right Is the Right? A Biblical and Balanced Approach to Politics* (Grand Rapids, Mich.: Zondervan, 1996), that attempts to construct a moderate evangelical position; Clyde Wilcox, *Onward, Christian Soldiers: The Religious Right in American Politics* (Boulder, Colo.: Westview, 1996); and Corwin E. Smidt, *Contemporary Evangelical Political Involvement: An Analysis and Assessment* (Lanham, Md.: University Press of America, 1985).

27. Many who criticized Falwell, Moral Majority, and cognate groups such as the Christian Coalition were quick to point out that the nuclear family idealized by the religious right was a recent phenomenon in American history, moving to center stage only after World War II.

28. See Duane M. Oldfield, *The Right and the Righteous: The Christian Right Confronts the Republican Party* (Lanham, Md.: Rowman and Littlefield, 1996).

29. Of the early studies, still insightful are Samuel S. Hill and Dennis E. Owen, *The New Religious Political Right in America* (Nashville: Abingdon, 1982), and Erling Jorstad, *The Politics of Moralism: The New Christian Right in American Life* (Minneapolis: Augsburg, 1981).

30. The aims of the Christian Coalition are set forth in Ralph Reed, *Active Faith: How Christians Are Changing the Soul of American Politics* (New York: Free Press, 1996).

31. Thomas C. Reeves, *The Empty Church: The Suicide of Liberal Christianity* (New York: Free Press, 1996), p. 29.

32. See ''Thou Shalt Not Endorse,'' *Christian Century* 113:29 (16 October 1996): 958.

33. See Randy Frame, ''Payback Time? Conservative Christians Support GOP 'Contract' as Profamily Agenda Takes a Back Seat,'' *Christianity Today* 39:3 (6 March 1995): 42–45.

34. These issues inform Heidi Schlumpf, ''How Catholic Is the Catholic Alliance,'' *Christianity Today* 40:6 (20 May 1996): 76; Matthew G. Monahan, ''The Christian Coalition's New 'Catholic Alliance' Crass and Unnecessary (View from a Pew),'' *America* 174:1 (13 January 1996): 7; G. W. Gerner, ''Catholics and the 'Religious Right',''  *Commonweal* 122 (5 May 1995): 15–20; and John M. Swomley, ''Catholics and the Religious Right (Watch on the Right),'' *The Humanist* 56:2 (March-April 1996): 36–37.

# 8
# American Evangelicalism Looks to the Future

At the end of the twentieth century, evangelicalism had come into its own. By some estimates, more than 40 million Americans, or approximately 15 percent of the nation's population, were evangelicals.[1] Numbers alone made evangelicalism a major force in American religious life. With evangelicalism's maturity came naysayers, many of them separatist fundamentalists but some simply students of religious movements, who saw hidden dangers that in time could mean that evangelicals, like those they criticized, sold their souls to the culture around them. For along with the evangelical surge lurked challenges to the seemingly secure niche evangelicalism carved for itself over the preceding half century.

One signal of evangelicalism's maturity came in the intellectual sphere. In the last half of the twentieth century, evangelicals mounted a formidable effort to build a solid intellectual base to equal, if not surpass, the intellectual rigor once conceded to alternative Christian perspectives.*Carl F. H. Henry, one of the original faculty at Fuller Seminary and founding editor of *Christianity Today*, paved the way for constructing a systematic theology for moderate evangelicalism distinct from fundamentalism with two early works, *Remaking the Modern Mind* and *The Uneasy Conscience of Modern Fundamentalism*.[2] Between 1976 and 1983 he published his five-volume *God, Revelation and Authority*.[3] In this magnum opus, Henry carefully argued for the necessity of supernatural revelation as the basis for theology, the traditional evangelical insistence on the authority (and also inerrancy) of the Bible, and the theism he believed central to biblical revelation. Before the final volume appeared, Henry had been elected president of the respected American Theological Society, whose members spanned the theological spectrum. Others also buttressed evangelicalism's intellectual foundations.*Edward John Carnell, with doctorates from both Harvard and Boston universities, worked with Henry at Fuller and served as Fuller's president for a time. Before his death in 1967, he wrote several books arguing that orthodox (i.e., evangelical) Christian belief, while based on revelation, affirmed no postulates contrary to reason. Particularly well known were his *Introduction to Christian Apologetics* and *The Case for Orthodox Theology*.[4] Some of Carnell's works were held in such esteem that reprint editions are available at century's end.

Carnell and Henry wrote for a theologically sophisticated audience. Among rank and file evangelicals, the writings of British Christian apologist C. S. Lewis had an enduring impact. Widely read among evangelical laity were also the works of *Francis A. Schaeffer. Born in Philadelphia, Schaeffer spent much of his career in Switzerland where he brought evangelicals together to reflect on history and culture at L'Abri, a study center he founded in 1955. Informed by the Reformed theological heritage, Schaeffer claimed that only the kind of absolute truth central to evangelical Christianity could provide meaning in life, but that western civilization had gradually, but steadily, abandoned absolute truth for shallow relativism. In turn, relativism's glorification of human freedom demolished biblical morality. Schaeffer's work cut across traditional academic disciplines in an effort to unify truth within a biblical framework. Critics, some from within evangelical circles, found his analyses superficial and simplistic, but many evangelicals found in them a viable Christian world-view.

Evangelicals moved in other ways to assure the intellectual credibility of orthodox Protestant thought. *Billy Graham, by the 1990s forced by age and declining health to curtail global evangelism, throughout his career sought to make evangelicalism as plausible as any other Christian perspective. One early sign was his critical role in founding *Christianity Today*. In 1970 he moved in another direction, as the Billy Graham Evangelistic Association undertook establishment of the Billy Graham Center, dedicated in 1980 on the Wheaton College campus. The center housed both archives documenting Graham's ministry and the Institute for the Study of American Evangelicals. The institute has amassed the foremost collection of primary sources dealing with North American evangelicalism from the seventeenth century to the present, with particular strength in nineteenth- and twentieth-century materials. The *Evangelical Studies Bulletin* appears quarterly under institute sponsorship. Although a host of other Wheaton programs operate through the Billy Graham Center, the institute and archives made it the premier location for sustained research on the evangelical heritage. Some institute initiatives targeted particular topics in the history of evangelicalism. For example, in late 1996 it launched a three-year study, funded by the Lilly Endowment, of the history of the financing of American evangelicalism.[5]

Evangelicals with academic interests in 1949 had formed a quasi-professional group, the Evangelical Theological Society, to pursue scholarly discussion and provide a medium for intellectual inquiry. Initially most members and participants came from the faculties of schools such as Wheaton, Fuller, or Gordon-Conwell Theological Seminary. It became a forum where nonevangelicals studying evangelical thought and kindred topics shared their work. Those oriented toward Pentecostal strains of evangelicalism also bolstered the intellectual and scholarly credulity of their enterprises. The Society for Pentecostal Studies, organized in 1970 during the ninth Pentecostal World Conference, since the spring of 1979 has published a semiannual scholarly journal, *Pneuma*. Serious study of evangelicalism and affirmation of evangelical belief and practice came in yet another way. In the last decades of the twentieth century, the Pew Charitable Trusts provided millions of dollars in grants to individuals and institutions. Most targeted particular themes or topics in American evangelicalism, with several administered by the Institute for the Study of American Evangelicals. Others allowed self-professing evangelicals from a variety of disciplines to study and write about how their evangelical affirmation related to their fields. Technological advances had an impact on evangelical intellectual life as electronic communication by computer via the Internet became commonplace. For example, evangelicals organized an electronic discussion list on the history of evangelicalism operating from Baylor University. Calvin College professor Quentin J. Schultze regularly published electronic lists of resources for evangelicals called the "Internet for Christians." Where radio once assisted evangelicals in networking, the computer was taking over that role.

More traditional means also indicated that evangelicalism had moved to the center of American cultural life. The annual convention of the Christian Booksellers Association (CBA), founded in 1950 to supply merchandise to Christian book stores, grew in size and scope to meet growing demand, although some industry analysts believe the market has now stabilized.[6] Some titles distributed through CBA rank as best sellers, although none appears on established best seller lists since sales through Christian retailers are excluded from tabulations. At the same time, the later twentieth-century evangelical explosion led commercial houses, some of which had dropped religious lines of a theological bent, to re-enter the field with books aimed at a mass audience. Available through major book store chains and outlets as diverse as supermarkets and airports, evangelically oriented books cover a wide range of topics. There are Christian romances and reprints or updates of classics, such as the books of Grace Livingston Hill written for young evangelical women in the 1920s through 1940s. Interest in self-help groups reverberated in evangelical publishing, with scores of titles appearing that treat such practical matters as managing stress, controlling weight, and improving marriage. Evangelical radio celebrities market their own books; some, such as James Dobson of "Focus in the Family," have their own publishing arms.

All these signs of intellectual maturity have a touch of irony, given the complex of forces shaping evangelicalism in the late nineteenth century when most evangelicals were suspicious of intellectual pursuits. In biblical criticism, liberal theology, study of other religions, and schools of thought associated with Darwin and evolutionary theory, they found distinct threats to orthodox evangelical belief. Historians often classified evangelicalism as anti-intellectual because of the way these evangelicals shunned intellectual currents of the day. Many early evangelicals would have applauded Princeton Theological Seminary professor Charles Hodge, who on ending his tenure as editor of the *Princeton Review* in 1871 wrote, "Whether it be a ground of reproach or of approbation, it is believed to be true that an original idea in theology is not to be found on the pages of the *Biblical Repertory and Princeton Review* from the beginning [1825] until now [1871]."[7] Evangelicals a century later could not make such a statement, so intent were they on securing a strong intellectual foundation for their expression of Christian belief.

Several other kinds of institutions also testify to the strength of evangelicalism at the dawn of the twenty-first century. Many evangelical colleges, once shadows of private and public schools, took their place in the front ranks of American colleges and universities. Wheaton College may be the most prominent, but through the Coalition for Christian Colleges and Universities, Wheaton is linked with such other schools as Michigan's Calvin College, an evangelical school in the Reformed tradition, and Westmont College in California. The clear distinction between such evangelical schools and those identified with separatist fundamentalism (such as Bob Jones University in Greenville, South Carolina) has augmented their public credibility. The burgeoning Christian school movement stood as another sign of evangelicalism's strength. If such schools owed their origins to convictions that secular humanism controlled public education and fears about racial integration, those concerns were consigned to the past. Enrolling more than 1 million students by the mid–1990s, Protestant day schools constituted a major component of the nation's educational systems. Not all schools were identified with moderate evangelicals; many were aligned with separatist fundamentalist churches or with denominations such as the evangelically inclined Lutheran Church–Missouri Synod or the Seventh-Day Adventists that had long maintained weekday schools. Providing curriculum resources and assuring that they met state-established standards were no small tasks. At the same time, there was a growing interest in home schooling, somewhat more among fundamentalists than moderate evangelicals.

In other educational arenas, the evangelical presence remained strong. Thanks in part to the Christian Coalition, strident evangelicals who won seats on local school boards often spearheaded efforts to reform curricula, usually first directing attention to the teaching of science. The issue was whether evolution would be taught as theory or fact and whether "creation science" would receive a hearing. The Institute for Creation Research, set up by civil engineer Henry Morris in 1972, provided textbook-type materials examining creation science.[8] Critics insisted that creation science was not a science at all, but religious teaching inappropriate for public schools. Another issue continuing to draw fire was the evangelical effort to restore some explicit religious element to public education.[9] In the political sector, debates surfaced, often in presidential election years, over having a constitutional amendment to make prayer in public schools legal. By century's end, the right of students to have extracurricular religiously oriented clubs meet on school property was generally recognized; some locales and school boards endorsed student-initiated prayer at events such as graduation ceremonies. What got lost in much of the public debate was the Supreme Court's having encouraged academic study of religion in public schools.

The steady growth of interest in parachurch movements such as Promise Keepers and Women's Aglow, the network of churches identifying with the contemporary Christian worship advocated by Willow Creek Community Church, and the near necessity of having evangelical congregations sponsor aerobics classes, parenting support groups, as well as the usual Alcoholics Anonymous and Narcotics Anonymous type groups likewise suggests the power of the evangelical presence in American religious life. Virtually all parachurch movements have evangelical dimensions; more traditional congregations of the oldline denominations that give them support, as when a United Methodist congregation sponsors a local unit of Promise Keepers but not the denominationally sanctioned United Methodist Men, enhance evangelicalism's strength indirectly. Christian radio and television continue to buttress evangelicalism's presence across the nation.

From many perspectives, evangelicalism's future as a major feature of American religious life appears secure. But there are challenges that could sabotage evangelicalism's current strength. Through much of evangelicalism's history, the work of key individuals (such as*Dwight L. Moody,*Billy Sunday,*Charles E. Fuller,*Oral Roberts,*Kathryn Kuhlman,*Billy Graham, and*Pat Robertson) shaped its course. The scandals effectively ending the ministries of Jimmy Swaggart and Jim and Tammy Faye Bakker tarnished the reputation of all, except perhaps Billy Graham, in the forefront of evangelical leadership. Robertson's political forays likewise raised questions about the intentions of those who were public voices for evangelicalism. At century's end, it appeared that the age of "giants" on the evangelical scene had passed; some figures commanded widespread respect, but leadership became more localized and diffuse. Could evangelicalism flourish without having a cluster of individuals to provide a symbolic focus around which the masses could rally?

Shifts in the religious culture of the nation also threaten evangelicalism. When modern American evangelicalism emerged, Christianity dominated the religious picture. There was pluralism, but one denoting the multiplicity of Protestant denominations. Roman Catholicism, the largest Christian body in the United States well before the twentieth century, became generally perceived simply as one Christian denomination among many. Until the massive immigration between the end of the Civil War and the outbreak of World War I, Jews constituted such a numerically small minority as to be almost statistically insignificant. Sociologist Will Herberg suggested at midcentury that the labels of Protestant, Catholic, and Jew had become functionally equivalent in American culture; all were popularly taken as valid ways of being religious.[10] By the late 1990s, the religious picture was more diverse; a new pluralism took root. Immigration patterns in the last third of the twentieth century swelled the Asian American population; Hindu temples appeared even in smaller cities. Scholars estimate that early in the twenty-first century Muslims will outnumber Jews in the United States; some believe that the number of Muslims already surpasses the number of Jews. Modern evangelicalism came to maturity in a culture where a multi-faceted Christian perspective could be assumed. Evangelicalism come of age does not enjoy that luxury. Whether evangelicalism will be able to sustain plausibility structures in an increasingly pluralistic religious milieu constitutes another major challenge.

Evangelicalism at heart presumes that individuals will have some deep, inner, often very personal experience of Jesus Christ. While that individualistic dimension gave evangelicalism some diversity, since one person's experience may not duplicate another's, acceptance of biblical revelation and authority set some parameters. For evangelicals, it has never been "anything goes" because of the primacy of individual experience. The difficulty in setting parameters sheds some light on the rift between moderate evangelicals and separatist fundamentalists, who wanted to insist on doctrinal conformity as well as personal experience to authenticate true faith. It also helps explain the uncertainty many evangelicals felt when more Pentecostal and charismatic expressions of faith became common; how could one evaluate such ecstatic phenomena to be certain that the Spirit motivated them? The spirituality of the baby boomers raised fresh challenges. While many were drawn to evangelical congregations where small groups provided support for individual needs and worship was often more casual and informal, boomers appeared to espouse a much more eclectic personal spirituality than evangelicalism historically accommodated. That spirituality might be inner-directed, but it might also tap nonbiblical sources and non-Christian approaches. For example, many women have drawn on traditional Christian resources familiar to evangelicals, but combined them with others—some would call them pagan—to fashion a spirituality that speaks to women's experience.[11] "New Age" phenomena that aroused the ire of so many evangelicals are appropriated by others as they mold an idiosyncratic spirituality. Much of this illustrates what sociologists identify as the privatization of religion, more common in highly complex, urban, industrial societies.[12] Evangelicalism is not exempt from this larger social-religious trend. James Davison Hunter, whose several studies probe contemporary evangelicalism, has called attention to the growing emphasis on private religious experience among those who are traditional and orthodox in belief.[13] The challenge lies in constructing boundaries around what is acceptable personal religious belief and practice in this more intensely individualized, privatized spiritual milieu.

Within evangelical circles, much internal variance must be acknowledged. Some revolves around worship. Not all evangelical congregations have espoused "contemporary Christian worship" with its informality and upbeat music. For some, worship does not require expensive sound systems and singing from words flashed on screens rather than hymnals. Even the formal underpinnings of evangelical thought span the gamut of the Christian theological heritage.[14]

Some strands look to Luther and the German Reformation; others are firmly in the tradition of John Calvin. Many evangelicals have historically identified with the theology associated with John Wesley, particularly the Wesleyan understanding of holiness and sanctification. Baptist evangelicals point to yet other theological roots. So, too, Pentecostals and charismatics, evangelical Mennonites, and a host of others who tout the centrality of an inner experience of faith and the authority of inspired Scripture have very different theological constructs supporting their particular discernment of what being evangelical actually means. The range of evangelical denominations also betrays the diversity in polity that marks American religious life. Some are fiercely local and independent; others are more connectional. Evangelicalism is not cut from a single mold when it comes to worship, theology, or organization, and one challenge of the twenty-first century is how to juggle that internal diversity while retaining enough of a common identity so that "evangelical" and "evangelicalism" point to recognizable realities.

These issues lead directly to another challenge. The history of modern American evangelicalism is one of fission rather than fusion. The division between fundamentalists and moderate evangelicals represents only one strand of this history of dividing when the Spirit seems to move evangelicals in different directions. The Holiness movement spawned numerous denominations; so did the Pentecostal movement as it spread nationally. Dynamic preachers have often severed their denominational ties to start independent ministries that in turn take on the trappings of denominations, until they, too, divide over some minor dispute. The way Willow Creek Community Church became the pivot for a network of local congregations, some identified with denominations and some independent, illustrates another facet of this potential for fission. Disagreement within evangelical circles about the tactics of Ralph Reed and the Christian Coalition, while they echo reservations evangelicals earlier held about Jerry Falwell and Moral Majority, points to another arena where dangers of a different kind of division lurk beneath the surface.

Evangelicals have long made extraordinarily deft use of communications media. At the dawn of the twenty-first century, the challenge here comes from the computer and the expanding opportunities offered through the Internet. Numerous religious "chat rooms" already bring people of like mind into electronic contact with each other. Will the evangelical chat room replace the local congregation as the focus for whatever religious community evangelical Christians of the computer generation require? The question mirrors concerns raised when evangelicals explored radio and television as vehicles to proclaim the gospel and nurture people in the faith. As Americans become a people of computers, evangelicals must wrestle with how to adopt and adapt the technological leaps made in communications media.

Evangelicalism come of age must also deal with forces that would formerly have been dismissed as alien. Perhaps the most prominent is psychology, once summarily rejected because the theories linked especially to Freud were seen as hostile to religious faith. But evangelicals now are as likely as others to be part of some twelve–step recovery program or seeking psychological counselling. As previously noted, part of the attractiveness of the megachurch is the array of such support groups and similar mechanisms for enhancing psychological health it provides. Add to that the chain of evangelically oriented New Life Clinics that offer Christian counseling, along with its cognate Women of Faith organization. Evangelicals are inextricably tied to the psychotherapy once spurned. The roots were there in the positive thinking of *Norman Vincent Peale and the possibility thinking of Robert Schuller. Gnawing questions remains. Will evangelical faith simply become good psychology? Has psychology already transformed evangelicalism?[15] Many of these concerns aroused a passionate critique already from within the evangelical family. Michael Scott Horton, a Reformed Episcopal priest active with the evangelically oriented parachurch group Christians United for Reformation (CURE), argued that evangelicals undermine truth when they sell out to "how to" consumer religion where it is "to each his own."[16] For Horton, only a return to the Reformed theological heritage will allow evangelicalism to retain its claim to truth.

The twentieth century brought modern American evangelicalism to maturity. Defying critics who dismissed evangelicalism as anachronistic and anti-intellectual, evangelicals established a host of institutions and drew on a dazzling array of resources that brought about an explosion of interest in evangelical faith in the last third of the century. With that maturity came the stability of no longer being on the defensive. Challenges remained, as did the peril of letting security lapse into stasis.[17] A static evangelicalism would be not only oxymoronic, but truly anachronistic.

## NOTES

1. The 40 million figure comes from Gustav Niebuhr, "Putting Life's Trials in a Sacred Context," *New York Times* (9 February 1997), 4: 4.

2. Carl F. H. Henry, *Remaking the Modern Mind* (Grand Rapids, Mich.: Eerdmans, 1946); idem, *The Uneasy Conscience of Modern Fundamentalism* (Grand Rapids, Mich.: Eerdmans, 1947). On the central role played by Fuller Theological Seminary in molding an evangelicalism that was distinct from separatist fundamentalism, see George M. Marsden, *Reforming Fundamentalism: Fuller Seminary and the New Evangelicalism* (Grand Rapids, Mich.: Eerdmans, 1987), passim. Also valuable is Henry's autobiography, *Confessions of a Theologian: An Autobiography* (Waco, Tex.: Word, 1986).

3. Carl F. H. Henry, *God, Revelation and Authority*, 5 vols. (Waco, Tex.: Word, 1976–83). Volumes are also titled individually.

4. Edward John Carnell, *An Introduction to Christian Apologetics* (Grand Rapids, Mich.: Eerdmans, 1948), and *The Case for Orthodox Theology* (Philadelphia: Westminster, 1959). *Christian Apologetics* was reprinted in 1996 and available through Green Leaf Press. See also Rudolph Nelson, *The Making and Unmaking of an Evangelical Mind: The Case of Edward Carnell* (New York: Cambridge University Press, 1987).

5. See the announcement of this program in *Evangelical Studies Bulletin* 13:4 (Winter 1996): 5.

6. Randall Balmer, *Mine Eyes Have Seen the Glory: A Journey into the Evangelical Subculture in America* (New York: Oxford University Press, 1989), pp. 155–70, describes a CBA convention. CBA also publishes a newsletter and offers an array of ancillary services to members.

7. Charles Hodge, "Retrospect of the History of the Princeton Review," *Biblical Repertory and Princeton Review: Index Volume from 1825 to 1868* (Philadelphia: Peter Walker, 1871), p. 11.

8. For a good overview of much of the early debate over creation science, see Ronald Numbers, "Creationism in 20th-Century America," *Science* 218 (1982): 534–44.

9. A valuable, although now dated, study is Robert Michaelsen, *Piety in the Public School: Trends and Issues in the Relationship Between Religion and the Public Schools in the U.S.* (New York: Macmillan, 1970).

10. Will Herberg, *Protestant, Catholic, Jew: An Essay in American Religious Sociology* (Garden City, N.Y.: Doubleday, 1955).

11. See Nancy A. Hardesty, "Seeking the Great Mother: The Goddess for Today," paper presented to the South Carolina Academy of Religion, February 1993.

12. In *Being Religious, American Style: A History of Popular Religiosity in the United States* (Westport, Conn.: Greenwood, 1994), Charles H. Lippy suggests that this tendency to eclecticism and privatization has been part of American religious life at least since the arrival of the first European settlers.

13. James Davison Hunter, *American Evangelicalism: Conservative Religion and the Quandary of Modernity* (New Brunswick, N.J.: Rutgers University Press, 1983), pp. 120–26.

14. This theological diversity becomes evident in *The Variety of Evangelicalism*, edited by Donald W. Dayton and Robert K. Johnston (Knoxville: University of Tennessee Press, 1991).

15. Some of these issues were pointedly raised by Gustav Niebuhr, "Putting Life's Trials in Sacred Context."

16. Michael Scott Horton, *Made in America: The Shaping of Modern American Evangelicalism* (Grand Rapids, Mich.: Baker, 1991), develops this criticism. Christians United for Reformation (CURE) promoted publication of the book.

17. Mark A. Shibley, in his *Resurgent Evangelicalism in the United States: Mapping Cultural Change Since 1970* (Columbia: University of South Carolina Press, 1997), concluded from his analysis of a Southern Baptist congregation and an Assemblies of God congregation in California that evangelicalism is now culture affirming, oriented toward a therapeutic focus, insistent on being highly individualistic, reticent about the political picture in the larger society, and becoming fixated on programming in local congregations. He suggests that this cultural accommodation and reflection of trends in American society more generally is the price evangelicalism has paid for its success.

# Bibliography for Part I

Abel, Theodore. *Protestant Missions to Catholic Immigrants*. New York: Institute of Social and Religious Research, 1933.

Abelman, Robert, and Stewart Hoover, eds. *Religious Television: Controversies and Conclusions*. Norwood, N.J.: Ablex Corp., 1990.

Alexander, Bobby C. *Televangelism Reconsidered: Ritual in the Search for Human Community*. American Academy of Religion Studies in Religion No. 68. Atlanta: Scholars Press, 1994.

Allen, A. A., with Walter Wagner. *Born to Lose, Bound to Win*. Garden City, N.Y.: Doubleday, 1970.

Ammerman, Nancy Tatom. *Baptist Battles: Social Change and Religious Conflict in the Southern Baptist Convention*. New Brunswick, N.J.: Rutgers University Press, 1990.

———. *Bible Believers: Fundamentalists in the Modern World*. New Brunswick, N.J.: Rutgers University Press, 1987.

———. "Golden Rule Christianity: Lived Religion in the American Mainstream." In *Lived Religion in America*. Edited by David D. Hall. Princeton, N.J.: Princeton University Press, 1997. An abbreviated version appreared in *Congregations* (January 1997).

Anderson, Robert Mapes. *Vision of the Disinherited: The Making of American Pentecostalism*. New York: Oxford University Press, 1979.

Armstrong, Ben. *The Electric Church*. Nashville, Tenn.: Thomas Nelson, 1979.

Armstrong, William C. "Demos Shakarian: A Man and His Message." *Logos Journal* (September-October 1971): 13–14.

Baker, Paul. *Why Should the Devil Have All the Good Music?* Waco, Tex.: Word, 1979.

Balmer, Randall. *Mine Eyes Have Seen the Glory: A Journey into the Evangelical Subculture in America*. New York: Oxford University Press, 1989.

Barna, George. *The Barna Report 1992–93*. Ventura, Calif.: Regal Books, 1992.

Barnhart, Joe E., with Steven Winzenburg. *Jim and Tammy: Charismatic Intrigue Inside PTL*. Buffalo: Prometheus Books, 1988.

Bass, Clarence B. *Backgrounds to Dispensationalism*. Grand Rapids, Mich.: Eerdmans, 1960.

Bebbington, David. *Evangelicals in Modern Britain: A History from the 1730s to the 1980s*. Grand Rapids, Mich.: Baker, 1992.

Bellah, Robert, Richard Madsen, William M. Sullivan, Ann Swidler, and Steven M. Tipton. *Habits of the Heart: Individualism and Commitment in American Life*. Berkeley: University of California Press, 1985.

Berkhofer, Robert F., Jr. *Salvation and the Savage: An Analysis of Protestant Missions and American Indian Response, 1787–1862*. Rev. ed. New York: Atheneum, 1972.

Bird, Brian. "FGBMFI: Facing Frustrations and the Future." *Charisma* 11 (June 1986); 25–26, 28.

———. "The Legacy of Demos Shakarian." *Charisma* 11 (June 1986): 20–25.

Bittlinger, Arthur, ed. *The Church Is Charismatic*. Geneva: World Council of Churches, 1981.

Blair, Ralph. "An Evangelical Look at Homosexuality." New York: Homosexual Community Counselling Center, 1972.

Bloch-Hoell, Nils. *The Pentecostal Movement*. London: Allen and Unwin, 1964.

Blumhofer, Edith L. "Divided Pentecostals: Bakker vs. Swaggart." *Christian Century* 103 (6 May 1987): 430–31.

Boone, Kathleen C. *The Bible Tells Them So: The Discourse of Protestant Fundamentalism*. Albany: State University of New York Press, 1989.

Bowden, Henry Warner. *American Indians and Christian Missions: Studies in Cultural Conflict*. Chicago: University of Chicago Press, 1981.

———. *Church History in an Age of Uncertainty: Historiographical Patterns in the United States, 1906–1990*. Carbondale, Ill.: Southern Illinois University Press, 1991.

Boyer, Paul S. *When Time Shall Be No More: Prophecy Belief in Modern American Culture*. Cambridge, Mass.: Belknap Press of Harvard University Press, 1992.

Bradbury, M. L., and James B. Gilbert, eds. *Transforming Faith: The Sacred and Secular in Modern American History*. Westport, Conn.: Greenwood, 1989.

Bratt, James D. *Dutch Calvinism in Modern America: A History of a Conservative Subculture*. Grand Rapids, Mich.: Eerdmans, 1984.

*A Brief History of the National Christian Association*. Chicago: Ezra A. Cook, 1875.

Bruce, Dickson D. *And They All Sang Hallelujah: Plain-Folk Camp-Meeting Religion, 1800–1845*. Knoxville: University of Tennessee Press, 1974.

Bruce, Steve. *Pray TV: Televangelism in America*. New York: Routledge, 1990.

Burch, Maxie B. *The Evangelical Historians: The Historiography of George Marsden, Nathan Hatch, and Mark Noll*. Lanham, Md.: University Press of America, 1996.

Burgess, Stanley M., and Gary B. McGee, eds. *Dictionary of Pentecostal and Charismatic Movements*. Grand Rapids, Mich.: Regency/Zondervan, 1988.

Calhoon, Robert M. "The African Heritage, Slavery, and Evangelicalism." *Fides et Historia* 21 (June 1989): 61–66.

Carnell, Edward John. *The Case for Orthodox Theology*. Philadelphia: Westminster, 1959.

———. *An Introduction to Christian Apologetics*. Grand Rapids, Mich.: Eerdmans, 1948.

Carnes, Mark C. *Secret Ritual and Manhood in Victorian America*. New Haven, Conn.: Yale University Press, 1989.

Carpenter, Joel A. "Fundamentalist Institutions and the Growth of Evangelical Protestantism, 1929–1942." *Church History* 49 (1980): 62–75.

———. *Revive Us Again: The Reawakening of American Fundamentalism*. New York: Oxford University Press, 1997.

———. "The Scope of American Evangelicalism: Some Comments on the Dayton-Marsden Exchange." *Christian Scholar's Review* 23:1 (September 1993): 53–61.

———, ed. *A New Evangelical Coalition: Early Documents of the National Association of Evangelicals*. New York: Garland, 1988.

———, ed. *The Youth for Christ Movement and Its Pioneers*. New York: Garland, 1988.

Carpenter, Joel A., and Kenneth W. Shipps, eds. *Making Higher Education Christian: The History and Mission of Evangelical Colleges in America*. Grand Rapids, Mich.: Eerdmans, 1987.

Cauthen, Kenneth. *The Impact of American Religious Liberalism*. New York: Harper & Row, 1962.

Carwardine, Richard. *Evangelicals and Politics in Antebellum America*. New Haven, Conn.: Yale University Press, 1993.

Chappell, Paul G. "The Divine Healing Movement in America." Ph.D. diss., Drew University, 1983.

Cherry, Conrad. *Hurrying Toward Zion: Universities, Divinity Schools, and American Protestantism*. Bloomington: Indiana University Press, 1995.

Clabaugh, Gary K. *Thunder on the Right: The Protestant Fundamentalists*. Chicago: Nelson-Hall, 1974.

Collins, Kenneth J. "Children of Neglect: American Methodist Evangelicals." *Christian Scholar's Review* 20:1 (September 1990): 7–16.

Colson, Charles, and Richard John Neuhaus, eds. *Evangelicals and Catholics: Toward a Common Mission Together*. Dallas: Word, 1995.

" 'Confessing' Statement Termed Divisive." *Christian Century* 113 (3 April 1996): 365.

Cross, Robert L., ed. *The Church and the City*. Indianapolis: Bobbs-Merrill, 1967.

Cunningham, Lawrence S., et al. *The Sacred Quest: An Invitation to the Study of Religion*. New York: Macmillan, 1991.

Danker, Frederick W., assisted by Jan Schambach. *No Room in the Brotherhood: The Preus-Otter Purge of Missouri*. St. Louis: Clayton Publishing House, 1977.

Darwin, Charles. *The Origin of Species and The Descent of Man*. New York: Random House, 1977.

Dayton, Donald W. "Another Layer of Onion, Or Opening the Ecumenical Door to Let the Riffraff In." *Ecumenical Review* 40:1 (January 1988): 87–110.

———. *Discovering an Evangelical Heritage*. 1976. Reprint, Peabody, Mass.: Hendrickson, 1988.

———. " 'The Search for the Historical Evangelicalism': George Marsden's History of Fuller Seminary as a Case Study." *Christian Scholar's Review* 23:1 (September 1993): 12–33.

———. *Theological Roots of Pentecostalism*. Peabody, Mass.: Hendrickson, 1987.

Dayton, Donald W., and Robert K. Johnston, eds. *The Variety of American Evangelicalism*. Knoxville: University of Tennessee Press, 1991.

Dockery, David S., ed. *Southern Baptists and American Evangelicals: The Conversation Continues*. Nashville: Broadman and Holman, 1993.

Dollar, George W. *A History of Fundamentalism in America*. Greenville, S.C.: Bob Jones University Press, 1973.

Dorgan, Howard. *The Airwaves of Zion: Radio and Religion in Appalachia*. Knoxville: University of Tennessee Press, 1993.

Dorsett, Lyle W. *Billy Sunday and the Redemption of Urban America*. Grand Rapids, Mich.: Eerdmans, 1991.

Douglas, Ann. *The Feminization of American Culture*. New York: Knopf, 1978.

Drummond, Lewis A. *Charles Grandison Finney and the Birth of Modern Evangelism*. London: Hodder and Stoughton, 1983.

Durasoff, Steve. *Bright Winds of the Spirit: Pentecostalism Today*. Englewood Cliffs, N.J.: Prentice-Hall, 1972.

Eliade, Mircea, ed. *Encyclopedia of Religion*. 16 vols. New York: Macmillan, 1987.

Ellwood, Robert S. *One Way: The Jesus Movement and Its Meaning*. Englewood Cliffs, N.J.: Prentice-Hall, 1973.

Enlow, David. *Men Aflame: The Story of Christian Business Men's Committee International*. Grand Rapids, Mich.: Zondervan, 1962.

Enroth, Ronald M., Edward Ericson Jr., and C. Breckinridge Peters. *The Jesus People: Old-Time Religion in the Age of Aquarius*. Grand Rapids, Mich.: Eerdmans, 1974.

Erickson, Hal. *Religious Radio and Television in the United States, 1921–1991: The Programs and Personalities*. Jefferson, N.C.: McFarland, 1992.

Ernst, Eldon G. *Moment of Truth for Protestant America: Interchurch Campaigns Following World War One*. Missoula, Mont.: Scholars Press, 1974.

Fackler, P. Mark, and Charles H. Lippy, eds. *Popular Religious Magazines of the United States*. Westport, Conn.: Greenwood, 1995.

Fea, John. "American Fundamentalism and Neo-Evangelicalism: A Bibliographic Survey." *Evangelical Journal* 11 (Spring 1993): 21–30.

Finke, Roger, and Rodney Stark. "How the Upstart Sects Won America: 1776–1850." *Journal for the Scientific Study of Religion* 28:1 (March 1989): 27–44.

Frady, Marshall W. *Billy Graham: Parable of American Righteousness*. Boston: Little, Brown, 1979.

Frame, Randall, and Alan Tharpe. *How Right Is the Right? A Biblical and Balanced Approach to Politics*. Grand Rapids, Mich.: Zondervan, 1996.

Frame, Randy. "The Evangelical Closet." *Christianity Today* 34 (5 November 1990): 56–57.

———. "Payback Time? Conservative Christians Support GOP 'Contract' as Profamily Agenda Takes a Back Seat." *Christianity Today* 39:3 (6 March 1995): 42–45.

———. "United Methodists Bury Theological Pluralism." *Christianity Today* 32 (17 June 1988): 60ff.

Frank, Douglas W. *Less Than Conquerors: How Evangelicalism Entered the Twentieth Century*. Grand Rapids, Mich.: Eerdmans, 1986.

Fuller, Robert. *Naming the Antichrist: The History of an American Obsession*. New York: Oxford University Press, 1995.

Gallup, George, Jr. *The Gallup Poll: Public Opinion, 1995*. Wilmington, Del.: Scholarly Resources, 1996.

Garrett, James Leo, Jr., E. Glenn Hinson, and James E. Tull. *Are Southern Baptists "Evangelicals"?*. Macon, Ga.: Mercer University Press, 1983.

Gaustad, Edwin S. *A Religious History of America*. Rev. ed. San Francisco: Harper & Row, 1990.

Gerner, G. W. "Catholics and the 'Religious Right'." *Commonweal* 122 (5 May 1995): 15–20.

Gifford, Carolyn DeSwarte, ed. *The Defense of Women's Rights to Ordination in the Methodist Episcopal Church.* New York and London: Garland, 1987.

———. *The Ideal of the "New Woman" According to the Women's Christian Temperance Union.* New York and London: Garland, 1987.

Gilbreath, Edward. "Manhood's Great Awakening." *Christianity Today* 39:2 (6 February 1995): 20–28.

Ginger, Ray. *Six Days or Forever? Tennessee v. John Thomas Scopes.* Boston: Beacon, 1958.

Goen, Clarence C. *Broken Churches, Broken Nation: Denominational Schisms and the Coming of the Civil War.* Macon, Ga.: Mercer University Press, 1985.

Goodman, Felicitas D. *Speaking in Tongues: A Cross-Cultural Study of Glossolalia.* Chicago: University of Chicago Press, 1972.

Griffith, Ruth Marie. "A Network of Praying Women: The Formation of Religious Identity in Women's Aglow Fellowship." Ph.D. diss., Harvard University, 1995.

Hall, David D., ed. *Lived Religion in America: Toward a Theory of Practice.* Princeton, N.J.: Princeton University Press, 1997.

Hambrick-Stowe, Charles E. *Charles G. Finney and the Spirit of American Evangelicalism.* Grand Rapids, Mich.: Eerdmans, 1996.

Handy, Robert T. "The American Religious Depression, 1925–1935." *Church History* 29 (1960): 2–16.

———. *A Christian America: Protestant Hopes and Historical Realities.* New York: Oxford University Press, 1971. 2nd ed., New York: Oxford University Press, 1984.

———. "The Protestant Quest for a Christian America, 1830–1930." *Church History* 22:1 (March 1952): 8–20.

Hardesty, Nancy A. "Seeking the Great Mother: The Goddess for Today." Paper presented to the South Carolina Academy of Religion, February 1993.

Hardman, Kevin. *Charles Grandison Finney, 1792–1875: Revivalist and Reformer.* Syracuse, N.Y.: Syracuse University Press, 1987.

Harrell, David E., Jr. *All Things Are Possible: The Healing and Charismatic Revivals in Modern America.* Bloomington: Indiana University Press, 1975.

Hart, D. G. "A Connoisseur of 'Rabble-Rousing,' 'Human Folly,' and 'Theological Pathology': H. L. Mencken on American Presbyterians." *American Presbyterians* 66:3 (Fall 1988): 195–204.

———. *Defending the Faith: J. Gresham Machen and the Crisis of Conservative Presbyterianism in America.* Baltimore: The Johns Hopkins University Press, 1994.

———, ed. *Reckoning with the Past: Historical Essays on American Evangelicalism from the Institute for the Study of American Evangelicals.* Grand Rapids, Mich.: Baker, 1995.

Hatch, Nathan O. *The Democratization of American Christianity.* New Haven, Conn.: Yale University Press, 1989.

———. *The Sacred Cause of Liberty: Republican Thought and the Millennium in Revolutionary New England.* New Haven, Conn.: Yale University Press, 1977.

———. "The Puzzle of Methodism." *Church History* 63:2 (June 1994): 175–89.

Hayes, Laurie Ann Schultz. "The Rhetoric of Controversy in the Lutheran Church-

Missouri Synod with Particular Emphasis on the Years 1969–1976." Ph.D. diss., University of Wisconsin at Madison, 1980.

"Healing in the Spirit." *Christianity Today* (20 July 1973): 4–10.

Hefley, James. *God Goes to High School*. Waco, Tex.: Word, 1970.

Henke, F. G. "The Gift of Tongues and Related Phenomena at the Present Day." *American Journal of Theology* 13 (1909): 196–201.

Henry, Carl F. H. *Confessions of a Theologian: An Autobiography*. Waco, Tex.: Word, 1986.

———. *God, Revelation and Authority*. 5 vols. Waco, Tex.: Word, 1976–83.

———. *Remaking the Modern Mind*. Grand Rapids, Mich.: Eerdmans, 1946.

———. *The Uneasy Conscience of Modern Fundamentalism*. Grand Rapids, Mich.: Eerdmans, 1947.

Hill, Samuel S., and Dennis E. Owen. *The New Religious Political Right in America*. Nashville: Abingdon, 1982.

Hocken, Peter. *One Lord, One Spirit, One Body*. Gaithersburg, Md.: Word Among Us, 1987.

Hodge, Charles. "Retrospect of the History of the Princeton Review." *Biblical Repertory and Princeton Review: Index Volume from 1825 to 1868*. Philadelphia: Peter Walker, 1871.

Hoffecker, W. Andrew. *Piety and the Princeton Theologians: Archibald Alexander, Charles Hodge, and Benjamin Warfield*. Grand Rapids, Mich.: Baker, 1981.

Hofstadter, Richard. *Anti-Intellectualism in American Life*. New York: Vintage, 1962.

Hoge, Dean R., and David A. Roozen, eds. *Understanding Church Growth and Decline, 1950–1979*. New York: Pilgrim, 1979.

Hollenweger, W. J. *The Pentecostals: The Charismatic Movement in the Churches*. Minneapolis: Augsburg, 1969.

Hopkins, C. Howard. *History of the Y.M.C.A. in North America*. New York: Association, 1951.

Horton, Michael. *The Agony of Deceit: What Some TV Preachers Are Teaching*. Chicago: Moody, 1990.

Horton, Michael Scott. *Made in America: The Shaping of Modern American Evangelicalism*. Grand Rapids, Mich.: Baker, 1991.

Hunter, George G., III. *Church for the Unchurched*. Nashville: Abingdon, 1996.

Hunter, James Davison. *American Evangelicalism: Conservative Religion and the Quandary of Modernity*. New Brunswick, N.J.: Rutgers University Press, 1983.

Hutchison, William R. *Errand to the World: American Protestant Thought and Foreign Missions*. Chicago: University of Chicago Press, 1987.

———. *The Modernist Impulse in American Protestantism*. Cambridge, Mass.: Harvard University Press, 1976.

———, ed. *Between the Times: The Travail of the Protestant Establishment in America, 1900–1960*. Cambridge, Eng.: Cambridge University Press, 1989.

Hybels, Lynne, and Bill Hybels. *Rediscovering Church: The Story and Vision of Willow Creek Community Church*. Grand Rapids, Mich.: Zondervan, 1995.

Jennings, Ted W. "The 'Houston Declaration' Is Heretical." *Christian Century* 105 (20 April 1988): 399–401.

Johnson, Benton, Donald A. Luidens, and Dean R. Hoge. *Vanishing Boundaries: The Religion of Mainline Protestant Baby Boomers*. Louisville, Ky.: Westminster/John Knox, 1994.

Johnson, Douglas, ed. *A Brief History of the International Fellowship of Evangelical Students*. London: InterVarsity, 1964.

Johnson, R. K. *Builder of Bridges*. Murphreesboro, Tenn.: Sword of the Lord, 1969.

Jordan, Philip D. *The Evangelical Alliance for the United States of America, 1847–1900: Ecumenism, Identity, and the Religion of the Republic*. Lewiston, N.Y.: Edwin Mellen, 1983.

Jorstad, Erling. *The Politics of Moralism: The New Christian Right in American Life*. Minneapolis: Augsburg, 1981.

———. *Popular Religion in America: The Evangelical Voice*. Westport, Conn.: Greenwood, 1993.

Kelley, Dean M. *Why Conservative Churches Are Growing*. Rev. ed. New York: Harper & Row, 1977.

Kellstedt, Lyman A., and John C. Green. "The Mismeasure of Evangelicals." *Books and Culture* 2:1 (January/February 1996): 14–15.

Kennedy, Gail, ed. *Evolution and Religion: The Conflict Between Science and Theology in Modern America*. Boston: D.C. Heath, 1957.

Kildahl, John P. *The Psychology of Speaking in Tongues*. New York: Harper & Row, 1972.

Kimbrough, David. *Taking Up Serpents: Snake Handlers of Eastern Kentucky*. Chapel Hill: University of North Carolina Press, 1995.

Klein, Patricia, et al. *Growing Up Born Again: A Whimsical Look at the Blessings and Tribulations of Growing Up Born Again*. Old Tappan, N.J.: Fleming H. Revell, 1987.

Kraus, C. Norman, ed. *Evangelicalism and Anabaptism*. Scottsdale, Pa.: Herald Press, 1979.

Kuhlman, Kathryn. *I Believe in Miracles*. Englewood Cliffs, N.J.: Prentice-Hall, 1962.

Kuykendall, John W. *"Southern Enterprize": The Work of National Evangelical Societies in the Antebellum South*. Westport, Conn.: Greenwood, 1982.

LaHaye, Tim. *The Battle for the Mind*. Old Tappan, N.J.: Revell, 1980.

Lamb, Robert Paul. "Jimmy Swaggart's Ministry." *Charisma* 3 (March 1977): 17–20.

Laurentin, Rene. *Catholic Pentecostalism*. Translated by Matthew J. O'Connell. Garden City, N.Y.: Doubleday, 1977.

Lawless, Elaine. *God's Peculiar People: Women's Voices and Folk Tradition in a Pentecostal Church*. Lexington: University of Kentucky Press, 1988.

———. *Handmaidens of the Lord: Pentecostal Women Preachers and Traditional Religion*. Philadelphia: University of Pennsylvania Press, 1988.

Leonard, Bill J. *God's Last and Only Hope: The Fragmentation of the Southern Baptist Convention*. Grand Rapids, Mich.: Eerdmans, 1990.

Levine, Lawrence W. *Defender of the Faith. William Jennings Bryan: The Last Decade, 1915–1925*. New York: Oxford University Press, 1965.

Lewis, Michael. "God Is In the Packaging: To Sell Bottled Water, or Eternal Life, Just Know the Customers and Meet Their Needs. Amen." *New York Times Magazine* (21 July 1996): 14ff.

Lindsell, Harold. *The Battle for the Bible*. Grand Rapids, Mich.: Zondervan, 1976.

———. *The Bible in the Balance*. Grand Rapids, Mich.: Zondervan, 1979.

Lindsey, Hal, with C. C. Carlson. *The Late Great Planet Earth*. Grand Rapids, Mich.: Zondervan, 1970.

————, with C. C. Carlson. *Satan Is Alive and Well on Planet Earth*. Grand Rapids, Mich.: Zondervan 1972.

Lippy, Charles H. "The Camp Meeting in Transition: The Character and Legacy of the Late Nineteenth Century." *Methodist History* 34:1 (October 1995): 3–17.

————. *Modern American Popular Religion: A Critical Assessment and Annotated Bibliography*. Westport, Conn.: Greenwood, 1996.

————, ed. *Religious Periodicals of the United States: Academic and Scholarly*. Westport, Conn.: Greenwood, 1986.

————, ed. *Twentieth-Century Shapers of American Popular Religion*. Westport, Conn.: Greenwood, 1989.

Lippy, Charles H., and Peter W. Williams, eds. *Encyclopedia of the American Religious Experience*. 3 vols. New York: Scribners, 1988.

Livingstone, David N. *Darwin's Forgotten Defenders: The Encounter between Evangelical Theology and Evolutionary Thought*. Grand Rapids, Mich.: Eerdmans, 1987.

Long, Kathryn. "The Power of Interpretation: The Revival of 1857–58 and the Historiography of Revivalism in America." *Religion and American Culture* 4:1 (Winter 1994): 77–105.

Longfield, Bradley J. *The Presbyterian Controversy: Fundamentalists, Modernists, and Moderates*. New York: Oxford University Press, 1991.

Lotz, David W., Donald W. Shriver, and John F. Wilson, eds. *Altered Landscapes: Christianity in America, 1935–1985*. Grand Rapids, Mich.: Eerdmans, 1989.

Luecke, David S. "Is Willow Creek the Way of the Future?" *Christian Century* 114:16 (14 May 1997): 479ff.

McCauley, Deborah Vansau. *Appalachian Mountain Religion: A History*. Urbana: University of Illinois Press, 1995.

McDannell, Colleen. *The Christian Home in Victorian America, 1840–1900*. Bloomington: Indiana University Press, 1986.

MacDonald, Fergus. *The Catholic Church and the Secret Societies in the United States*, edited by Thomas J. McMahon. United States Catholic Historical Society Monograph Series 22. New York: United States Catholic Historical Society, 1946.

McDonnell, Killian. *Charismatic Renewal in the Churches*. New York: Seabury, 1976.

McDowell, John P. *The Social Gospel in the South: The Woman's Home Mission Movement in the Methodist Episcopal Church, South, 1886–1939*. Baton Rouge: Louisiana State University Press, 1982.

McGrath, Alister. *Evangelicalism and the Future of Christianity*. Downers Grove, Ill.: InterVarsity, 1995.

McHugh, Robert, ed. *The Bathtub Hoax and Other Blasts and Bravos from the Chicago Tribune*. New York: Knopf, 1958.

McIntire, C. T., and Ronald A. Wells, eds. *History and Historical Understanding*. Grand Rapids, Mich.: Eerdmans, 1984.

McKinley, Edward H. *Marching to Glory: The History of the Salvation Army in the United States, 1880–1992*. 2nd ed. Grand Rapids, Mich.: Eerdmans, 1995.

McLoughlin, William G. *Revivals, Awakenings, and Reform: An Essay on Religion and Social Change in America, 1607–1977*. Chicago History of American Religion Series, edited by Martin E. Marty. Chicago: University of Chicago Press, 1978.

————, ed. *The American Evangelicals, 1800–1900*. New York: Harper & Row, 1968.

Magnuson, Norris. *Salvation in the Slums: Evangelical Social Work, 1865–1920*. Metuchen, N.J.: Scarecrow, 1977.

Marsden, George M. *Fundamentalism and American Culture: The Shaping of Twentieth-Century Evangelicalism, 1870–1925*. New York: Oxford University Press, 1980.
———. *The Outrageous Idea of Christian Scholarship*. New York: Oxford University Press, 1997.
———. *Reforming Fundamentalism: Fuller Seminary and the New Evangelicalism*. Grand Rapids, Mich.: Eerdmans, 1987.
———. *Religion and American Culture*. San Diego: Harcourt Brace Jovanovich, 1990.
———. "Response to Don Dayton." *Christian Scholar's Review* 23:1 (September 1993): 34–40.
———. *The Soul of the American University: From Protestant Establishment to Established Nonbelief*. New York: Oxford University Press, 1994.
———. *Understanding Fundamentalism and Evangelicalism*. Grand Rapids, Mich.: Eerdmans, 1991.
———, ed. *Evangelicalism and Modern America*. Grand Rapids, Mich.: Eerdmans, 1984.
Martin, Donald L. "The Thought of Amzi Clarence Dixon." Ph.D. diss., Baylor University, 1989.
Martin, William C. *With God on Our Side: The Rise of the Religious Right in America*. New York: Bantam Books, 1996.
Marty, Martin E. *Modern American Religion*. Vol. 2, *The Noise of Conflict, 1919–1941*. Chicago: University of Chicago Press, 1991.
———. "Onward, Christian Shoulders." *Christian Century* 103:38 (10 December 1986): 1135.
———. *Modern American Religion*. Vol. 3, *Under God, Indivisible: 1941–1960*. Chicago: University of Chicago Press, 1996.
Mencken, H. L. *Prejudices: Fourth Series*. New York: Knopf, 1924.
Menendez, Albert J. *Evangelicals at the Ballot Box*. Buffalo: Prometheus Books, 1996.
Michaelsen, Robert. *Piety in the Public School: Trends and Issues in the Relationship Between Religion and the Public Schools in the U.S.* New York: Macmillan, 1970.
Minkowitz, Donna. "In the Name of the Father." *Ms.* 6:3 (November-December 1995): 64–71.
Monahan, Matthew G. "The Christian Coalition's New 'Catholic Alliance' Crass and Unnecessary (View from a Pew)," *America* 174:1 (13 January 1996): 7.
Moody, Dale, "The Eschatology of Hal Lindsey." *Review and Expositor* 72 (Summer 1975): 271–78.
Moore, James R. *The Post-Darwinian Controversies: A Study of the Protestant Struggle to Come to Terms with Darwin in Great Britain and America, 1870–1900*. Cambridge, Eng.: Cambridge University Press, 1979.
Moore, R. Laurence. *Religious Outsiders and the Making of Americans*. New York: Oxford University Press, 1986.
Morgan, David T. *The New Crusades, The New Holy Land: Conflict in the Southern Baptist Convention, 1969–1991*. Tuscaloosa: University of Alabama Press, 1996.
Morris, James. *The Preachers*. New York: St. Martin's, 1973.
Mosier, Richard D. *Making the American Mind: Social and Moral Issues in the McGuffey Readers*. New York: King's Crown Press, 1947.
Murch, James DeForest. *Cooperation Without Compromise*. Grand Rapids, Mich.: Eerdmans, 1956.
———. *Protestant Revolt*. Arlington, Va.: Crestwood Books, 1967.

Murdoch, Norman H. *Origins of the Salvation Army*. Knoxville: University of Tennessee Press, 1994.

Nash, Ronald H. *Evangelicals in America: Who They Are, What They Believe*. Nashville: Abingdon, 1987.

Nason, Michael, and Donna Nason. *Robert Schuller: The Inside Story*. Waco, Tex.: Word, 1983.

Nelson, Rudolph. *The Making and Unmaking of an Evangelical Mind: The Case of Edward Carnell*. New York: Cambridge University Press, 1987.

Niebuhr, Gustav. "Putting Life's Trials in a Sacred Context." *New York Times* (9 February 1997): 4: 4.

Niebuhr, Reinhold. "Liberalism, Individualism, and Billy Graham." *Christian Century* 73 (1956): 640–42.

Noll, Mark A. *Between Faith and Criticism: Evangelicals, Scholarship, and the Bible in America*. New York: Harper and Row, 1986.

———. *A History of Christianity in the United States and Canada*. Grand Rapids, Mich.: Eerdmans, 1992.

———. *The Scandal of the Evangelical Mind*. Grand Rapids, Mich.: Eerdmans, 1994.

———. "Scientific History in America: A Centennial Observation from a Christian Point of View." *Fides et Historia* 14:1 (Fall-Winter 1981): 21–37.

———, ed. *The Princeton Theology, 1812–1921*. Grand Rapids, Mich.: Baker, 1983.

Numbers, Ronald. "Creationism in 20th-Century America." *Science* 218 (1982): 534–44.

O'Connor, Edward D. *The Pentecostal Movement and the Catholic Church*. Notre Dame, Ind.: Ave Maria Press, 1971.

Oldfield, Duane M. *The Right and the Righteous: The Christian Right Confronts the Republican Party*. Lanham, Md.: Rowman and Littlefield, 1996.

Parsons, Paul F. *Inside America's Christian Schools*. Macon, Ga.: Mercer University Press, 1987.

Peck, Janice. *The Gods of Televangelism: The Crisis of Meaning and the Appeal of Religious Television*. Cresskill, N.J.: Hampton, 1993.

Phillips, Clifton Jackson. *Protestant America and the Pagan World*. Cambridge, Mass.: Harvard University Press for the Harvard University East Asian Research Center, 1969.

Plantinga, Alvin, and Nicholas Wolterstorff, eds. *Faith and Rationality: Reason and Belief in God*. Notre Dame, Ind.: University of Notre Dame Press, 1983.

Porter, Daryl A. "*Christianity Today*: Its History and Development." Th.M. thesis, Dallas Theological Seminary, 1978.

Pritchard, Gregory Allen. "The Strategy of Willow Creek Community Church: A Study in the Sociology of Religion." Ph.D. diss., Northwestern University, 1994.

"The Promise of a Promise Keeper." *Good News* (September-October 1995): 12–17.

Quebedeaux, Richard. *The New Charismatics: The Origins, Development, and Significance of Neo-Pentecostalsim*. Garden City, N.Y.: Doubleday, 1976.

———. *The New Charismatics II: How a Christian Renewal Movement Became a Part of the American Religious Mainstream*. San Francisco: Harper & Row, 1983.

———. *The Worldly Evangelicals*. San Francisco: Harper & Row, 1978.

———. *The Young Evangelicals: Revolution in Orthodoxy*. New York: Harper & Row, 1974.

Queen, Edward L., II, Stephen R. Prothero, and Gardiner H. Shattuck Jr. *Encyclopedia of American Religious History*, 2 vols. New York: Facts on File, 1996.

Raabe, Tom. *The Ultimate Church: An Irreverent Look at Church Growth, Megachurches, and Ecclesiastical "Show-Biz."* Grand Rapids, Mich.: Zondervan, 1991.

Ranaghan, Kevin, and Dorothy Ranaghan. *As the Spirit Leads Us*. New York: Paulist, 1971.

————. *Catholic Pentecostals*. New York: Paulist, 1969.

Raser, Harold E. *Phoebe Palmer: Her Life and Thought*. Lewiston, N.Y.: Edwin Mellen, 1987.

Rausch, David A. *Arno C. Gaebelein, 1861–1945: Irenic Fundamentalist and Scholar*. Lewiston, N.Y.: Edwin Mellen, 1983.

Reed, Ralph. *Active Faith: How Christians Are Changing the Soul of American Politics*. New York: Free Press, 1996.

Reese, Boyd T. "Resistance and Hope: The Interplay of Theological Synthesis, Biblical Interpretation, Political Analysis, and Praxis in the Christian Radicalism of 'Sojourners' Magazine." Ph.D. diss., Temple University, 1991.

Reeves, Thomas C. *The Empty Church: The Suicide of Liberal Christianity*. New York: Free Press, 1996.

Reich, Jutta. *Amerikanischer Fundamentalismus: Geschichte und Erscheinung der Bewegung um Carl McIntire*. 2nd ed. Heildesheim, Germany: H. A. Gerstenberg, 1972.

Riss, Richard M. *A Story of Twentieth-Century Revival Movements in North America*. Peabody, Mass.: Hendrickson, 1988.

Roberts, Clarence N. "The Crusade Against Secret Societies and the National Christian Association." *Journal of the Illinois State Historical Society* 64 (Winter 1971): 382–400.

Roof, Wade Clark. *A Generation of Seekers: The Spiritual Journeys of the Baby Boom Generation*. San Francisco: HarperSanFrancisco, 1994.

————, ed. *Religion in the Nineties. Annals of the American Academy of Political and Social Science* 527. Newbury Park, Calif.: Sage Periodicals, 1993.

Roof, Wade Clark, and William McKinney. *American Mainline Religion: Its Changing Shape and Future*. New Brunswick, N.J.: Rutgers University Press, 1994.

Roy, Ralph Lord. *Apostles of Discord: A Study of Organized Bigotry and Disruption on the Fringes of Protestantism*. Boston: Beacon, 1953.

Ruether, Rosemary Radford, and Rosemary Skinner Keller, eds. *In Our Own Voices: Four Centuries of American Women's Religious Writing*. San Francisco: HarperSanFrancisco, 1995.

Sandeen, Ernest R. *The Roots of Fundamentalism: British and American Millenarianism, 1800–1930*. Chicago: University of Chicago Press, 1970.

Sargeant, Kimon Howland. "Faith and Fulfillment: Willow Creek and the Future of Evangelicalism." Ph.D. diss., University of Virginia, 1996.

Saunders, Lowell Sperry. "The National Religious Broadcasters and the Availability of Commercial Radio Time." Ph.D. diss., University of Illinois, 1968.

Scanzoni, Letha Dawson, and Nancy A. Hardesty. *All We're Meant to Be: Biblical Feminism for Today*. 3rd ed. Grand Rapids, Mich.: Eerdmans, 1992.

Schlumpf, Heidi. "How Catholic Is the Catholic Alliance?" *Christianity Today* 40:6 (20 May 1996): 76.

Schultze, Quentin J., ed. *American Evangelicals and the Mass Media*. Grand Rapids, Mich.: Academie Books of Zondervan, 1990.

Setta, Susan M. "Healing in Suburbia: The Women's Aglow Fellowship." *Journal of Religious Studies* 12:2 (1986): 46–56.

Shakarian, Demos. "FGBMFI Struggles Toward the Future." *Charisma* 13 (March 1988): 24.

Shapiro, Joseph. "Heavenly Promises." *U.S. News & World Report* 119:13 (2 October 1995): 68–70.

Shelley, Bruce L. *Evangelicalism in America*. Grand Rapids, Mich.: Eerdmans, 1967.

———. "Sources of Pietistic Fundamentalism." *Fides et Historia* 5 (Spring 1973): 68–78.

Shepard, Charles E. *Forgiven: The Rise and Fall of Jim Bakker and the PTL Ministry*. New York: Atlantic Monthly Press, 1989.

Sherrill, John. *They Speak with Other Tongues*. New York: Pyramid Books, 1964.

Shibley, Mark A. *Resurgent Evangelicalism in the United States: Mapping Cultural Change Since 1970*. Columbia: University of South Carolina Press, 1997.

Smidt, Corwin E. *Contemporary Evangelical Political Involvement: An Analysis and Assessment*. Lanham, Md.: University Press of America, 1985.

Smith, Robert Wayne. "A Study of the Speaking in the Anti-Secrecy Movement, 1862–1882, with Special Reference to the National Christian Association." Ph.D. diss., State University of Iowa, 1956.

Smith, Timothy L. *Called Unto Holiness: The Story of the Nazarenes, the Formative Years*. Kansas City, Mo.: Nazarene Publishing House, 1962.

———. "The Evangelical Kaleidoscope and the Call to Christian Unity." *Christian Scholar's Review* 15:2 (1986): 125–40.

———. *Revivalism and Social Reform: American Protestantism on the Eve of the Civil War*. Baltimore: The Johns Hopkins University Press, 1980; originally issued as *Revivalism and Social Reform in Mid-Nineteenth-Century America*. New York: Abingdon, 1957.

Smith-Rosenberg, Carroll. *Religion and the Rise of the American City: The New York City Mission Movement, 1812–1870*. Ithaca, N.Y.: Cornell University Press, 1971.

Spring, Beth. "Norman Lear's Lobbying Style Troubles Some Supporters." *Christianity Today* 26 (12 November 1982): 78–80.

Stelzle, Charles. *Christianity's Storm Centre: A Study of the Modern City*. New York: Fleming H. Revell, 1907.

Stewart, Don, with Walter Wagner. *The Man from Miracle Valley*. Long Beach, Calif.: Great Horizons, 1971.

Stoeffler, F. Ernest. *The Rise of Evangelical Pietism*. Leiden: E. J. Brill, 1971.

Streiker, Lowell D. *The Jesus Trip: Advent of the Jesus Freaks*. Nashville: Abingdon, 1971.

Strobel, Lee. *Inside the Mind of Unchurched Harry and Mary: How to Reach Friends and Family Who Avoid God and the Church*. Grand Rapids, Mich.: Zondervan, 1993.

Strong, Josiah. *The Challenge of the City*. New York: Missionary Education Movement, 1907.

———. *Our Country*, edited by Jurgen Herbst. Cambridge, Mass.: Belknap Press of Harvard University Press, 1963.

Sweeney, Douglas A. "The Essential Evangelicalism Dialectic: The Historiography of the Early Evangelical Movement and the Observer-Participant Dilemma." *Church History* 60:1 (March 1991): 70–84.

Sweet, Leonard I. "Wise as Serpents, Innocent as Doves: The New Evangelical Historiography." *Journal of the American Academy of Religion* 56:3 (1988): 397–416.

———, ed. *Communication and Change in American Religious History.* Grand Rapids, Mich.: Eerdmans, 1993.

———, ed. *The Evangelical Tradition in America.* Macon, Ga.: Mercer University Press, 1984.

Swomley, John M. "Catholics and the Religious Right (Watch on the Right)." *The Humanist* 56:2 (March-April 1996): 36–37.

Synan, Vinson. *The Holiness-Pentecostal Movement in the United States.* Grand Rapids, Mich.: Eerdmans, 1971.

———. *In the Latter Days: The Outpouring of the Holy Spirit in the Twentieth Century.* Ann Arbor, Mich.: Servant Books, 1984.

———. *The Twentieth-Century Pentecostal Explosion: The Exciting Growth of the Pentecostal and Charismatic Renewal Movements.* Altamonte Springs, Fla.: Creation House, 1987.

———. *Under His Banner: History of Full Gospel Business Men's Fellowship International.* Costa Mesa, Calif.: Gift Publications, 1992.

Szasz, Ferenc Morton. *The Divided Mind of Protestant America, 1880–1930.* University: University of Alabama Press, 1982.

Tebbel, John. *A History of Book Publishing in the United States.* Vol. 1, *The Expansion of an Industry, 1865–1919.* New York: Bowker, 1975. Vol. 4, *The Great Change, 1940–1980.* New York: Bowker, 1981.

"Thou Shalt Not Endorse." *Christian Century* 113:29 (16 October 1996): 958.

Tidball, Derek J. *Who Are the Evangelicals? Tracing the Roots of the Modern Movements.* London: Marshall Pickering, 1994.

Tietjen, John H. *Memoirs in Exile: Confessional Hope and Institutional Conflict.* Minneapolis: Fortress, 1990.

Tingley, Sabrina. "Willow Creek Community Church and Holy Covenant United Methodist Church: A Comparison." *Chicago Theological Seminary Register* 76:3 (Fall 1996): 2–11.

Trent, John, et al. *Go the Distance: The Making of a Promise Keeper.* Colorado Springs, Colo.: Focus on the Family Publishing, 1996.

Trollinger, William Vance, Jr. *God's Empire: William Bell Riley and Midwestern Fundamentalism.* Madison: University of Wisconsin Press, 1990.

Truehart, Charles. "Welcome to the Next Church." *Atlantic Monthly* 277 (August 1996): 37–58.

Tuveson, Ernest Lee. *Redeemer Nation: The Idea of America's Millennial Role.* Chicago: University of Chicago Press, 1968.

"UMC Evangelicals Dissent." *Christian Century* 109 (5–12 February 1992): 120.

"United Methodists Form Confessing Movement." *Christian Century* 112 (7 June 1995): 600–601.

van Biema, David. "In the Name of the Father." *Time* 147:20 (13 May 1996): 75.

Van Leeuwen, Mary Stewart. "Servanthood or Soft Patriarchy? A Christian Feminist Looks at the Promise Keepers Movement." *Journal of Men's Studies* 5:3 (February 1997): 233–61.

Voskuil, Dennis. *Mountains into Goldmines: Robert Schuller and the Gospel of Success*. Grand Rapids, Mich.: Eerdmans, 1983.

Wacker, Grant. "The Holy Spirit and the Spirit of the Age in American Protestantism, 1880–1920." *Journal of American History* 72 (1985): 45–62.

Wagenheim, Jeff. "Among the Promise Keepers." *Utne Reader* No. 73 (January-February 1996): 74–77.

Wagner, Melinda Bollar. *God's Schools: Choice and Compromise in American Society*. New Brunswick, N.J.: Rutgers University Press, 1990.

Wallis, Jim. *Revive Us Again: A Sojourners Story*. Nashville: Abingdon, 1983.

————. *The Soul of Politics: A Practical and Prophetic Vision for Change*. New York: New Press, 1994. Reissued as *The Soul of Politics: Beyond Religious Right and Secular Left*. San Diego: Harcourt Brace, 1995.

Watson, Russell, et al. "Holy War: Heaven Can Wait." *Newsweek* 109 (8 June 1987): 58–62.

Watt, David Harrington. *A Transforming Faith: Explorations of Twentieth-Century American Evangelicalism*. New Brunswick, N.J.: Rutgers University Press, 1991.

Webber, Robert E. *Common Roots: A Call to Evangelical Maturity*. Grand Rapids, Mich.: Zondervan, 1978.

Weber, Timothy P. *Living in the Shadow of the Second Coming: American Premillennialism, 1875–1982*. Enl. ed. Chicago: University of Chicago Press, 1987.

Weiss, Ellen. *City in the Woods: The Life and Design of an American Camp Meeting on Martha's Vineyard*. New York: Oxford University Press, 1987.

Wells, David F., and John D. Woodbridge, eds. *The Evangelicals: What They Believe, Who They Are, Where They Are Changing*. Nashville: Abingdon, 1975.

Wells, William W. *Welcome to the Family: An Introduction to Evangelical Christianity*. Downers Grove, Ill.: InterVarsity, 1979.

Werning, Waldo J. *Making the Missouri Synod Functional Again*. Fort Wayne, Ind.: Biblical Renewal Publications, 1992.

Westerhoff, John H. *McGuffey and His Readers: Piety, Morality, and Education in Nineteenth Century America*. Nashville: Abingdon, 1978.

White, Charles E. *The Beauty of Holiness: Phoebe Palmer as Theologian, Revivalist, Feminist, and Humanitarian*. Grand Rapids, Mich.: Zondervan (Francis Asbury Press), 1986.

Wilcox, Clyde. *Onward, Christian Soldiers: The Religious Right in American Politics*. Boulder, Colo.: Westview, 1996.

Willard, Frances. *Women in the Pulpit*. Chicago: Women's Christian Temperance Publishing Association, 1889. Reprinted in *The Defense of Women's Rights to Ordination in the Methodist Episcopal Church*, edited by Carolyn DeSwarte Gifford. New York: Garland, 1987.

Wilson, Charles Reagan. *Baptized in Blood: The Civil Religion of the Lost Cause, 1865–1920*. Athens: University of Georgia Press, 1980.

Wilson, Elizabeth. *Fifty Years of Association Work Among Young Women, 1866–1916*. New York: National Board of the Young Women's Christian Association of the United States of America, 1916. Reprint, New York and London: Garland, 1987.

Wittenmyer, Annie Turner. *Women's Work for Jesus*. New York: Nelson and Phillips, 1873. Reprint, New York: Garland, 1987.

Woodward, Kenneth L. "King of Honky-Tonk Heaven." *Newsweek* 101 (30 May 1983): 89ff.

————. "Swaggart's One-Edged Sword." *Newsweek* 102 (9 January 1984): 65.

Woodward, Kenneth L., et al. "Born Again!" *Newsweek* 90 (25 October 1976): 68–76.

*The World's Most Famous Court Trial: Tennessee Evolution Case*. Cincinnati: National Book Company, 1925.

Wuthnow, Robert. *The Struggle for America's Soul: Evangelicals, Liberals, and Secularism*. Grand Rapids, Mich.: Eerdmans, 1989.

————, ed. *"I Come Away Stronger": How Small Groups Are Shaping American Religion*. Grand Rapids, Mich.: Eerdmans, 1994.

Zipperer, John. "United Methodists: Confessing Movement Grows amid Doctrinal Disputes." *Christianity Today* 39 (2 October 1995): 105.

# Part II
# Themes and Issues in Modern American Evangelicalism

# 9
# Understanding the Word of God: Evangelical Religious Thought

The diversity of evangelicalism makes it difficult to formulate one approach to religious thought that can be called distinctively "evangelical." But common concerns make it possible to characterize evangelical thought as a whole in an overarching fashion. First and foremost, what sets evangelicals apart is the subculture's affection for the Bible. Indeed, a proper normative description of evangelicalism is its biblicism. As John Stott has stated, "We evangelicals are a Bible people."[1] Although disagreement arises over how to interpret the Scriptures, evangelicals habitually return to the Bible as the focal point of their faith.

Closely related to Bible study is theology. According to one evangelical, "Christian theology" is "that discipline which strives to give a coherent statement of the doctrines of the Christian faith, based primarily on the Scriptures. . . ."[2] Theology is an attempt to bring systematic order to the various assertions found in the Bible. Evangelicals may engage in foot washing, closed communion, glossolalia, and other practices, but to be genuinely evangelical they will attempt to justify those practices through a theological study of the Scriptures. This foundational attachment to biblicism and the attendant need to express that biblical attachment theologically form the focus of this chapter.

The twentieth century was a tumultuous period for evangelical Bible study. The critical notions of theological liberalism repeatedly challenged traditional assumptions about the literal veracity of the Scriptures. One sees the impact of this criticism within one generation of scholars at Princeton Theological Seminary. In the mid–1800s, *Charles Hodge, a theological conservative, could admit to errors in the Bible while characterizing them as specks of sandstone in the marble of the Parthenon. By 1881 however, Hodge's son Alexander and his student *Benjamin Breckinridge Warfield had formulated the doctrine of inerrancy to safeguard the absolute truthfulness of the biblical texts in the original autographs.[3] The Hodge-Warfield statement of 1881 arose largely in reaction to the corrosive attacks of theological liberalism.[4]

By 1910 the inerrancy defense had hardened into the primary plank of the growing fundamentalist movement as evidenced by the "five fundamentals" statement of the General Assembly of the (Northern) Presbyterian Church, USA.[5] Adopted without reflection by many Presbyterians, Baptists, and other conservative evangelicals, it was felt that to relinquish the belief in an inerrant Bible was to compromise one's faith.

Many fundamentalists were nurtured theologically on the *Scofield Reference Bible* (1909), a version of the Scriptures whose annotations advanced a dispensational premillennial interpretation of the text. Although dispensationalism strengthened the traditional biblicism of evangelicals by stressing the supernatural character of the Bible and the need to read it carefully, the anti-historical and anti-intellectual tendencies of the viewpoint had a chilling affect on scholarly biblical research. Dispensationalists tended to equate any application of historical-critical methods to the Bible with theological liberalism.[6] Despite the fact that the dispensational scheme was so highly interpretative as to seem at odds with a doctrine of inerrancy, most fundamentalists were willing to overlook the apparent contradiction. Thus, for most early twentieth-century fundamentalists, inerrancy and dispensationalism tended to go hand-in-hand.

The fundamentalist-dispensational approach to Bible study was known as "proof-texting" or "the Bible Reading." This method consisted of stringing together a series of scriptural passages on a given topic with the aid of a concordance in the expectation that the Holy Spirit would "speak" through the train of verses.[7] An alternative to proof-texting that still tried to interpret the Scriptures at face value was the synthetic approach popularized by James M. Gray, president of Moody Bible Institute. In opposition to literary criticism, which, Gray argued, tore the Bible apart, his synthetic method urged an examination of the Bible "in its fullness." Specifically, Gray suggested that the student first read the Scriptures in their entirety. Only then should one proceed to the study of individual books. At the book level, Gray advised: (1) read the book completely in one sitting, (2) read it without regard to chapter or verse divisions, (3) read it repeatedly until one has a feel for the flow of the book, (4) read it independently of any outside aid, and (5) read it prayerfully. As with proof-texting, Gray's approach gained a tremendous following among the early American fundamentalist community.[8]

In the 1940s a new openness to an academic investigation of the Bible began to well up in the evangelical bosom. Reacting against the separatist fundamentalism of their youth, a band of young evangelicals in the 1930s and 1940s, including *Edward John Carnell, *Carl F. H. Henry, and *George Eldon Ladd, attended and earned graduate degrees from educational institutions like Harvard that were thought to be irreconcilably opposed to everything that evangelicals held dear.[9] A key goal of these "new evangelicals" was to liberate evangelical biblical studies from the confines of dispensationalism and a wooden, static view of inerrancy without compromising the infallible nature of the Bible.[10] With regard to dispensationalism, the work of Ladd was especially significant. Beginning with his *Crucial Questions About the Kingdom of God*, Ladd chastised the dispensationalists for ignoring contemporary historical research. He was probably most responsible for legitimating a conservative scholarly evangelical interpretation of biblical eschatology that was respectful of both the divine and historical dimensions of the Scriptures.[11]

It should be noted, however, that the "new evangelical" approach to biblical interpretation has not been received by the evangelical faithful without a good deal of controversy. For one thing, there is no one "new evangelical" approach, but rather a myriad of approaches that are differentiated from one another primarily by the degree to which the biblical text is subjected to historical criticism. This reality leads to the question: What are the acceptable bounds of biblical criticism within the American evangelical community? As evangelicals have been unable to answer this question with any unanimity, it has formed the context for the "battles over the Bible" that have waxed and waned within the subculture since World War II.

The epicenter for this conflict for most of the past fifty years has been Fuller Theological Seminary, the original citadel of the "new evangelicalism." The early Fuller faculty valued scholarship and wanted to use their advanced academic training to restore evangelicalism to the position of societal prominence it had enjoyed in the nineteenth century. Although its scholars never agreed on an agenda to accomplish this goal, Fuller seemed to be moving the center of gravity of American evangelicalism away from dispensational fundamentalism by the mid–1950s.[12]

The commitment of the new generation of evangelicals to a more rigorous variety of biblical criticism seemed strong. There were apparent signs at every turn; not only the works of scholars like Ladd and the appropriation of ideas from British evangelicals such as F. F. Bruce and C. H. Dodd, but also in widespread evangelical involvement in academic forums like the Society for Biblical Literature (SBL), the formation of the Evangelical Theological Society (ETS) in 1949, and the willingness of evangelical presses like Eerdmans to publish works like the *New International Commentary on the New Testament* (beginning in 1951).[13]

This era of good feelings began to evaporate almost as quickly as it first coalesced. The cracks appeared as early as 1954 when Carnell succeeded *Harold John Ockenga as president of Fuller, and suggested in his inaugural address (17 May 1955) that the vistas of scholarly investigation at Fuller might be broader than the seminary's founders had envisioned. Although some were shocked at the implications of Carnell's speech, given Fuller's prior commitment to a more rigorous academic methodology, it was almost inevitable that the approach would lead some of its scholars in creative directions that would seem beyond the pale of traditional evangelicalism. The only apparent safeguard against this "slippage" was to institute some guidelines as to what biblical research was "acceptable" and "unacceptable." This recourse was unpalatable to most of the Fuller faculty because of their revolt against the obscurantist side of fundamentalism and the seminary's nondenominational status.[14]

The door set ajar by Carnell in the mid–1950s was pushed wide open on 1 December 1962, popularly referred to as "Black Saturday" by many associated with Fuller. On that date, Daniel Fuller, son of the seminary's founder and the dean-elect of the school, contended against the biblical inerrantists on the faculty that there were errors in the Bible that could not be judged merely as copyist errors. This declaration directly challenged the views of Henry, *Harold Lindsell, and others who were wedded to a strict inerrantist viewpoint. Fuller's statement touched off a protracted power struggle at the seminary that resulted in the departure of the more conservative faculty and the installation of David A. Hubbard, a noninerrantist Old Testament scholar, as Fuller's president in 1963.[15]

The reverberations from the Fuller shakeup echoed until 1976 when they emerged from the evangelical subculture in an uproarious cacaphony through the publication of Lindsell's *The Battle for the Bible*. In his book, Lindsell both asserted a strident defense of the doctrine of inerrancy—that the Bible "does not contain error of any kind" and is absolutely trustworthy in all its references to history, cosmology, and science, as well as in matters of faith and practice—and an extended attack on evangelical denominations (Missouri Synod Lutherans, Southern Baptists, Evangelical Covenanters) and institutions (the ETS and Fuller Seminary) where the author believed that inerrancy was being abandoned in favor of historical criticism.[16]

Lindsell's book ignited a firestorm within American evangelicalism. For the rest of the 1970s and well into the 1980s the conflict raged. At institutions as conservative as Westmont College, Biola College, Gordon-Conwell Seminary, and Southern Baptist Theological Seminary, biblical instructors were forced to resign their positions for failing to give assent to a strict doctrine of inerrancy like the one advanced by Lindsell.[17] Emboldened by Lindsell's attack, which was further advanced by his *The Bible in the Balance*,[18] many biblical inerrantists banded together to form the International Council for Biblical Inerrancy (ICBI) in October 1978.[19] Throughout the period in question, any semblance of agreement over biblical interpretation was torn to shreds by the inerrancy debate, an argument that grew even more complicated and protracted when various evangelical scholars began to advance alternative theories of inerrancy that differed from Lindsell's in both nuance and scope.[20]

The situation remains muddled. The Missouri Synod Lutherans and the Southern Baptists have suffered divisions over the inerrancy issue.[21] On the popular level, American evangelicals continue to display a suspicious attitude toward academic biblical scholarship; many retain a preference for proof-texting the Scriptures. Although some rather jarring adjustments on traditional dispensationalism have been offered recently by Dallas Seminary scholars,[22] the older eschatology still exerts considerable sway as evidenced by the strong sales of *The New Scofield Bible* (1967) and the works of *Hal Lindsey. The debate in the 1950s over the publication of the *Revised Standard Version* of the Bible as well as the more recent conflict over Zondervan's plan to publish a gender-neutral *New International Version* is continuing evidence that a sizable portion of the evangelical subculture is not going to yield on the inerrancy issue.[23] Evangelicals are clearly biblicists, and most of them would prefer to ignore or finesse interpretive questions so as to avoid having to deal with the Pandora's box of literary criticism.

Evangelical theology in the later twentieth century has evinced this similar strain between the academic and popular approaches. Ever since Calvinism began to lose its interpretive grip over evangelicalism in the early nineteenth century, theology has tended to divide the various evangelical constituencies. Indeed, none of the best-known revivalists of the nineteenth and twentieth centuries has been known as a theologian in the systematic sense. To the contrary, all have deliberately deemphasized highly articulate theological statements as an impediment to the ecumenical nature of their core gospel message: "repent and be saved."

To the extent that structured theology has been influential among American evangelicals, an enduring force has been Charles Hodge's *Systematic Theology* (1872). Conceived as a simplified version of François Turretini's 2,000-page *Institutio Theologiae Elencticae* (1674), Hodge's book took the facts of the Scriptures and in true Enlightenment fashion, arranged them in an orderly manner under four divisions: God, man, salvation, and "end things."[24] Although he labored in the religious milieu of old school Presbyterianism, Hodge developed a theology that had influence far beyond his own denomination. This can be seen most vividly by the fact that Basil Manly and James P. Boyce, the first two professors of Southern Baptist Theological Seminary (founded 1859), were students of Hodge, although both were Baptists. Until 1917 the textbook for "the special and more erudite" course on theology at Southern remained Turretini's *Institutio*.[25]

Northern Baptists, who at the end of the nineteenth century were more influenced by historical-critical scholarship than their brethren to the south, looked to A. H. Strong, professor of theology at Rochester Theological Seminary, for theological guidance. Strong's *Systematic Theology* (1876; 8th ed., 1907) influenced several generations of evangelicals both within and outside the Baptist tradition.[26] Unlike the Princetonians, Strong attempted to wrestle seriously with the problems raised by the historical-critical school while adhering to a conservative evangelical theology as much as possible. This mediating position left Strong open to attacks from both sides of the American theological continuum.[27] Yet the influence of his theology, particularly during the early part of this century, cannot be denied.

To some degree *E. Y. Mullins, president and professor of theology at Southern Baptist Seminary at the beginning of the twentieth century, followed Strong's approach. As with Strong, one notes a less than tidy mixture of conservative evangelical theology with a greater openness to historical criticism in

Mullins's thinking. Although he stoutly defended the authority of the Bible in the life of the Christian believer, Mullins was not an inerrantist. Rather, his defense of biblical theology on the basis of the religious experience of the believer was more in line with the approach of the German theologian, Friedrich Schleiermacher. Despite his seemingly more liberal approach to Baptist theology, Mullins has probably influenced more theologians than anyone else in the generally conservative Southern Baptist Convention through his main theological works *The Axioms of Religion* (1908) and *The Christian Religion in Its Doctrinal Expression* (1917). The latter book succeeded Turretini's text as the main theological textbook at Southern Seminary in 1917.[28]

With the coming of dispensational premillennialism to prominence in the 1920s, the work of *Lewis Sperry Chafer assumed greater importance. Chafer personified the populist, almost anti-intellectual approach of American fundamentalists to theology. More than once Chafer expressed his thankfulness that his study of the Bible had not been prejudiced by formal theological training.[29] To the extent that his theology can be categorized, it might be called broadly Presbyterian, reflecting Chafer's own theological mentors who were *Dwight L. Moody and *C. I. Scofield. Chafer's methodology, which was deeply informed by dispensationalism, educated scores of theologians at Dallas Theological Seminary before being published in multivolume book form in 1948.

As with biblical studies, it was the dispensational approach to theology that prompted the "new evangelicalism" of the post–World War II era. Two individuals are especially important on this front: Carl Henry and Edward Carnell. Henry's first major work, *The Uneasy Conscience of Modern Fundamentalism* (1947), although it was not an extended statement of theological beliefs, was instrumental in challenging the separatist mentality of dispensational fundamentalism.[30] To the extent that a new generation of evangelicals was willing to adopt Henry's premise that fundamentalism was a theologically warped version of historical American evangelicalism, *The Uneasy Conscience* became a manifesto of the "new evangelicalism."

A more comprehensive theological assault on dispensational fundamentalism came from Carnell. Carnell's first significant work, *An Introduction to Christian Apologetics* (1948), was a rationalistic defense of traditional evangelical Christianity that reflected his own theological training at Wheaton College and Westminster Theological Seminary.[31] As one of the progenitors of the new evangelicalism, however, Carnell always seemed more psychologically troubled by his fundamentalist Baptist upbringing. This unsettled state erupted into a full-blown polemic in *The Case for Orthodox Theology* (1959). In a scathing assessment, Carnell defined fundamentalism as "orthodoxy gone cultic." Its "ideological thinking" was dismissed as "rigid, intolerant, and doctrinaire."[32] Specifically, Carnell attacked fundamentalism by way of its dispensationalism, its separatism, and its inerrant view of the Scripture. Although he did not repudiate the Princetonian doctrine of inerrancy that he had championed in his 1948 work, Carnell did assert that authors of the Scriptures may have given

infallible accounts of fallible sources.[33] This disingenuous sleight-of-hand atten-
tuated the Hodge-Warfield doctrine, which maintained that the "original autographs" of the Bible had been preserved from every error except the most minor
copyist mistake. It also opened the door to a broader view of the Scriptures at
Fuller (as evidenced by "Black Saturday" in 1962).

With the coming of the 1960s, there was a proliferation of diverse viewpoints
that impacted American theology in various ways.[34] Although evangelicals had
little to do with such exotic formulations as liberation, feminist, process, and
black theologies, a survey of the subculture since then reveals a surprising diversity of expression.

Some evangelicals like Bernard Ramm, for example, suggested that Karl
Barth's neo-orthodox theology offered fundamentalists a way out of their seem-
ing impasse with an empirical and skeptical scientific methodology.[35] In the
wake of the Enlightenment, particularly Immanuel Kant's argument in his *Critique of Pure Reason* that it is impossible to have rational knowledge of objects
that transcend sensory experience, evangelicals found it increasingly difficult to
assert the veracity of the Scriptures through propositional theology. Simply put,
propositional theology insisted that the revelation of God was transmitted to
humanity in the form of intelligible statements from the Word of God or the
Bible. The propositional approach was the primary apologetical argument employed by such distinguished evangelicals as Warfield, Henry, Carnell, and others. Yet the corrosive effects of literary-critical theory on the biblical texts, along
with the skeptical metaphysics of Kant and others, meant that the traditionalists
were constantly struggling to defend the "truth claims" of the Scriptures against
the critical assertions of their skeptics. Ramm believed that Barth offered evangelicals an escape from the dilemma of historical criticism because the Swiss
theologian had formulated his ideas in light of, not in opposition to, contemporary rationalism.[36]

Ramm would consider Barth an evangelical of sorts, but an evangelical who
framed his theology in the context of the basic assumptions of the Enlightenment. There are other contemporary evangelicals who are more wedded
procedurally to the amorphous epistemological viewpoint known as "postmod-
ernism." Theologically, these "postconservative evangelicals" tend to reject
propositional truths enshrined in doctrines in favor of the narrative-shaped experience of the believing Christian community. In addition, this group eschews
what they view as a static approach to the Scriptures, like inerrancy, in favor
of the continual working of the Holy Spirit through the biblical narratives. Millard Erickson calls the advocates of this approach the "Evangelical Left" and
singles out Clark Pinnock, John Sanders, and Stanley Grenz as representatives
of the perspective. Although there is a good deal of variability in the approaches
of these postconservative evangelicals, all of them operate under the assumption
that the empirical, rationalist epistemology of the Enlightenment has been thoroughly discredited, giving the supernatural metaphysics of traditional evangelicalism an opportunity to reassert itself.[37]

Although postconservatism has stirred a good deal of interest within the evangelical academy, it is an alien concept to most of the American evangelical subculture. Rather than displaying sympathy for esoteric theological formulations, most evangelicals reflexively genuflect toward the pragmatic, practical, and populist. In other words, evangelicals gravitate to what "works" for them theologically. At the end of the twentieth century, this tendency tended to atomize even further the theological viewpoint of American evangelicalism. Hence, in addition to the traditional propositional viewpoint advanced by Carl Henry in his *God, Revelation, and Authority* (6 vols., 1976), one finds "theologies" of many stripes distributed under the broad banner of evangelicalism. Examples include a "Methodist theology" by Thomas Oden, a "Pentecostal theology" by Stanley Horton, a "Baptist theology" by James Leo Garrett, an "evangelical theology" by Donald Bloesch, and, yes, a "neo-evangelical theology" by Paul Jewett.[38]

All theological trends within evangelicalism suggest further fragmentation, particularly in light of the breakdown of denominations like the Southern Baptist Convention and the rise of nondenominational megachurches like Calvary Chapel of Santa Ana, California, and Willow Creek Community Church of South Barrington, Illinois. As these congregations create themselves with little reference to tradition, their theology will surely form either by consensus (what is agreeable to the majority of the assembly) or by fiat (what the church leadership believes is the mandate of God).[39] Neither of these alternatives may lead to a coherent evangelical theology in the twenty-first century, but one or the other may be inevitable.

## NOTES

1. John R. W. Stott, *What Is an Evangelical?* (London: Church Pastoral Aid Society, 1977), p. 5.

2. Millard J. Erickson, *Christian Theology*, vol. 1 (Grand Rapids, Mich.: Baker, 1983), p. 21.

3. Charles Hodge, *Systematic Theology*, vol. 1 (New York: Scribners, 1871), p. 170.

4. A. A. Hodge and B. B. Warfield, "Inspiration," *Presbyterian Review* 2 (April 1881): 225–60. This essay has been reprinted in book form as Hodge and Warfield, *Inspiration*, intro. by Roger Nicole (Grand Rapids, Mich.: Baker, 1979).

5. Edwin Scott Gaustad, *A Religious History of America*, new rev. ed. (San Francisco: Harper & Row, 1990), p. 258.

6. Mark A. Noll, *Between Faith and Criticism: Evangelicals, Scholarship, and the Bible in America*, 2nd ed. (Grand Rapids, Mich.: Baker, 1991), pp. 58–60.

7. Timothy P. Weber, "The Two-Edged Sword: The Fundamentalist Use of the Bible," in *The Bible in America: Essays in Cultural History*, edited by Nathan O. Hatch and Mark A. Noll (New York: Oxford University Press, 1982), p. 110.

8. Ibid., pp. 112–13.

9. Carnell is an excellent representative of this new scholarly attitude that suffused some in the fundamentalist community. Carnell's goals and their attendant psychic strains

are ably presented in Rudolf Nelson, *The Making and Unmaking of an Evangelical Mind: The Case of Edward Carnell* (Cambridge, Eng.: Cambridge University Press, 1987), pp. 54–57.

10. There was, however, considerable division even among the "new evangelicals" with regard to inerrancy. As Douglas Sweeney has pointed out, Ockenga, Henry, Carnell, and Lindsell all maintained their allegiance to the doctrine and continued to think of themselves as "fundamentalists" well after the 1947 date commonly given as the start of the "neo-evangelical" movement. See Douglas A. Sweeney, "Fundamentalism and the Neo-Evangelicals," *Fides et Historia* 24:2 (Winter/Spring 1992): 81–96.

11. George Eldon Ladd, *Crucial Questions About the Kingdom of God* (Grand Rapids, Mich.: Eerdmans, 1952), p. 59. See also idem, *The New Testament and Criticism* (Grand Rapids, Mich.: Eerdmans, 1967).

12. Carl F. H. Henry, "American Evangelicals in a Turning Time," *Christian Century* (5 November 1980): 1060.

13. Mark A. Noll, "Evangelicals and the Study of the Bible," in *Evangelicalism and Modern America*, edited by George Marsden (Grand Rapids, Mich.: Eerdmans, 1984), pp. 104–5.

14. George M. Marsden, *Reforming Fundamentalism: Fuller Seminary and the New Evangelicalism* (Grand Rapids, Mich.: Eerdmans, 1987), pp. 147–50.

15. Ibid., pp. 208–24.

16. Harold Lindsell, *The Battle for the Bible* (Grand Rapids, Mich.: Zondervan, 1976), pp. 72–131.

17. Donald A. Hagner, "The Battle for Inerrancy: An Errant Trend Among the Inerrantists," *Reformed Journal* 34:4 (April 1984): 19–22.

18. Harold Lindsell, *The Bible in the Balance* (Grand Rapids, Mich.: Zondervan, 1979).

19. J. I. Packer, *Beyond the Battle for the Bible* (Westchester, Ill.: Cornerstone Books, 1980), pp. 48–49. The 300 scholars meeting under ICBI auspices wrote a 3,000 word "Chicago Statement on Biblical Inerrancy" which was signed by 90 percent of those attending. The long statement can be found in J. Gordon Melton and James Sauer, *The Encyclopedia of American Religions: Religious Creeds*, 2 vols. (Detroit: Gale Research, 1994), 2: 269–73, and the "Five Point," 200 word summary that opens the longer statement is printed in full in Packer's book (p. 48).

20. The range of perspectives is sampled nicely in Robert M. Price, "Inerrant the Wind: The Troubled House of North American Evangelicals," *Evangelical Quarterly* 55:3 (July 1983): 129–44. Price delineates five "noninerrantist" groups that move in a more liberal continuum away from Lindsell's strict view: (1) limited inerrantists; (2) partial infallibilists; (3) pluriform canonists; (4) biblical deabsolutists; and (5) orthodoxfordists. Price's scheme is interesting, but does not seem to have been adopted in any widespread fashion by the commentators on inerrancy.

21. A large body of articles and books has been written on the travails of these denominations. Two representative titles are James E. Adams, *Preus of Missouri and the Great Lutheran Civil War* (New York: Harper & Row, 1977) and David T. Morgan, *New Crusades, The New Holy Land Conflict in the Southern Baptist Convention, 1969–1991* (Tuscaloosa: University of Alabama Press, 1996).

22. Craig A. Blaising and Darrell L. Bock, *Progressive Dispensationalism* (Wheaton, Ill.: BridgePoint, 1993).

23. Regarding the uproar over the RSV, see Bruce M. Metzger, "The Revised Stan-

dard Version," in *The Word of God: A Guide to English Versions of the Bible*, edited by Lloyd R. Bailey (Atlanta: John Knox, 1979), pp. 32–34. The controversy over the NIV became public by way of a series of provocative articles in *World* magazine by Susan Olasky in 1997. These articles were: Susan Olasky, "The Feminist Seduction of the Evangelical Church: Femme Fatale," *World* 12:2 (29 March 1997): 12–15; idem, "The Battle For the Bible," *World* 12:5 (19 April 1997): 14–18; and idem, "Bailing Out of the Stealth Bible," *World* 12:10 (14/21 June 1997): 12–17.

24. Turretini (1623–87) was the Reformed chair of theology at the University of Geneva for thirty-four years. He is known as a "Reformed scholastic" because his theological approach mimicked not John Calvin, but Thomas Aquinas. The *Institutio* emphasized "precise definition and systematic, scientific statement." See Jack B. Rogers and Donald K. McKim, *The Authority and Interpretation of the Bible: An Historical Approach*, foreword by Ford Battles (New York: Harper & Row, 1979), pp. 172–73. Archibald Alexander, the founder of Princeton Seminary, centered the school's theological studies around Turretini's text, which is where they remained until Hodge published his *Systematic*. See David F. Wells, "The Stout and Persistent Theology of Charles Hodge," *Christianity Today* 18 (30 August 1974): 15.

25. Timothy George, "Systematic Theology at Southern Seminary," *Review and Expositor* 82 (Winter 1985): 31.

26. The major divisions of the *Systematic* were: prolegomena; the existence of God; the Scriptures; the natures, decrees, and works of God; anthropology; and soteriology. See Augustus Hopkins Strong, *Systematic Theology: A Compendium*, 8th ed., 3 vols. (Philadelphia: American Baptist Publication Society, 1907).

27. Strong's difficulty in synthesizing traditional evangelicalism with the historical-critical methodology is illustrated in Grant Wacker, *Augustus H. Strong and the Dilemma of Historical Consciousness* (Macon, Ga.: Mercer University Press, 1985).

28. David S. Dockery, *Christian Scripture: An Evangelical Perspective on Inspiration, Authority, and Interpretation* (Nashville: Broadman & Holman, 1995), pp. 194–96. Mullins's key works are E. Y. Mullins, *The Axioms of Religion: A New Interpretation of the Baptist Faith* (Philadelphia: American Baptist Publication Society, 1908), and idem, *The Christian Faith in Its Doctrinal Expression* (Nashville: Broadman, 1917).

29. F. Lincoln, "Biographical Sketch," prefaced to Lewis Sperry Chafer, *Systematic Theology*, vol. 8 (Dallas: Dallas Theological Seminary, 1948), pp. 5–6.

30. Carl F. H. Henry, *The Uneasy Conscience of Modern Fundamentalism* (Grand Rapids, Mich.: Eerdmans, 1947).

31. Edward John Carnell, *An Introduction to Christian Apologetics* (Grand Rapids, Mich.: Eerdmans, 1948).

32. Edward John Carnell, *The Case For Orthodox Theology* (Philadelphia: Westminster, 1959), pp. 113–14.

33. Ibid., pp. 99–110.

34. A good background essay is Sydney E. Ahlstrom, "The Radical Turn in Theology and Ethics: Why It Occurred in the 1960s," *Annals of the American Academy of Political and Social Sciences* 387 (1970): 1–13.

35. Bernard Ramm, *After Fundamentalism: The Future of Evangelical Theology* (San Francisco: Harper & Row, 1983), pp. 11–15.

36. Ibid., pp. 29–31.

37. Millard J. Erickson, *The Evangelical Left: Encountering Postconservative Evangelical Theology* (Grand Rapids, Mich.: Baker, 1997).

38. Carl F. H. Henry, *God, Revelation, and Authority*, 6 vols. (Waco, Tex.: Word, 1976); Thomas C. Oden, *Systematic Theology*, 3 vols. (San Francisco: HarperCollins, 1992); Stanley M. Horton, *Systematic Theology: A Pentecostal Perspective* (Springfield, Mo.: Logion Press, 1994); James Leo Garrett Jr., *Systematic Theology: Biblical, Historical, and Evangelical*, 2 vols. (Grand Rapids, Mich.: Eerdmans, 1990); Donald G. Bloesch, *Essentials of Evangelical Theology*, 2 vols. (San Francisco: Harper & Row, 1978–79); and Paul K. Jewett, *God, Creation, and Revelation: A Neo-Evangelical Theology* (Grand Rapids, Mich.: Eerdmans, 1991).

39. In a study of J. I. Packer's theology, Alister McGrath points out the dangers that evangelicals face when they ignore the instructive nature of the Christian tradition. See Alister E. McGrath, "The Importance of Tradition for Modern Evangelicalism," in *Doing Theology for the People of God: Studies in Honor of J. I. Packer*, edited by Donald Lewis and Alister McGrath (Downers Grove, Ill.: InterVarsity, 1996), pp. 159–73.

# 10
# Transforming Culture: Evangelicals and the Social Order

Evangelicalism's passion for individual conversion endows its public expression of faith with considerable ambiguity. "The world" is a zone fraught with evil, luring the unconverted into sin and tantalizing the believer with temptation. Yet daily activity occurs in that world, and evangelism plunges the faithful into the world to find souls still lost. Those born again are, in images drawn from the Fourth Gospel, "in, but not of the world." This ambivalent relationship to society has had far-reaching consequences. It is simplistic, albeit somewhat accurate, to conclude that evangelicalism has eschewed direct involvement in the political realm because it was intrinsically evil and therefore dangerous. Historians often highlight evangelicalism's stress on personal over social ethics; some even assert that most American evangelicalism has lacked a social ethic. That extreme is as much a distortion as its opposite, that other expressions of Christianity lack concern for the individual soul. Some analysts describe the tension between these orientations by contrasting a "reform" motif with a "rescue" motif.[1] The former arises from the conviction that altering social structures can render them more reflective of religious values and thus more conducive to conversion and religious nurture. The latter presumes that the primary religious duty is to rescue individual sinners from the clutches of an evil society; social change follows only through the actions of redeemed individuals. Evangelicalism's favoring the rescue approach receives clear confirmation in the rescue mission movement that first worked with those pushed to the margins in the nation's rapidly growing cities in the later nineteenth century.[2] Some remain in operation today. Of those, perhaps the most famous is Chicago's Pacific Garden Mission that began in 1877. It received the enthusiastic endorsement of revivalist *Dwight L. Moody, and its ministry helped bring about *Billy Sunday's conversion.[3] Like Pacific Garden, other rescue missions (such as the Water Street

Mission in New York City's Bowery District that began in 1872) were located in slum areas that abounded with gambling centers, saloons, and houses of prostitution. Many evangelicals believed that the homeless and unemployed were responsible for their own situation; it resulted from sin and could be cured by conversion. Rescue missions did meet immediate physical needs by providing food and shelter; many of those still functioning offer temporary quarters for homeless and abused women, medical and dental clinics for the indigent, and occasional day care centers for children. Pacific Garden Mission has promoted its many ministries through films and a regular syndicated radio program, "Unshackled." In cities that were points of entry for immigrants, many missions in the later nineteenth and early twentieth century provided programs designed to ease the transition of immigrants into American life.

American evangelicalism's relationship to and engagement with the social and political orders are more complex than its penchant for the rescue motif suggests. During the twentieth century, evangelicals developed new strategies and structures for appropriate political action, but their substance remained constant. Formerly persons so inclined might identify with a group with a single social or political mission, such as the Anti-Saloon League, but more might act as individuals, not aligning with any group. A few organizations, such as the Salvation Army or the Volunteers of America, have addressed more wide-ranging social issues, but in tandem with efforts to convert individuals. Since the antebellum period, social stands taken by evangelicals have also reflected the interweaving of region and historical circumstance. Chattel slavery in the South, even as the South was becoming an evangelical bastion, contributed to the emphasis on personal over social ethics there. Stressing personal ethics allowed Southern evangelicals to sidestep wrestling with moral issues surrounding slavery. In the North, debates about slavery also serve as a barometer for marking greater openness to religiously informed social action. An episode at Oberlin College, which numbered evangelical revivalist Charles Grandison Finney among its founders in 1833 (and later its president), provides a convenient symbol. Two years after opening, Oberlin welcomed as students a group of abolitionists who had withdrawn from evangelically oriented Lane Seminary in Cincinnati; consequently, a passion for social reform fused with one strand of Northern evangelicalism.[4]

Equally nuanced is modern American evangelicalism's relation to social change. Built into evangelicalism is an inertia that springs in part from its biblicism. Evangelicals by and large have understood the New Testament to demand respect and honor for established political institutions, as, for example, in Romans 13:1–7:

Let every soul be subject unto the higher powers. For there is no power but of God; the powers that be are ordained of God. Whosoever therefore resisteth the power, resisteth the ordinance of God: and they that resist shall receive to themselves damnation. For rulers are not a terror to good works, but to the evil. Wilt thou then be afraid of the power? do that which is good, and thou shalt have praise of the same: For he is the minister of God to thee for good. But if thou do that which is evil, be afraid; for he beareth not the sword in vain: for he is the minister of God, a revenger to execute wrath upon him that doeth evil. Wherefore ye must needs be subject, not only for wrath, but also for conscience sake. For this cause pay ye tribute also: for they are God's ministers, attending continually upon this very thing. Render therefore to all their dues: tribute to whom tribute is due; custom to whom custom; fear to whom fear; honour to whom honour. (KJV)

If political powers have God's blessing, the social order—even if fraught with temptation and evil—is also part of the divine scheme. Hence, evangelicalism tends to accept the status quo as normative, particularly when those who exercise political power appear to share evangelical standards, principles, and values. So long as evangelicals believe their approach represents a cultural consensus, there is little reason to challenge the social or political modus operandi.

Evangelicalism's traditional support for the powers that be comes into sharp relief in looking at two phenomena, evangelicalism's support for the American cause in both world wars and its strident anticommunism after World War II. Apart from those identified with historic peace churches, most evangelicals supported the American cause in the Great War, perhaps in part because Calvinist theology and its homiletic tradition shaped the oratorical style and rhetoric of President Woodrow Wilson. Robert Linder points out that most evangelical preachers, like their more liberal counterparts, were either militant or moderate supporters of the war effort. Revivalist Billy Sunday merged evangelicalism and patriotism when he preached, "If you turn hell upside down, you will find 'Made in Germany' stamped on the bottom."[5] Evangelical congregations joined other religious communities in flying the American flag in their buildings, promoting the sale of war bonds, and soliciting and packaging nonmilitary supplies for armed forces personnel. No one foresaw that the emotions stirred by a patriotism that required hating an enemy would spill over into the fundamentalist-modernist controversy of the 1920s.

The Second World War brought some division among evangelicals, particularly between the emerging moderate stream of evangelicalism with its zealous patriots and fundamentalists and/or those on the far right politically, including several who virulently opposed the New Deal of the 1930s. Gerald B. Winrod, leader of the fundamentalist Defenders of the Christian Faith and since 1926 publisher of *Defender Magazine*, was among those the federal government took to court for conspiring to cause insubordination in the armed forces. Gerald L. K. Smith, one-time Disciples of Christ minister and later associate of infamous Louisiana politician Huey Long, avoided such charges, but like Winrod was highly critical of the U.S. position. Both Winrod and Smith became strident antisemitists as the war progressed.[6] But the majority of evangelicals supported the war effort, and, like others, had to wrestle with the new moral issues that came with dropping atomic bombs on Hiroshima and Nagasaki in the closing weeks of the war. At the same time, the war stimulated new forms of evangelical ministry and mission. Hundreds of evangelical military chaplains experienced both the horrors of war and opportunities for sustained interaction with persons of other religious persuasions. At the same time, postings on the war front stimulated evangelicals to ponder missionary possibilities that could be developed when the war ended. The Far Eastern Gospel Crusade, organized in 1947 and renamed SEND International in 1981, owes its genesis to military personnel stationed in the Pacific who returned home eager to support evangelization efforts in Asia.

As the nation moved from World War to Cold War, evangelicals reaped the surface benefits of the so-called "revival" of religion of the 1950s, building new churches and adding members in sometimes record numbers. Public voices across the evangelical spectrum also took up the anticommunism crusade. In the early years of his evangelistic ministry, *Billy Graham frequently peppered sermons with references to the specter of "godless communism" and contrasted his vision of a converted America as a bastion of righteousness with the Soviet Union and its satellites, which signalled the pervasiveness of evil.[7] Some evangelicals described Cold War combatants in terms of the final struggle at Armageddon. Many applauded Wisconsin senator Joseph McCarthy's efforts to ferret out Communists presumed serving in the U.S. military. Evangelist Billy James Hargis, a master of the medium of radio, exemplified the ties between conservative Protestantism and anticommunist patriotism in his widely broadcast radio message "For God and Against Communism." Hargis turned his Christian Crusade organization into an anticommunist propaganda machine to such an extent that it lost tax-exempt status in 1966.[8] In time, it became a commonplace that evangelicals identified government positions, sometimes without careful examination, with truth, for government was ordained by God.[9]

Also ordained by God for many evangelicals are cultural roles first assigned to women in the Victorian era. Although women have consistently outnumbered men on the rolls of evangelical congregations, with the exception of evangelists like *Kathryn Kuhlman or *Aimee Semple McPherson, few stand in the front ranks of evangelical leadership. Indeed, one fairly consistent undercurrent in evangelical social thought is opposition to change in women's roles. Such can first be seen in the women's suffrage movement. Although historians claim that male Protestant clergy were more likely to support women's suffrage than other men, there was less support among evangelical clergy, particularly those in the fundamentalist orbit. Suffragists found ammunition for their cause in the pages of Scripture, even without resorting to extremes like the commentaries in Elizabeth Cady Stanton's *Woman's Bible*.[10] So did their opponents. The appearance of the *Woman's Bible* in 1895, just as higher criticism gained currency in theological circles, cemented in the minds of some evangelicals the conviction that biblical authority was under attack; they opposed woman's suffrage under the guise of protecting the authority of Scripture. But as Aileen Kraditor pointed out decades ago, at the end of the nineteenth century "most people believed that the Bible opposed any change in the status of women."[11] In order not to forfeit religious support for women's suffrage, the National American Woman Suffrage Association repudiated the *Woman's Bible*. That hardly assuaged evangelical fears that giving women the vote would disrupt home life and church life.

Parallel with the suffrage effort was the temperance movement, leading to the national experiment with Prohibition. Women, including evangelicals, provided critical leadership, particularly through the Women's Christian Temperance Union (WCTU), founded in 1874.[12] The Anti-Saloon League of America, begun in 1895, also relied heavily on evangelical support, although men dominated its leadership. The WCTU, guided for many years by *Frances Willard who was a confirmed suffragist and proponent of the ordination of women, was the largest women's organization in the nation at the turn of the century. Evangelically inclined Methodists provided much energy for the temperance movement, even in the antebellum period, and Southern Methodist Bishop James Cannon became known as the ''dry messiah'' for his leadership of prohibition forces early in the twentieth century. There were some Methodists, particularly in the South, who were suspicious of having local congregations sponsor WCTU units because they provided women speakers with a forum men did not control. Nonetheless, evangelical support for the endeavor to ban the manufacture, sale, and consumption of alcoholic beverages remains a signal example of how evangelicals interacted with and influenced common life. The constitutional amendments granting women the vote and launching Prohibition both went into effect in 1920, just as the fundamentalist-modernist controversy was brewing and the nation was returning to peacetime living after World War I. Betty DeBerg argues cogently that fear of the changing role of women and a desire to equate Victorian gender roles with scriptural truth, thereby assuring the control of men over women in both church and society, energized fundamentalism in the 1920s.[13] The strongest continuing support for insisting that woman's place is in the home and that the primary roles of woman are as wife subordinate to her husband and mother nurturing her children comes from the fundamentalist wing of evangelicalism.

Two other instances of resisting change in the role of women must suffice: calls for ordination of women and debates in the 1970s and 1980s over the proposed Equal Rights Amendment to the U.S. Constitution. Evangelicalism again represents a paradox when it comes to the ordination of women.[14] In the nineteenth century, the Salvation Army recognized the ministry of women, and women were in the forefront of the Holiness movement and its churches. Pentecostals also have a heritage of women preachers, although some have resisted women pastors; as Elaine Lawless demonstrates, Pentecostal women can receive the gifts of the Spirit as powerfully as men, but women preachers are expected to remain subordinate to their husbands in the context of marriage and family.[15] Individual evangelical women have also achieved national prominence; Aimee Semple McPherson, Kathryn Kuhlman, and Ruth Carter Stapleton represent only three examples. Yet since the beginning of the twentieth century, resistance to ordaining women has grown. Within the Southern Baptist Convention, for example, formal resolutions discourage ordaining women, although local churches have done so. For most, the arguments are similar to those that prevail in Roman Catholic teaching, namely that Jesus called only men as "disciples," the New Testament restricts the role of women in the churches (1 Timothy 2: 8–15), biblical references to deacons and elders presume men in those roles, and in general the New Testament insists on the subordination of women to men.

Evangelicals by and large opposed the proposed constitutional amendment that would have guaranteed equal rights for women. For many the Equal Rights Amendment (ERA) captured all the fears that surrounded feminism. From the Moral Majority's *Jerry Falwell to less fundamentalist evangelicals, the proposed amendment signaled destruction of the family and the final blow to the presumed biblical view of the husband as head of the household and the one to whom women should be submissive. Falwell repeatedly attacked feminism and the ERA on the lecture circuit and in his widely distributed *Listen America!*.[16] What made the Equal Rights Amendment so threatening was its following on the heels of *Roe v. Wade*, the 1973 Supreme Court decision legalizing abortion in many situations. Falwell and evangelicals of all varieties regarded abortion as murder and believed that its legalization continued the assault on the nuclear family unit headed by a godly, benevolent husband.[17] Evangelical theologian *Francis A. Schaeffer and radio personality, theologian, and educator *James C. Dobson Jr. not only renounced abortion, but urged evangelicals to use their influence in persuading legislators to enact laws that would again make abortion illegal.[18] For them, the "pro-choice" insistence that abortion gave a woman control over her body undercut traditional gender roles and promoted moral decay. Some evangelicals of the 1970s and 1980s spoke of feminists and pro-choice advocates in much the same terms that others used to condemn Communists in the 1950s. The Evangelical Women's Caucus and the Sojourners community represented the most vocal dissenters among evangelicals on some of these issues.

At the same time, evangelicals have recognized in subtle ways that the world has changed when it comes to gender issues.[19] For evangelicals in whose homes and families shifts away from Victorian gender roles became daily reality, tension and paradox prevailed. Both the Council on Biblical Manhood and Womanhood and Christians for Biblical Equality attempt to carve a *via media* that affirms biblical norms while acknowledging that Victorian gender roles have vanished.[20] In 1978 evangelical publisher Fleming H. Revell introduced the monthly magazine *Today's Christian Woman*, acquired by Christianity Today, Inc., a decade later. Although the primary foci for articles remain a woman's relationship to God, to her husband, to her children, and to herself, content reflects the ways that feminism has penetrated the evangelical consciousness. Issues such as abortion, divorce, rape, AIDS, sexual harassment, alcoholism, and extramarital affairs have been featured; even addressing such topics reminds

readers that they are part of the life experience of evangelicals. Other evangelically oriented periodicals designed for a female audience include *Joyful Woman*
and *Virtue*, but neither has attracted the circulation of *Today's Christian Woman*
or addressed current issues as forthrightly. Evangelicals understand that gender
roles have shifted even if they remain suspicious of the changes.

Concerns about homosexuality have also drawn evangelicals into the public
arena. Evangelical interpretation of Scripture usually concludes that homosexuality is a sin condemned by the Bible or an intrinsically evil aberration.[21] Most
often passages in Leviticus are combined with the Sodom and Gomorrah story
as evidence of Old Testament proscriptions of homosexual acts, and Paul's letter
to the Romans joins with passages in 1 Timothy to provide the same for the
New Testament. As calls for equal rights for homosexuals mounted in the 1970s
and 1980s and those for legalizing homosexual "marriages" or same-gender
unions became more strident in the 1990s, most evangelical writers continued
to see homosexuality as one sign of moral decay that must be resisted at all
costs. Indeed, the tone becomes more shrill when evangelicals talk about homosexuality than when they discuss feminism. For Falwell, for example, any
legal action making homosexuality appear normal or natural and therefore acceptable invites divine judgment on the nation more severe than what Scripture
describes as the destruction of Sodom and Gomorrah. Some arguments advanced
against gay rights are similar to those used to condemn feminism, for homosexuals are portrayed as agents undermining traditional family structures, and
those advocating ordination of "practicing" homosexuals receive greater rebuke
than those who ordain women. Many evangelicals rejoiced in 1996 when President Bill Clinton signed the so-called Defense of Marriage Act that decreed
that individual states did not have to recognize marriages between persons of
the same gender that might be legal in other states. In 1997, the Southern Baptist
Convention bade the faithful to boycott Disney World and all products associated with any Disney enterprise because the parent corporation was thought too
supportive of homosexuals. Again there are dissenting evangelical voices. The
Evangelical Women's Caucus has offered encouragement to lesbians, while
Evangelicals Concerned has provided not only alternative interpretations of
Scripture used to condemn homosexuality, but also opportunities for homosexual
evangelicals to network together.

Social historians see cultural concern for the status of women and homosexuals as a concomitant to the civil rights movement. Yet evangelical response to
the civil rights movement represents an even greater paradox.[22] African American churches steeped in evangelical ways nurtured the movement's leaders.
*Martin Luther King Jr., a Baptist pastor, is the most conspicuous example; his
civil rights organization was intentionally named the Southern *Christian* Leadership Conference. In the movement's opening years, many evangelicals ob-
jected to the use of nonviolent civil disobedience, arguing that because
government was ordained by God, such action was contrary to the divine will.
White Southern evangelicals generally mirrored attitudes of the culture around

them, straining to insist that Scripture mandated racial separation and the infe-
riority of blacks to whites; many castigated white clergy who joined the movement for abandoning their responsibility to seek the conversion of souls.
Southern Presbyterians tried to avoid tackling racism by claiming that the "spirituality of the church" required aloofness from political and social issues. Pentecostal and charismatic evangelicals remained racially separated, even though
at the dawn of the century, many Pentecostal congregations had been racially
mixed. As congregations clustered into denominations, most organized along
racial lines. Billy Graham, the herald of white moderate evangelicalism, early
on demanded that separate seating by race be ended at his crusades.[23] Graham
illustrates the tension pervading evangelical circles, for evangelicals knew that
the Bible speaks of love and justice in terms that would require denouncing
racism and segregation. Half a century after the civil rights movement rocked
American life, the churches (whether or not evangelical) remain the most segregated public institutions, although virtually all evangelicals now reject the use
of Scripture to condone racism.

Paradox also marks evangelical involvement in controversies over public
schools. For generations evangelicals had been among the most vocal advocates
of public education, criticizing those who supported public financial assistance
for parochial schools or other private religious schools. Evangelicalism's suspicion of Roman Catholicism fueled some of this feeling, since most private
schools with a religious orientation had Roman Catholic ties. At the same time,
American public education in the later nineteenth century assumed an evangelically informed world-view in instruction, curriculum, and teaching materials.
Not until evangelicals sensed that this consensus was in danger, if it had not
already eroded, did attitudes toward public education shift.[24] U.S. Supreme Court
cases since World War II help track evangelical concerns. In *McCollum v. Board
of Education* (1948), the Court struck down released time for religious instruction held on school property, although four years later (*Zorach v. Clausen*) the
Court upheld dismissing students for religious instruction held off school property. Most controversial were two decisions in the early 1960s. In *Engel v. Vitale*
(1962), the Court declared unconstitutional the required recitation of a generic
daily prayer authorized by the New York State Board of Regents to replace the
practice, more common in areas other than New York, of beginning the school
day with either the Lord's Prayer or another prayer. In 1963, the Court struck
down recitation of the Lord's Prayer and reading portions of the Bible for devotional purposes (*Abington v. Schempp*) in public schools. Many evangelicals,
particularly in areas where multifaith pluralism was not part of the landscape,
believed these decisions thwarted inculcation of moral values basic to education.
Few noted that the Court encouraged academic study of religion and also of the
Bible (and other sacred texts) as literature. Later court cases struck down laws
prohibiting teaching of evolutionary theory (*Epperson v. Arkansas*, 1968), requiring posting the Ten Commandments in classrooms (*Stone v. Graham*, 1980),
mandated a daily time of silence for meditation or prayer (*Wallace v. Jaffree*,

1985), and requiring teaching creation science if theories of evolution were taught (*Edwards v. Aquillard*, 1987). Only one decision brought some comfort. In *Widmar v. Vincent* (1981), a case involving the University of Missouri with implications for public schools since the university was a public institution, the Court ruled that student religious groups could meet on school property if other student social and political groups did so.

Restoring prayer to public schools or at least sanctioning times of silence became a rallying cry for evangelicals convinced that public morality had eroded. Many local school boards moved to sanction some religious exercises, particularly if they were student initiated or led. The Christian Coalition has tried in selected communities across the nation to engineer election of school board members in order to control school policy. In many instances, issues involving curriculum materials, required reading, books in libraries, and sex education classes became more controversial than school prayer. In numerous communities, congregations began private "Christian" schools as alternatives to public schools so that prayer, Bible reading, and other religious activities could occur without violating the law. The move to private schools represented a sharp break with the historic support evangelicals offered to public education in theory and in practice.

A rather different focus of evangelical political concern, one aspect of U.S. foreign policy, requires mention. Evangelicals have supported Israel and its interests almost without question since the creation of Israel as a nation in the late 1940s. The reason is theological and stretches back to the dispensationalist currents that gave shape to both modern evangelicalism and fundamentalism. Simply put, evangelicals came to believe that the existence and security of Israel are intimately tied to the eschatological events issuing in Christ's return to earth. Most of this support comes in sermons and speeches by evangelicals and through individual action in the political arena.

Although evangelicals insist that salvation of individual souls remains their primary interest, they have also consistently taken an interest in political and social issues sweeping the nation. In many cases, evangelicals have tried to preserve a culture that was changing too rapidly. This helps explain evangelical interest in temperance and Prohibition, in opposing woman's suffrage and the Equal Rights Amendment, and in working to reverse Supreme Court decisions regarding religious activity in public schools. In other cases, evangelicals have acted because of their understanding of scriptural mandate. The unquestioning patriotism central to much evangelical life in the twentieth century, the opposition to abortion and homosexuality, and the support for Israel all reflect the ways evangelicals have attempted to imprint on public life perspectives emerging from their interpretation of the Bible. How evangelical political and social action have changed in the twentieth century is in the formation of groups such as the Moral Majority and the Christian Coalition with wide-ranging political and social interests. Prior to the last quarter of the century, evangelicals eschewed forming religious agencies that had such obvious political orientations, preferring instead to encourage persons to act as individuals or to join groups such as the Anti-Saloon League of America that had single issues as their focus. After all, at the heart of most evangelical political and social action prior to the close of the twentieth century lay the conviction that the world would change only as individuals changed through a direct, personal experience of Jesus Christ. Paradox also prevailed, for in attempting to buttress ways of the past, evangelicals always, even if unwittingly, were adjusting their message to meet a new age.

## NOTES

1. See particularly Jean Miller Schmidt's doctoral dissertation, published as *Souls or the Social Order: The Two-Party System in American Protestantism* (Brooklyn, N.Y.: Carlson, 1991). Martin E. Marty, *Protestantism in the United States: Righteous Empire*, 2nd ed. (New York: Scribners, 1986) also uses this contrast. For a more chronological analysis, see Robert D. Linder, "The Resurgence of Evangelical Social Concern (1925–1975)," in *The Evangelicals: What They Believe, Who They Are, Where They Are Changing*, edited by David D. Wells and John D. Woodbridge (Nashville: Abingdon, 1975), pp. 189–210. Some of the issues discussed here are also considered in the essay by George H. Williams and Rodney L. Petersen in that same volume, pp. 211–48: "Evangelicals: Society, the State, the Nation (1925–1975)."

2. The standard overview is Norris A. Magnuson, *Salvation in the Slums: Evangelical Social Work, 1865–1920* (Metuchen, N.J.: Scarecrow, 1977).

3. See James R. Adair, *The Old Lighthouse: The Story of the Pacific Garden Mission* (Chicago: Moody, 1966).

4. On the "Lane rebels" and other ways Oberlin merged social reform with evangelicalism, see Robert S. Fletcher, *A History of Oberlin College: From Its Foundation through the Civil War*, 2 vols. in 1 (New York: Arno, 1971).

5. Robert D. Linder, "World War I," in *Dictionary of Christianity in America*, edited by Daniel G. Reid et al. (Downers Grove, Ill.: InterVarsity, 1990), p. 1278. The classic study is Ray Abrams, *Preachers Present Arms* (New York: Round Table, 1933), but see also John F. Piper Jr. *The American Churches in World War I* (Athens: Ohio University Press, 1985).

6. Still valuable are Leo P. Ribuffo, *The Old Christian Right: The Protestant Right from the Great Depression to the Cold War* (Philadelphia: Temple University Press, 1983), and Ralph Lord Roy, *Apostles of Discord: A Study of Organized Bigotry and Disruption on the Fringes of Protestantism* (Boston: Beacon, 1953).

7. William Martin, Graham's biographer, makes frequent mention of the evangelist's attitudes toward communism, including Graham's moderating his sharp critique as he became more sensitive to the complexity of global economic and political dilemmas. See William C. Martin, *Prophet with Honor: The Billy Graham Story* (New York: Morrow, 1991), esp. pp. 115, 119, 165–67, 197, 208–9, 270–71, 277–78.

8. The most compelling direct statement is Billy James Hargis, *Communist America—Must It Be?* (Butler, Ind.: Highley Huffman, 1960). On Hargis, see also James Morris, *The Preachers* (New York: St. Martin's, 1973), pp. 257–314. On the religious response to communism, see Martin E. Marty, *Modern American Religion, vol. 3, Under God, Indivisible: 1941–1960* (Chicago: University of Chicago Press, 1996), pp. 354–75,

and Erling Jorstad, *The Politics of Doomsday: Fundamentalists and the Far Right* (New York: Abingdon, 1970), passim.

9. On the angst this position has produced and the complexities it involves, see Mark A. Noll, Nathan O. Hatch, and George M. Marsden, *The Search for Christian America* (Westchester, Ill.: Crossway Books, 1983; reprinted, Colorado Springs, Colo.: Helmers and Howard, 1989).

10. Elizabeth Cady Stanton et al., *The Woman's Bible, Parts I and II* (New York: European Publishing, 1895, 1898).

11. Aileen S. Kraditor, *The Ideas of the Woman Suffrage Movement, 1890–1920* (New York: Columbia University Press, 1965), p. 86. This classic work was reissued in 1981 by W. W. Norton.

12. See Ruth Bordin, *Women and Temperance: The Quest for Power and Liberty, 1873–1900* (1981; reprint, New Brunswick, N.J.: Rutgers University Press, 1990).

13. Betty A. DeBerg, *Ungodly Women: Gender and the First Wave of American Fundamentalism* (Minneapolis: Fortress, 1990).

14. A helpful resource is Bonnidell Clouse and Robert G. Clouse, *Women in Ministry: Four Views* (Downers Grove, Ill.: InterVarsity, 1989). See also Stan Ingersoll, "Holiness Women: Recovering a Tradition," *Christian Century* 111:20 (29 June 1994): 632.

15. Elaine J. Lawless, *Handmaidens of the Lord: Pentecostal Women Preachers and Traditional Religion* (Philadelphia: University of Pennsylvania Press, 1988), and idem, *God's Peculiar People: Women's Voices and Folk Tradition in a Pentecostal Church* (Lexington: University Press of Kentucky, 1988).

16. Jerry Falwell, *Listen America!* (New York: Doubleday, 1980).

17. Recent discussion includes Ron Sider, "Our Selective Rage: A Pro-Life Ethic Means More than Being Anti-Abortion," *Christianity Today* 40:9 (12 August 1996): 14–15, and Frederica Mathewes-Green, "Pro-Life, Pro-Choice: Can We Talk?" *Christian Century* 113:1 (3 January 1996): 12–14. On evangelical views of the family, see Bill Gothard, *Research in Principles of Life* (Oak Brook, Ill.: Institute in Basic Youth Conflicts, 1986).

18. Although practices such as picketing at abortion clinics and other direct action techniques to make it more difficult for women to obtain abortions lie beyond the scope of the present discussion, many who engage in such exercises are evangelicals, and many who have been arrested have testified in court that evangelical religious faith motivated their conduct.

19. On this issue more generally see Judith Stacey and Susan Elizabeth Gerard, " 'We Are Not Doormats': The Influence of Feminism on Contemporary Evangelicals in the United States," in *Uncertain Terms: Negotiating Gender in American Culture*, edited by Faye Ginsburg and Anna Lowenhaupt Tsing (Boston: Beacon, 1990), pp. 98–117. Also insightful is Erling Jorstad, *Popular Religion in America: The Evangelical Voice* (Westport, Conn.: Greenwood, 1993), chap. 4.

20. The basic "text" for the Council is John Piper and Wayne A. Grudem, eds., *Recovering Biblical Manhood and Womanhood* (Westchester, Ill.: Crossway, 1991).

21. Two older, but representative statements are Carl F. H. Henry, "In and Out of the Gay World," in *Is Gay Good? Ethics, Theology, and Homosexuality*, edited by W. Dwight Oberholtzer (Philadelphia: Westminster, 1971), pp. 104–115, and Ruth Tiffany Barnhouse, "Homosexuality: A Symbolic Confusion," in *Homosexuality and Ethics*, edited by Edward Batchelor Jr. (New York: Pilgrim, 1980), pp. 79–85.

22. A recent study informed by a religious perspective is Andrew Young, *An Easy*

*Burden: The Civil Rights Movement and the Transformation of America* (San Francisco: HarperCollins, 1996). The classic study is David J. Garrow, *Bearing the Cross: Martin Luther King, Jr., and the Southern Christian Leadership Conference* (New York: Random House, 1986).

23. See Martin, *Prophet with Honor*, pp. 168–72.

24. Grant Wacker argues that evangelical parents moved to assert greater control over their children's education because they fear their children will come to scorn them. See Grant Wacker, "Searching for Norman Rockwell: Evangelicalism in Contemporary America," in *The Evangelical Tradition in America*, edited by Leonard I. Sweet (Macon, Ga.: Mercer University Press, 1984), pp. 289–315.

# 11
# Evangelical Spirituality

Alister McGrath effusively states in *Evangelicalism and the Future of Christianity*, "The Christian vision of the future now seems increasingly to belong to evangelicalism. . . ." His optimistic paean continues, "Evangelicalism is a high-octane faith that seems set to continue its upswing into the next millennium."[1] If there is a discouraging word to be found in McGrath's rosy scenario, it is with regard to "evangelical spirituality." In this crucial area McGrath fears evangelicals "may neglect the needs of the human heart" in spite of their many other achievements.[2]

Others with a more personal perspective on the issue lament the absence of a contemporary evangelical spirituality. Among these witnesses is Robert Webber, professor of theology at Wheaton College. Webber, son of a fundamentalist Baptist missionary and one-time minister in the Reformed Presbyterian Church, left his former faith in 1972 to enter the Episcopal denomination. He left evangelicalism for a more sacramental and liturgical tradition after concluding that the faith of his forebears "took away the mystery and power of the resurrection and turned it into a dry fact that had little to do with my personal struggle to live a Christian life."[3] Webber described his own search for spirituality in his *Evangelicals on the Canterbury Trail.*[4]

The word "spirituality" is notoriously difficult to define with precision although an adequate attempt is offered by Stanley Grenz. He says, "Spirituality, then, is the quest under the direction of the Holy Spirit, but with the cooperation of the believer for holiness. It is the pursuit of the life lived to the glory of God, in union with Christ and out of obedience to the Holy Spirit."[5] A number of points should be noted here. First, spirituality is the work of the third person of the Trinity on the willing heart of the believer. Second, Grenz follows the definition in his text by stating that the Christian concept of holiness must be firmly tied to the Scriptures.[6] Thus, the New Testament enjoins the believer to deny oneself through a mystical inner union with Christ, yet not at the expense of genuine service to others. Hence, a bona fide Christian spirituality contains a creative tension. It is not, as Donald Bloesch has noted, a neo-Platonic escape from the physical world, nor a "naturalistic mysticism, which celebrates the instinctual drives of man and the will to power and success."[7]

The observation of McGrath and the testimony of Webber support the perception that traditional evangelicalism often lacks this biblically centered form of spirituality. Instead, evangelicals tend to regard spirituality as a cognitive understanding of the biblical text rather than an emotional interaction with Scripture through extrarational human faculties like the imagination. The ethos of the Enlightenment, as seen in the neoscholastic approaches to Bible study and apologetics bequeathed to contemporary evangelicalism by seventeenth-century Reformed theologians like Turretini (and continued by the Princeton school), has transmuted "the Living Word" into Webber's dry "textbook of facts."[8]

This rationalistic style of spirituality appears in the attempts of evangelicals to program their approaches to the devotional life. This tendency stands out in the practice of evangelism and the use of the quiet time, a daily period of individual Bible reading, meditation, and prayer. No American evangelical group has been more rigorous in its attempt to program evangelism than the Southern Baptists. Although many examples could be cited to illustrate this programmatic tendency, one will suffice. In a 1961 work entitled *You Can Win Souls*, C. E. Autrey noted the urgency for individual evangelism ("it is the only way to reach the great masses of lost people"), then described a typical approach that Christians might use to share their faith with others. Several chapters attempted to deal with "hard cases" (the anxious, indifferent, Jews, Catholics, spiritists, and doubters) who resisted the generic approach. The rationale behind Autrey's work was that soul winning, which Southern Baptists believe is commanded by the Bible and thus part of the ideal spiritual life, can be routinized by a scripted, programmatic methodology that seeks to anticipate every eventuality.[9] What Autrey suggested was presented in painstaking detail one year later in *Evangelism Explosion*, a programmed guide to personal evangelism developed by *D. James Kennedy, the pastor of Coral Ridge Presbyterian Church in Fort Lauderdale, Florida.[10] By the 1980s, *Evangelism Explosion* was used by several evangelical denominations to train individuals in sharing their faith.

The quiet time is another example of evangelical programmed piety. A regular fixture of Christianity since its earliest history, it became a signature ritual of contemporary evangelicalism through the Higher Life movement by the dawn of the twentieth century.[11] Parachurch organizations like *Dawson Trotman's Navigators particularly have encouraged the practice of the quiet time in their discipleship literature since World War II.[12] Guides that instruct the believer step-by-step in the exercise roll off evangelical presses at a brisk pace even today.

The danger of programmed guides to spirituality, whether for instruction in witnessing or for one's devotional life, is that the practices they promote can become empty; the mere performance of the act is what confers a greater sense of spirituality. Of course, any spiritual exercise in any religious tradition, liturgical or evangelical, can become an empty form. Yet, because many evangelicals have adopted a rationalistic and routinized attitude toward spirituality, the reduction of evangelical piety to formalism serves only to accentuate the tenuous nature of the spirituality itself.[13]

However, it is misleading to assert that modern evangelicalism is devoid of a rigorous emphasis on the spiritual life. Heretofore, this examination has been restricted to what we have called elsewhere "intentional or card carrying evangelicals," that relatively small group of Christians who consider evangelicalism to be their primary category of religious identification. These are primarily the "neoevangelicals," the direct descendants of the early twentieth-century Baptist and Reformed tradition fundamentalists. If we expand our view to the much larger group of "unintentional evangelicals," the picture changes significantly.

Evangelicals who trace their religious lineage to Wesleyan Methodism consistently have emphasized the work of the Holy Spirit in the Christian life. John Wesley, in his *Plain Account of Christian Perfection* (1766), asserted that to be "perfect" was "to be sanctified throughout; even to have a heart so all-flaming with the love of God . . . as to continually offer up every thought, word, and work, as a spiritual sacrifice, acceptable to God, through Christ."[14] As Albert Outler has noted, Wesley's perfectionism was not absolute. Rather, it was "the fulfillment of faith's desire to love God above all else and all else in God, so far as conscious will and deliberate action are concerned."[15] This emphasis on the sanctified life as the heart of Christian spirituality came to the fore in American Methodism in the first half of the nineteenth century. Phoebe Palmer was instrumental in popularizing the notion of "entire sanctification" or "the baptism of the Holy Spirit." Unlike Wesley, who indicated that Christian perfection was a dynamic process, Palmer viewed sanctification as a state of grace distinct from salvation that was instantly attainable by faith.[16] By the end of the Civil War, a sizable Holiness faction had formed within Methodism. This group eventually coalesced into separate Holiness denominations and Pentecostal groups within American evangelicalism. In addition, a separate, although allied, non-Methodist strain of Holiness teachings matured into the Oberlin Perfectionism of Asa Mahan and Charles Finney, the Higher Life movement of William Boardman, and the American Keswick movement led by *Robert C. McQuilkin Jr. and *Charles G. Trumbull.

In the twentieth century, the greatest emphasis on evangelical spirituality as evidenced in the pursuit of the sanctified life has come from the various Holiness and Pentecostal groups. The Holiness movement antedates Pentecostalism and forms a link between the latter group and Wesleyan perfectionism.[17] Steven Land refers to Pentecostalism as a "third force in Christianity" alongside the Catholic/Eastern Orthodox and Protestant churches, and divides the worldwide movement into three main subgroups: (1) Pentecostals proper, (2) charismatics, and (3) "third-wavers."[18] An adequate examination of evangelical spirituality demands a closer look at the Holiness and Pentecostal groups.

Randall Balmer examined the Holiness movement in the 1980s through a visit to the Camp Freedom retreat center in St. Petersburg, Florida. At that time Balmer noted the distinctives of the Holiness tradition as an emphasis on sanctification or the "second blessing" of the Holy Spirit that followed the experience of salvation; a conviction that gifts of the Spirit, such as divine healing, were still operative in the Church; and a lively brand of worship. An overwhelming emphasis on personal holiness meant that the true Christian must be "separate" from the dominant trends of the nonbelieving world. Says Balmer: "[M]oral strictures and behavioral taboos are common, even though they have eased somewhat in recent years. Dancing, card playing, alcohol, motion pictures, and 'worldly' music are all viewed askance in holiness circles. They are entertainments of the devil that lure the unwitting into sin, debauchery, and prurience."[19]

The modern American Holiness movement has a long tradition of social reform that can be traced back to the early nineteenth century.[20] This reform impulse appeared in the abolitionist platform of the Wesleyan Methodists; the work of *A. B. Simpson, a Presbyterian minister, who was greatly motivated by Holiness spirituality to form the Christian and Missionary Alliance in 1887 in order to minister to the poor of New York City; and the greater role granted to women in the holiness ministry.[21] A prominent example of the latter is the itinerant revivalism of *Maria B. Woodworth-Etter at the turn of the twentieth century. However, Balmer finds little contemporary evidence of this social concern in his examination. Instead, the overwhelming emphasis is on personal holiness and separation from the larger world. Donald Dayton blames this "great reversal" on the influence of dispensational premillennialism on the Holiness movement, a desire on the part of Holiness cause to distance itself from the liberal Social Gospel movement, and the Wesleyan belief that one can "fall from grace" which necessitates constant self-examination and separation from temptation and evil.[22] Although significant as a force within the history of evangelical spirituality, the modern Holiness movement is much less vibrant than it was in the late nineteenth century.

On the other hand, Pentecostal or "third force" spirituality is a powerful presence within contemporary evangelicalism. This spirituality is best understood through an analysis of Pentecostalism's rituals and characteristics. These are: (1) a high degree of physical activity as evidence of the work of the Holy Spirit in the believer, (2) a primarily oral and narrative liturgy and theology, (3) an "already-not yet" eschatological view of the work of God, (4) a dualistic perspective of key aspects of the Christian life, and (5) an appreciation of spiritual maturity that is both crisis (isolated event) and development (continuous process).[23]

Pentecostals, as a whole, express the work of the Spirit through bodily expression. Examples of this activity are raising the hands in praise, clapping to the glory of God, extending the hand of fellowship, joining hands for prayer, dancing, swaying, prostration (being "slain in the Spirit"), fasting, and divine healing.[24] Divine healing may be the most characteristic of Pentecostal expressions. Healing is rooted in the presupposition that all sickness ultimately is related to sin and Satan. Hence, if one possesses the Pentecostal power over sin and Satan as evidenced Acts 2–3, the sanctified believer also has power over sickness. While various Holiness revivalists pioneered the notion of a faith healing ministry in nineteenth-century America, a genuine "healing revival" did not emerge in Pentecostal circles until the post–World War II era. The two giants of this revival were *William M. Branham and *Oral Roberts. The two evangelists were polar opposites in their demeanor; Branham was quiet and humble, while Roberts was gregarious and flamboyant. Yet, as they ministered to thousands of souls in hundreds of nights of tent meetings, the impact of their respective ministries on the popularization of divine healing within Pentecostalism is undeniable.[25] In addition, Branham and Roberts were largely responsible for fueling the growth of the nondenominational "charismatic movement," of which *Kathryn Kuhlman was probably the best-known faith healer.

Pentecostal spirituality also emphasizes a highly oral and narrative liturgy and theology. Russell Spittler notes that as part of a relatively young religious movement, Pentecostals "have not yet produced any substantial theological literature."[26] Nevertheless, a lively oral tradition, expressed both in words and music, exists. "Speaking in tongues" is viewed as a sign of the baptism of the Holy Spirit. Although Pentecostals differ over whether or not tongues are a necessary sign of the truly sanctified believer, they freely employ the practice both in their personal devotional lives and corporate worship services. Whether viewed as a unknown prayer language (*glossolalia*) or an unlearned foreign language (*xenoglossolalia*), tongues are part of the spiritual testimony that issues from the personal religious experience of the believer. As with preaching, teaching, words of wisdom and knowledge, and prophecy, the intent of this spiritual gift is to edify the Church.[27]

A key presupposition that undergirds all Pentecostal spirituality is an "already-not yet" eschatology. The earliest American Pentecostals like *Charles Fox Parham and *William J. Seymour were convinced that the signs and wonders they observed at the beginning of the twentieth century were precursors of a new spiritual age.[28] Modern Pentecostals implicitly retain that expectation, yet realize that the new age will not be consummated fully until the final victory of Christ over Satan at the end of human history. Through Pentecostal worship, the sanctified believer experiences a foretaste of the full blessings of the end of the age as manifested in spiritual events like divine healing, speaking in tongues, answered prayer, anointed preaching, and praise.[29]

While "already-not yet" speaks more to the Pentecostal awareness of how history ultimately will be disposed, the present world-view of the movement is fundamentally dualistic in structure. Some dualistic elements are mutually exclusive; for example, God and Satan, saint and sinner, and light and darkness.

Other elements are less dualistic, although the first element is valued more than the second. Thus, it is the "heart," as the place where reason, will, and emotions are integrated, that takes precedence over the "mind" when it comes to discerning spiritual matters. Similarly, Scripture, as the bearer of the living Holy Spirit, takes precedence over "creeds."[30] This conviction partly explains the devotion Pentecostals have for the Bible and also why they are less troubled by the various inerrancy battles that have consumed other American evangelical groups.[31]

Finally, Pentecostal spirituality can be viewed as both a series of isolated events and as a continuous process. Salvation through receiving Christ as personal savior and sanctification through the baptism of the Holy Spirit are events in time and space. Yet both these events are not truly isolated. Rather, they are like links in a chain that represents the sovereign work of God from the beginning of time until the end of history. The result of this process is not only the redemption and sanctification of the individual; it is also the creation of the eschatological Kingdom of God through which Christ eventually will be manifested as "all in all."

Thus, Pentecostal spirituality can be identified through a series of rituals and beliefs. Although creating a common pattern, they are not practiced uniformly by all Pentecostal groups. In fact, some rather controversial variations within contemporary Pentecostal spirituality have had an impact on the larger evangelical subculture. Two of these better known aberrations are the Word of Faith movement and the power religion teachings of *John Wimber and the Vineyard Christian Fellowship.

The Word of Faith movement exerts a powerful pull on contemporary Pentecostal spirituality. The people who have popularized its beliefs are some of the most widely recognized names in contemporary evangelicalism: Kenneth Hagin, Kenneth and Gloria Copeland, Charles Capps, and Robert Tilton. Through a canny use of the media and an appealing message, these individuals have attracted a host of disciples to their ministries. The basic presupposition of Word of Faith adherents is that there are two types of knowledge: revelation (which is not mediated by the senses but comes from God) and sense (which is cognitive). Revelation knowledge is the power behind the positive confession that permits the believer to declare victory in faith over sickness and poverty through the utterance of the promises of God from the Scriptures. Deuteronomy 28 is used to demonstrate that sickness is a curse of the law. Then Galatians 3:13 is quoted to prove that Christ has redeemed believers from the curse of the law which, in this view, includes sickness. Thus Kenneth Hagin states unequivocally: "Don't ever tell anyone sickness is the will of God for us [Christians]. It isn't! Healing and health are the will of God for mankind. If sickness were the will of God, heaven would be filled with sickness and disease."[32] A similar hermeneutical approach is used to confirm the Word of Faith conviction that all believers should enjoy material prosperity. The key biblical verses on this theme are God's pledge to make Joshua's way prosperous (Joshua 1:8) and various passages promising prosperity to the righteous (Nehemiah 2:20; Psalm 1:3; Psalm 35:27; and 3 John 2). Word of Faith advocates insist that believers live under the provisions of the Abrahamic covenant. Just as Abraham was blessed by God in a spiritual, physical, and financial fashion, so should contemporary Christians expect to "name and claim" financial blessings. To quote Gloria Copeland: "Make this quality decision concerning your prosperity: God's blessing of prosperity belongs to me. I WILL receive it. Make this decision and you will begin to enjoy the financial blessing that has belonged to you since you became a believer in Jesus Christ.[33]

To suggest that such a set of beliefs has caused an uproar in contemporary evangelicalism is an understatement. Pentecostals have been especially energetic in their refutations of Word of Faith doctrines, fearing that the uninitiated might misconstrue "name it and claim it" theology as orthodox Pentecostal belief. D. R. McConnell and H. Terris Neuman have demonstrated that the key convictions of the Word of Faith movement came from nineteenth-century mind-healing sects like New Thought, Christian Science, and the Unity School.[34] The two cardinal beliefs of all these groups were that sickness is an illusion that could be overcome through "right thinking" and that material prosperity is the legitmate birthright of all children of God. As early as 1980, Charles Farah noted the gnostic elements within the Word of Faith movement. Calling the movement an idolization of the American concept of success, Farah referred to it as "a burgeoning heresy."[35]

Despite the call to alarm by many and the sensational public fall of a key advocate like Robert Tilton,[36] the Word of Faith doctrines remain popular in contemporary evangelical spirituality. Key elements appear more subtly in the writings of *Norman Vincent Peale and Robert Schuller, not to mention the motivational teachings of Zig Ziglar.[37] Whether the Word of Faith group owes its popularity to a crassly materialistic modern culture or to appeals to the basic human longings for comfort and success, it is not going to lose its appeal in the near future. To that end some might say that the movement's own "success" is the best validation of its beliefs.

Contrary to the "self" orientation of the Word of Faith following, the "power religion" movement associated with John Wimber found its origins in an evangelistic imperative. Wimber, formerly an unbelieving jazz musician, became a Christian in 1962. Although he was highly successful as a Bible teacher, Wimber did not experience real joy and power in his devotional life until he accepted the validity of miraculous healing and supernatural spiritual gifts in 1977. Shortly thereafter Wimber started a prayer group that eventually became the Vineyard Christian Fellowship, a church in Anaheim, California, that, although officially non-Pentecostal and noncharismatic, focused on miracles and the exercise of supernatural gifts as signs of the powerful working of God.[38] Within the first ten years of its existence, the Vineyard church grew from seventeen to more than 6,000 members and spawned hundreds of other "affiliated" Vineyard congregations all over the world.[39]

The rapid growth of the Vineyard congregation and its emphasis on power religion caught the attention of Peter Wagner, a former missionary to Bolivia and head of the Fuller Seminary School of World Mission. Independently of Wimber, Wagner had concluded that an emphasis on signs and wonders was a major reason behind the phenomenal growth of Pentecostal Christianity, particularly in Third World countries. Wagner believed that a ministry built upon these signs and wonders would be a powerful evangelistic tool in the world Christian missionary movement. The perspectives of Wagner and Wimber converged when the two united to teach a course, "The Miraculous and Church Growth (MC510)," on the Fuller campus from 1982 to 1986. The course, which included laboratory sessions in which demons were exorcised, words of knowledge were received, and divine healings were performed, quickly became the most popular and controversial ever taught at the Pasadena institution.[40] So controversial was MC510 that the president of Fuller, David Hubbard, suspended it in 1986 and appointed a faculty task force to study the course and suggest under what form it should be continued. The task force recommended that the course be retained, but without the problematic laboratory requirement with its emphasis on the miraculous.[41] Wimber continued his association with Fuller but concentrated increasingly on his pastoral duties at the Vineyard. He also clarified his theology in two books: *Power Evangelism* (1986) and *Power Healing* (1987). The gist of both works is that supernatural phenomena should be normative in the exercise of Christian faith in the present age. The display of the power of God's working (hence the appellation "power religion") in the form of miraculous healings, prophetic and unusual utterances, even raisings from the dead, is the surest sign of the genuineness of Christianity to an unbelieving world.[42]

Wimber and his like-minded associates were especially keen to bring "power evangelism" to the secularized Western nations so that churches might experience the kind of growth and renewal their counterparts were enjoying in Africa, South America, and Asia. Wimber defined power evangelism as "a spontaneous, Spirit-inspired, empowered presentation of the gospel. Power evangelism is evangelism that is preceded and undergirded by supernatural demonstrations of God's presence. . . . In power evangelism, resistance to the gospel is overcome by the demonstration of God's power in supernatural events."[43] Wimber contrasted power evangelism with "programmatic evangelism," a presentation of the gospel to passive listeners through rational arguments and without a display of signs and wonders.[44] The fact that it is not based on a visible demonstration of God's power makes programmatic evangelism an incomplete form of witnessing in Wimber's estimation.[45]

Clearly Wimber's Vineyard movement is a dynamic and growing force within contemporary evangelicalism. The movement is difficult to categorize because it replicates the traditional Pentecostal/charismatic emphasis on spiritual gifts and miracles while eschewing the usual Pentecostal/charismatic labels.[46] Its focus on the Kingdom of God's breaking into human history to combat Satan's kingdom through power encounters is attractive to many evangelicals who believe that the Bible validates the supernatural and the miraculous.[47] The evangelistic rationale behind the teachings of Wimber also resonates with the historical concern of evangelicals for leading souls to the Christian faith. The otherworldliness of the Vineyard movement is a very attractive alternative to a modern culture saturated with naturalism and materialism.

However, the "signs and wonders" approach to Christianity has been criticized by numerous evangelicals as inadequate. Tim Stafford quotes theologian *J. I. Packer, who has said that many Christians "see the powers of the kingdom operating, but mainly in regeneration, sanctification, the Spirit as comforter, [and] the transformation of the inner life, rather than in physical miracles." Packer implies that the power of God is evidenced genuinely not in the performance of miracles that remove suffering, but in the living of a godly life in the midst of suffering.[48] Wallace Benn and Mark Burkill note that Wimber tends to establish a metaphysical dualism between God and Satan—"two gods battling it out with the kingdom front being extended by miracles and power encounters." The authors contend that this approach reduces humans to mere pawns and minimizes the sovereignty of God's dominion "over all aspects of human life."[49] Finally, Donald Kammer questions the highly provocative suggestion made by Wimber in *Power Healing* that Christians can be "demonized," or possessed by malevolent beings that adversely affect them "physically, mentally, and spiritually."[50]

How might one summarize the state of evangelical spirituality at the end of the twentieth century? That judgment is contingent on the group of evangelicals under study. "Intentional evangelicals" appear somewhat unsettled with their current devotional condition. Their legacy from the Enlightenment—an overriding emphasis on "routinizing" personal piety in a cognitive fashion through programs of evangelism and manuals of "learned holiness"—has caused many like Webber to search for spirituality in more liturgical traditions. Others, such as McGrath and Packer, have pointed to the wealth of spiritual wisdom found in the writings of the Protestant Reformers and the Puritans.[51] Even while rationalism dominated Western thinking in the eighteenth century, those whom we have labeled "unintentional evangelicals" (principally those who trace their theological heritage to Wesleyan Methodism) made the search for personal holiness an important part of their religious pilgrimages. In America that quest materialized into the Holiness movement and the various "waves" of Pentecostalism with all their diverse beliefs and rituals. The fact that Pentecostalism is no longer merely a faith of the "disinherited" in America is seen in the adoption of many Pentecostal worship practices by non-Pentecostal evangelicals (the use of praise choruses, a much more physical style of worship, more openness to the validity of spiritual gifts and supernatural phenomena) that were formerly rejected as unseemly and unacceptable.[52] Although the growing popularity of the "praise and worship" phenomenon still causes consternation among some evangelicals, the impact of these practices on evangelical worship may have advanced to the point that we can speak legitimately of the "pentecostalization" of evangelical spirituality.[53] In fact, Donald Miller has declared that in an increasingly postmodern climate when many assumptions of Enlightenment thought have been challenged, Pentecostalism's emphasis on profound religious experience that does not necessarily "conform to the norms of logic and rational discourse" will enable it to reinvent American Protestantism in the next millennium.[54] It remains to be seen whether or not Miller is a prophet on this issue, although all the signs suggest that his thesis is valid.

## NOTES

1. Alister McGrath, *Evangelicalism and the Future of Christianity* (Downers Grove, Ill.: InterVarsity, 1995), p. 10.

2. Ibid., p. 120.

3. Robert E. Webber, *Evangelicals on the Canterbury Trail: Why Evangelicals Are Attracted to the Liturgical Church* (Waco, Tex.: Word, 1985), p. 24.

4. Other evangelicals have entered the Roman Catholic and Eastern Orthodox traditions for similar reasons. The most prominent individual to make this move recently is Franky Schaeffer, the son of Francis Schaeffer, who detailed his spiritual trek from evangelicalism to orthodoxy in *Dancing Alone: The Quest for Orthodox Faith in the Age of False Religion* (Brookline, Mass.: Holy Cross Orthodox Press, 1994).

5. Stanley J. Grenz, *Revisioning Evangelical Theology: A Fresh Agenda for the 21st Century* (Downers Grove, Ill.: InterVarsity, 1993), p. 42.

6. Ibid.

7. Donald G. Bloesch, *The Future of Evangelical Christianity: A Call for Unity amid Diversity* (Garden City, N.Y.: Doubleday, 1983), p. 132.

8. Webber, *Evangelicals on the Canterbury Trail*, p. 23.

9. C. E. Autrey, *You Can Win Souls* (Nashville: Broadman, 1961).

10. The development of *Evangelism Explosion* as an integral part of Kennedy's ministry is detailed in Herbert L. Williams, *D. James Kennedy: The Man and His Ministry* (Nashville: Thomas Nelson, 1990).

11. See the discussion in D. G. Reid, "Spirituality: Protestant," in *Dictionary of Christianity in America*, edited by Daniel G. Reid et al. (Downers Grove, Ill.: InterVarsity, 1990), pp. 1123–27.

12. A good example of this is the pamphlet by Warren and Ruth Myers entitled *How to Have a Quiet Time* (Colorado Springs, Colo.: NavPress, 1989).

13. McGrath, *Evangelicalism and the Future of Christianity*, pp. 128–29. McGrath suggests the obsolescence of the traditional quiet time saying it is "a virtual impossibility" for many contemporary evangelicals to whom "personal space is a rare and cherished luxury" (p. 128).

14. John Wesley, *A Plain Account of Christian Perfection* (reprint, London: Epworth, 1983), p. 30.

15. "Introduction," in *John Wesley*, edited by Albert C. Outler (New York: Oxford University Press, 1964), pp. 31–32.

16. Jean Miller Schmidt, "Holiness and Perfection," in *Encyclopedia of the American Religious Experience*, edited by Charles H. Lippy and Peter W. Williams, 3 vols. (New York: Scribners, 1988), 2:814.

17. The standard work on the subject remains John L. Peters, *Christian Perfection and American Methodism* (New York: Abingdon, 1956).

18. Steven J. Land, "Pentecostal Spirituality: Living in the Spirit," in *Christian Spirituality: Post-Reformation and Modern, World Spirituality: An Encyclopedic History of the Religious Quest*, vol. 18, edited by Louis Dupré and Don E. Saliers in collaboration with John Meyendorff (New York: Crossroad, 1989), pp. 481–83. Land's classification is taken from C. Peter Wagner, *The Third Wave of the Holy Spirit: Encountering the Power of Signs and Wonders* (Ann Arbor, Mich.: Servant Books, 1988), p. 13. In Wagner's typology, "Pentecostals proper" refers to the established Pentecostal denominations; "charismatics" are those who subscribe to many Pentecostal beliefs (especially a postconversion baptism in the Holy Spirit) but who remain in non-Pentecostal denominations; and "third-wavers" are primarily those who have experienced a renewal of the Spirit but do not recognize it as an experience separate from conversion. Land states that the emphasis of "third-wavers" is on "signs and wonders, healings, and power encounters" (p. 483).

19. Randall Balmer, *Mine Eyes Have Seen the Glory: A Journey into the Evangelical Subculture in America* (New York: Oxford University Press, 1989), p. 192.

20. See Donald W. Dayton, *Discovering an Evangelical Heritage* (Peabody, Mass.: Hendrickson, 1976).

21. For an examination of A. B. Simpson's spirituality, which formed the core of his social ministry, see Bill Pitts, "Holiness as Spirituality: The Religious Quest of A. B. Simpson," in *Modern Christian Spirituality: Methodological and Historical Essays*, edited by Bradley C. Hanson (Atlanta: Scholars Press, 1990), pp. 223–48.

22. Dayton, *Discovering an Evangelical Heritage*, pp. 121–35.

23. Land, "Pentecostal Spirituality," pp. 484–91.

24. Daniel E. Albrecht, "Pentecostal Spirituality: Looking Through the Lens of Ritual," *Pneuma* 14:2 (Fall 1992): 111–14.

25. See David Edwin Harrell Jr., *All Things Are Possible: The Healing and Charismatic Revivals in Modern America* (Bloomington: Indiana University Press, 1975), pp. 27–52.

26. Russell P. Spittler, "Spirituality, Pentecostal and Charismatic," in *Dictionary of Pentecostal and Charismatic Movements*, edited by Stanley M. Burgess and Gary B. McGee (Grand Rapids, Mich.: Zondervan, 1988), p. 805.

27. This is the claim made in Larry Christenson, *Speaking in Tongues and Its Significance for the Church* (Minneapolis, Minn.: Dimension, 1968), pp. 110–24.

28. Cecil M. Robeck Jr., "Faith, Hope, Love, and the Eschaton," *Pneuma* 14:1 (Spring 1992): 1–3.

29. For an explanation of how Pentecostals view history, see Grant Wacker, "Are the Golden Oldies Still Worth Playing? Reflections on History Writing among Early Pentecostals," *Pneuma* 8:2 (Fall 1986): 84–85.

30. Land, "Pentecostal Spirituality," pp. 486–89.

31. Russell P. Spittler, "Scripture and the Theological Enterprise: View From a Big Canoe," in *The Use of the Bible in Theology: Evangelical Options*, edited by Robert K. Johnston (Atlanta: John Knox, 1985), pp. 56–77.

32. Kenneth E. Hagin, *Redeemed from Poverty, Sickness, and Death* (Tulsa, Okla.: Faith Library Publications, 1983), p. 16.

33. Gloria Copeland, *God's Will Is Prosperity* (Fort Worth, Tex.: KC Publications, 1978), p. 38.

34. D. R. McConnell, *A Different Gospel*, updated ed. (Peabody, Mass.: Hendrickson, 1995), and H. Terris Neuman, "Cultic Origins of Word-Faith Theology within the Charismatic Movement," *Pneuma* 12:1 (Spring 1990): 32–55.

35. Charles Farah Jr., "A Critical Analysis: The 'Roots' and 'Fruit' of Faith Formula Theology," paper presented to the Society for Pentecostal Studies, Tulsa, Oklahoma, November 1980, p. 26.

36. See John W. Kennedy, "End of the Line for Tilton?" *Christianity Today* 37 (13 September 1993): 82.

37. The Word of Faith elements in the teachings of Peale and Schuller are noted in Neuman, "Cultic Origins of Word-Faith Theology," pp. 49–50. Ziglar's doctrines are examined in Cynthia Schaibles, "The Gospel of the Good Life," *Eternity* 32:2 (February 1981): 27.

38. John Wimber with Kevin Springer, *Power Evangelism* (San Francisco: Harper & Row, 1986), pp. xv-xxi.

39. C. Peter Wagner, "Foreword" to *Power Evangelism*, p. x. As of 1997 the Vineyard "movement" had 400 churches in the United States and almost 200 abroad. See Donald E. Miller, *Reinventing American Protestantism: Christianity in the New Millennium* (Berkeley: University of California Press, 1997), p. 50.

40. Donald Kammer, "The Perplexing Power of John Wimber's Power Encounters," *Churchman* 106:1 (1992): 46–47.

41. The report of the faculty task force was published in *Ministry and the Miraculous: A Case Study at Fuller Theological Seminary*, edited by Lewis B. Smedes with a foreword by David Allan Hubbard (Pasadena, Calif.: Fuller Theological Seminary, 1987).

42. Wimber, *Power Evangelism*, p. 16.

43. Ibid., p. 35.

44. This could be construed as a criticism of the traditional routinized approach to evangelism mentioned earlier in this chapter.

45. Wimber, *Power Evangelism*, pp. 45–47.

46. Wagner has specifically refused the charismatic label while avowing "nothing but admiration and praise for the so-called charismatic movement." See Wagner, *Third Wave of the Holy Spirit*, p. 54.

47. This interpretation of "Kingdom theology" is a major theme of George Eldon Ladd and is best presented in his work *A Theology of the New Testament* (Grand Rapids, Mich.: Eerdmans, 1974), pp. 45–134.

48. Tim Stafford, "Testing the Wine from John Wimber's Vineyard," *Christianity Today* 30 (8 August 1986): 22.

49. Wallace Benn and Mark Burkill, "A Theological and Pastoral Critique of the Teachings of John Wimber," *Churchman* 101:2 (1987): 102.

50. Kammer, "The Perplexing Power of John Wimber's Power Encounters," p. 50. See also the chapter entitled "Healing the Demonized" in Wimber, *Power Healing*, pp. 97–125. Edward N. Gross, *Miracles, Demons, and Spiritual Warfare: An Urgent Call for Discernment* (Grand Rapids, Mich.: Baker, 1990), takes Wimber to task for asserting that born-again Christians can be sufficiently inhabited by demons and that deliverance can only be obtained by exorcism (p. 163).

51. See Alister E. McGrath, *Spirituality in an Age of Change: Rediscovering the Spirit of the Reformers* (Grand Rapids, Mich.: Zondervan, 1994), and J. I. Packer, *A Quest for Godliness: The Puritan Vision of the Christian Life* (Wheaton, Ill.: Crossway, 1990).

52. The disinherited theme of American Pentecostalism was developed at length in

Robert Mapes Anderson, *Vision of the Disinherited: The Making of American Pentecostalism* (New York: Oxford University Press, 1979).

53. See the critique in Darryl G. Hart, ''Post-Modern Evangelical Worship,'' *Calvin Theological Journal* 30:2 (November 1995): 451–59.

54. Miller, *Reinventing American Protestantism*, p. 23.

# 12
# Parachurch Movements: Sustaining Modern American Evangelicalism

American Christianity has long relied on auxiliary agencies not controlled by individual churches or denominations to accomplish particular goals or provide needed services. Because individuals or groups supported their work on a voluntary basis, such agencies in the antebellum period were often called ''voluntary societies.'' Historians have spoken of them as collectively constituting a ''benevolent empire,'' a designation that also reflected the aim of such groups to advance the well-being or benevolence of society. Now analysts call such groups ''parachurch movements'' to emphasize how these organizations flourish alongside of the churches in a complementary and symbiotic relationship.[1] Historian Joel Carpenter convincingly argues that modern American evangelicals and their fundamentalist cousins built and nourished networks of parachurch organizations that sustained an evangelical identity in a hostile cultural ethos and laid the groundwork for the evangelical resurgence of the later twentieth century.[2]

Classifying parachurch movements poses many challenges, for the sheer variety of evangelical interests they represent is staggering. Evangelical forays into the political realm, for example, spawned a host of parachurch movements. Endeavors to use every communications medium generated different kinds of parachurch organizations, ranging from publishing houses and booksellers associations to the National Religious Broadcasters. The broadest inclusive understanding of parachurch movements also includes the many educational ventures of American evangelicals. Another kind of parachurch group links together evangelicals with common professional interests or who offer professional services to individuals or evangelical businesses. The Wesleyan Theological Society, an organization for scholarly inquiry into the Holiness tradition, illustrates the first, as does the American Scientific Affiliation, an outfit primarily for conservative Christian scientists. The Christian Ministries Management Institute is among the more significant nondenominational agencies that provide a range of services to evangelical businesses. Then, too, there are countless Christian support groups that arose primarily in the later twentieth century for evangelical Christians with shared personal needs or interests. Included here would also be organizations such as the Christian Business Men's Committee U.S.A. (founded in 1937 and headquartered in Glen Elyn, Illinois), the Full Gospel Business Men's Fellowship International (FGBMFI), Women's Aglow Fellowship, Christian Women's Clubs (with national offices at Stonecroft Ministries in Kansas City, Missouri), the Patricia French Christian Charm Schools and Patricia French Cosmetics, and others.[3] Another that emerged in the 1990s is Promise Keepers, which draws thousands of men to large conferences and rallies and then to small support groups sponsored by local congregations across the nation. Organizations with a single-issue focus form yet another type of parachurch group. The Rutherford Institute, for example, deals exclusively with religious freedom issues; the Creation Science Institute exists solely to refute evolutionary theories of the development of species.

Here the focus falls primarily on those organizations whose aim is evangelistic; that is, they labor to bring individuals into a personal relationship with Jesus Christ. Some work outside the United States, although their support comes from Americans and in most cases their headquarters are in the United States. Others follow in the wake of the Christian Endeavor Society, founded in 1881, in targeting adolescents and young adults in order to assure transmission of the truth to future generations. A secondary focus encompasses parachurch agencies connecting independent congregations with each other or bringing evangelical denominations and groups into cooperative association. Among moderate evangelicals, the most well-known example of the latter is the National Association of Evangelicals. The former includes groups as different as the Christian Holiness Association, with roots in nineteenth-century camp meetings, and the American Council of Christian Churches, established by separatist fundamentalist Carl McIntire. Not every parachurch group falls neatly into one category. The National Association of Evangelicals, for example, counts more than fifty evangelical denominations as constituent members. But hundreds of schools, local and state associations of churches, other organizations, and individuals also hold membership. The Young Men's Christian Association (YMCA) began with evangelism as its primary mission at its founding in England in 1844, but today has a more diverse character. The Evangelical Women's Caucus has developed as a support group for evangelical feminist pastors and academics, while still prodding evangelicals about issues of concern to women. The story of parachurch movements lures one into a maze with countless nooks and crannies, but all at some point have promoted personal religious experience and a Christian life informed by scripture and evangelical truth.

Promoting conversion lies at the heart of evangelicalism, and the Great Commission in Matthew 28, "Go ye therefore, and teach all nations" (KJV), has inspired hundreds of evangelical missionary endeavors.[4] Many emerged in the antebellum period, but interest in global evangelization mushroomed in the last third of the nineteenth century, especially with the founding of "faith missions" where organizers and missionaries believed that God would provide the necessary financial backing. No salary guarantees were offered missionaries, and unsolicited contributions from individuals and churches were preferred over direct appeals for support. The prototype was the China Inland Mission (CIM), organized in England in 1865 but an integral part of American evangelical missions since 1888. That year CIM founder James Hudson Taylor spoke in North America at the premillennial dispensationalist Niagara Bible Conference and at a conference sponsored by revivalist *Dwight L. Moody. As its name suggests, CIM's focus was evangelizing China. After the Communist regime forced missionaries to leave the People's Republic of China, CIM expanded the geographic scope of its work, changed its name to the Overseas Missionary Fellowship, and began to recruit Asians to serve along with North Americans and Europeans.[5] Cognate endeavors include the Central American Mission (1890; now CAM International), Sudan Interior Mission (1893), and the Africa Inland Mission (1895). The last has headquarters in Bristol, England, but its origins are American; Scottish immigrant Peter Cameron Scott organized the Africa Inland Mission with the support of the Philadelphia Missionary Society and the evangelical Philadelphia Bible Institute.[6] The Scandinavian Alliance Mission, known today as The Evangelical Alliance Mission (TEAM) has sponsored a more diverse ministry than most almost since its inception in 1890. Founded by Fredrik Franson, the group intended to send missionaries to China, gathering most of its support from Scandinavian immigrants since Franson was Swedish by birth. In addition to evangelism, it has supported medical missions, Christian camping, church development on a global scale, and other programs to spread the gospel.

In time, some umbrella organizations emerged to support mission agencies by coordinating publications, providing promotional conferences, and facilitating cooperative undertakings. The Interdenominational Foreign Missions Association, started in 1917, counts nearly 100 individual mission societies and efforts as members; the Evangelical Foreign Missions Association, which emerged from the National Association of Evangelicals in 1945, has around ninety constituent members. The two organizations work together in Evangelical Missions Information Service, publisher of *Evangelical Missions Quarterly*. World Gospel Mission, started in 1910 as the National Holiness Missionary Society, serves as a coordinating agency for missionaries from churches linked to the Christian Holiness Association; as with so many others, China was its target, but today World Gospel Mission sponsors work in Latin America, Asia, and Africa. Several enterprises have undertaken to provide Bibles and evangelical Christian literature for missionary use. The World Literature Crusade, founded in Canada in 1946 but opened a U.S. office in 1952 and now operating from Chatsworth, California, hopes to place evangelical literature in every home throughout the world. This goal has required recruiting evangelicals from numerous countries to translate materials into their indigenous languages. Translation of the Bible into every known language has been the goal of Wycliffe Bible Translators since its founding in 1934. Its work has included some missionary activities of its own as well as organizing highly regarded linguistic institutes, an unintended offshoot of its translation efforts. Wycliffe Bible Translators has also worked closely with the World Home Bible League in its efforts to place in every home the text of the Scriptures in the language of its residents.[7] American evangelicals support more than 200 other foreign missionary agencies and organizations. One is as humanitarian as evangelistic, however. Evangelist Bob Pierce started World Vision International in 1950 to raise funds for Koreans who had suffered loss and for children orphaned during the Korean conflict. Its work spread elsewhere in Asia, and then to Latin America and Africa. By century's end, World Vision supported between 4,000 and 5,000 separate projects, including emergency relief and community development endeavors. But assisting children in need remained its overarching focus.[8]

Reaching American youth with the gospel has motivated numerous evangelical parachurch organizations, although many have also expanded the scope of their work over time. Of longest standing is the YMCA, founded in London in 1844. The YMCA opened its first U.S. center in Boston in 1851. In the later nineteenth century, it was a major evangelical vehicle to reach unchurched young men in the nation's urban industrial centers, as well as on campuses. It received the enthusiastic support of Dwight L. Moody, who worked for a time with the Chicago YMCA. Today the YMCA operates more as a health club and social service agency, but for much of its history, providing housing and meals for laborers, distributing Bibles, offering Bible study and religious education classes, and assisting the poor were central to its program. The Young Women's Christian Association (YWCA), a cognate but separate agency, began its U.S. labors in 1866, offering low-cost housing in a wholesome, Christian environment to young unmarried women who came to cities for employment. By the later twentieth century, both the YMCA and YWCA had lost a distinctive evangelical cast.[9] But the YMCA did spur one of the earliest ministries oriented to college and university students, the Student Volunteer Movement (SVM), originally the Student Volunteer Movement for Foreign Missions, which began in 1886, also with the encouragement of Dwight L. Moody.[10] Robert Wilder, one of its founders, toured American campuses, recruiting students to enter foreign missions work after graduation. As the SVM became more a medium for ecumenical campus ministry, albeit still oriented to community and social service, it lost some of its evangelical flavor. One result was the formation in 1936 of the Student Foreign Missions Fellowship by students from Wheaton College and Columbia Bible College who believed that SVM had lost direction and purpose. Another was the merger of the SVM with other ecumenical campus ministry agencies in 1959 to create the National Student Christian Federation, which in turn was absorbed into the University Christian Movement until its demise in 1969. Historians suggest, however, that the SVM spurred some 20,000 students in the United States and Canada to embark on missionary careers.

Most evangelical ministries to college and university students are twentieth-century parachurch organizations. Three of the most well-established are InterVarsity Christian Fellowship (IVCF), Campus Crusade for Christ, and the Navigators.[11] IVCF arose when several independent ministries in England came together in the late nineteenth century; its first U.S. group was established at the University of Michigan in 1939. Like other parachurch movements, IVCF is transdenominational, reaching out to students regardless of formal affiliation. With groups on some 750 U.S. campuses, it has attracted media attention because of its Urbana Missionary Conference, held every three years at the University of Illinois. Conference attendance approaches 20,000. InterVarsity supports other ministries through its publishing arm, InterVarsity Press, which produces academic and popular materials linking an evangelical understanding of Christian faith to many areas of inquiry. Campus Crusade for Christ was the name *Bill Bright gave in 1951 to his ministry at the University of California at Los Angeles.[12] Campus Crusade has developed around its founder's teachings, particularly Bright's "four spiritual laws" that have been distributed in printed form to more than a billion people around the world: (1) God loves all people and has a plan for everyone's life, (2) sin separates people from God, making it impossible for them to know God's love and plan, (3) that love and plan can be realized through Christ, (4) all that is necessary is personal conversion and commitment to Christ.[13] Campus Crusade targeted especially the "Jesus people" of the 1970s, sponsoring Explo '72, a gathering that drew around 85,000 young people to Dallas, Texas. A similar event in Korea two years later attracted an audience estimated at more than 1.25 million. More recent endeavors have used the latest communications technology; Explo '85, for example, linked persons at some 100 sites through satellite hookups. The Navigators tracks its origins to the ministry of *Dawson Trotman, who in 1933 began evangelistic work among navy personnel (hence the name) in San Pedro, California.[14] Although a presence at many colleges, Navigators has never been exclusively a campus ministry and at first was primarily an outreach to persons on U.S. military bases. In the Navigators' lexicon, their aim is to "disciple" new believers, to help nurture spiritual growth and development through Bible study and prayer. By the end of the twentieth century, the Navigators were developing programs for business people and expanding evangelistic efforts outside the United States. The core of campus ministry for virtually all these groups revolves around regular Bible study programs, prayer sessions, social activities, and special interest groups. The common conviction is that surrounding evangelical youth with like-minded peers and immersing them in religious activities will strengthen their personal faith and lessen the chances that they will drop out of the evangelical orbit while in college. Some ministries, such as the Fellowship of Christian Athletes, single out particular types of students as the focus of their work, although the activities are nearly identical.

Other parachurch ventures work with younger students. The oldest modern transdenominational evangelical youth ministry began in 1881 in Portland, Maine, prompted by the work of Francis E. Clark. Known popularly as Christian

Endeavor, the movement spread both nationally (as the United Christian Endeavor Society) and internationally (as the World's Christian Endeavor Union). Its program was in many ways a prototype for both Youth for Christ and denomination-based youth ministries; prayer, Bible study, social service, advocating high moral standards, and supporting local church programs were at its core. By the later twentieth century, other evangelical and denominational ventures had largely eclipsed Christian Endeavor, although it retained considerable vitality in developing nations as part of the larger missionary movement. Wheaton College provided the impetus for another youth-oriented parachurch movement targeted toward youth, one designed to nurture boys in Christian faith. Joseph Coughlin, while a Wheaton student, supplemented his efforts as a Sunday School teacher of sixth grade boys with additional programs of Bible study and recreation. Thus was born the Christian Service Brigade, formally organized in 1940.[15] Coughlin and others wanted to provide a strong male evangelical presence particularly for boys whose fathers were in military service during World War II. Benefiting from the surge of interest in religious activities of the immediate postwar years, the Christian Service Brigade expanded rapidly throughout the 1950s, even launching programs in more than a dozen nations. When its traditional base dwindled, the brigade enlarged its ministry to include single parents, African Americans, and fathers with daughters, among others. Still nondenominational in its national organization, it was adopted by the Church of God (Cleveland, Tennessee), one of the nation's larger Pentecostal denominations, as its official youth agency in the early 1980s.

Among other evangelical parachurch agencies with ministries to youth are Young Life, Youth for Christ, and Youth With a Mission. Young Life began in 1938 as part of the ministry of Presbyterian Jim Rayburn, then enrolled at Dallas Theological Seminary.[16] Rayburn took high school special interest clubs as a model and inaugurated an evangelical club, combining entertainment with serious Bible study, which met in private homes on a weeknight. Rayburn knew that some came to Young Life meetings because of the entertainment, but hoped that their involvement would eventuate in conversion. By meeting on weeknights, Young Life complemented rather than competed with local church youth ministries, a key ingredient of any parachurch movement. By the end of the twentieth century, Young Life claimed its local clubs reached nearly 100,000 teenagers each week. Youth for Christ (YFC), not officially organized until 1945, had roots in evangelistic rallies held during the Great Depression years in New York.[17] Spreading to other cities in the early 1940s, YFC held meetings usually on Saturday nights to offer youth a wholesome alternative to other weekend amusements. During World War II, YFC added a ministry to military personnel, but after the war, it concentrated on establishing Bible study groups for high school students, known as Campus Life Clubs, along with weekly rallies. In some areas, YFC launched summer camping programs designed for potential juvenile delinquents. Among the more well-known staff of YFC in its early years was evangelist *Billy Graham. By the late 1990s, YFC sponsored more than 1,000 high school groups. Although its aim is evangelistic, YFC has made nurturing the faith of evangelical youth its major focus. Somewhat different in focus is Youth With a Mission (YWAM), begun by Assemblies of God pastor Loren Cunningham in 1960.[18] YWAM recruits youth to engage in short-term evangelistic work, usually during the summer break from school, in more than 100 countries. One aim is distribution of Bibles; another is providing humanitarian relief where natural disasters strike. The most lofty goal of YWAM, yet to be realized, is to support professional educational opportunities for evangelical youth throughout the world so that a lively personal faith might be integrated into every line of employment.

Evangelistic parachurch groups are by no means limited to student-based ministries. Virtually all modern revivalists have formally incorporated associations that promote their work, manage finances (and hope to avoid scandal), and publish materials ranging from gospel tracts to home Bible study programs. The Billy Graham Evangelistic Association is the most well known, but there are hundreds of others. Other evangelistic parachurch groups have roots in evangelicalism's ambivalent relation to Judaism grounded in the dispensational premillennialism shaping American evangelicalism a century ago.[19] As God's "chosen people," Jews occupy a position of privilege in the divine scheme; a respect for Jews and their religion runs through most evangelical undertakings. But most evangelicals also insist that accepting Jesus as the Messiah or Christ sent by God as Savior is essential to salvation; hence, Jews are without salvation and objects of evangelism. The American Board of Missions to the Jews arose from efforts of Hungarian Jewish immigrant and Christian convert Leopold Cohn to take the gospel to Jews in Brooklyn in the 1890s. It took its present name in 1924 when similar endeavors were organized in other cities in the United States, Canada, and Europe. In the 1970s, some younger Jewish converts to Christianity who identified with the Jesus Movement began calling themselves Jews for Jesus. They formed a separate parachurch group in 1973, spinning off from the American Board of Missions to the Jews because many of them wanted to become Christians without abandoning all Jewish practice. Jews for Jesus was also more aggressive in its approach to evangelism. An older group took a rather different tactic. The Chicago Hebrew Mission, which flourished before the First World War, set up schools and summer camp opportunities for Jewish children, staffed centers where those interested could read about the Christian faith, and recruited Jewish converts to take its message to other Jews.

In recent years, in part reacting to reports that the Nation of Islam had gained many converts among prison inmates, evangelical parachurch groups that offer religious counsel to prisoners, seek their conversion, and nurture them in faith have formed. The most conspicuous effort is the Prison Fellowship Ministries (PFM) organized in 1976 by *Charles Colson, onetime aide to President Richard Nixon, as a result of spiritual needs he experienced while incarcerated on Watergate-related charges. PFM began as a support network for furloughed prisoners in the hopes that personal conversion and association with other evangelical ex-prisoners would prevent recidivism. It has added efforts to reform the criminal justice system through its Justice Fellowship, and set up an international association of prison ministries.[20]

Not all parachurch enterprises have been self-consciously evangelistic. Some of the most vital have provided forums for churches, groups, and individuals to connect with each other. The National Association of Evangelicals (NAE) has its roots in the formation of the New England Fellowship in 1929, as the fundamentalist-modernist controversy left evangelicals feeling pushed to the margins. One of its leaders, Boston evangelical pastor *Harold John Ockenga, was instrumental in urging the group to expand its vision on a national basis. That vision became reality at the National Conference for United Action among Evangelicals held in St. Louis in 1942. When the gathering proved eager for a viable alternative to the more liberal Federal Council of Churches (since 1950 the National Council of Churches) and the separatist fundamentalist American Council of Christian Churches, NAE was born. Calling for "cooperation without compromise," NAE has spurred formation of other cooperative movements, including the National Religious Broadcasters and the Evangelical Foreign Missions Association.[21] Headquartered in Wheaton, Illinois, NAE gives evangelicals a forum for addressing current issues and making statements on matters ranging from apartheid in South Africa to pornography, although they are not binding on members.

Since 1941 the American Council of Christian Churches (ACCC) has provided a home for fundamentalist denominations and congregations intent on maintaining doctrinal purity; only a few will even cooperate with groups such as the National Council of Churches.[22] Many also belong to the International Council of Christian Churches (ICCC), another body organized by Carl McIntire to counter the apostate ecumenism he found in other Protestant bodies. The ICCC's passion for separatism means that it refuses membership to any body affiliated with the World Council of Churches. In the 1970s, the ACCC edged McIntire out of formal leadership, although his many enterprises remain vital to both the ACCC and the ICCC. Separate from both are the Independent Fundamental Churches of America, founded in 1930 by persons drawn to the ACCC but wanting to network with fundamentalist congregations and pastors within oldline denominations,[23] and the World's Christian Fundamentals Association, formed in 1919 to combat the teaching of evolutionary theory in the nation's schools and colleges. The latter group endeavored to become an umbrella organization for evangelicals after the Scopes trial removed the force of its focus, but slowly faded after NAE established itself as a more all-encompassing moderate fellowship.

Churches and denominations identified with the Holiness strand of evangelicalism have two cooperative agencies, the Christian Holiness Association and the Interdenominational Holiness Association. The former began as the Methodist-oriented National Campmeeting Association for the Promotion of Christian Holiness in 1867. Never an official arm of any Methodist denomination, it was really a fellowship of Holiness-inclined revivalists who worked the camp meeting circuit. As camp meetings dwindled in number and importance, the association evolved into an organization for Holiness churches and denominations in the Wesleyan tradition. The shift was formalized in 1971 with the adoption of the Christian Holiness Association name. Even earlier, around 1955, some who balked at presumably more liberalizing trends among member churches split off to form the Interdenominational Holiness Association. Emerging from a different kind of theological concern is the National Black Evangelical Association (NBEA), founded as the National Negro Evangelical Association in 1963 at the height of the civil rights movement. Two concerns propel NBEA. One is a conviction that the heritage of slavery gave African American churches a more profound social consciousness than most white counterparts; NBEA fuses that social consciousness with evangelical spiritual concerns. The other is a recognition that because many African American evangelicals came from predominantly white denominations or received their education in white institutions, there was a need to identify and preserve what is distinctive to African American evangelical Christianity. Relatively small numerically, NBEA remains an association of individuals, not groups, although its presence has been felt in many denominations and through the conferences it organizes.[24]

Evangelicalism is impossible to define easily and even difficult to describe adequately. Some of that dilemma emerges because evangelicalism has been sustained by such a broad array of parachurch organizations—some of them like denominations, some with special interests to promote, some intent on evangelizing the world, some geared to sustaining the commitment of persons already in the evangelical fold—that a single understanding or approach mutilates the history and vitality of the evangelical impulse in American religious life. Yet these same parachurch organizations have kept evangelicalism alive and continue to cultivate its prospering on the nation's religious soil.

## NOTES

1. Critics claim parachurch movements sap commitment from local congregations and replace them as the focus of individual loyalty. More generally see Jerry W. White, *The Church and the Parachurch: An Uneasy Marriage* (Portland, Ore.: Multnomah, 1983), and the chapter on "Parachurch Organizations" in Richard G. Hutcheson Jr., *Mainline Churches and the Evangelicals* (Atlanta: John Knox, 1981).

2. Joel A. Carpenter, "Fundamentalist Institutions and the Growth of Evangelical Protestantism, 1929–1942," *Church History* 49 (1980): 62–75; idem, "The Fundamentalist Leaven and the Rise of an Evangelical United Front," in *The Evangelical Tradition in America*, edited by Leonard I. Sweet (Macon, Ga.: Mercer University Press, 1984), pp. 257–88; and idem, "Revive Us Again: Alienation, Hope and the Resurgence of Fundamentalism, 1930–1950," in *Transforming Faith: The Sacred and Secular in Modern American History*, edited by M. L. Bradbury and James B. Gilbert (Westport, Conn.: Greenwood, 1989), pp. 105–25. The most sustained treatment is Carpenter, *Revive Us*

*Again: The Reawakening of American Fundamentalism* (New York: Oxford University Press, 1997).

3. Only a few scattered works discuss these groups; most are written from an uncritical "insider" perspective. See, for example, David Enlow, *Men Aflame: The Story of Christian Business Men's Committee International* (Grand Rapids, Mich.: Zondervan, 1962); Brian Bird, "The Legacy of Demos Shakarian," *Charisma* 11 (June 1986): 20–25; idem, "FGBMFI: Facing Frustrations and the Future," *Charisma* 11 (June 1986): 25, 26, 28; Demos Shakarian, "FGBMFI Struggles toward the Future," *Charisma* 13 (March 1988): 24. Critical acumen marks Ruth Marie Griffith, "A Network of Praying Women: The Formation of Religious Identity in Women's Aglow Fellowship" (Ph.D. diss., Boston University, 1995). See also Susan M. Setta, "Healing in Suburbia: The Women's Aglow Fellowship," *Journal of Religious Studies* 12:2 (1986): 46–56.

4. A brief but insightful summary is the entry for "Missions, Evangelical Foreign" by Harvie M. Conn in *Dictionary of Christianity in America*, edited by Daniel G. Reid et al. (Downers Grove, Ill: InterVarsity, 1990), pp. 749–53. Among the more helpful overviews are R. Pierce Beaver, ed., *American Missions in Bicentennial Perspective* (Pasadena, Calif.: William Carey Library, 1977); Patricia R. Hill, *The World Their Household: The American Women's Foreign Missions Movement and Cultural Transformation, 1877–1920* (Ann Arbor: University of Michigan Press, 1985); William R. Hutchison, *Errand to the World: American Protestant Thought and Foreign Missions* (Chicago: University of Chicago Press, 1987); and the classic study of Stephen Neill, *A History of Christian Missions* (New York: Viking Penguin, 1964).

5. The most comprehensive, albeit somewhat triumphalist, treatment is the six volume work by A. J. Broomhall: *Hudson Taylor and China's Open Century* (Littleton, Colo.: OMF Books, 1981–88).

6. See Catherine S. Miller, *The Life of Peter Cameron Scott: The Unlocked Door* (London, Eng.: Parry Jackman, 1955).

7. On Wycliffe Bible Translators, there are two older studies: Ethel Emily Wallis and Mary Angela Bennett, *Two Thousand Tongues to Go: The Story of the Wycliffe Bible Translators* (New York: Harper, 1959), and George M. Cowan, *The Word That Kindles* (Chappaqua, N.Y.: Christian Herald Books, 1979).

8. See W. Franklin Graham with Jeannette Lockerbie, *Bob Pierce: This One Thing* (Waco, Tex.: Word, 1983), and Norm B. Rohrer, *Open Arms* (Wheaton, Ill.: Tyndale House, 1987). On its major publication, see Ken Waters, "World Vision," in *Popular Religious Magazines of the United States*, edited by P. Mark Fackler and Charles H. Lippy (Westport, Conn.: Greenwood, 1995), pp. 537–42.

9. Both the YMCA and YWCA deserve histories to bring their stories through the twentieth century. The standard ones are nearly a half century old: C. Howard Hopkins, *History of the Y.M.C.A. in North America* (New York: Association Press, 1951), and Mary S. Sims, *The Y.W.C.A.: An Unfolding Purpose* (New York: Women's Press, 1950).

10. See Ben Harder, "The Student Volunteer Movement for Foreign Missions and Its Contributions to Twentieth Century Missions," *Missiology* 8 (April 1980): 141–54.

11. IVCF and several other of the youth and student oriented evangelical parachurch endeavors form the focus of Bruce L. Shelley, "The Rise of Evangelical Youth Movements," *Fides et Historia* 18 (1986): 47–63. On InterVarsity, see also Richard Quebedeaux, *The Young Evangelicals: Revolution in Orthodoxy* (New York: Harper & Row, 1974), pp. 90–94, and Douglas Johnson, ed., *A Brief History of the International Fellowship of Evangelical Students* (London: InterVarsity, 1964).

12. See Richard Quebedeaux, *I Found It! The Story of Bill Bright and Campus Crusade* (San Francisco: Harper & Row, 1979), and idem, *The Worldly Evangelicals* (San Francisco: Harper & Row, 1978), pp. 55–59.

13. See Bill Bright, *Have You Heard of the Four Spiritual Laws?* (San Bernardino, Calif.: Campus Crusade, 1965).

14. See Betty L. Skinner, *Daws: A Man Who Trusted God* (Colorado Springs, Colo.: NavPress, 1994).

15. See Paul H. Heidebrecht, *God's Man in the Marketplace: The Story of Herbert J. Taylor* (Downers Grove, Ill.: InterVarsity, 1990).

16. See Quebedeaux, *Worldly Evangelicals*, pp. 104–5. Quebedeaux indicates that the Young Life ministry was formally organized in 1941.

17. See James Hefley, *God Goes to High School* (Waco, Tex.: Word, 1970), Quebedeaux, *Worldly Evangelicals*, pp. 103–4; and Carpenter, *Revive Us Again*, pp. 161–76.

18. See Loren Cunningham, *Is That Really You, God? Hearing the Voice of God* (Seattle: YWAM Publishing, 1984).

19. Instructive are the essays in Martin E. Marty and Frederick E. Greenspahn, eds., *Pushing the Faith: Proselytizing and Civility in a Pluralistic World* (New York: Crossroad, 1988). See especially Nancy Tatom Ammerman's essay, "Fundamentalists Proselytizing Jews."

20. Colson described his move into prison ministry in *Life Sentence* (1979; reprint, Grand Rapids, Mich.: Baker, 1991). Daniel Van Ness, first director of PFM's Justice Fellowship, wrote about its aims and approach in *Crime and Its Victims* (Downers Grove, Ill.: InterVarsity, 1986).

21. See James DeForest Murch, *Cooperation without Compromise* (Grand Rapids, Mich.: Eerdmans, 1956).

22. The formation and early history of the ACCC and mention of some of the other separatist fundamentalist groups are discussed in Louis Gasper, *The Fundamentalist Movement, 1930–1956* (1963; reprint, Grand Rapids, Mich.: Baker, 1981).

23. See James O. Henry, *For Such a Time as This: A History of the Independent Fundamental Churches of America* (Westchester, Ill.: Independent Fundamental Churches of America, 1983).

24. On the beginnings of NBEA, see William H. Bentley, *National Black Evangelical Association: Evolution of a Concept in Ministry*, rev. ed. (Chicago: William H. Bentley, 1979). Bentley was president of the National Black Evangelical Association at the time these reflections were written (1974). There is also a chapter on NBEA in Mary R. Sawyer, *Black Ecumenism: Implementing the Demands of Justice* (Valley Forge, Pa.: Trinity Press International, 1994).

# 13
# To God Be the Glory: Evangelical Worship and Music

Evangelical worship owes much to the Reformed wing of the Protestant Reformation, the "free church" heritage with its own roots in the Reformation, and the revivalism (particularly the frontier camp meeting) central to American Protestantism. In varying degrees, evangelical worship's emphasis on preaching developed from all three. The Reformed tradition, identified initially with John Calvin, placed proclamation of the Word through Scripture and sermon at the heart of worship. Nearly 500 years later, most evangelical worship still has the sermon as its focal point. The "free church" heritage brought preaching to the fore by playing down sacramental celebration and abandoning a liturgical structure for worship. Since the Great Awakening, revivalism has held preaching as fundamental. Those accepting the Calvinist idea of election found in revival preaching occasions when individuals might be stirred to sense not only their own depravity, but also the signs of God's having chosen them for salvation. Those of an Arminian bent saw preaching as a device to make persons aware of their need to repent and accept the free gift of salvation offered through Jesus Christ. These strands coalesced in modern American evangelicalism to make worship both an expression of praise and thanksgiving to God and a time when individuals might undergo the intensive, personal experience of salvation.[1]

When worship's aim is to gain converts, connections to revivalism become patent. Inviting those under conviction to come to a place set apart goes back to the frontier camp meeting. In the urban revivalism of Charles Grandison Finney, the "anxious bench" replaced the camp meeting's pen; calling sinners to the bench became the direct precursor of the modern altar call. Also connected to revivalism is an openness to emotional expression in worship. Well known from the camp meeting era are descriptions of physical "exercises" offered by early nineteenth-century Methodist revivalist Peter Cartwright in his autobiography. The "jerking exercise" and "barking exercise" that Cartwright noted are forms of ecstatic experience that gained renewed life in later revivalism, albeit in more muted form, when persons undergoing conversion might burst into prolonged bouts of crying or near convulsions of remorse at one's sin. If the lines of those who came forward to shake evangelist *Billy Sunday's hand to signal their religious commitment seem more subdued, the emotional frenzy of Sunday's preaching style more than compensated. Acceptance of emotional expression in worship allowed evangelicals drawn to Pentecostalism to see worship as the setting where spiritual gifts such as speaking in tongues would manifest themselves. Intoxicated with the power of the Spirit, Pentecostals might resemble those overcome by physical exercises at frontier camp meetings in their exuberance and emotional turbulence. The popular stereotype of the "holy roller" owes its genesis to the seemingly excessive ardor that consumed those empowered by the Spirit. More complex is the way African American preaching and emotional sensibilities also paved the way for modern American evangelical worship. A call and response pattern came to mark black preaching, merging African expression with what transpired when slave preachers exhorted while toiling in the fields. That format echoes in shouts of "Amen" that accompany powerful preaching in some evangelical circles. As the response authenticates black preaching, interaction with congregants enhances the plausibility of evangelical emotion-packed worship.[2]

For at least a century after the close of the Civil War, several of the more evangelical denominations and groups gradually lessened overt emotional expression in worship. Historians track this "move to respectability" to socioeconomic shifts that are obvious by the later Victorian period. When educational opportunities broadened, more cerebral approaches supplanted emotional expression. As millions of evangelicals moved into the ranks of the urban middle class, emotional excess became consigned to the lower classes. By the time of the fundamentalist-modernist controversy, many willingly jettisoned an emotion-filled style in a defensive reaction against the condemnation of detractors. In retrospect, evangelicals were simply constraining emotional abandon by relegating exuberance to particular occasions and settings. Upscale urban evangelical churches might have more subdued worship services on Sunday morning, but more emotion-filled, evangelistic ones Sunday evening. Emotional exuberance was still acceptable; it was merely channeled into times and places that were deemed appropriate and then disdained at other times. The Holiness, higher life, and victorious life movements of the later nineteenth century also illustrate this development of acceptable avenues for emotional expression. These movements are distinctive in part because their appeal is to those already converted, not those undergoing an initial religious experience of the saving power of Christ. Surrendering all to Jesus and embarking on a higher life of holiness represented a recommitment or deeper commitment on the part of the believer, usually without the profusion of emotional expression that frequently accompanied conversion. The act of surrender became a way both to constrain emotion and to channel it in a proper manner. Among Pentecostal groups, ecstatic experience remained more common, but from the 1920s until the neo-Pentecostal and charismatic revival of the 1960s, other evangelicals often consigned Pentecostals to the periphery.

Modern American evangelical worship has remained nonliturgical and essentially nonsacramental. The rejection of liturgy stems from the same theological conviction that propelled preaching into prominence, the belief that no human invention (such as fixed prayer) should fetter the Divine. Rather, worship should give free rein to the Word and power of God. Among many evangelicals there still prevails a view that written prayer (other than the Lord's Prayer), recitation of creeds, and following a lectionary elevate human contrivance above movement of the Spirit. Such does not mean that evangelical worship is without ritual form. There is a pattern to the "free church" worship characteristic of modern American evangelicalism with a clear movement and intention to it. The hymns and other musical renditions, a pastoral prayer, announcements, an offering, and reading of a Scripture lesson even in the most subdued service builds to an affective peak as the sermon reaches its climax and an invitation is extended for persons to yield to conversion or recommitment of life. Even when there is no altar call, there is usually a hymn of invitation symbolizing response to the Word.

The neo-Pentecostal and charismatic revival that began in the 1960s gave renewed legitimation to more direct emotional expression in worship beyond creating an atmosphere conducive to the manifestation of charismatic gifts like speaking in tongues.[3] Increasingly common in all evangelical services are clapping hands to the rhythm of lively praise music and raising hands toward heaven to signify surrender and submission, both characteristic of Pentecostalism. These physical gestures represent a contemporary form of the physical exercises that accompanied the frontier camp meeting. Hands raised toward heaven, for example, have become a ritual form, a means to express inner emotion in a physical, yet socially acceptable way. As well, the identification of many televangelists' Pentecostal religious communions buttressed the plausibility of more impassioned worship. Their mix of emotion-charged preaching and commentary with lively entertainment made it possible for viewers to vent their own emotions in the privacy of their homes. What might be too exuberant for public worship was acceptable at home.

A more recent contribution of evangelicalism to American worship styles is the "seeker service" pioneered by the Willow Creek Community Church in South Barrington, Illinois. Although many churches have adapted the Willow Creek format to fit local needs, some elements are fairly common: multimedia presentations, use of drama as a didactic tool, upbeat music using the latest audio technology, and preaching oriented more to practical issues than to personal salvation. Conspicuous because of its absence in most seeker services is overt Christian content reflected in traditional Christian symbols, music, or even Scripture. The rationale relates to the audience that the seeker service attempts to attract: members of the "baby boomer" generation and "Generation X" who are alienated from traditional religion, but nevertheless seek spiritual nurture and uplift. If the music and drama of the seeker service entertain, they also provide subtle examples about how to structure personal life and how to build a sense of self-identity that endures. At first glance, the seeker service may appear to be a departure from the kind of worship that sustained modern American evangelicalism for more than a century. Such a view fails to recognize that adaptability and openness to new forms are central to American evangelicalism. The camp meeting that once fed evangelicalism was, for its time, a radical departure from traditional worship and a conscious endeavor to respond to the needs of a frontier audience untouched by religious institutions. As revivalism adapted some camp meeting practices, it demonstrated a willingness to use forms not found in ordinary worship services to reach the unchurched. Where the seeker service differs is in its willingness to defer calls for conversion and acceptance of salvation, instead nudging seekers to reflect on their lives and move at their own pace toward religious commitment. Many seekers do not realize that most churches, like Willow Creek, that are independent of denominational affiliation have formal statements of faith or doctrine that are clearly evangelical, if not fundamentalist, in content. So the evangelical insistence on personal salvation, authority of Scripture, and centrality of Jesus Christ underlie the seeker service in a subtle manner.

The seeker service is one manifestation of a larger phenomenon called "contemporary Christian worship."[4] In this context, contemporary has a particular nuance. It does not mean worship occurring at the present time, but worship that relies heavily on current communications technology. Here, too, the influence of the televangelists is obvious, for contemporary Christian worship entertains as much as it nurtures. In some congregations, key points in the sermon are highlighted by being flashed on a screen as the preacher is speaking; worshippers are able to see as well as hear the salient issues being discussed. In contemporary Christian worship one rarely finds hymnals used for congregational singing. Rather, words are flashed on a large screen. The traditional organ or piano may not provide accompaniment, but instead keyboard, guitar, and drums or even recorded music is piped over elaborate sound systems. Much of the music seems indistinguishable from what one hears on radio stations appealing to teenage listeners.

But for centuries, American evangelicals have been at the forefront of developing a music that echoed the popular forms of the day, but reshaped them as expressions of evangelical faith.[5] The evangelical revivals of the eighteenth century, for example, generated the thousands of hymns written by Methodist Charles Wesley, who was briefly a missionary in Georgia. Wesley's "O for a Thousand Tongues to Sing" and "Love Divine All Loves Excelling" remain popular among evangelicals. From the eighteenth century, too, come the hymns of Isaac Watts, including perennial evangelical favorites such as "O God, Our Help in Ages Past" and "When I Survey the Wondrous Cross." The camp meeting drew heavily on popular musical genres, even songs that with other lyrics were more associated with carousing and distinctly unevangelical behavior, often adding snappy refrains to older hymns and giving them a syncopated beat that mirrored the raw energy of the frontier. One example is the camp meeting refrain appended to the text of Isaac Watts's "Alas and Did My Savior Bleed." The "gospel hymn" tracks its heritage to collections of camp meeting songs prepared for use in adult Sunday schools, although its popularity came largely from its association with the urban revivals of the later nineteenth century;[6] half a century ago historian of hymnody Robert Stevenson called the gospel hymn "America's most typical contribution to Christian song."[7]

*Dwight L. Moody was one of the first modern American revivalists to recognize the power of music and to employ a full-time musician, Ira D. Sankey, to accompany him on revival campaigns.[8] Since then, virtually every evangelist has relied on a professional to oversee and incorporate music into the revival service. Homer Rodeheaver had a long association with Billy Sunday; Cliff Barrows and singer George Beverly Shea worked for decades with *Billy Graham. Sankey was also a composer, penning the tunes for many gospel hymns. Perhaps the most well-known evangelical hymn writer is *Fanny Crosby. Author of some 8,500 hymn texts, Crosby achieved renown in part because she was a blind woman with a contagious enthusiasm for her evangelical faith. Among her most popular hymns still used in evangelical worship are "Blessed Assurance" (with its polka beat), "Jesus, Keep Me Near the Cross," "I Am Thine, O Lord," and "To God Be the Glory." Most of Crosby's texts illuminate familiar evangelical themes in the praise of God who through the death of Christ on the cross offered an unworthy humanity salvation. The emphasis on total surrender to the Divine will in the "higher life" and "victorious life" wings of later nineteenth-century evangelicalism also found expression in hymns such as J. W. Deventer's 1896 text, "I Surrender All," and the almost doleful "Is Your All on the Altar." The millennialist fervor behind many strands of early modern American evangelicalism also inspired hymns; *J. Wilbur Chapman, Presbyterian evangelist and sometime associate of Dwight L. Moody, captured that spirit in his "One Day," the refrain of which crescendos and moves to a higher pitch as it points to Christ's return. Evangelists, their musicians, and gospel hymn writers understood instinctively that catchy phrases and tunes lingered in the minds of those who heard and sang them, etching into the subconscious basic tenets of evangelical faith. The hymns created a sense of community among those linked by a shared evangelical sensibility that transcended denominational lines. Historian Sandra Sizer sees the resulting common identity as an example of social religion, for the gospel hymns help sustain a religious society that bypasses traditional labels.[9]

Gospel hymns also informed an emerging Pentecostal musical tradition. In Pentecostal worship, music, whether performed by soloists or the familiar gospel quartet or sung exuberantly by the congregation, may seem to predominate over preaching in terms of the time allocated to it during a service.[10] Pentecostals were particularly open to the movement from the more formal gospel hymn to the gospel song by the 1930s.[11] During the Depression era, the gospel song celebrated a world where the redeemed would triumph over the adversities prevailing in this life. One example of this genre, now also found in some hymnals of oldline denominations, is "Victory in Jesus." Another, sometimes dismissed by critics for espousing a simplistic escapism, is the energetic "I'll Fly Away," written in 1932. A parallel tradition emerged from African American evangelical circles, where the spiritual fed into the blues that in turn issued in so-called "black gospel."[12] Drawing on African rhythmic patterns and accompanied by clapping and foot stomping reminiscent of African tribal celebrations, some spirituals in the days of slavery offered thinly disguised messages of hope and liberation. The dimension of protest against oppression continued as legalized segregation supplanted slavery in the later nineteenth century. When modern Pentecostalism gained currency in some African American circles, its style fused with this distinctive heritage to produce a hymnody that quickly spread among African American churches. Integral to this process was an African American Methodist pastor from Philadelphia, Charles Albert Tindley (1851–1933), whose more widely known hymns include "Stand By Me," "Leave It There," and "We'll Understand It Better By and By." Thomas A. Dorsey, who was familiar with Tindley's work, drew directly on blues and ragtime in producing his still popular "Precious Lord, Take My Hand."[13]

In their quest for respectability and endeavors to sustain the plausibility of evangelical belief in a presumably hostile world, moderate evangelicals by the middle third of the twentieth century often relegated more exuberant singing to Sunday evening and midweek services or consigned it to their Pentecostal cousins and others on the periphery of evangelicalism. Part of the concern was a perception that using blues and ragtime, as Dorsey did, enmeshed believers in the forms of an impure world. Not always recalling that gospel hymns and songs had roots in popular folk music, evangelicals backed away from religious music that had too ready an association with secular styles. In the 1970s, however, thanks to the infectious energy of the Jesus Movement and its openness to appropriating and transforming material taken from popular culture, evangelical music again entered into a symbiotic relationship with popular secular music. One result was "contemporary Christian music."[14] On the secular side, the symbiotic relationship between gospel and rock music began earlier. Personal ties to Pentecostal religious expression strongly influenced rock icon Elvis Presley; even the physical gyrations that many found shocking mimicked bodily movements common to Pentecostal ecstatic experience.[15] Presley was far from alone; analysts have called attention to the Pentecostal influence on other popular singers such as Tammy Wynette and Jerry Lee Lewis.[16]

By the 1970s evangelical musicians were also giving birth to yet another genre of American religious music. Composers such as *Andrae Crouch and *Bill Gaither (whose wife, *Gloria, penned the lyrics for many of his songs and choruses) offered the evangelical message in a fresh way that drew heavily on harmonics and syncopation common to rock music. Recording artist *Amy Grant was among the first evangelical vocalists whose work attracted a mass audience outside of religious circles, with two early albums (*Age to Age* and *Straight Ahead*) topping the best-seller charts. Grant and others like her became known as "crossover" artists because they appealed to both religious and secular audiences and moved easily from singing songs of divine praise to ones about secular love. Popularity with nonevangelicals and dabbling with musical approaches some saw as Satanic raised suspicions. In the late 1990s, for example, Pat Boone was condemned in some evangelical circles for shedding his traditional image as a Christian artist whose music reflected religious values, even when topics were secular, when he released an album entitled *In a Metal Mood* that had obvious affinities with secular heavy metal music.

The growth of religious radio, especially stations devoted to "contemporary Christian music," provided a ready outlet for such music. As well, by the late 1970s the magazine *Contemporary Christian Music* was launched. With profiles of gospel musicians, itineraries of concert tours, slick advertisements for their products, and reviews of new music, the journal became a kind of clearinghouse for the latest evangelical contribution to religious music. It has since been joined by a host of others, including *Gospel Metal*, *The Cutting Edge*, and *Heaven's Metal*. The innovative character of contemporary Christian music and worship also spawned specialty publishing houses to print and distribute appropriate materials. They join other companies, such as Lorenz Publishing Co., in catering to the evangelical market, and their materials include new editions of older evangelical hymnals such as *Church Hymnal*, which appeared in 1951 for the Church of God, but garnered much wider usage, and collections without a denominational imprimatur. Among the newer companies are Pathway Music, Lexicon-Light Music, Hosanna-Integrity Music, and Melody Music.[17] At century's end, contemporary Christian music has become sufficiently recognized as a genre in its own right that an awards program comparable to the Grammy awards in the popular secular music industry had emerged. Like the Grammy awards, the Dove awards mark achievements, honor stars, and recognize newcomers to the field.

The genius of popular music, regardless of genre, lies in part in its being easily recalled by the masses. Such instant recognition comes partly through catchy, syncopated melody lines, but also through lyrics that are repetitive and, hence, readily remembered. Thus most of the new hymnody, as found in the work of the Gaithers or Andrae Crouch, uses the old format of a refrain that repeats after each stanza.[18] In addition, what is popularly called the "praise song" or "praise chorus," reminiscent of sacred ditties written for Sunday school children of an earlier generation, has gained increasing use. Illustrative of this category of Christian music is Andrae Crouch's "Soon Very Soon," which exalts the heavenly future awaiting the believer. As oldline denominations issued new editions of official hymnals in the closing decades of the century, several of the more well-known works of Crouch, the Gaithers, Grant, and Ralph Carmichael made their way into them.

Evangelical worship and music have had an impact on American religious life that extends well beyond the evangelical denominations and thousands of independent congregations in the evangelical orbit. Over the last century, but particularly since the resurgence of evangelicalism in the last third of the twentieth century, the free church approach to worship has gained fresh credibility. In the late 1960s, following the Roman Catholic ecumenical council (Vatican II), many Protestant denominations were drawn into the liturgical renewal movement that brought experimentation with "high church" elements in a more sustained manner than previously. The net result was a greater openness to investigating a much wider range of approaches to worship. Thus some oldline congregations added crucifers and sung responses to their Sunday morning worship, drawing on more liturgical and high church traditions, but also incorporated singing gospel hymns and praise songs or use of recorded electronic instrumental accompaniment for some choir anthems or other musical presentations. At the same time, some evangelical congregations have appropriated more liturgical features.[19] But on balance, Protestant worship in many individual congregations has become much more diverse than it was a century ago, with a stronger evangelical influence meshing with others to create variety.[20] Evangelicalism's genius in combining worship and entertainment has also affected American Christian worship across many traditions. Because evangelicals have been particularly adept at taking advantage of developments in communications technology, they early realized how the medium of television, for example, catered to a very short attention span on the part of viewers and thus required more rapid movement from point to point. American Christian worship has had to recognize that and adjust the structure of worship in ways pioneered by evangelicals to sustain the congregational interest, albeit for ever shorter periods of time.

From the emphasis on the Word proclaimed from the pulpit to the evangelistic message of revivals, evangelical worship has consistently sought to identify its audience and develop formats to reach that audience. The same motivation helps explain evangelicalism's willingness to take over secular musical forms and make them vehicles of faith. That passion to reach the masses with the message of redemption and salvation helped generate not only the gospel hymn, praise song, and the array of phenomena that constitute contemporary Christian music, but also a willingness to experiment with worship format and style.

## NOTES

1. On worship in the Christian tradition more generally, see James F. White, *Introduction to Christian Worship* (Nashville: Abingdon, 1990). There is no contemporary

scholarly history of worship in America, although there are a few studies that focus on worship in individual denominations and traditions.

2. See James Cone, "Black Worship," in *The Study of Spirituality*, edited by Cheslyn Jones, Geoffrey Wainwright, and Edward Yarnold, S.J. (New York: Oxford University Press, 1986).

3. See D. N. Malz, "Joyful Noise and Reverent Silence: The Significance of Noise in Pentecostal Worship," in *Perspectives in Silence*, edited by Deborah Tannen and Muriel Saville-Truike (Greenwich, Conn.: Ablex Publishing Corp., 1985).

4. Providing resources is *Worship Leader*, a periodical offered by CCM Publishers in Nashville since 1992.

5. For a broad overview, see Don Hustad, *Jubilate! Church Music in the Evangelical Tradition* (Carol Stream, Ill.: Hope, 1981).

6. See Don Cusic, *The Sound of Light: A History of Gospel Music* (Bowling Green, Ohio: Bowling Green State University Popular Press, 1992). See also Lois S. Blackwell, *Wings of the Dove: The Story of Gospel Music in America* (Norfolk, Va.: Donning, 1978), and Jesse Burt and Duane Allen, *History of Gospel Music* (New York: Robert Sterling, 1971). A helpful resource is Robert M. Anderson and Gail North, *Gospel Music Encyclopedia* (New York: Sterling, 1979).

7. Robert M. Stevenson, *Patterns of Protestant Church Music* (Durham, N.C.: Duke University Press, 1953), p. 162.

8. See Mel R. Wilhoit, "Sing Me a Song: Ira D. Sankey and Congregational Singing," *The Hymn* 42 (January 1991): 13–19, and Rupert Murrell Stevenson, "Ira D. Sankey and 'Gospel Hymnody'," *Religion in Life* 20 (1950–51): 81–88.

9. Sandra Sizer [Tamar Frankiel], *Gospel Hymns and Social Religion: The Rhetoric of Nineteenth-Century Revivalism* (Philadelphia: Temple University Press, 1978).

10. Delton L. Alford, *Music in the Pentecostal Church* (Cleveland, Tenn.: Pathway, 1967).

11. As radio became a venue for gospel music and gospel hymns gave birth to gospel songs, all rooted in variant folk traditions, the courts in time often had to decide awkward questions of copyright. See David Crawford, "Gospel Songs in Court: From Rural Music to Urban Industry in the 1950's," *Journal of Popular Culture* 11 (1977): 557–67.

12. Invaluable is Jon Michael Spencer, *Black Hymnody: A Hymnological History of the African-American Church* (Knoxville: University of Tennessee Press, 1992). Somewhat dated, but still solid, is Troy Heilbut, *The Gospel Sound: Good News and Bad Times* (Garden City, N.Y.: Anchor Books, 1975). See also Jon Michael Spencer, *Blues and Evil* (Knoxville: University of Tennessee Press, 1993); idem, "God in Secular Music Culture: The Theodicy of the Blues as the Paradigm of Truth," *Journal of Black Sacred Music* 3 (Fall 1989): 17–49; and idem, "A Theology for the Blues," *Journal of Black Sacred Music* 2 (Spring 1988): 1–20.

13. See Michael W. Harris, *The Rise of Gospel Blues: The Music of Thomas Andrew Dorsey in the Urban Church* (New York: Oxford University Press, 1992).

14. See Paul Baker, *Contemporary Christian Music*, rev. ed. (Westchester, Ill.: Crossway Books, 1985), and Donald P. Ellsworth, *Christian Music in Contemporary Witness: Historical Antecedent and Contemporary Practice* (Grand Rapids, Mich.: Baker, 1979). On connections to the Jesus movement, see Paul Baker, *Why Should the Devil Have All the Good Music?* (Waco, Tex.: Word, 1979). See also Nicholas Dawidoff, "No Sex. No Drugs. But Rock 'n' Roll (Kind of)," *New York Times Magazine* (5 February 1995): 40–44, 66, 68–69, 72.

15. Van K. Brock, "Assemblies of God: Elvis and Pentecostalism," *Bulletin of the Center for the Study of Southern Culture and Religion* 3 (April 1979): 9–15, and Charles M. Wolfe, "Presley and the Gospel Tradition," *Southern Quarterly* 18 (Fall 1979): 135–50.

16. See, for example, Stephen R. Tucker, "Pentecostalism and Popular Culture in the South: A Study of Four Musicians," *Journal of Popular Culture* 16 (Winter 1982): 68–80.

17. See William D. Romanowski, "Rock 'n' Roll Religion: A Socio-Cultural Analysis of the Contemporary Christian Music Industry" (Ph.D. diss., Bowling Green State University, 1990). Some of the most salient points are capsuled in his "Contemporary Christian Music: The Business of Music Ministry," in *American Evangelicals and the Mass Media*, edited by Quentin J. Schultze (Grand Rapids, Mich.: Zondervan, 1990), pp. 143–69. See also James Long, "Christian Record Publishers," *Christianity Today* 26 (12 November 1982): 80–81, and Richard D. Dinwiddie, "Moneymakers in the Church: Making the Sounds of Music," *Christianity Today* 25 (26 June 1981): 853–56.

18. See Don Hustad, "The Explosion of Popular Hymnody," *The Hymn* 33 (July 1982): 159–67. See also Milburn Rice, "The Impact of Popular Culture on Congregational Song," *The Hymn* 44 (January 1993): 1–19.

19. See Robert Webber, *Evangelicals on the Canterbury Trail: Why Evangelicals Are Attracted to the Liturgical Church* (Waco, Tex.: Word, 1985).

20. See especially James F. White, *Protestant Worship: Traditions in Transition* (Louisville, Ky.: Westminster/John Knox, 1990). Also suggestive is Robert Webber, *Signs of Wonder: The Phenomenon of Convergence in Modern Liturgical and Charismatic Churches* (Nashville: Abbott Martyn, 1992).

# 14
# The Meeting of Evangelicalism and Popular Culture

The interaction of modern American evangelicalism with mass culture provides a valuable prism through which to see how religious styles both influence and are influenced by the world around them. On a theoretical level American evangelicalism has long held mass culture at arm's length. In the antebellum period when popular novels gained wider circulation and the stage became more accepted as an entertainment medium, evangelicals were suspicious. Reading pulp fiction usurped time that could be spent reading the Scriptures; attending the theater distracted one from pursuits healthy for the soul. Similarly, twentieth-century evangelicals first looked askance at radio and television, but then embraced both as means to proclaim the gospel and nurture believers. Popular amusements from theater to sports, mass market literature, material culture forms such as art for the home—evangelicals have become at ease with them all, yet all are still suspect to some degree. Evangelicals no longer cavalierly condemn mass culture, but many believe that forces of evil lurk in its accoutrements and that the ways of the world tempt the faithful to abandon what is holy and pure for what leads to destruction. When talking about mass culture or popular culture, one also plunges into a scholarly morass. In recent decades, analysts have begun to take mass culture seriously, but no consensus has emerged as to how to study it or how to construct interpretive paradigms. Much of the inquiry links popular culture with "popular religion," again without careful definition of terms.[1] As well, because of the sheer numbers of Americans calling themselves evangelicals, some regard evangelicalism as an expression of popular religion. Analysis here, however, focuses on how popular culture or mass culture and modern American evangelicalism have become increasingly intertwined. Evangelicals in the later Victorian period viewed much of popular culture with suspicion, but they were also accommodating evangelical practice to culturally

accepted mores and adapting expressions of popular culture to serve their purposes. In time evangelicals co-opted some manifestations of mass culture, transforming them into vehicles for the proclamation and nurture of evangelical faith.

Evangelical attitudes toward sport and athletics manifest this range of attitudes.[2] When the greater leisure time available in an urban, industrial society
made competitive sports more popular in the later Victorian age, evangelicals
were not of a single mind as to their value. Revivalist *Billy Sunday provides
a good case in point. Sunday began a career as a baseball player before his
religious conversion, but felt he could not continue as a professional athlete
once he became a professing Christian. Athletes had a reputation for "high
living" and immoral personal behavior, as did those who surrounded them. The
benefits to health and maintaining a strong physical body that resulted from
participating in sports were overwhelmed by the negative dimensions. As a
revivalist, however, Sunday organized special meetings to appeal to men and
peppered his sermons with sports analogies and the slang thought typical of
masculine vernacular speech. Sunday abandoned a sports career, but he knew
that the audience he hoped to attract would respond to athletic imagery and
analogy. At the same time, city congregations were building what that generation
called "institutional churches," forerunners of today's megachurches. Often
these had gymnasia; many included sports activities as part of their outreach to
Christian working men and, in some cases, to the immigrants swelling the urban
population. The Men and Religion Forward movement of 1911–12, a carefully
orchestrated series of religious rallies designed to draw Euro-American men into
active church life, called for a physically active, "muscular" Christianity manifested in social service. Later analysts note that promoting "muscular Christianity" meant adding sports teams and athletic events to the programs of larger
urban Protestant churches. As well, opportunities for athletic activity were integral to the strategy of the YMCA movement as it expanded rapidly in the later
nineteenth and early twentieth centuries. Indeed, at the close of the twentieth
century, the YMCA was known in many communities primarily as a "health
club" and a venue for physical activity.

The surge of interest in professional and collegiate sports in the decades after
World War II evoked a different sort of response among some evangelicals.
Now many athletes came from evangelical backgrounds, as did some coaches
and members of their staffs. As a result, more evangelicals began to regard
athletics as "clean and healthy" and sports competition as a way to "build
good character" because of the discipline involved in training.[3] Some still
thought that sports undermined Christian morality and that competition often
became an obsession with winning requiring a hatred of opponents that nullified
evangelical love for one's fellow human beings.[4] The shifting response to sports
led to organizations for athletes who were evangelicals.[5] The Fellowship of
Christian Athletes (FCA), a ministry initially directed primarily to high school,
college, and university students, emerged in 1955 and continues to offer a slate
of prayer and Bible study opportunities, summer camps, and other programs for

spiritual nurture. Most FCA events are also open to coaches and sports enthu-
siasts. By the 1970s, FCA penetrated professional sports as players and coaches
associated with FCA moved from the collegiate to the professional level. Campus Crusade for Christ, the organization founded by *Bill Bright in the 1950s,
early on started a subsidiary, Athletes in Action. Like other Campus Crusade
ventures, Athletes in Action also included a vigorous evangelistic component
that targeted athletes for conversion. Some evangelical involvement in sports
activity took a different twist; a former Athletes in Action staff member, for
example, launched the Institute for Athletic Perfection that developed a training
program for athletes touted as reflecting biblical principles.[6]

The extent of evangelical presence in professional sports became obvious in
the early 1970s when Dallas Cowboys coach Tom Landry began to speak publicly about his personal faith and former Cowboy Roger Staubach, raised a
Roman Catholic, published his autobiography with a major evangelical press.[7]
Soon players in many professional sports were talking about their personal faith
in interviews, frequently claiming that belief in God gave them the ability to
perform and that victory in competitive sports came only with divine aid.[8] By
century's end, team prayer meetings, especially prior to games, were commonplace,[9] but some open expressions of religiosity were becoming controversial.
Many wondered whether faith or pride propelled those who scored touchdowns
in football games to fall on their knees, presumably in prayer, and whether such
actions suggested a theology in which divine blessing fell only on winners and
divine disfavor on losers. Recently, a highly publicized blending of evangelicalism and the ethos of sports came in the Promise Keepers movement, founded
by former University of Colorado football coach Bill McCartney in 1990. Mc-
Cartney, a onetime Roman Catholic drawn to the charismatic Vineyard Fellowship, established this evangelical effort to revitalize male spirituality and
commitment. Recognizing that men are comfortable in sports settings, Promise
Keepers holds rallies in football stadiums, arenas, and other locations identified
with athletic competition. Part of the rationale is that in such locales are men
free to express their emotions and bond with other men.

Another dimension of mass culture where ambivalence has yielded to acceptance and accommodation is in appropriation of print materials, ranging from
popular novels and inspirational books to periodicals designed to reach evangelical audiences. As noted, when popular novels became widely accessible in
the nineteenth century, evangelicals questioned their value. Many of the most
popular ones that addressed religious questions did not echo an evangelical
perspective; some tackled matters of whether orthodox belief was viable in a
scientific age.[10] St. Elmo by Augusta J. Evans (Wilson) on one level tells a story
familiar to the evangelically inclined among the more than 1 million who purchased it after its publication in 1867: The heroine, a deeply pious woman,
refuses to marry the title character, St. Elmo Murray, until he undergoes a conversion experience.[11] Elizabeth Stuart Phelps, whose The Gates Ajar sold steadily but not spectacularly after it appeared in 1868, portrayed a heaven that came

alive to evangelical readers because it was an extension of the best in human life.[12] Historical fiction, such as the wildly popular *Ben Hur*, written by a man who lacked formal religious affiliation, also appealed to late Victorian evangelicals.[13] But none achieved more enduring success than *In His Steps*, by Topeka, Kansas, pastor Charles M. Sheldon.[14] Ironically, Sheldon was influenced by the Social Gospel movement that contemporary evangelicals shunned because they thought that it stressed social concerns over individual salvation. But the novel's personal message, with characters vowing to ask "what would Jesus do?" before making decisions in every aspect of daily life, was compatible with the evangelical individualistic approach to ethics. Still in print from an evangelical publishing house, *In His Steps* also appeared in comic book form in the late 1970s at the height of the Jesus people movement.

Conventional wisdom holds that more women than men read fiction. In the twentieth century, evangelical writers have presented a growing body of novels, especially Christian romance, aimed at women readers. Among the most widely published writers of Christian romance is Grace Livingston Hill (1865–1947), who also wrote under her mother's name, Marcia MacDonald. Hill's nearly eighty novels, many updated and reissued over the last decade or so, portray heroines whose faith brings triumph over adversity, although along the way virtually all meet a "good Christian man" whom they marry or plan to marry by the novel's conclusion.[15] Intended to attract a male and female readership that spanned the Protestant spectrum were the many novels of Congregational pastor Lloyd C. Douglas, including the well-known *Magnificent Obsession*, *The Robe*, and *The Big Fisherman*; the latter two are examples of historical fiction.[16] *The Robe* especially was designed to appeal to men, for it makes affirmation of religious faith an act of powerful courage. It seemed to matter little that Douglas's own theological leanings were more liberal than those of most evangelical readers. Several of Douglas's novels were made into feature films; *Magnificent Obsession* appeared in 1935 with a remake released in 1954, while film rights to *The Robe* were purchased even before the novel was published. Although evangelicals scorned the new medium of film when its popularity soared in the 1920s and 1930s, film versions of "safe" novels and biographies convinced evangelicals that film could be a vehicle for sound religious expression. Ambivalence to popular film eroded further when evangelical *Catherine Marshall's *A Man Called Peter*, the biography of her first husband, Presbyterian pastor and U.S. senate chaplain Peter Marshall, became a commercial success when released by Twentieth Century-Fox in 1955.[17] The most significant signal that evangelicals no longer feared film came when the Billy Graham Evangelistic Association in 1951 began regular production of feature films with a clear evangelistic focus.

Catherine Marshall's other books provide a useful means to note some forms of literature that have always found an audience among evangelicals.[18] She became a best-selling author with a collection of sermons preached by her husband, *Mr. Jones Meet the Master*.[19] Later she produced several devotional or inspirational works, a literary genre with a steady evangelical clientele.[20] One novel, *Christy*, sold some 8 million copies in its first decade in print and provided the stimulus for a television series of the same name.[21] Marshall had experienced something akin to conversion in the early 1940s. While recovering from tuberculosis, she read a classic inspirational work still popular in evangelical circles, *The Christian's Secret of a Happy Life* by Hannah Whitall Smith, which was first published in 1875. Smith, raised a Quaker, experienced the "second blessing" advocated in Methodist Holiness circles, and penned her work to promote the evangelical conviction that happiness results only from complete surrender of the self to God.[22]

Daily devotional materials have also found a secure niche among evangelical reads. *Our Daily Bread*, now with a circulation in excess of 7 million, had its roots in a popular radio Bible class conducted by *Martin R. DeHaan, who left the Reformed Church in America because he believed it had strayed from its evangelical heritage. It first appeared in 1956, and like its United Methodist-based counterpart *The Upper Room*, it includes a daily devotional essay, Scripture reading, and "thought for the day."[23] Some books of daily devotional readings have remained in print for more than half a century. For example, the first of a series of devotional guides called *Streams in the Desert* was published by Mrs. Charles E. Cowman in 1925. In some years selling more than 1 million copies, it remains in print along with other similar works by Lettie Bird Cowman.[24]

Some of the titles most popular among evangelicals fall into the spiritual "self-help" genre; they are designed to help individuals develop not only their spiritual lives, but also their individual abilities and capacities. Among the more perennially popular since its publication in 1952 has been *Norman Vincent Peale's *The Power of Positive Thinking*.[25] Soon after its initial appearance, it was joined by *Billy Graham's *Peace with God*, the first of more than a dozen religious best sellers by Graham.[26] For more than a quarter century, Robert Schuller's books on "possibility thinking," akin to Peale's "positive thinking," have reached the evangelical masses. There is no precise way to determine what proportion of readers of books by Peale, Graham, and Schuller are evangelicals. Nor is there a precise estimate of the evangelical readership of popular inspirational writers like M. Scott Peck or novelist James Redfield, who appeal to both sophisticated and mass market audiences. The same holds for the popularization of premillennial dispensationalism in the best-selling works of *Hal Lindsey, written with Carole Carlson. In its first twenty years, Lindsey's *The Late Great Planet Earth*, an interpretation of contemporary events ranging from the movement of killer bees north from Brazil to the increasing incidence of skin cancer, sold more than 20 million copies.[27] Lindsey collaborated with Carlson on the best-selling sequel, *Satan Is Alive and Well on Planet Earth*.[28] Few readers probably know that Lindsey is a graduate of the evangelical Dallas Theological Seminary and a one-time staff member of Campus Crusade for Christ, for they come from across the religious spectrum. More recently, a spate of books on angels has brought one aspect of popular evangelical belief into the public consciousness, reinforced in the late 1990s by the highly rated television series, "Touched by an Angel," starring Della Reese.[29]

Of course, among evangelicals, the leading religious title remains the Bible. The most conservative retain a strong preference for the King James Version. Particularly popular have been the *Scofield Reference Bible* and the *Thompson Chain-Reference Bible*.[30] Both received new editions after the revised King James appeared in 1967. Many evangelicals have been drawn to paraphrases because they seem more expressive of textual nuance; translators argue that paraphrases distort the literal meaning of the Hebrew and Greek texts and introduce theological biases in such a way that readers regard them as words of Scripture. Among the more popular are *The Living Bible* and *The Amplified Bible*.[31] Modern translations favored by evangelicals include *The New International Version* and *Today's English Version*.[32] Most suspect, and rejected in many evangelical circles, is the *Revised Standard Version* and its update, the *New Revised Standard Version*, in part because of connections between this translation and the National Council of Churches, an ecumenical agency many evangelicals regard as the epitome of liberal views.[33]

Behind this growing body of print material are several publishing houses geared toward the evangelical market. In recent years, most have enjoyed spectacular growth, making them targets for takeovers by publishing conglomerates eager to tap into the mushrooming interest in evangelical books over the last quarter century. *Fleming H. Revell Jr., brother-in-law of revivalist *Dwight L. Moody, began an independent religious publishing company in Chicago in the late 1860s. Now a subsidiary of Baker Book House with headquarters in New Jersey, by 1890 it had become one of the largest religious publishing houses in the nation.[34] Heavy immigration of persons of Reformed heritage to Michigan led to the establishment of several independent evangelical publishing operations in the Grand Rapids, Michigan, area. Among them are William B. Eerdmans, Zondervan, and Baker Book House. Leading secular publisher HarperCollins recently acquired Zondervan. Waco, Texas, was home to another major player in evangelical publishing, Word Books, prior to its move to Nashville. The evangelical nexus around Chicago is now the center of operations for Christianity Today, Inc., with its empire of evangelical periodicals, as well as InterVarsity Press. Thomas Nelson, a leading Bible publisher, has expanded its evangelical line as well, from its headquarters in Nashville, Tennessee, where both the United Methodist Church and Southern Baptist Convention maintain major publishing businesses. Other publishing ventures specialized in materials for use in local church Sunday schools and education programs. Among those of longest standing is the company founded by Methodist layman David C. Cook in 1875 (now headquartered in Elgin, Illinois). As well, some evangelical denominations maintain publishing arms that serve both members and nonmembers. Representative is Warner Press, formerly the Gospel Trumpet Company, which developed to meet the needs of the Church of God (Anderson, Indiana), but has now expanded well beyond that denominational focus. One must add to this array the publishing enterprises of prominent evangelical revivalists (such as World Wide Publications of the Billy Graham Evangelistic Association) and of radio and television personalities (such as *James C. Dobson Jr.'s Focus on the Family publishing operation). Indeed, these many publishing ventures signal a vital means by which evangelicals have forged networks and alliances for more than a century.

However, since the eighteenth century when the first religious magazine was published in the North American English colonies, periodicals have undoubtedly been the most significant print medium for connecting evangelicals with each other and creating a transdenominational evangelical community with a shared identity.[35] Both the Holiness and Pentecostal strands of evangelicalism relied heavily on periodicals to spread their particular perspectives. Among nineteenth-century Holiness periodicals are the *Guide to Holiness* (started by Phoebe Palmer), *Times of Refreshing*, *Word of Life*, and *Service for Jesus*. Daniel Warner, for whom the Indiana publishing house is named, for many years edited the *Herald of Gospel Freedom* and its better known successor, the *Gospel Trumpet*. "Victorious life" Holiness teaching penetrated many local congregations through the *Sunday School Times* after *Charles G. Trumbull became editor in 1910. Early Pentecostals had *Apostolic Faith*, started by *William J. Seymour, among others. *Aimee Semple McPherson was one of many evangelists to have her own magazine, the *Bridal Call*. Later twentieth-century charismatics connected for a decade through *Logos*; today the primary charismatic periodical is *Charisma and Christian Life*, which came from the merger of two predecessor journals. In addition to the *Scofield Reference Bible*, periodicals provided a vital means for disseminating premillennial dispensationalism. From 1874 until 1921, *Watchword and Truth* and its predecessor magazines carried dispensationalism's prophetic message into thousands of American homes. *Christian Herald*, identified more with the Reformed heritage within evangelicalism, began in 1878 as a premillennialist journal, although by the time of World War I it reflected the emerging moderate evangelical viewpoint. Later moderate evangelicals, spurred by Billy Graham (who has his own magazine, *Decision*), since the 1950s have been linked together by *Christianity Today* and in time by several other journals appearing under the auspices of Christianity Today, Inc. *Today's Christian Woman* is only one example. Those oriented more to fundamentalist evangelicalism have *Jerry Falwell's *Fundamentalist Journal*. Add to these the host of magazines, newsletters, and related print communications from various parachurch organizations (such as *Campus Life* and *World Vision*), those associated with evangelical educational enterprises (such as *Moody Magazine*), and the numerous magazines produced by evangelical denominations, and it becomes evident that periodicals have provided much of the symbolic glue that has held evangelicals together and granted them a cohesive common identity.

A final area in which evangelicalism has a history of ambivalence relates to material culture.[36] Evangelicals have long produced various religious items for personal use, ranging from bookmarks with Scripture quotations or inspirational verse to picture puzzles and coloring books on religious themes designed for children. Mass production also transformed Warner Sallman's *Covenant Companion* magazine cover, *Head of Christ*, into an evangelical icon; scarcely a church is without at least one print, and this representation of Jesus is the one most commonly found in evangelical homes.[37] All of these were, in one sense, legitimate because they all had some explicit religious purpose, usually to inspire or to teach. The ambivalence toward other expressions of popular material culture came from the conviction that those with a personal experience of Jesus Christ should be distinct from others; to follow the latest fashions and fads would not do, for they were marks of "the world" left behind.

At least two forces began to nudge evangelicals to appreciate other aspects of material culture. One was the growing desire of evangelicals to give public expression to their faith as evangelicalism became socially acceptable in the latter half of the twentieth century. Evangelicals wanted to display items that reflected their faith. American businesses recognized the potential market and generated product lines to appeal to evangelicals. In addition to the ever-popular inspirational verses by Helen Steiner Rice on greeting cards manufactured by Gibson, for example, Hallmark and other greeting card producers by the 1980s introduced or amplified the number of greeting cards with an explicitly religious message. Others produced resources such as the *Christian Yellow Pages* so consumers could take their business to persons whose religious persuasion mirrored their own. Christian resorts and theme parks became a growing industry as evangelicals sought places to spend vacations and pursue leisure activities where their beliefs and values would be reinforced and temptation to sample alternatives minimized. The other force was the Jesus Movement of the 1970s, propelled by evangelicals who refused to forsake the youth culture of the day or their evangelical faith. One result was the rapid growth of industries, such as Insight Creations, that produce everything from T-shirts and automobile bumper stickers with evangelical messages to "Scripture cookies" and "Scripture tea" (both from Word of Life Scriptures in Florida). Registration fees for Promise Keepers rallies generally include a T-shirt and baseball cap bearing the program theme or logo. This explosion of evangelical material culture allows evangelicals to immerse themselves totally in a religious world, transforming what once was secular into that which is sacred and holy. In another sense, the artifacts of material culture provide ready badges of identity for evangelicals. Who but a fellow evangelical, for example, would drive an auto bearing a "Real Men Love Jesus" bumper sticker? As always, evangelicals would insist that there is also an evangelistic dimension; nonbelievers might strike up a conversation with someone attired in a "Biking for Christ" T-shirt, thereby opening the doors for personal witness and perhaps even conversion.

Modern American evangelicals have looked askance at virtually every element of popular culture. But they have also demonstrated tremendous elasticity in being able to use the media of popular culture for evangelical purposes and transform what would otherwise be regarded as sinful and evil into vehicles to promote evangelical truth and cultivate deeper commitment to the life of faith.

## NOTES

1. Catherine L. Albanese examines much of the scholarly discussion in "Religion and American Popular Culture: An Introductory Essay," *Journal of the American Academy of Religion* 64:4 (Winter 1996): 733–42.

2. On Christianity and sport more generally, see the essays in Shirl J. Hoffman, ed., *Sport and Religion* (Champaign, Ill.: Human Kinetics Books, 1992), and also David Chidester, "The Church of Baseball, the Fetish of Coca-Cola, and the Potlatch of Rock 'n' Roll: Theoretical Models for the Study of Religion in American Popular Culture," *Journal of the American Academy of Religion* 64:4 (Winter 1996): 743–65.

3. Richard Quebedeaux, *The Worldly Evangelicals* (San Francisco: Harper & Row, 1978), p. 76.

4. Many of these concerns were expressed in the popular press. See, for example, "Are Sports Good for the Soul?" *Newsweek* 77 (11 January 1971): 51–52.

5. Also insightful in probing the significance of evangelical efforts to embrace sports is Carol Flake, *Redemptorama: Culture, Politics, and the New Evangelicalism* (Garden City, N.Y.: Doubleday, 1984), esp. pp. 91–113.

6. Wes Neal, the institute's founder, described his approach in his *The Handbook on Athletic Perfection* (Milford, Mich.: Mott Media, 1981).

7. Roger Staubach, *First Down, Lifetime to Go* (Waco, Tex.: Word, 1974).

8. Representative are the interviews in Bob Hill, *The Making of a Super Pro* (Atlanta: Cross Roads Books, 1979).

9. See Lori Rotenberk, "Pray Ball," in Hoffman, ed., *Sport and Religion*, pp. 177–81. Rotenberk, a newspaper reporter, first published this piece in the *Chicago Sun-Times* in 1988.

10. For example, *Robert Elsmere*, by the British writer Mrs. Humphrey Ward, portrayed a Church of England cleric who ultimately rejected most Christian doctrine (but not ethical principles) in the name of science. The novel portrays his struggle to be both a man of faith and a man of intellectual integrity. It sold more than a half million copies in the United States in 1888 when it appeared. Mrs. Humphrey Ward, *Robert Elsmere* (Chicago: J. S. Ogilvie, 1888).

11. Augusta J. Evans, *St. Elmo* (New York: George W. Carleton, 1867).

12. Elizabeth Stuart Phelps, *The Gates Ajar*, edited by Elizabeth Sootin Smith (Cambridge, Mass.: Harvard University Press, 1964). The novel was originally published in Boston by Fields, Osgood, and Co., in 1868.

13. Lew Wallace's *Ben Hur: A Tale of the Christ* was reissued as recently as 1993 by Regnery in Washington, D.C.

14. Charles M. Sheldon, *In His Steps: What Would Jesus Do?* (Chicago: Advance, 1897). The novel was published the year before in serial form. On the novel, see Wayne Elzey, " 'What Would Jesus Do?': *In His Steps* and the Moral Codes of the Middle Class," *Soundings* 58 (1975): 463–89, and Paul S. Boyer, "*In His Steps:* A Reappraisal," *American Quarterly* 13 (1971): 60–71. The comic book edition mentioned above was published by Fleming H. Revell in 1977.

15. There is a dearth of material about Hill other than biographical sketches in the

standard reference works. The only monograph is short on analysis, but does include a complete bibliography of Hill's works: Jean Karr, *Grace Livingston Hill, Her Story and Her Writings* (New York: Greenberg, 1948).

16. Lloyd C. Douglas, *Magnificent Obsession* (Chicago: Wilett, Clark, and Colby, 1929); idem, *The Robe* (Boston: Houghton Mifflin, 1942); and idem, *The Big Fisherman* (Boston: Houghton Mifflin, 1948). The most complete analyses of Douglas's work are found in the following doctoral dissertations: Edward Richard Barkowsky, "The Popular Christian Novel in America, 1918–1953" (Ed.D. diss., Ball State University, 1975); Raymond Arthur Detter, "A Ministry to Millions: Lloyd C. Douglas, 1877–1951" (Ph.D. diss., University of Michigan, 1975); Mary Ann Underwood Russell, "Lloyd C. Douglas and His Larger Congregation: The Novels and a Reflection of Some Segments of the American Popular Mind of Two Decades" (Ph.D. diss., George Peabody School for Teachers, 1970); and Richard Leon Stoppe, "Lloyd C. Douglas" (Ph.D. diss., Wayne State University, 1966). See also Carl Bode, "Lloyd Douglas: Lost Voice in the Wilderness," *American Quarterly* 2 (1950): 340–58.

17. Catherine Marshall, *A Man Called Peter* (New York: McGraw-Hill, 1951).

18. On Marshall herself, see Paul Boyer, "Minister's Wife, Widow, Reluctant Feminist: Catherine Marshall in the 1950s," *American Quarterly* 30 (Winter 1978): 703–21, and Mary Elisabeth Goin, "Catherine Marshall: Three Decades of Popular Religion," *Journal of Presbyterian History* 56 (Fall 1978): 219–35.

19. Catherine Marshall, ed., *Mr. Jones Meet the Master: Sermons and Prayers of Peter Marshall* (New York: Fleming H. Revell, 1949).

20. Representative are Catherine Marshall, *Adventures in Prayer* (Chappaqua, N.Y.: Chosen Books, 1975); idem, *Meeting God at Every Turn* (Lincoln, Va.: Chosen Books, 1980); and idem, *My Personal Prayer Diary* (New York: Epiphany-Ballantine, 1983). The last was co-authored with her second husband, *Guideposts* editor Leonard LeSourd.

21. Catherine Marshall, *Christy* (New York: McGraw-Hill, 1967).

22. Among contemporary editions is Hannah Whitall Smith, *The Christian's Secret of a Happy Life*, edited by Melvin E. Dieter (Grand Rapids, Mich.: Zondervan, 1994). See also Marle Henry, *The Secret Life of Hannah Whitall Smith* (Grand Rapids, Mich.: Baker, 1984).

23. On the launching of *Our Daily Bread*, see James R. Adair, *M. R. De Haan: The Man and His Ministry* (Grand Rapids, Mich.: Zondervan, 1969).

24. Mrs. Charles E. Cowman, *Streams in the Desert* (Los Angeles: Oriental Missionary Society, 1925). The current edition is published by Zondervan.

25. Norman Vincent Peale, *The Power of Positive Thinking* (Englewood Cliffs, N.J.: Prentice-Hall, 1952).

26. Billy Graham, *Peace with God* (1953; rev. ed., Waco, Tex.: Word, 1984). Many of the titles appealing to evangelicals are marketed primarily through so-called Christian bookstores and other religious outlets that are not included in the surveys of sales figures that go into computation of national best seller lists. However, the major book retailing chains such as Waldenbooks, Books-a-Million, and Barnes and Noble began by the mid–1980s to increase their inventory of religious titles that would appeal primarily to evangelically oriented or informed buyers.

27. Hal Lindsey with Carole C. Carlson, *The Late Great Planet Earth* (Grand Rapids, Mich.: Zondervan, 1970).

28. Hal Lindsey with Carole C. Carlson, *Satan Is Alive and Well on Planet Earth* (Grand Rapids, Mich.: Zondervan, 1972).

29. Among the early books on angels was one by perennial evangelical favorite Billy Graham, *Angels: God's Secret Agents* (New York: Doubleday, 1975).

30. Oxford University Press publishes the *Scofield Reference Bible*, while for years B. B. Kirkbride Bible Co. in Indianapolis issued the *Thompson Chain-Reference Bible*.

31. Ayer Publishing in North Stratford, N.H., issues the *Living Bible*, while Zondervan publishes the *Amplified Bible*.

32. Zondervan is a primary publisher of the *New International Version*; Thomas Nelson offers *Today's English Version*.

33. Numerous publishers have printed editions of both the Revised and New Revised Standard Versions; the National Council of Churches holds the copyright to both.

34. See "Revell: Seventy-Five Years of Religious Book Publishing," *Publishers Weekly* (9 December 1944): 2232–36.

35. Some, but not all, of the titles mentioned are profiled in P. Mark Fackler and Charles H. Lippy, eds., *Popular Religious Magazines of the United States* (Westport, Conn.: Greenwood, 1995).

36. The leading studies are both by Colleen McDannell. Her *The Christian Home in Victorian America, 1840–1900* (Bloomington: Indiana University Press, 1986) offers keen insight into domestic architecture and religious artifacts for the home, comparing both (primarily evangelical) Protestant and Roman Catholic approaches for the period when modern American evangelicalism was emerging. Her *Material Christianity: Religion and Popular Culture in America* (New Haven, Conn.: Yale University Press, 1996) offers in chapter 8 keen observations on Christian mass retailing in the later twentieth century. On that topic, see also Randall Balmer, *Mine Eyes Have Seen the Glory: A Journey into the Evangelical Subculture in America* (New York: Oxford University Press, 1989), pp. 155–70. Helpful, but more narrow, is Robert L. Gambone, *Art and Popular Religion in Evangelical America, 1915–1940* (Knoxville: University of Tennessee Press, 1989).

37. See the essays in David Morgan, ed., *Icons of American Protestantism: The Art of Warner Sallman* (New Haven, Conn.: Yale University Press, 1996).

# 15
# Modern American Evangelicals Embrace Education

Evangelicalism in the United States has a rich, complex relationship with education and its institutions. The evangelical revivals of the eighteenth century known as the Great Awakening, for example, propelled the founding of what is now Princeton University to provide an evangelically oriented alternative, particularly to Harvard and Yale, for training colonial clergy. In the early years of the Republic, Andover Seminary emerged to sustain more orthodox theological approaches when Harvard moved in a Unitarian direction. Almost from its beginnings, American evangelicalism has harbored a concern for education, particularly to preserve and protect ideas, values, and methods congenial to evangelical world-views from the dangerous and false. As well, evangelicalism has seen formal education as an appropriate, but not exclusive, means to prepare individuals for careers in ministry, missions, or Christian education. What tempered evangelical educational involvement is evangelicalism's emphasis on personal religious experience. No amount of formal education or intellectual reasoning could supplant conversion as the turning point that launched the individual on the way to salvation. Inner experience became even more pronounced among those in the Pentecostal and charismatic streams of evangelicalism; for them, direct experience of the presence and power of the Holy Spirit that could not be attained through learning became integral to authentic Christian living. Accompanying this appreciation for the centrality of religious feeling was a fear that too much education, rational reflection, or intellectual speculation would weaken, if not destroy, faith. The greater the significance attached to ecstatic experience (like glossolalia), the greater is apprehension that education could be detrimental to Christian faith. Hence, those of more charismatic and Pentecostal leanings have been slower than other evangelicals to organize educational institutions.

A direct call from God to the ministry or the mission field also determines how evangelicals discern what qualifies individuals for religious careers. Just as learning could not replace conversion or baptism in the Spirit, education could not replace the sense of divine call. Yet many evangelicals recognize that sensing a call and having the talents for effective ministry represent different, albeit complementary, gifts. Hence providing training for clergy and other religious professionals has been regarded as a legitimate endeavor, even by those who refuse to require specific educational certification as a precondition of engaging in ministry. Indeed, preparing persons to proclaim the gospel to future generations has been the most compelling force that led evangelicals to found scores of colleges and seminaries in the antebellum period.[1] As the population moved westward, evangelicals planted schools along the frontier so that the people would not be left without clergy to care for their souls. Today, numerous colleges and universities trace their origins to the Congregationalists, Methodists, Presbyterians, or other antebellum evangelical groups. Oberlin College, the nation's first coeducational and multiracial school of higher learning, owed its genesis in the 1830s to evangelicals associated with revivalist Charles Grandison Finney. Further west, Wesleyan Methodist abolitionists founded the Illinois Institute in the 1840s; evangelically inclined Congregationalists gave the school its present name, Wheaton College, in 1860.[2] This heritage nudged later nineteenth-century evangelicals to embark on educational ventures to train men and women to nurture others in the faith.

Bible institutes and then Bible colleges were among the first educational enterprises started to meet the fresh demands of that urbanizing, industrializing age.[3] One of the earliest, Moody Bible Institute (originally the Chicago Training Institute), still exerts a powerful presence in evangelical circles.[4] Founded by revivalist *Dwight L. Moody in 1889 to train lay workers for local churches and urban ministries, the institute grew quickly. In a half century, its campus expanded from a single building to more than thirty buildings and its enrollment grew to more than 2,000 students annually. In time, the institute added its own radio station, a pioneer in evangelical broadcasting, and a publishing arm. Similar in focus was a school begun in New York City in 1882 by former Presbyterian pastor and Christian and Missionary Alliance founder *A. B. Simpson. Initially called the New York Missionary Training Institute, the school today is known as Nyack College (also the name of the suburban town where it is located).[5] Like Moody Bible Institute, Nyack prepares lay workers (many of whom in the early years would probably not have satisfied entry requirements to other colleges) for ministry in local churches and overseas missions. Some estimates suggest that around 40 percent of those attending Nyack in its first two decades served on foreign mission fields. Although today the college offers a traditional arts and sciences education from an evangelical perspective, many of its graduates still intend careers in some form of ministry; the related Alliance Theological Seminary offers appropriate professional training. On the west coast, the Bible Institute of Los Angeles (popularly known as Biola) ranks among the older evangelical schools. Congregationalist pastor and dispensationalist *Reuben A. Torrey served as its dean for twelve years starting in 1912; Torrey had earlier been superintendent of the Chicago Training School (Moody Bible Institute). Like Moody and Nyack, Biola gradually broadened its curriculum, now offering numerous courses of study as the fully accredited Biola University in La Mirada, California.

The independent Bible school or institute became a major educational venue for Pentecostal evangelicals in the early decades of the Pentecostal revival. *Charles Fox Parham briefly headed short-lived Bible institutes in both Topeka, Kansas, and Houston, Texas. Unlike Moody, Nyack, and Biola, Parham's schools and most other early Pentecostal ventures had modest educational aims, offering their full course of study in six- to eight-week sessions that concentrated almost exclusively on Bible study and Pentecostal doctrinal interpretation. Schools managing to survive more than a year or two often expanded their offerings; many developed first a two-year course and then a three-year program focused on biblical, doctrinal, and practical matters. Among Pentecostally oriented schools in operation today that trace their heritage back to these early Bible institutes is the Holmes Theological Seminary in Greenville, South Carolina. Founded in 1898, it came into the Pentecostal orbit in 1907 and now is affiliated with the Pentecostal Holiness denomination. The burst of interest in foreign missions in the later nineteenth century also spurred founding institutes; most broadened curricular offerings as they became stable and secure. One example is the Boston Missionary Training School, started by *A. J. Gordon in 1889. Gordon was a good friend of Dwight L. Moody and a major supporter of the prophetic Bible conferences that disseminated premillennial dispensationalism. As the school matured, it added more traditional arts and sciences studies, in time taking Gordon's name as a college. Russell H. Conwell, Gordon's contemporary, illustrates another way that evangelicals started colleges, one still popular a century later. Conwell organized a school identified with the Baptist Temple, the church in Philadelphia that he served as pastor; countless others have started schools linked to congregations they pastored. Taking its name from Conwell's church, the school became Temple University. Although the university eventually became publicly supported, its theological wing merged with Gordon College's counterpart in 1969 to form the Gordon-Conwell Theological Seminary. Greater coherence came to the Bible institutes and colleges nationally after the National Association of Evangelicals formed in the 1940s. Under its auspices, a coordinating body, the Bible Institute Accrediting Association, was founded in 1947. Now the American Association of Bible Colleges, this agency moved to assure some comparability in training and quality of curriculum, instruction, and resources among affiliated schools. Many Bible institutes still do not qualify for, nor do they seek, accreditation by one of the regional associations that fix standards for other public and private institutions.

Some evangelical colleges owe their beginnings to the growing concern in the late nineteenth and early twentieth centuries that dangerous ideas were taking over the nation's academies. For evangelical Protestants, anything that smacked of "modernism" was potentially harmful. Modernism took in clusters of ideas ranging from evolutionary theories to use of critical method in studying the Bible. Independent revivalist Bob Jones Sr. began an educational venture designed to resist encroaching modernism in 1926 in Florida.[6] Jones, a prominent separatist fundamentalist, moved the school to the Pentecostal stronghold of Cleveland, Tennessee, during the Great Depression and then to Greenville, South Carolina, in 1947. Eschewing regional accreditation on religious principle, Bob Jones University (which dubs itself "The World's Most Unusual University") offers courses of study through the doctoral level and houses a world-class art museum, while remaining a strident voice for separatist fundamentalism. Also in South Carolina is Columbia Bible College, founded by *Robert C. McQuilkin Jr. in 1923. That school and its graduate school of missions were also started in part to have educational institutions devoid of modernism's inroads. Whereas Bob Jones and his school identified proudly with separatist fundamentalism, McQuilkin and his school identified more with the "victorious life" theology strand of modern evangelicalism.

When Bob Jones University left Cleveland, Tennessee, its former campus became the new home of Lee College, a school affiliated with the Church of God (Cleveland, Tennessee). Lee illustrates a recurring pattern among Pentecostal evangelicals who gradually forsook their hostility to education by forming schools that they themselves controlled. Like numerous others, it began as a Bible institute, known as the Bible Training School, in 1918, to provide rudimentary, practical education for persons preparing for ministry in this Pentecostal denomination. As its many counterparts, the Bible Training School was modest in size, beginning with a dozen students and one faculty member who worked together in a room located above the denomination's print shop. But the upward socioeconomic movement of Pentecostal evangelicals and the transformation of the Church of God from a Pentecostal sect to a stable denomination brought demands for greater educational opportunities. A two-year course of study that paralleled junior college offerings was added in 1941. Its success led to further expansion in both size and curriculum when the school took over the former Bob Jones campus in 1947 and was renamed Lee College (now University), in memory of the Church of God's second general overseer. In 1969, Lee received regional accreditation for the first time. Other denominations from the Pentecostal wing of modern American evangelicalism have established their own colleges. Among the older colleges is Emmanuel College in Franklin Springs, Georgia, which was founded in 1919 by the Pentecostal Holiness Church.

In the last half of the twentieth century, two forces brought rapid expansion to evangelical colleges and the formation of several new centers for higher learning. One was the return to civilian life of World War II veterans who were of evangelical persuasion. The educational boom that swept the nation in the postwar decade brought significant growth to colleges of every stripe. The G.I.

Bill that offered financial support for veterans who pursued college degrees created educational opportunities for thousands of Americans who otherwise would have been unable to afford them. It indirectly spurred many evangelical schools to upgrade standards and facilities, for schools had to meet basic requirements set by the government to receive money through the G.I. Bill. Also in some ways a result of the war was the increased affluence that came to millions of those evangelicals whom H. Richard Niebuhr labeled the "disinherited."[7] Many could finance a college education, even without the assistance of the G.I. Bill. The second factor was the coming of age of evangelicalism itself. As evangelicalism emerged from the shadows where it had amassed strength over the decades, individuals launched colleges to perpetuate their personal ministries or started schools to meet the demands for alternatives to secular higher education. When evangelicalism became fashionable, there were greater demands for quality educational institutions to train people not just for ministry or missionary work, but for every conceivable type of employment.

One school with origins reflecting the interaction of these forces is Evangel College, maintained by the Assemblies of God in Springfield, Missouri, home of the denomination's headquarters. The Assemblies of God started its first educational venture in Auburn, Nebraska, in 1920, six years after the denomination organized. But suspicion of formal education was so strong that necessary financial support did not materialize; the school closed after nine months. Undaunted, the Assemblies' leadership opened the Central Bible Institute that same fall (1921), in Springfield. Its goals were familiar: to provide basic instruction in Bible and doctrine and pragmatic training for ministry. Central flourished, receiving certification from the Accrediting Association of Bible Colleges (later the American Association of Bible Colleges) in 1947. When calls came to expand Assemblies-sponsored educational opportunities after the war, the decision was made not to change the direction of the Central Bible Institute (Central Bible College since 1965), but to start Evangel College in 1955 on a new, nearly sixty-acre campus. The denomination also maintains a graduate theological school in Springfield.

Those who began their own schools as evangelicalism soared to prominence in the last third of the twentieth century include *Oral Roberts, *Jerry Falwell, *Pat Robertson, and Jimmy Swaggart. Oral Roberts opened the university bearing his name in 1964, determined that it would quickly achieve academic excellence. Then at the peak of his career as a healing evangelist, Roberts had been deeply pained by the low credibility much of the public and the media granted his ministry. Starting a university was one way to dispel the perception that Roberts's brand of evangelicalism and healing lacked intellectual and rational support. Roberts realized great success. The school received accreditation in 1970, after just six years in operation; by the mid–1990s, it enrolled nearly 3,000 students in its undergraduate, graduate, and professional schools and also boasted a top-ranked basketball program.[8] Jerry Falwell, with the support of his independent Thomas Road Baptist Church, formed Liberty Baptist College (now

Liberty University) in Lynchburg, Virginia, in 1971, the year before he set up
the Lynchburg Christian Academy for children through the twelfth grade. Although Falwell is popularly identified with evangelicalism's fundamentalist
strand, his school is more centrist, attracting *Billy Graham, the symbol of
moderate evangelicalism, as its 1997 commencement speaker. Although Pat
Robertson was ordained in the Southern Baptist Convention when he started the
school in 1977, he kept CBN University (now Regent University) as part of his
personal evangelistic empire rather than connecting it to the denomination. The
school has faced investigations because of allegations that efforts to bring biblical truth to bear on every area of academic inquiry resulted in inappropriate
censorship of course content and impinged on academic freedom. Nonetheless,
Regent has set up graduate schools of biblical studies, business administration,
communication, education, journalism, law, and public policy on its Virginia
Beach, Virginia, campus.[9] Jimmy Swaggart Bible College, begun in Baton
Rouge, Louisiana, in 1982, has not attained the success of the others. Narrower
in focus, it suffered from the negative publicity that came to Swaggart in late
1987 when he admitted to liaisons with a prostitute and saw his Assemblies of
God ordination revoked. Undeterred, Swaggart responded to the crisis by expanding his educational activities, the next year opening the Jimmy Swaggart
Theological Seminary with its commitment to biblical inerrancy, dispensationalism, Pentecostal practice, and global evangelism.

Most evangelical colleges and universities seek to provide education equal to
that offered by the nation's leading secular institutions. Critics believe this desire
for recognition and acceptance by secular academics has been deleterious, resulting in erosion of an evangelical base. Consequently, some evangelical universities differ little from their secular counterparts, other than perhaps in
requiring Bible and religion courses or attendance at chapel services. The coun-
terargument holds that a solid evangelical faith had nothing to fear from any
area of inquiry since all knowledge is a divine gift. In the late 1990s, several
prominent evangelical scholars, including *George M. Marsden and Mark Noll,
wrote extensively about evangelical higher education to call attention to what
was or could be unique about such ventures.[10] Many schools building solid
educational programs informed by evangelical religious philosophy came together in what is now the Coalition for Christian Colleges and Universities,
based in Washington, D.C. With predecessor groups such as the Christian College Consortium (1971) and the Christian College Coalition (1976), the coalition
has fostered a spirit of intercollegiate cooperation, allowing institutions to combine resources and offer programs for students, faculty, and administrators that
none could finance individually. It also publishes materials to help secondary
school students select a Christian college. By 1996, the coalition counted more
than ninety schools in the United States and Canada as members and several
others, including a handful in Europe, Asia, and South America, as affiliates.[11]

Well into the twentieth century, many evangelicals (particularly those with
fundamentalist leanings) eschewed traditional theological education through

seminaries and theological schools, relying instead on the old Bible schools and institutes. The belief that modernism pervaded most Protestant theological education was widespread. Most denominational seminaries taught biblical criticism and were to some extent influenced by liberal theological currents, but they did not necessarily dismiss sacred writ or deny biblical authority. Nonetheless, evangelicals were slower to establish full-fledged theological schools and seminaries than they were to initiate other educational enterprises, and fewer of them have come into being. Another reason for the smaller number is the changing focus of many of the Bible schools and institutes; as they enhanced their curricula and upgraded academic standards, they began to resemble theological seminaries.[12] Among the older evangelical theological ventures is Dallas Theological Seminary in Texas.[13] Founded as the Evangelical Theological College in 1924, the school owed its genesis to evangelist and Bible teacher *Lewis Sperry Chafer, and for many years reflected Chafer's theological preferences: premillennial dispensationalism combined with Keswick Holiness, intense biblical study, and personal spiritual formation. By the later 1930s, Dallas Seminary identified with separatist fundamentalism, but in response to changing religious currents in the larger culture, by the 1980s it had moved more toward the evangelical center as one of the nation's leading centers for training evangelical clergy. Also once heavily tilting toward the fundamentalist end of the evangelical spectrum, though much less so today, is Westminster Theological Seminary, founded by *J. Gresham Machen and his conservative allies in 1929 after they resigned from the faculty of Presbyterian Princeton Theological Seminary to protest inroads of liberalism there.

When moderate evangelicalism came into its own in the 1940s, no seminaries independent of denominational ties and also highly respected academically espoused its position. Evangelist *Charles E. Fuller and prominent evangelical Boston pastor *Harold John Ockenga were both eager to establish a theological school that would wrestle with modern theological thought and scholarship, avoid the rancor of separatist fundamentalism, and promote evangelicalism's vision for global evangelism. Out of their passion came Fuller Theological Seminary, which opened in Pasadena, California, in 1947.[14] Regarding fundamentalism as anti-intellectual, Ockenga, Fuller's first president, moved the school securely into the fold of the "new evangelicalism." It remains on the evangelical forefront, with a center for the study of spirituality, a school of psychology, a highly regarded school of world missions, and programs designed to attract women, African Americans, and even Pentecostals to its student body. Smaller but also intent on bringing modern scholarship and evangelical convictions into dialogue is Trinity Evangelical Divinity School (and its complement, Trinity University) in Deerfield, Illinois, almost in the shadow of Wheaton College.

Pentecostals have been slower to support seminaries meeting accreditation standards of the Association of Theological Schools. The first emerged within a predominantly African American Pentecostal denomination, the Church of God in Christ. Opening in 1970, the Charles H. Mason Theological Seminary quickly associated itself with other theological initiatives in the Atlanta area serving primarily an African American constituency. The consortium, the Inter-denominational Theological Center (ITC), is better known than the Church of God in Christ school. For a decade after it opened in 1973, one seminary that was connected to Pentecostal evangelist David Wilkerson's Melodyland Chris-tian Center in Anaheim, California, received much publicity and sparked ex-citement among Pentecostals who yearned for a Pentecostal school as respected as Fuller Seminary. Within five years, it enrolled more than 200 students, but soon confronted financial and doctrinal problems, the latter over having faculty sign a statement supporting biblical inerrancy. The disputes became so bitter that many students and faculty left; despite reorganization, the school folded in the mid–1980s. The Church of God (Cleveland, Tennessee) maintains a school of theology adjacent to Lee University, while the Assemblies of God have sup-ported the Assemblies of God Theological Seminary (originally the Assemblies of God Graduate School) in Springfield, Missouri, since 1973.

More recently, evangelical educational activity has turned to elementary and secondary ventures. For decades, evangelicals looked favorably on public schools, largely because they developed when an unofficial evangelical consen-sus permeated American public life. As that eroded, evangelicals became con-cerned that public schools were becoming hostile territory. For some, they were centers of a secular humanism out to destroy evangelical faith, a view that gained currency after the U.S. Supreme Court banned prayers and public Bible reading in the schools.[15] Particularly in the South, moves to integrate schools racially made them dangerous for those who espoused any notion of white supremacy. Sex education also raised suspicion among those who believed such was solely the prerogative of parents. The net result was a steady growth in the number of private Christian schools in the last half of the twentieth century.[16] At the same time, some separatist fundamentalists and others moved in the direction of home schooling, believing that only in the home could parents retain total control over what their children were taught. Both Christian academies and home schooling ventures required instructional materials that reflected evangelical ideology. De-veloping them has been a major challenge because those used in teaching so-called secular subjects must meet criteria set by the states. Slowly a full range of materials has emerged. For Pentecostal schools, for example, the Assemblies of God developed the *Radiant Bible Curriculum* to use in religious instruction. Some colleges have introduced courses of study designed for those embarking on teaching careers in Christian schools. Continuing demand has also brought about organizations to set standards and offer resources to individual schools, especially those connected to independent congregations. Among them are the Association of Christian Schools International, the National Association of As-semblies of God Christian Schools, and a cognate group linking schools affili-ated with the Church of God (Cleveland, Tennessee).

Another form of educational ministry targeting children and youth is the sum-mer camp. The Holiness camp meetings and prophetic Bible conferences vital to early modern American evangelicalism offered activities that attracted entire families. Where permanent camp grounds were established, families would often build summer residences or tent encampments for the season. With the metamorphosis of some of these camp grounds into resorts that were not explicitly religious and, by the time of the Great Depression, the decline in the number of families able to maintain separate summer residences at camp grounds came a lacuna in providing summer educational activity in an evangelical environment for children and youth. Many denominations moved to establish summer camping programs for children and youth, sometimes on the site of old camp meeting grounds, after World War II; so did evangelicals. One example must suffice. In 1946, Jack Wyrtzen purchased a ninety-acre island at the north end of Schroon Lake in New York's Adirondack mountains.[17] Wyrtzen and his Word of Life Fellowship organized a camp and a ranch on the island where children and youth could enjoy recreational activities hard to find in urban areas, be instructed in evangelical ways, and perhaps undergo conversion. Over the next half century, Word of Life Fellowship acquired a great deal more land in the Schroon Lake area, adding an inn, family campground, and Bible institute to its center in the mountains. It also now sponsors radio broadcasts, overseas mission activities, itinerant evangelists, and local Word of Life clubs to keep its vision alive.

As in so many areas of society and culture, education evoked different responses among modern American evangelicals. While some are still apprehensive of formal learning even for clergy, other evangelicals embraced and established an array of educational institutions from Bible institutes and theological seminaries to day schools and universities. Evangelicals have evinced a tenacious ability to take what otherwise might be spiritually dangerous and transform it into a device to further the gospel. Like other institutions that evangelicals have adapted for their own purposes, the various schools have not only created a network that binds evangelicals together, they have helped assure transmission of the evangelical vision to successive generations.

## NOTES

1. For overviews, see Arthur F. Holmes, *The Idea of a Christian College* (Grand Rapids, Mich.: Eerdmans, 1987) and William C. Ringenberg, *The Christian College: A History of Protestant Higher Education in America* (Grand Rapids, Mich.: Eerdmans for Christian University Press, 1984). A helpful reference work is Thomas C. Hunt and James C. Carper, eds., *Religious Higher Education in the United States: A Source Book*, Source Books on Education 46 (New York: Garland, 1996).

2. See Paul M. Bechtel, *Wheaton College: A Heritage Remembered, 1860–1985* (Wheaton, Ill.: H. Shaw, 1984).

3. The best published study to date is Virginia L. Brereton, *Training God's Army: The American Bible School, 1880–1940* (Bloomington: Indiana University Press, 1990). See also Harold Watson Boon, "The Development of the Bible College and Institute in the United States and Canada Since 1880 and Its Relationship to the Field of Theological Education in America" (Ed.D. diss., New York University, 1950).

4. See Gene A. Getz, *MBI: The Story of Moody Bible Institute* (Chicago: Moody Press, 1969), for an "insider" account.

5. There is some discussion of the school's founding in Pat Dys and Linda Corbin, *He Obeyed God: The Story of Albert Benjamin Simpson* (Camp Hill, Pa.: Christian Publishers, 1986), and Charles W. Nieukirchen, *A. B. Simpson and the Pentecostal Movement: A Study in Continuity, Crisis, and Change* (Peabody, Mass.: Hendrickson, 1992).

6. There are two older, basically uncritical histories of Bob Jones University: Melton Wright, *Fortress of Faith* (Grand Rapids, Mich.: Eerdmans, 1960), and Margaret Beall Tice, *Bob Jones University* (Greenville, S.C.: Bob Jones University Press, 1976).

7. H. Richard Niebuhr, *The Social Sources of Denominationalism* (New York: Henry Holt, 1929).

8. Roberts himself drafted a brief, appreciative history in *Oral Roberts University, 1965–1983: "True to a Heavenly Vision,"* Newcomen Publication No. 1192 (New York: Newcomen Society of the United States, 1983).

9. See Harvey Cox, "The Warring Visions of the Religious Right," *Atlantic Monthly* 276:5 (November 1995): 59–62ff.

10. Marsden has addressed these issues in several works, including *The Soul of the American University: From Protestant Establishment to Established Nonbelief* (New York: Oxford University Press, 1994); *The Outrageous Idea of Christian Scholarship* (New York: Oxford University Press, 1997); and the collection edited with Bradley J. Longfield, *The Secularization of the Academy* (New York: Oxford University Press, 1992). Noll's most important published contribution to the discussion is *The Scandal of the Evangelical Mind* (Grand Rapids, Mich.: Eerdmans, 1994). Also insightful are the essays in Richard T. Hughes and William B. Adrian, *Models for Christian Higher Education: Strategies for Success in the Twenty-First Century* (Grand Rapids, Mich.: Eerdmans, 1997).

11. See Karen A. Longman, "Coalition for Christian Colleges and Universities: Celebrating Twenty Years of Service, 1976–1996" (Privately printed by the Coalition for Christian Colleges and Universities, 1996). The Coalition also publishes an annual "year in review" report, a resource catalogue, and a host of other materials.

12. On theological education more generally, see D. G. Hart and R. Albert Mohler Jr., eds., *Theological Education in the Evangelical Tradition* (Grand Rapids, Mich.: Baker, 1996).

13. See John D. Hannah, "The Social and Intellectual Origins of the Evangelical Theological College" (Ph.D. diss., University of Texas at Dallas, 1988).

14. George M. Marsden, *Reforming Fundamentalism: Fuller Seminary and the New Evangelicalism* (Grand Rapids, Mich.: Eerdmans, 1987), remains a model for looking at evangelical theological institutions.

15. Some of these issues are also discussed in chapter 11 above.

16. Most insightful are the works of Melinda Bollar Wagner: *God's Schools: Choice and Compromise in American Society* (New Brunswick, N.J.: Rutgers University Press, 1990); "Christian Schools: Walking the Christian Walk the American Way," in *Religion in the Contemporary South*, edited by O. Kendall White Jr., and Daryl White (Athens: University of Georgia Press, 1995); and "Generic Conservative Christianity: The Demise of Denominationalism in Christian Schools," *Journal for the Scientific Study of Religion*

36:1 (March 1997): 13–24. See also Susan D. Rose, *Keeping Them Out of the Hands of Satan: Evangelical Schooling in America* (New York: Routledge, 1988).

17. See Randall Balmer, "Adirondack Fundamentalism," *Mine Eyes Have Seen the Glory: A Journey into the Evangelical Subculture in America* (New York: Oxford University Press, 1989), pp. 92–108.

# Bibliography for Part II

Abrams, Ray. *Preachers Present Arms*. New York: Round Table, 1933.

Adair, James R. *M. R. DeHann: The Man and His Ministry*. Grand Rapids, Mich.: Zondervan, 1969.

—————. *The Old Lighthouse: The Story of the Pacific Garden Mission*. Chicago: Moody, 1966.

Adams, James E. *Preus of Missouri and the Great Lutheran Civil War*. New York: Harper & Row, 1977.

Ahlstrom, Sydney E. "The Radical Turn in Theology and Ethics: Why It Occurred in the 1960s." *Annals of the American Academy of Political and Social Sciences* 387 (1970): 1–13.

Albanese, Catherine L. "Religion and American Popular Culture: An Introductory Essay." *Journal of the American Academy of Religion* 64:4 (Winter 1996): 733–42.

Albrecht, Daniel E. "Pentecostal Spirituality: Looking Through the Lens of Ritual." *Pneuma* 14:2 (Fall 1992): 107–25.

Alford, Delton L. *Music in the Pentecostal Church*. Cleveland, Tenn.: Pathway, 1967.

Anderson, Robert Mapes. *Vision of the Disinherited: The Making of American Pentecostalism*. New York: Oxford University Press, 1979.

Anderson, Robert, and Gail North. *Gospel Music Encyclopedia*. New York: Sterling, 1979.

"Are Sports Good for the Soul?" *Newsweek* 77 (11 January 1971): 51–52.

Autrey, C. E. *You Can Win Souls*. Nashville: Broadman, 1961.

Bailey, Lloyd R., ed. *The Word of God: A Guide to English Versions of the Bible*. Atlanta: John Knox, 1979.

Baker, Paul. *Contemporary Christian Music*. Rev. ed. Westchester, Ill.: Crossway, 1985.

—————. *Why Should the Devil Have All the Good Music?* Waco, Tex.: Word, 1979.

Balmer, Randall. *Mine Eyes Have Seen the Glory: A Journey into the Evangelical Subculture in America*. New York: Oxford University Press, 1989.

Barkowsky, Edward Richard. "The Popular Christian Novel in America, 1918–1953."
   Ed.D. diss., Ball State University, 1975.
Batchelor, Edward, Jr., ed. *Homosexuality and Ethics*. New York: Pilgrim, 1980.
Beaver, R. Pierce. *American Missions in Bicentennial Perspective*. Pasadena, Calif.: William Carey Library, 1977.
Bechtel, Paul M. *Wheaton College: A Heritage Remembered, 1860–1985*. Wheaton, Ill.:
   H. Shaw, 1984.
Benn, Wallace, and Mark Burkill. "A Theological and Pastoral Critique of the Teachings
   of John Wimber." *Churchman* 101:2 (1987): 101–13.
Bentley, William H. *National Black Evangelical Association: Evolution of a Concept in
   Ministry*. Rev. ed. Chicago: William H. Bentley, 1979.
Bird, Brian. "FGBMFI: Facing Frustrations and the Future." *Charisma* 11 (June 1986):
   25, 26, 28.
———. "The Legacy of Demos Shakarian." *Charisma* 11 (June 1986): 20–25.
Blackwell, Lois S. *Wings of the Dove: The Story of Gospel Music in America*. Norfolk,
   Va.: Donning, 1978.
Blaising, Craig A., and Darrell L. Bock. *Progressive Dispensationalism*. Wheaton, Ill.:
   BridgePoint, 1993.
Bloesch, Donald G. *Essentials of Evangelical Theology*. 2 vols. San Francisco: Harper
   & Row, 1978–79.
———. *The Future of Evangelical Christianity: A Call for Unity amid Diversity*. Garden
   City, N.Y.: Doubleday, 1983.
Bode, Carl. "Lloyd Douglas: Lost Voice in the Wilderness." *American Quarterly* 2
   (1950): 340–58.
Boon, Harold Watson. "The Development of the Bible College and Institute in the United
   States and Canada Since 1880 and Its Relation to the Field of Theological Education in America." Ed.D. diss., New York University, 1950.
Bordin, Ruth. *Women and Temperance: The Quest for Power and Liberty, 1873–1900*.
   1981. Reprint, New Brunswick, N.J.: Rutgers University Press, 1990.
Boyer, Paul S. "*In His Steps*: A Reappraisal." *American Quarterly* 13 (1971): 60–71.
———. "Minister's Wife, Widow, Reluctant Feminist: Catherine Marshall in the
   1950s." *American Quarterly* 30 (Winter 1978): 703–21.
Bradbury, M. L., and James B. Gilbert, eds. *Transforming Faith: The Sacred and Secular
   in Modern American History*. Westport, Conn.: Greenwood, 1989.
Brereton, Virginia L. *Training God's Army: The American Bible School, 1880–1940*.
   Bloomington: Indiana University Press, 1990.
Bright, Bill. *Have You Heard of the Four Spiritual Laws?* San Bernardino, Calif.: Campus
   Crusade, 1965.
Brock, Van K. "Assemblies of God: Elvis and Pentecostalism." *Bulletin of the Center
   for the Study of Southern Culture and Religion* 3 (April 1979): 9–15.
Broomhall, A. J. *Hudson Taylor and China's Open Century*. Littleton, Colo.: OMF
   Books, 1981–88.
Burgess, Stanley M., and Gary B. McGee, eds. *Dictionary of Pentecostal and Charismatic
   Movements*. Grand Rapids, Mich.: Zondervan, 1988.
Burt, Jesse, and Duane Allen. *History of Gospel Music*. New York: Robert Sterling, 1971.
Carnell, Edward John. *The Case for Orthodox Theology*. Philadelphia: Westminster,
   1959.
———. *An Introduction to Christian Apologetics*. Grand Rapids, Mich.: Eerdmans, 1948.

Carpenter, Joel A. "Fundamentalist Institutions and the Growth of Evangelical Protestantism, 1929–1942." *Church History* 49 (1980): 62–75.

———. *Revive Us Again: The Reawakening of American Fundamentalism.* New York: Oxford University Press, 1997.

Chafer, Lewis Sperry. *Systematic Theology.* 8 vols. Dallas: Dallas Theological Seminary, 1948.

Chidester, David. "The Church of Baseball, the Fetish of Coca-Cola, and the Potlatch of Rock 'n' Roll: Theoretical Models for the Study of Religion in American Popular Culture." *Journal of the American Academy of Religion* 64:4 (Winter 1996): 743–65.

Christenson, Larry. *Speaking in Tongues and Its Significance for the Church.* Minneapolis, Minn.: Dimension, 1968.

Clouse, Bonnidell, and Robert G. Clouse. *Women in Ministry: Four Views.* Downers Grove, Ill.: InterVarsity, 1989.

Colson, Charles. *Life Sentence.* Reprint, Grand Rapids, Mich.: Baker, 1991.

Copeland, Gloria. *God's Will Is Prosperity.* Fort Worth, Tex.: KC Publications, 1978.

Cowan, George M. *The Word That Kindles.* Chappaqua, N.Y.: Christian Herald Books, 1979.

Cowman, Mrs. Charles E. *Streams in the Desert.* Los Angeles: Oriental Missionary Society, 1925.

Cox, Harvey. "The Warring Voices of the Religious Right." *Atlantic Monthly* 276:5 (November 1995): 59–62ff.

Crawford, David. "Gospel Songs in Court: From Rural Music to Urban Industry in the 1950's." *Journal of Popular Culture* 11 (1977): 557–67.

Cunningham, Loren. *Is That Really You, God? Hearing the Voice of God.* Seattle: YWAM Publishing, 1984.

Cusic, Don. *The Sound of Light: A History of Gospel Music.* Bowling Green, Ohio: Bowling Green State University Popular Press, 1992.

Dawidoff, Nicholas. "No Sex. No Drugs. But Rock 'n' Roll (Kind of)." *New York Times Magazine* (5 February 1995): 40–44, 66, 68–69, 72.

Dayton, Donald W. *Discovering an Evangelical Heritage.* Peabody, Mass.: Hendrickson, 1976.

DeBerg, Betty A. *Ungodly Women: Gender and the First Wave of American Fundamentalism.* Minneapolis: Fortress, 1990.

Detter, Raymond Arthur. "A Ministry to Millions: Lloyd C. Douglas, 1877–1951." Ph.D. diss., University of Michigan, 1975.

Dinwiddie, Richard D. "Moneymakers in the Church: Making the Sounds of Music." *Christianity Today* 25 (26 June 1981): 853–56.

Dockery, David S. *Christian Scripture: An Evangelical Perspective on Inspiration, Authority, and Interpretation.* Nashville: Broadman & Holman, 1995.

Douglas, Lloyd C. *The Big Fisherman.* Boston: Houghton Mifflin, 1948.

———. *Magnificent Obsession.* Chicago: Wilett, Clark, and Colby, 1929.

———. *The Robe.* Boston: Houghton Mifflin, 1942.

Dupré, Louis, and Don E. Saliers, eds., in collaboration with John Meyendorff. *Christian Spirituality: Post-Reformation and Modern.* Vol. 18, *World Spirituality: An Encyclopedic History of the Religious Quest*, vol. 18. New York: Crossroad, 1989.

Dys, Pat, and Linda Corbin. *He Obeyed God: The Story of Albert Benjamin Simpson.* Camp Hill, Pa.: Christian Publishers, 1986.

Ellsworth, Donald P. *Christian Music in Contemporary Witness: Historical Antecedent and Contemporary Practice*. Grand Rapids, Mich.: Baker, 1979.

Elzey, Wayne. " 'What Would Jesus Do?': *In His Steps* and the Moral Codes of the Middle Class." *Soundings* 58 (1975): 463–89.

Enlow, David. *Men Aflame: The Story of Christian Business Men's Committee International*. Grand Rapids, Mich.: Zondervan, 1962.

Erickson, Millard J. *Christian Theology*. 3 vols. Grand Rapids, Mich.: Baker, 1983.

———. *The Evangelical Left: Encountering Postconservative Evangelical Theology*. Grand Rapids, Mich.: Baker, 1997.

Evans, Augusta J. *St. Elmo*. New York: George W. Carleton, 1867.

Fackler, P. Mark, and Charles H. Lippy, eds. *Popular Religious Magazines of the United States*. Westport, Conn.: Greenwood, 1995.

Falwell, Jerry. *Listen America!* New York: Doubleday, 1980.

Farah, Charles, Jr. "A Critical Analysis: The 'Roots' and 'Fruit' of Faith Formula Theology." Paper presented to the Society for Pentecostal Studies, Tulsa, Oklahoma, November 1980.

Flake, Carol. *Redemptorama: Culture, Politics, and the New Evangelicalism*. Garden City, N.Y.: Doubleday, 1984.

Fletcher, Robert S. *A History of Oberlin College: From Its Foundation through the Civil War*. 2 vols. in 1. New York: Arno, 1971.

Gambone, Robert L. *Art and Popular Religion in Evangelical America, 1915–1940*. Knoxville: University of Tennessee Press, 1989.

Garrett, James Leo, Jr. *Systematic Theology: Biblical, Historical, and Evangelical*. 2 vols. Grand Rapids, Mich.: Eerdmans, 1990.

Garrow, David J. *Bearing the Cross: Martin Luther King, Jr., and the Southern Christian Leadership Conference*. New York: Random House, 1986.

Gasper, Louis. *The Fundamentalist Movement, 1930–1956*. 1963. Reprint, Grand Rapids, Mich.: Baker, 1981.

Gaustad, Edwin Scott. *A Religious History of America*. New rev. ed. San Francisco: Harper & Row, 1990.

George, Timothy. "Systematic Theology at Southern Seminary." *Review and Expositor* 82 (Winter 1985): 31–47.

Getz, Gene A. *MBI: The Story of Moody Bible Institute*. Chicago: Moody Press, 1969.

Ginsburg, Faye, and Anna Lowenhaupt Tsing, eds. *Uncertain Terms: Negotiating Gender in American Culture*. Boston: Beacon, 1990.

Goin, Mary Elisabeth. "Catherine Marshall: Three Decades of Popular Religion." *Journal of Presbyterian History* 56 (Fall 1978): 219–35.

Gothard, Bill. *Research in Principles of Life*. Oak Brook, Ill.: Institute in Basic Youth Conflicts, 1986.

Graham, Billy. *Angels: God's Secret Agents*. New York: Doubleday, 1975.

———. *Peace with God*. Rev. ed. Waco, Tex.: Word, 1984.

Graham, W. Franklin, with Jeannette Lockerbie. *Bob Pierce: This One Thing*. Waco, Tex.: Word, 1983.

Grenz, Stanley J. *Revisioning Evangelical Theology: A Fresh Agenda for the 21st Century*. Downers Grove, Ill.: InterVarsity, 1993.

Griffith, Ruth Marie. "A Network of Praying Women: The Formation of Religious Identity in Women's Aglow Fellowship." Ph.D. diss., Harvard University, 1995.

Gross, Edward N. *Miracles, Demons, and Spiritual Warfare: An Urgent Call for Discernment.* Grand Rapids, Mich.: Baker, 1990.

Hagin, Kenneth E. *Redeemed from Poverty, Sickness, and Death.* Tulsa, Okla: Faith Library Publications, 1983.

Hagner, Donald A. ''The Battle for Inerrancy: An Errant Trend Among the Inerrancists.'' *Reformed Journal* 34:4 (April 1984): 19–22.

Hannah, John D. ''The Social and Intellectual Origins of the Evangelical Theological College.'' Ph.D. diss., University of Texas at Dallas, 1988.

Hanson, Bradley C., ed. *Modern Christian Spirituality: Methodological and Historical Essays.* Atlanta: Scholars Press, 1990.

Harder, Ben. ''The Student Volunteer Movement for Foreign Missions and Its Contributions to Twentieth Century Missions.'' *Missiology* 8 (April 1980): 141–54.

Hargis, Billy James. *Communist America—Must It Be?* Butler, Ind.: Highley Huffman, 1960.

Harrell, David Edwin, Jr. *All Things Are Possible: The Healing and Charismatic Revivals in Modern America.* Bloomington: Indiana University Press, 1975.

Harris, Michael W. *The Rise of Gospel Blues: The Music of Thomas Andrew Dorsey in the Urban Church.* New York: Oxford University Press, 1992.

Hart, D. G., and R. Albert Mohler Jr., eds. *Theological Education in the Evangelical Tradition.* Grand Rapids, Mich.: Baker, 1996.

Hart, Darryl G. ''Post-Modern Evangelical Worship.'' *Calvin Theological Journal* 30:2 (November 1995): 451–59.

Hatch, Nathan O., and Mark A. Noll, eds. *The Bible in America: Essays in Cultural History.* New York: Oxford University Press, 1982.

Hefley, James. *God Goes to High School.* Waco, Tex.: Word, 1970.

Heidebrecht, Paul H. *God's Man in the Marketplace: The Story of Herbert J. Taylor.* Downers Grove, Ill.: InterVarsity, 1990.

Heilbut, Troy. *The Gospel Sound: Good News and Bad Times.* Garden City, N.Y.: Anchor, 1975.

Henry, Carl F. H. ''American Evangelicals in a Turning Time.'' *Christian Century* (5 November 1980): 1058–62.

———. *God, Revelation, and Authority.* 6 vols. Waco, Tex.: Word, 1976.

———. *The Uneasy Conscience of Modern Fundamentalism.* Grand Rapids, Mich.: Eerdmans, 1947.

Henry, James O. *For Such a Time as This: A History of the Independent Fundamental Churches of America.* Westchester, Ill.: Independent Fundamental Churches of America, 1983.

Henry, Marle. *The Secret Life of Hannah Whitall Smith.* Grand Rapids, Mich.: Baker, 1984.

Hill, Bob. *The Making of a Super Pro.* Atlanta: Cross Roads Books, 1979.

Hill, Patricia R. *The World Their Household: The American Women's Foreign Missions Movement and Cultural Transformation, 1877–1920.* Ann Arbor: University of Michigan Press, 1985.

Hodge, A. A., and B. B. Warfield. ''Inspiration.'' *Presbyterian Review* 2 (April 1881): 225–60. Reprinted in book form, Grand Rapids, Mich.: Baker, 1979.

Hodge, Charles. *Systematic Theology.* 3 vols. New York: Scribners, 1871.

Hoffman, Shirl J., ed. *Sport and Religion.* Champaign, Ill.: Human Kinetics Books, 1992.

Holmes, Arthur F. *The Idea of a Christian College*. Grand Rapids, Mich.: Eerdmans, 1987.

Hopkins, C. Howard. *History of the Y.M.C.A. in North America*. New York: Association Press, 1951.

Horton, Stanley M. *Systematic Theology: A Pentecostal Perspective*. Springfield, Mo.: Logion Press, 1994.

Hughes, Richard T., and William B. Adrian, eds. *Models for Christian Higher Education: Strategies of Success in the Twenty-First Century*. Grand Rapids, Mich.: Eerdmans, 1997.

Hunt, Thomas C., and James C. Carper, eds. *Religious Higher Education in the United States: A Source Book*. Source Books on Education 46. New York: Garland, 1996.

Hustad, Don. "The Explosion of Popular Hymnody." *The Hymn* 33 (July 1982): 159–67.

———. *Jubilate! Church Music in the Evangelical Tradition*. Carol Stream, Ill.: Hope, 1981.

Hutcheson, Richard G., Jr. *Mainline Churches and the Evangelicals*. Atlanta: John Knox, 1981.

Hutchison, William R. *Errand to the World: American Protestant Thought and Foreign Missions*. Chicago: University of Chicago Press, 1987.

Ingersoll, Stan. "Holiness Women: Recovering a Tradition." *Christian Century* 111:20 (29 June 1994): 632.

Jewett, Paul K. *God, Creation, and Revelation: A Neo-Evangelical Theology*. Grand Rapids, Mich.: Eerdmans, 1991.

Johnson, Douglas, ed. *A Brief History of the International Fellowship of Evangelical Students*. London: InterVarsity, 1964.

Johnston, Robert K., ed. *The Use of the Bible in Theology: Evangelical Options*. Atlanta: John Knox, 1985.

Jones, Cheslyn, Geoffrey Wainwright, and Edward Yarnold, S.J., eds., *The Study of Spirituality*. New York: Oxford University Press, 1986.

Jorstad, Erling. *The Politics of Doomsday: Fundamentalists and the Far Right*. New York: Abingdon, 1970.

———. *Popular Religion in America: The Evangelical Voice*. Westport, Conn.: Greenwood, 1993.

Kammer, Donald. "The Perplexing Power of John Wimber's Power Encounters." *Churchman* 106:1 (1992): 45–64.

Karr, Jean. *Grace Livingston Hill, Her Story and Her Writings*. New York: Greenberg, 1948.

Kennedy, John W. "End of the Line for Tilton?" *Christianity Today* 37 (13 September 1993): 78, 82.

Kraditor, Aileen S. *The Ideas of the Woman Suffrage Movement, 1890–1920*. New York: Columbia University Press, 1965. Reprint, New York: W. W. Norton, 1981.

Ladd, George Eldon. *Crucial Questions About the Kingdom of God*. Grand Rapids, Mich.: Eerdmans, 1952.

———. *The New Testament and Criticism*. Grand Rapids, Mich.: Eerdmans, 1967.

———. *A Theology of the New Testament*. Grand Rapids, Mich.: Eerdmans, 1974.

Lawless, Elaine J. *God's Peculiar People: Women's Voices and Folk Tradition in a Pentecostal Church*. Lexington: University Press of Kentucky, 1988.

———. *Handmaidens of the Lord: Pentecostal Women Preachers and Traditional Religion*. Philadelphia: University of Pennsylvania Press, 1988.

Lewis, Donald, and Alister McGrath, eds. *Doing Theology for the People of God: Studies in Honor of J. I. Packer*. Downers Grove, Ill.: InterVarsity, 1996.

Lindsell, Harold. *The Battle for the Bible*. Grand Rapids, Mich.: Zondervan, 1976.

———. *The Bible in the Balance*. Grand Rapids, Mich.: Zondervan, 1979.

Lindsey, Hal, with Carole C. Carlson. *The Late Great Planet Earth*. Grand Rapids, Mich.: Zondervan 1970.

———, with Carole C. Carlson. *Satan Is Alive and Well on Planet Earth*. Grand Rapids, Mich.: Zondervan, 1972.

Lippy, Charles H., and Peter W. Williams, eds. *Encyclopedia of the American Religious Experience*. 3 vols. New York: Scribners, 1988.

Long, James. "Christian Record Publishers Tap into the Exercise Craze." *Christianity Today* 26 (12 November 1982): 80–81.

Longman, Karen A. "Coalition for Christian Colleges and Universities: Celebrating Twenty Years of Service, 1976–1996." Privately printed by the Coalition for Christian Colleges and Universities, 1996.

McConnell, D. R. *A Different Gospel*. Updated ed. Peabody, Mass.: Hendrickson, 1995.

McDannell, Colleen. *The Christian Home in Victorian America, 1840–1900*. Bloomington: Indiana University Press, 1986.

———. *Material Christianity: Religion and Popular Culture in America*. New Haven, Conn.: Yale University Press, 1996.

McGrath, Alister. *Evangelicalism and the Future of Christianity*. Downers Grove, Ill.: InterVarsity, 1995.

———. *Spirituality in an Age of Change: Rediscovering the Spirit of the Reformers*. Grand Rapids, Mich.: Zondervan, 1994.

Magnuson, Norris A. *Salvation in the Slums: Evangelical Social Work, 1865–1920*. Metuchen, N.J.: Scarecrow, 1977.

Marsden, George M. *The Outrageous Idea of Christian Scholarship*. New York: Oxford University Press, 1997.

———. *Reforming Fundamentalism: Fuller Seminary and the New Evangelicalism*. Grand Rapids, Mich.: Eerdmans, 1987.

———. *The Soul of the American University: From Protestant Establishment to Established Nonbelief*. New York: Oxford University Press, 1994.

Marsden, George M., ed. *Evangelicalism and Modern America*. Grand Rapids, Mich.: Eerdmans, 1984.

Marsden, George M., and Bradley J. Longfield, eds. *The Secularization of the Academy*. New York: Oxford University Press, 1992.

Marshall, Catherine. *Adventures in Prayer*. Chappaqua, N.Y.: Chosen Books, 1975.

———. *A Man Called Peter*. New York: McGraw-Hill, 1951.

———. *Christy*. New York: McGraw-Hill, 1967.

———. *Meeting God at Every Turn*. Lincoln, Va.: Chosen Books, 1980.

———, ed. *Mr. Jones, Meet the Master: Sermons and Prayers of Peter Marshall*. New York: Fleming H. Revell, 1949.

Marshall, Catherine, with Leonard LeSourd. *My Personal Prayer Diary*. New York: Epiphany-Ballantine, 1983.

Martin, William C. *Prophet with Honor: The Billy Graham Story*. New York: Morrow, 1991.

Marty, Martin E. *Protestantism in the United States: Righteous Empire*. 2nd ed. New
    York: Scribners, 1986.
———. *Modern American Religion*. Vol. 3, *Under God, Indivisible: 1941–1960*. *Modern
    American Religion* 3. Chicago: University of Chicago Press, 1996.
Marty, Martin E., and Frederick E. Greenspahn, eds. *Pushing the Faith: Proselytizing
    and Civility in a Pluralistic World*. New York: Crossroad, 1988.
Mathewes-Green, Frederica. "Pro-Life, Pro-Choice: Can We Talk?" *Christian Century*
    113:1 (3 January 1996): 12–14.
Melton, J. Gordon, and James Sauer. *The Encyclopedia of American Religions: Religious
    Creeds*. Detroit: Gale Research, 1994.
Miller, Catherine S. *The Life of Peter Cameron Scott: The Unlocked Door*. London, Eng.:
    Parry Jackman, 1955.
Miller, Donald E. *Reinventing American Protestantism: Christianity in the New Millen-
    nium*. Berkeley: University of California Press, 1997.
Morgan, David, ed. *Icons of American Protestantism: The Art of Warner Sallman*. New
    Haven, Conn.: Yale University Press, 1996.
Morgan, David T. *New Crusades, The New Holy Land Conflict in the Southern Baptist
    Convention, 1969–1991*. Tuscaloosa: University of Alabama Press, 1996.
Morris, James. *The Preachers*. New York: St. Martin's, 1973.
Mullins, E. Y. *The Axioms of Religion: A New Interpretation of the Baptist Faith*. Phil-
    adelphia: American Baptist Publication Society, 1908.
———. *The Christian Faith in Its Doctrinal Expression*. Nashville: Broadman, 1917.
Murch, James DeForest. *Cooperation without Compromise*. Grand Rapids, Mich.: Eerd-
    mans, 1956.
Myers, Warren, and Ruth Myers. *How to Have a Quiet Time*. Colorado Springs, Colo.:
    NavPress, 1989.
Neal, Wes. *The Handbook on Athletic Perfection*. Milford, Mich.: Mott Media, 1981.
Neill, Stephen. *A History of Christian Missions*. New York: Viking Penguin, 1964.
Nelson, Rudolf. *The Making and Unmaking of an Evangelical Mind: The Case of Edward
    Carnell*. Cambridge, Eng.: Cambridge University Press, 1987.
Neuman, H. Terris. "Cultic Origins of Word-Faith Theology within the Charismatic
    Movement." *Pneuma* 12:1 (Spring 1990): 32–55.
Niebuhr, H. Richard. *The Social Sources of Denominationalism*. New York: Henry Holt,
    1929.
Nieukirchen, Charles W. *A. B. Simpson and the Pentecostal Movement: A Study in Con-
    tinuity, Crisis, and Change*. Peabody, Mass.: Hendrickson, 1992.
Noll, Mark A. *Between Faith and Criticism: Evangelicals, Scholarship, and the Bible in
    America*. 2nd ed. Grand Rapids, Mich.: Baker, 1991.
———. *The Scandal of the Evangelical Mind*. Grand Rapids, Mich.: Eerdmans, 1994.
Noll, Mark A., Nathan O. Hatch, and George M. Marsden. *The Search for Christian
    America*. Westchester, Ill.: Crossway Books, 1983. Reprint, Colorado Springs,
    Colo.: Helmers and Howard, 1989.
Oberholtzer, W. Dwight, ed. *Is Gay Good? Ethics, Theology, and Homosexuality*. Phil-
    adelphia: Westminster, 1971.
Oden, Thomas C. *Systematic Theology*. 3 vols. San Francisco: HarperCollins, 1992.
Olasky, Susan. "Bailing Out of the Stealth Bible." *World* 12:10 (14/21 June 1997): 12–
    17.
———. "The Battle for the Bible." *World* 12:5 (19 April 1997): 14–18.

————. "The Feminist Seduction of the Evangelical Church: Femme Fatale." *World* 12: 2 (29 March 1997): 12–15.

Packer, J. I. *Beyond the Battle for the Bible*. Westchester, Ill.: Cornerstone Books, 1980.

————. *A Quest for Godliness: The Puritan Vision of the Christian Life*. Wheaton, Ill.: Crossway, 1990.

Peale, Norman Vincent. *The Power of Positive Thinking*. Englewood Cliffs, N.J.: Prentice-Hall, 1952.

Peters, John L. *Christian Perfection and American Methodism*. New York: Abingdon, 1956.

Phelps, Elizabeth Stuart. *The Gates Ajar*. Edited by Elizabeth Sootin Smith. Cambridge, Mass.: Harvard University Press, 1964. First published, Boston: Fields, Osgood, and Co., 1868.

Piper, John, and Wayne A. Grudem, eds. *Recovering Biblical Manhood and Womanhood*. Westchester, Ill.: Crossway, 1991.

Piper, John F., Jr. *The American Churches in World War I*. Athens: Ohio University Press, 1985.

Price, Robert M. "Inerrant the Wind: The Troubled House of North American Evangelicals." *Evangelical Quarterly* 55:3 (July 1983): 129–44.

Quebedeaux, Richard. *I Found It! The Story of Bill Bright and Campus Crusade*. San Francisco: Harper & Row, 1979.

————. *The Worldly Evangelicals*. San Francisco: Harper & Row, 1978.

————. *The Young Evangelicals: Revolution in Orthodoxy*. New York: Harper & Row, 1974.

Ramm, Bernard. *After Fundamentalism: The Future of Evangelical Theology*. San Francisco: Harper and Row, 1983.

Reid, Daniel G., et al., eds. *Dictionary of Christianity in America*. Downers Grove, Ill.: InterVarsity, 1990.

"Revell: Seventy-Five Years of Religious Publishing." *Publishers Weekly* (9 December 1944): 2232–36.

Ribuffo, Leo P. *The Old Christian Right: The Protestant Right from the Great Depression to the Cold War*. Philadelphia: Temple University Press, 1983.

Rice, Milburn. "The Impact of Popular Culture on Congregational Song." *The Hymn* 44 (January 1993): 1–19.

Ringenberg, William C. *The Christian College: A History of Protestant Higher Education in America*. Grand Rapids, Mich.: Eerdmans for Christian University Press, 1984.

Robeck, Cecil M., Jr. "Faith, Hope, Love, and the Eschaton." *Pneuma* 14:1 (Spring 1992): 1–3.

Roberts, Oral. *Oral Roberts University, 1965–1983: "True to a Heavenly Vision."* Newcomen Publication No. 1192. New York: Newcomen Society of the United States, 1983.

Rogers, Jack B., and Donald K. McKim. *The Authority and Interpretation of the Bible: An Historical Approach*. Foreword by Ford Battles. New York: Harper & Row, 1979.

Rohrer, Norm B. *Open Arms*. Wheaton, Ill.: Tyndale House, 1987.

Romanowski, William D. "Rock 'n' Roll Religion: A Socio-Cultural Analysis of the Contemporary Christian Music Industry." Ph.D. diss., Bowling Green State University, 1990.

Rose, Susan D. *Keeping Them Out of the Hands of Satan: Evangelical Schooling in America*. New York: Routledge, 1988.

Roy, Ralph Lord. *Apostles of Discord: A Study of Organized Bigotry and Disruption on the Fringes of Protestantism*. Boston: Beacon, 1953.

Russell, Mary Ann Underwood. "Lloyd C. Douglas and His Larger Congregation: The Novels and a Reflection of Some Segments of the American Popular Mind of Two Decades." Ph.D. diss., George Peabody School for Teachers, 1970.

Sawyer, Mary R. *Black Ecumenism: Implementing the Demands of Justice*. Valley Forge, Pa.: Trinity Press International, 1994.

Schaeffer, Franky. *Dancing Alone: The Quest for Orthodox Faith in the Age of False Religion*. Brookline, Mass.: Holy Cross Orthodox Press, 1994.

Schaibles, Cynthia. "The Gospel of the Good Life." *Eternity* 32:2 (February 1981): 21–27.

Schmidt, Jean Miller. *Souls or the Social Order: The Two-Party System in American Protestantism*. Brooklyn, N.Y.: Carlson, 1991.

Schultze, Quentin J., ed. *American Evangelicals and the Mass Media*. Grand Rapids, Mich.: Zondervan 1990.

Setta, Susan. "Healing in Suburbia: The Women's Aglow Fellowship." *Journal of Religious Studies* 12:2 (1986): 46–56.

Shakarian, Demos. "FGBMFI Struggles toward the Future." *Charisma* 13 (March 1988): 24.

Sheldon, Charles M. *In His Steps: What Would Jesus Do?*. Chicago: Advance, 1897.

Shelley, Bruce L. "The Rise of Evangelical Youth Movements." *Fides et Historia* 18 (1986): 47–63.

Sider, Ron. "Our Selective Rage: A Pro-Life Ethic Means More than Being Anti-Abortion." *Christianity Today* 40:9 (12 August 1996): 14–15.

Sims, Mary S. *The Y.W.C.A.: An Unfolding Purpose*. New York: Women's Press, 1950.

Sizer, Sandra [Tamar Frankiel]. *Gospel Hymns and Social Religion: The Rhetoric of Nineteenth-Century Revivalism*. Philadelphia: Temple University Press, 1978.

Skinner, Betty L. *Daws: A Man Who Trusted God*. Colorado Springs, Colo.: NavPress, 1994.

Smedes, Lewis B., ed. *Ministry and the Miraculous: A Case Study at Fuller Theological Seminary*. Pasadena, Calif.: Fuller Theological Seminary, 1987.

Smith, Hannah Whitall. *The Christian's Secret of a Happy Life*. Edited by Melvin E. Dieter. Grand Rapids, Mich.: Zondervan, 1994.

Spencer, Jon Michael. *Black Hymnody: A Hymnological History of the African-American Church*. Knoxville: University of Tennessee Press, 1992.

———. *Blues and Evil*. Knoxville: University of Tennessee Press, 1993.

———. "God in Secular Music Culture: The Theodicy of the Blues as the Paradigm of Truth." *Journal of Black Sacred Music* 3 (Fall 1989): 17–49.

———. "A Theology for the Blues." *Journal of Black Sacred Music* 2 (Spring 1988): 1–20.

Spittler, Russell P. "Scripture and the Theological Enterprise: View from a Big Canoe." In *The Use of the Bible in Theology: Evangelical Options*, 56–77. Edited by Robert K. Johnston. Atlanta: John Knox, 1985.

Stafford, Tim. "Testing the Wine from John Wimber's Vineyard." *Christianity Today* 30 (8 August 1986): 17–22.

Stanton, Elizabeth Cady, et al. *The Woman's Bible, Parts I and II*. New York: European Publishing, 1895, 1898.

Staubach, Roger. *First Down, Lifetime to Go*. Waco, Tex.: Word, 1974.

Stevenson, Robert M. *Patterns of Protestant Church Music*. Durham, N.C.: Duke University Press, 1953.

Stevenson, Rupert Murrell. "Ira D. Sankey and 'Gospel Hymnody'." *Religion in Life* 20 (1950–51): 81–88.

Stoppe, Richard Leon. "Lloyd C. Douglas." Ph.D. diss., Wayne State University, 1966.

Stott, John R. W. *What Is an Evangelical?* London: Church Pastoral Aid Society, 1977.

Strong, Augustus Hopkins. *Systematic Theology: A Compendium*. 8th ed. 3 vols. Philadelphia: American Baptist Publication Society, 1907.

Sweeney, Douglas A. "Fundamentalism and the Neo-Evangelicals." *Fides et Historia* 24:2 (Winter/Spring 1992): 81–96.

Sweet, Leonard I., ed. *The Evangelical Tradition in America*. Macon, Ga.: Mercer University Press, 1984.

Tannen, Deborah, and Muriel Saville-Truike, eds. *Perspectives in Silence*. Greenwich, Conn.: Ablex Publishing Corp., 1985.

Tice, Margaret Beall. *Bob Jones University*. Greenville, S.C.: Bob Jones University Press, 1976.

Tucker, Stephen R. "Pentecostalism and Popular Culture in the South: A Study of Four Musicians." *Journal of Popular Culture* 16 (Winter 1982): 68–80.

Van Ness, Daniel. *Crime and Its Victims*. Downers Grove, Ill.: InterVarsity, 1986.

Wacker, Grant. "Are the Golden Oldies Still Worth Playing? Reflections on History Writing among Early Pentecostals." *Pneuma* 8:2 (Fall 1986): 81–100.

———. *Augustus H. Strong and the Dilemma of Historical Consciousness*. Macon, Ga.: Mercer University Press, 1985.

Wagner, C. Peter. *The Third Wave of the Holy Spirit: Encountering the Power of Signs and Wonders*. Ann Arbor, Mich.: Servant Books, 1988.

Wagner, Melinda Bollar. "Generic Conservative Christianity: The Demise of Denominationalism in Christian Schools." *Journal for the Scientific Study of Religion* 36:1 (March 1997): 13–24.

———. *God's Schools: Choice and Compromise in American Society*. New Brunswick, N.J.: Rutgers University Press, 1990.

Wallace, Lew. *Ben Hur: A Tale of the Christ*. 1880. Reprint, Washington, D.C.: Regnery, 1993.

Wallis, Ethel Emily, and Mary Angela Bennett. *Two Thousand Tongues to Go: The Story of the Wycliffe Bible Translators*. New York: Harper, 1959.

Ward, Mrs. Humphrey. *Robert Elsmere*. Chicago: J. S. Ogilvie, 1888.

Webber, Robert. *Evangelicals on the Canterbury Trail: Why Evangelicals Are Attracted to the Liturgical Church*. Waco, Tex.: Word, 1985.

———. *Signs of Wonder: The Phenomenon of Convergence in Modern Liturgical and Charismatic Churches*. Nashville: Abbott Martyn, 1992.

Wells, David D., and John D. Woodbridge, eds. *The Evangelicals: What They Believe, Who They Are, Where They Are Changing*. Nashville: Abingdon, 1975.

Wells, David F. "The Stout and Persistent Theology of Charles Hodge." *Christianity Today* 18 (30 August 1974): 10–15.

White, James F. *Introduction to Christian Worship*. Nashville: Abingdon, 1990.

————. *Protestant Worship: Traditions in Transition*. Louisville, Ky.: Westminster/John Knox, 1990.

White, Jerry W. *The Church and the Parachurch: An Uneasy Marriage*. Portland, Ore.: Multnomah, 1983.

White, O. Kendall, Jr., and Daryl White, eds. *Religion in the Contemporary South*. Athens: University of Georgia Press, 1995.

Wilhoit, Mel R. "Sing Me a Song: Ira D. Sankey and Congregational Singing." *The Hymn* 42 (January 1991): 13–19.

Williams, Herbert L. *D. James Kennedy: The Man and His Ministry*. Nashville: Thomas Nelson, 1990.

Wimber, John, with Kevin Springer. *Power Evangelism*. San Francisco: Harper & Row, 1986.

Wolfe, Charles M. "Presley and the Gospel Tradition." *Southern Quarterly* 18 (Fall 1979): 135–50.

Wright, Melton. *Fortress of Faith*. Grand Rapids, Mich.: Eerdmans, 1960.

Young, Andrew. *An Easy Burden: The Civil Rights Movement and the Transformation of America*. San Francisco: HarperCollins, 1996.

# Part III
# A Biographical Dictionary of Modern American Evangelical Leaders

# Abbreviations for Standard Reference Sources

| | |
|---|---|
| *ACSL* | *Biographical Dictionary of American Cult and Sect Leaders*, edited by J. Gordon Melton (New York & London: Garland, 1986). |
| *BT* | *Baptist Theologians*, edited by Timothy George and David S. Dockery (Nashville, Tenn.: Broadman, 1990). |
| *CANR* | *Contemporary Authors*, new revised series, various editors (Detroit: Gale, 1981—). |
| *CT* | *Christianity Today.* |
| *DARB* | *Dictionary of American Religious Biography*, 2nd ed., edited by Henry Warner Bowden (Westport, Conn.: Greenwood, 1993). |
| *DCA* | *Dictionary of Christianity in America*, edited by Daniel G. Reid, Robert D. Linder, Bruce L. Shelley, and Harry S. Stout (Downers Grove, Ill.: InterVarsity, 1990). |
| *DPCM* | *Dictionary of Pentecostal and Charismatic Movements*, edited by Stanley M. Burgess, Gary B. McGee, and Patrick H. Alexander (Grand Rapids, Mich.: Zondervan, 1988). |
| *EAAR* | *Encyclopedia of African American Religions*, edited by Larry G. Murphy, J. Gordon Melton, and Gary L. Ward (New York & London: Garland, 1993). |
| *HET* | *Handbook of Evangelical Theologians*, edited by Walter A. Elwell (Grand Rapids, Mich.: Baker, 1993). |
| *MTC* | *More Than Conquerors*, edited by John D. Woodbridge (Chicago: Moody, 1992). |
| *PTR* | *Prime-Time Religion: An Encyclopedia of Religious Broadcasting*, edited by J. Gordon Melton, Phillip Charles Lucas, and Jon R. Stone (Phoenix, Ariz.: Oryx Press, 1997). |

*RLA*                    *Religious Leaders of America*, edited by J. Gordon Melton (Detroit: Gale, 1991).

*TDCB*                   *Twentieth-Century Dictionary of Christian Biography*, edited by J. D. Douglas (Grand Rapids, Mich.: Baker, 1995).

*TSAPR*                  *Twentieth-Century Shapers of American Popular Religion*, edited by Charles H. Lippy (Westport, Conn.: Greenwood, 1989).

# B

---

**BRANHAM, WILLIAM M.** (6 April 1909, Burkesville, KY–24 December 1965, Amarillo, TX). *Education*: Marginal. *Career*: Professional boxer, 1928–33; preacher and healing revivalist, 1933–65.

One of the most significant evangelical faith healers, Branham was born into severe poverty in central Kentucky. His early life in Jefferson, Indiana, was made even more difficult by his father's alcoholism. Receiving little formal education and no religious training to speak of, Branham found refuge in an internal world that he later claimed was filled with many mystical experiences.

Searching for an escape from his bleak home life, Branham moved to Phoenix, Arizona, at age nineteen and became a professional boxer. He returned home to Indiana upon the death of his brother and began an effort to "find God." Shortly thereafter he started to preach and was ordained as an independent Baptist preacher. His revivalist career commenced in 1933, and almost immediately he attracted thousands of people to his tent services. After the death of his wife and child in 1937, Branham associated himself with "Jesus Only" Pentecostalism, a nontrinitarian sect that believed the Godhead was revealed in the person of Jesus only.

After World War II, Branham became a leader in the healing revival that swept American Pentecostalism. On 7 May 1946, Branham told his congregation that he had received an angelic commission both to preach and to heal. Following that announcement, his fame increased dramatically. The heyday of his ministry lasted just over ten years, beginning with a June 1946 revival in Jonesboro, Arkansas, that had over 25,000 attendees. A year later, Branham hired Gordon Lindsay as his manager. It was Lindsay who started the *Voice of Healing* magazine to publicize Branham's ministry. In time, *Voice of Healing* became the major publicity organ not only for Branham, but for dozens of healing evangelists.

During the peak years of his ministry, three events stand out. The first was a January 1950 revival meeting in Houston, Texas. At that meeting, Branham received national press coverage for a debate with W. E. Best, pastor of the Houston Tabernacle Baptist Church, over the biblical justification for faith healing. The second significant event was Branham's European evangelistic tour in April 1950 that brought international attention to the emerging worldwide healing revival movement. The third event was Branham's healing in 1951 of U.S. Congressman William Upshaw of Georgia who had been crippled for fifty-nine years. After the Upshaw incident Branham was regarded as a legend in Pentecostal circles and the model for a host of young healing revivalists from the equally famous *Oral Roberts to many more obscure evangelists.

By the late 1950s Branham's popularity began to ebb. The healing revival within Pentecostalism broadened in the 1950s into a larger charismatic movement that emphasized all the gifts of the Holy Spirit. Branham did not keep pace with this change. His ministry also experienced severe financial difficulties in the mid–1950s as local Pentecostal pastors began to vie with the healing revivalists for money. Branham's situation was worsened by his indifference toward financial management, a shortsighted attitude that got him in trouble with the Internal Revenue Service in 1956. Finally, Branham began to emphasis some controversial doctrinal teachings over faith healing. During his most successful period of revivalism, Branham minimized doctrine and was able to build a large group of ecumenical followers. By 1960, he espoused many beliefs that tended to alienate his core group of supporters, such as strict traditional roles for women, a condoning of divorce, a "Jesus only" position with regard to the Godhead and baptism, a denial of eternal hell, and the doctrine of the serpent's seed. This latter belief concerned the literal transmission of the "seed of the devil" through procreation from Eve down to the present. Thus, the race of Satan continues today as evidenced by those who reject the Gospel.

Although Branham remained one of the most popular of all the healing revivalists, he never recaptured the prominence he enjoyed from 1946–56. A genuinely humble person who believed that he was given a great gift by God, Branham had an unprepossessing demeanor that seemed to belie the mighty feats he was able to perform. In fact, his prominence among his closest disciples was so great that after he was killed in a traffic accident in December 1965, many awaited Branham's physical resurrection with genuine expectancy. At the time of his death, the movement he helped to create seemed to have left him behind, yet the imprint he placed upon it is undeniable.

*Bibliography*

A. *Footprints on the Sands of Time*, 2 vols. (Jeffersonville, Ind.: Spoken Word Publications, 1975).

B. *ACSL* 38–39; *DARB* 71–72; *DCA* 182; *DPCM* 95–97; Gordon Lindsay, *William Branham: A Man Sent From God* (Jefferson, Ind.: William Branham, 1950); C. Douglas

Weaver, *The Healer-Prophet, William Marrion Branham* (Macon, Ga.: Mercer University Press, 1987).

**BRIGHT, WILLIAM R. (BILL)** (19 October 1921, Coweta, OK—). *Education*: B.S., Northeastern State College (OK), 1943; Princeton Theological Seminary; Fuller Theological Seminary. *Career*: Teacher, 1943–44; businessman, 1944–51; president, Campus Crusade for Christ, 1951—.

Bill Bright was born in Coweta, Oklahoma, the son of a pious Methodist mother and a success-driven father. After a brief teaching stint in the early 1940s, Bright headed to California to earn his fortune as a businessman. Although indifferent to spiritual matters, he met *Dawson Trotman, the founder of the Navigators, on his very first day in Los Angeles. Bright quickly became a fixture in the Trotman household, developed a close friendship with Daniel Fuller, the son of *Charles E. Fuller, and joined Hollywood's First Presbyterian Church, nicknamed "Hollywood Pres."

As a member of Hollywood Pres, Bright grew serious about his religious life. Under the instruction of Henrietta Mears, the director of Christian education at the church, Bright committed his life to Christ in a personal way. Slowly he began to spend more time at church, praying, reading his Bible, and witnessing. In time, Bright resolved to attend seminary to become a Presbyterian minister. He enrolled in Princeton Theological Seminary in 1946, and transferred to Fuller the following year. In 1948, Bright married Vonette Zachary, a former acquaintance from Oklahoma with whom he had reestablished ties in California.

Campus Crusade for Christ was organized on the campus of UCLA in 1951. In the beginning, it was largely an extension of the college class of Hollywood Pres. Anxious to minister to the students at UCLA, Bright left Fuller before graduation and moved with Vonette into a rented house one block from campus. The couple particularly concentrated on reaching athletic teams, fraternities, and sororities, recognizing them as the centers of greatest influence on a college campus. Activities included prayer meetings, Bible studies, and discipleship programs. The Brights enjoyed sufficient success that within one year that they were able to recruit a six-person staff and establish chapters of Campus Crusade at other colleges and universities in California and Washington.

As of 1997, Campus Crusade had approximately 13,000 staffers working on 1,120 college campuses in 152 countries. A 1995 budget amounted to $270 million. Yet, through some forty different ministries, the organization operates under the same mandate it possessed nearly fifty years ago. Significant ministries of Campus Crusade include: Athletes in Action; Here's Life, America; Here's Life, World, which uses a film about the life of Jesus to take the Gospel to national groups all over the globe; as well as specialized efforts aimed at African Americans, Hispanics, inner city dwellers, prisoners, and high school students.

Combining a keen sales and marketing acumen with a heart for ministry, Bright conceived "The Four Spiritual Laws" in the 1960s as a concise way to introduce people to the Christian faith and bring them to the point of praying to "receive Christ as savior." The four laws are: (1) God loves you and has a plan for your life, (2) sin separates us from God, (3) Jesus is the only provision for man's sin, and (4) we must individually receive Christ as savior. The booklet closes with a sample "prayer of salvation." Although Bright's approach has been criticized as simplistic and formulaic, it is claimed that thousands have been introduced to the Christian faith through the pamphlet.

In many ways, Bright epitomized the distinctively American emphasis on pragmatism that dominated twentieth-century evangelicalism. One can see this in the meticulous planning associated with the varied ministries of Campus Crusade as well as the "Explo" mass rallies of 1972, 1974, 1985, and 1990. So thoroughly has Bright left his imprint on Campus Crusade that even sympathetic insiders have noted his authoritarian leadership style. Key associates like *Hal Lindsey have left the fold due to differences with Bright over the focus and objectives of the ministry. Dissent has also come from other quarters, particularly from denominational college ministries that see Campus Crusade as offering itself as an alternative, rather than as a complement, to the local church. More critically, Bright has been taken to task for his WASPish, pro-American, upper middle-class view of Christianity that seems oblivious to nuances of culture, gender, and ethnicity.

What is indisputable about Bill Bright is his prominence in late twentieth-century American evangelicalism, particularly in the operation of parachurch ministries. In this area no one has done a better and more efficient job, as witnessed by a 1995 *Money* magazine survey that singled out Campus Crusade for the highest percentage of contributor dollars that go directly to ministry programs. Further, Bright's achievements were recognized by the Templeton Foundation, which awarded him its Prize for Progress in Religion in March 1996. Consistent with his evangelistic goals, Bright pledged that the prize of $1.07 million would be used to promote the themes of prayer and fasting.

*Bibliography*

A. *Come Help Change Our World* (San Bernardino, Calif.: Campus Crusade for Christ International, 1979); *The Holy Spirit, The Key to Supernatural Living* (San Bernardino, Calif.: Campus Crusade for Christ International, 1980).

B. *DCA* 188–89; *MTC* 292–97; *TSAPR* 48–56; Wendy Zorba, "Bill Bright's Wonderful Plan for the World," *CT* 41:8 (14 July 1997): 14–27; Richard Quebedeaux, *I Found It! The Story of Bill Bright and Campus Crusade* (San Francisco: Harper & Row, 1979).

**BUSWELL, (J)AMES OLIVER, JR.** (16 January 1895, Burlington, WI–3 February 1977, St. Louis, MO). *Education*: A.B., University of Minnesota, 1917; B.D., McCormick Theological Seminary, 1923; M.A., University of Chicago,

1924; Ph.D., New York University, 1949. *Career*: Army chaplain, 1918–19; pastor, 1919–26; president, Wheaton College, 1926–40; professor, 1926–70.

Perhaps no person better symbolized the contradictions within pre–World War II American fundamentalism than J. Oliver Buswell. An army chaplain during the First World War, Buswell enjoyed a brief career as a Northern Presbyterian pastor in Milwaukee, Wisconsin, and Brooklyn, New York, before he was named president of Wheaton College in 1926. At Wheaton, Buswell had the unenviable task of succeeding Jonathan and Charles Blanchard, the father and son team who led Wheaton for a total of sixty-five years (1860–1925). Immediately, Buswell set about transforming the school from a small Bible college into perhaps the most important undergraduate institution in twentieth-century American evangelicalism.

During Buswell's tenure, Wheaton's student population nearly quadrupled, and for three years, it led all American liberal arts colleges in growth of enrollment. Most important for Wheaton's educational future, Buswell instituted widespread curricular reform. The classical offerings of the old-time college were scrapped in favor of modern courses in the physical and natural sciences, an increase in electives, proliferation of new departments and majors, and establishment of professional and vocational programs. Doctoral-bearing professors were hired in abundance, and Wheaton consistently went far beyond the minimal requirements for accreditation in the North Central Association. Buswell's efforts won for Wheaton the designation, "Harvard of the Bible Belt."

Yet, all these progressive reforms were balanced by a consistent commitment to the fundamentalist wing of American evangelicalism. The uneasy institutional balance mirrored the balance that Buswell strove for in his own religious life. In some ways, he was less successful in achieving this equilibrium than Wheaton. Indeed, Buswell's career as president of Wheaton showed a clear tendency toward radical separatist fundamentalism. Allied with the conservatives in the Northern Presbyterian denominational battles of the 1920s, Buswell followed *J. Gresham Machen into the Orthodox Presbyterian Church in 1936, then split with Machen to form the Bible Presbyterian Church with Carl McIntire one year later. Denominational controversy only intensified his separatist tendencies. Eventually this radicalism grew thin with the Wheaton College trustees who were interested in maintaining the school's growing interdenominational constituency. Pugnacious and intransigent, Buswell was forced to resign from the Wheaton presidency in 1940.

From Wheaton, Buswell migrated to Faith Theological Seminary in Wilmington, Delaware (1940–47); the National Bible Institute (later Shelton College) in New York City (1941–55); and Covenant College (1956–64) and Covenant Theological Seminary (1956–70) in St. Louis, Missouri. A professor of theology who authored eleven books, Buswell's most enduring scholarly effort was his two-volume, *Systematic Theology of the Christian Religion* (1962–63). His greater fame however, is the sizable imprint he left on the developing "neoevangelical" movement in America as president of Wheaton College.

*Bibliography*

A. *A Systematic Theology of the Christian Religion*, 2 vols. (Grand Rapids, Mich.: Zondervan, 1962–63).

B. *DCA* 203–4; *TDCB* 80; Michael S. Hamilton, "The Fundamentalist Harvard: Wheaton College and the Continuing Vitality of American Evangelicalism, 1919–1965," (Ph.D. diss., University of Notre Dame, 1994).

# C

**CARNELL, EDWARD JOHN** (28 June 1919, Antigo, WI–25 April 1967, Oakland, CA). *Education*: B.A., Wheaton College, 1941; Th.B., Th.M., Westminster Theological Seminary, 1944; Th.D., Harvard University, 1948; Ph.D., Boston University, 1949. *Career*: Baptist pastor, 1945–46; college professor and theologian, 1945–54; 1959–67; president, Fuller Theological Seminary, 1954–59.

Edward John Carnell was probably the most significant theologian to emerge from the post–World War II American "neoevangelical" subculture. Born and raised in a separatist fundamentalist Baptist household, he followed the path taken by several of his contemporaries who were interested in preserving the theological integrity of conservative evangelicalism while seeking to engage the larger American culture both socially and intellectually. Evangelicals like Carnell were convinced that Christianity could hold its own in the marketplace of ideas through a rigorous apologetic witness.

After a lackluster academic performance in high school, Carnell began to blossom intellectually at Wheaton under the tutelage of Gordon H. Clark, professor of philosophy. Clark's apologetic methodology, which argued for the logical consistency of Christianity against other faiths, made a tremendous impression on Carnell. Set on the career path of teacher and theologian, Carnell went on to Westminster Theological Seminary where he studied philosophy in greater depth under Cornelius Van Til. Concurrent doctoral studies at Harvard and Boston universities helped the young scholar sharpen his theological approach. Carnell learned as much from struggling with the existentialism of Reinhold Niebuhr as from the more palatable teachings of D. Elton Trueblood and Edgar S. Brightman.

In the midst of grueling graduate studies, Carnell pastored at the First Baptist Church of Marblehead (Mass.) and taught philosophy and religion at Gordon College and Divinity School. By 1948 he had developed into something of an academic prodigy, with two earned doctorates and a prize-winning book, *An Introduction to Christian Apologetics*. That year, at the invitation of *Harold John Ockenga, Carnell became one of the first professors at the new Fuller

Theological Seminary in Pasadena, California. Throughout the early years of Fuller, Carnell shared the teaching of apologetics and systematic theology with his friend and former Boston University classmate, *Carl F. H. Henry.

At Fuller with Henry, Carnell played a major role in shaping the theological agenda of neoevangelicalism. In addition to his work on Christian apologetics, he wrote several other significant books including *The Theology of Reinhold Niebuhr* (1950); *Television, Servant or Master?* (1950); *A Philosophy of the Christian Religion* (1952); and *Christian Commitment* (1957). In 1954 Carnell left the classroom to take up administrative duties as Fuller's president. Despite his lack of administrative experience and his reticence to engage in presidential duties like fund raising, Carnell's leadership earned Fuller accreditation from the Association of American Theological Schools in 1957.

Still, the presidential years took a toll on Carnell's health. Fuller's persistent financial difficulties were a constant worry for Carnell, exacerbating a severe insomnia problem from which he had suffered since his youth. Carnell was also troubled that he was unable to maintain the illustrious publication record of his early academic career. It has been suggested that Carnell's core difficulty was the severe emotional strain he experienced from his divided loyalties between the old fundamentalism of his youth and the new evangelicalism of his later years. In any case, few were surprised when an exhausted Carnell suffered a complete emotional breakdown shortly after resigning the Fuller presidency in 1959.

Carnell's last years were spent battling the demons of mental depression. Periodic shock treatments and psychotherapy helped him to return to the classroom, but Carnell seemed at times a shell of his former self. He remained one of Fuller's most popular teachers although students were increasingly embarrassed by his uneven pedagogical performances. Carnell used a copious amount of sleeping pills to deal with his chronic insomnia. It was an overdose of the pills that caused his death at a conference on 25 April 1967.

Deeply rooted in the Reformed tradition, Carnell was a conservative evangelical who wanted to move his religious subculture beyond what he called "cultic" fundamentalism. As one of the most prominent theological architects of the "new evangelicalism," Carnell stood in the line of theologians—*Charles Hodge, *Benjamin Breckinridge Warfield, and *J. Gresham Machen—who were convinced that Christianity was a thoroughly reasonable faith. As such, Carnell's approach to apologetics was a logical one based on the conviction that the human mind could cognitively receive the divine propositions of God. In the modern age, Carnell's methodology was an attractive one, and it made him one of the most respected and influential theologians in American evangelicalism.

*Bibliography*

A. *An Introduction to Christian Apologetics* (Grand Rapids, Mich.: Eerdmans, 1948); *The Case for Orthodox Theology* (Philadelphia: Westminster, 1959).

B. *BT* 606–26; *DCA* 225; *HET* 321–37; *RLA* 85–86; Rudolph Nelson, *The Making and*

*Unmaking of an Evangelical Mind: The Case of Edward Carnell* (Cambridge: Cambridge University Press, 1987).

**CARTER, JAMES EARL, JR. (JIMMY)** (1 October 1924, Plains, GA—). *Education*: B.S., United States Naval Academy, 1946. *Career*: Naval officer, 1946–53; farmer, 1953–63, 1967–71, 1975–77; Georgia legislator, 1963–67; Georgia governor, 1971–75; U.S. president, 1977–81; businessman and educator, 1981—.

The most insistently religious president since Woodrow Wilson, Jimmy Carter was born in the heart of the Bible Belt and was spiritually nurtured on the Christian Scriptures. Raised a Southern Baptist, he professed faith in Christ at age eleven and joined the local Baptist church in Plains, Georgia. As a young adult he became a Sunday School teacher—a duty that joyfully engaged him even after he became president of the United States.

A bright, intense young man, Carter broke out of the parochialism that overwhelmed so many southern males of his generation and received officer training and studied nuclear engineering at the U.S. Naval Academy. After graduating in 1946, Carter had thoughts of becoming a career naval officer, but resigned his commission in 1953 upon the death of his father to take over the family peanut farm. By the time he returned to Plains, he had started a family, having married his childhood sweetheart, Rosalynn Smith, shortly after his graduation from Annapolis.

Although he experienced success as a farmer, Carter had an agile mind that found greater challenges in the world of politics. After dabbling in local politics, he was elected to the Georgia state senate in 1962. In the midst of two successive terms, he unsuccessfully challenged incumbent Lester Maddox for the governorship of Georgia in 1966. To some Georgians, Carter's progressive views on race were too radical. However, Carter was able to win the statehouse on his second try in 1970 as one of the "New South" breed of politicians.

When Carter ran for the U.S. presidency in 1976, most dismissed his candidacy. Yet, events were conspiring in an advantageous way for Carter. Years of political and social unrest, culminating with an unsatisfactory end to the war in Vietnam, racial upheaval, and the Watergate political scandal, created an openness among many Americans toward electing a Washington "outsider" as president. Carter's obvious evangelical faith that promised an honest government seemed refreshing after the disgraced Nixon administration. As Carter began a slow ascent in the polls, he was also assisted by a growing media fascination with all things evangelical. Carter's candidacy seemed to represent a legitimation of the beliefs and practices of the evangelical subculture—a reversal of the banishment of conservative Christianity to the cultural periphery that had been in effect since the 1920s. Carter's campaign also appealed powerfully to the pride of southerners to elect one of their "own" to the presidency.

All these factors contributed to Carter's improbable win in 1976. Ironically however, the distinctively evangelical aspects of his character seemed to contribute to Carter's undoing as president. A Christian realist in the tradition of Reinhold Niebuhr, Carter believed that power tends to corrupt essentially sinful human beings. At times, his insistence on temperance and moderation, particularly in foreign affairs, made him seem indecisive and vacillating. Additionally, his Baptist upbringing, which emphasized a strict separation between church and state, made Carter reluctant to use religious symbolism to promote his political agenda. Critics interpreted his strong display of moralism as self-righteousness and an unwillingness to compromise. The outsider status that helped get him elected was a liability when it came time to govern; political coalitions were forged with only the greatest difficulty as Carter found few natural allies in Washington.

Carter's record as president was decidedly uneven. Domestic successes, particularly in the area of governmental reform, were outweighed by increasing inflation, unemployment, and federal deficits. The situation was brighter in foreign affairs: Full diplomatic recognition was accorded to the People's Republic of China, a new Panama Canal treaty was ratified, and the Camp David peace accord ended the age-old conflict between Israel and Egypt. Ironically, all these successes were largely undone when Carter was stymied by the taking of American hostages in the aftermath of the Iranian revolution (1979–80).

To win reelection in 1980, it was obvious that Carter would have to retain the support of southern evangelicals. Regarding this objective, he failed miserably. His inclination to govern as a political moderate ran against the growing conservative impulse in evangelicalism. Groups like the Moral Majority succeeded in vilifying Carter for the "selling out" of Taiwan, the "giveaway" of the Panama Canal, and his ineptitude in handling the Iranian hostage crisis. In the 1980 campaign, Carter was largely outflanked by Ronald Reagan, the former actor, who skillfully appealed to disaffected evangelicals through appeals to nostalgia and political symbolism. Losing the presidency in a landslide, Carter returned to Georgia to assume the life of a private citizen.

After 1981, Carter enjoyed a public rehabilitation. His efforts to establish a research center at Emory University in Atlanta, his service as special diplomatic envoy, and his work for Habitat for Humanity, an evangelical organization that provides economical housing for the poor, reinforced the better characteristics of the evangelical persona that Carter so assiduously displayed as president. Without violating the high moral principles of his southern evangelical worldview, Carter found vindication for both himself and those guiding principles.

*Bibliography*

A. *Why Not the Best?* (New York: Bantam, 1975); *Keeping Faith: Memoirs of a President* (New York: Bantam, 1982); *Living Faith* (New York: Times Books, 1996).

B. *DCA* 227–28; James Baker, *A Southern Baptist in the White House* (Philadelphia: Westminster, 1977); Peter G. Bourne, *Jimmy Carter: A Comprehensive Biography from Plains to Post-Presidency* (New York: Scribners, 1997).

**CHAFER, LEWIS SPERRY** (27 February 1871, Rock Creek, OH–22 August 1952, Seattle, WA). *Education*: Oberlin College. *Career*: Revivalist, 1889–1911; assistant pastor, 1899–1901; Bible institute teacher and administrator, 1911–22; pastor, 1922–24; president and professor of systematic theology, Dallas Theological Seminary, 1924–52.

As a revivalist, teacher, and theologian, Lewis Sperry Chafer did more than most to popularize dispensationalism among American evangelicals in this century. Chafer was the son of a Congregationalist pastor in Rock Creek, Ohio. His father died when Chafer was only eleven years old, and he was left with his brother and sister in the care of his mother. Early on, two passions gripped the young man: music and the ministry. Seeking to combine them in some fashion, Chafer attended Oberlin College and Conservatory. However, while still in his teens, he joined the evangelistic team of A. T. Reed. Ministering with Reed for some five years as revivalist singer and choir director, Chafer found that the pressure of an itinerant life forced him to end his studies at Oberlin in 1891.

After marrying a former Oberlin classmate in 1896, Chafer formed his own revival team and conducted evangelistic meetings throughout the middle Atlantic states and the Southeast until the turn of the century. Through his involvement in musical evangelism, Chafer met and befriended Ira Sankey and George Stebbins, two prominent associates of *Dwight L. Moody. After a brief stint as assistant pastor at the First Congregational Church of Buffalo, New York, Chafer moved to East Northfield, Massachusetts, where he became an important figure in the Moody Northfield Conference ministry.

Through his association with the Moody circle at Northfield, Chafer was introduced to some of the most prominent Bible teachers and revivalists in American evangelicalism. By far the most important acquaintance that Chafer made was *C. I. Scofield. When Chafer met Scofield in 1901, the latter was already a well-known figure in Congregationalism as a pastor, administrator, and featured speaker at Bible and prophecy conferences throughout North America. Working closely with Scofield at Northfield, Chafer came to see the man as a spiritual mentor. During the first years of the twentieth century, Scofield was preoccupied with the production of a new reference Bible. The interpretative schema ("Scofield's Notes"), which would be a prominent part of the Bible when it was published in 1909, greatly influenced Chafer in his approach to biblical exegesis. Like Scofield, Chafer became a thoroughgoing dispensationalist.

As Scofield's primary associate, Chafer helped his mentor establish the Scofield School of Bible in New York City in 1911 and the Philadelphia School of the Bible in 1914. For both institutes, Chafer served as administrator and teacher of Bible and theology. He also published many of his books during this period: *True Evangelism* (1911), *The Kingdom in History and Prophecy* (1915), and *Salvation* (1917). One year after Scofield's death, Chafer moved to Dallas where he assumed his friend's former pastorate at the First Congregational Church (renamed Scofield Memorial Church). Concerned that theological seminaries failed to train prospective ministers as effective Bible teachers, Chafer organized the Evangelical Theological College in 1924. The school became Dallas Theological Seminary in 1936.

The financial and administrative burden of starting and sustaining a nondenominational seminary was sizable, but it was a challenge that Chafer undertook with great enthusiasm. As president and professor of systematic theology from 1924 until his death in 1952, Chafer succeeded in establishing Dallas Seminary as one of the key theological institutions in American fundamentalism. Like Chafer, Dallas was characterized by a conservative Reformed approach to theology tinctured throughout by dispensational premillennialism. Chafer's own theological approach was spelled out in depth in his eight-volume *Systematic Theology* (completed in 1948). Along with the Bible bearing his mentor's name, Chafer's *Systematic Theology* was extremely important in popularizing dispensationalism in the conservative evangelical subculture of America.

*Bibliography*

A. *Systematic Theology*, 8 vols. (Dallas: Dallas Seminary Press, 1947–48).

B. *DCA* 237–38; *HET* 83–96; *RLA* 91–92; C. F. Lincoln, "Biographical Sketch of the Author," in Lewis Sperry Chafer, *Systematic Theology* (Dallas: Dallas Seminary Press, 1948), 8:3–6.

**CHAPMAN, (J)OHN WILBUR** (17 June 1859, Richmond, IN–25 December 1918, New York, NY). *Education*: Oberlin College; B.A., Lake Forest College (IL), 1879; B.D., Lane Seminary, 1882. *Career*: Presbyterian pastor, 1881–1902; corresponding secretary, Presbyterian General Assembly Committee on Evangelism, 1901–2; independent revivalist, 1903–18.

In the unofficial hierarchy of American revivalists, J. Wilbur Chapman is often accorded a place as the most significant personality between *Dwight L. Moody and *Billy Sunday. Joining the Presbyterian Church at age sixteen, Chapman prepared for the pastoral ministry during his college years, first at Oberlin College (1876–77), then at Lake Forest College (1877–79). Even before completing his theological work at Lane Seminary in Cincinnati, Ohio, Chapman was licensed to the ministry of the (Northern) Presbyterian Church USA (1881). Throughout the remainder of the nineteenth century, he served a succession of Presbyterian and Reformed churches: a circuit of two churches in Ohio and Indiana (1882); the Old Saratoga Dutch Reformed Church of Schuylerville, New York (1883–85); the First Dutch Reformed Church of Albany, New York (1885–90); the Bethany Presbyterian Church of Philadelphia (1890–93; 1896–99); and the Fourth Presbyterian Church of New York City (1899–1902).

During the early 1890s, Chapman met Moody. Assisting the great evangelist at the Chicago World's Fair campaign of 1893, Chapman soon became one of Moody's closest associates. For the rest of the 1890s, Chapman gravitated increasingly toward revivalism both through his friendship with Moody and through the ministry of Benjamin Mills, a college classmate. After serving for two years as corresponding secretary of the Presbyterian General Assembly Committee on Evangelism (1901–2), Chapman found his vocational fate sealed. Resigning the pastorate, he teamed with musician Charles Alexander and assumed a full-time revivalist ministry. For the last fifteen years of his life Chapman labored together with Alexander.

By the end of the first decade of the twentieth century, Chapman had taken up Moody's mantle as the greatest living urban evangelist. Significant revival campaigns took place in Boston (1909) and Chicago (1910). No mere imitator of Moody however, Chapman is credited with introducing the innovation of the simultaneous campaign to urban evangelism. In this, Chapman's organization conducted numerous small meetings around the city of focus with an eye toward directing them to the main meeting led by Chapman himself. A gifted speaker and indefatigable worker, Chapman regularly pushed himself to the point of physical collapse, often preaching as many as six times a day during revival campaigns.

In addition to his work as a revivalist, Chapman founded in 1885 and served as the first director of the Winona Lake Bible Conference in Indiana. By enlisting the services of some of the best pastors and religious speakers in the country, the Winona Lake Conference exerted a sizable influence over the lives of countless ministers. Chapman also extended his influence through the thirty-plus books he authored and edited. The most important of these was probably *The Secret of a Happy Life* (1899).

A lesser known aspect of Chapman's life was his association with Billy Sunday, an evangelist whose fame came to eclipse that of Chapman. After meeting Sunday in 1893, Chapman made the former baseball player his full-time assistant. For twenty-three crucial months, the novice Sunday learned how to conduct a revival minstry from one of the most accomplished evangelists in the nation.

Chapman's ministerial career was capped by his election in 1917 to the position of moderator of the Northern Presbyterian church. Less than two years later, like the circuit riders of old, he was physically spent. After emergency surgery on Christmas Day 1918, he died.

*Bibliography*

A. *The Power of a Surrendered Life* (Chicago: Moody, 1900).

B. *DARB* 109–10; *DCA* 240–41; Bernard DeRemer, "J. Wilbur Chapman: Evangelist to the World," *Fundamentalist Journal* 7 (January 1988): 47–50; John C. Ramsay, *John Wilbur Chapman, the Man, his Methods and his Message* (Boston: Christopher Publishing, 1962).

**COLSON, CHARLES** (16 October 1931, Boston, MA—). *Education*: A.B., Brown University, 1953; J.D., George Washington University, 1959. *Career*: U.S. Marine Corps officer, 1953–55; assistant to the assistant secretary of the

U.S. Navy, 1955–56; administrative assistant to U.S. senator Leverett Salton-stall, 1956–61; lawyer, 1961–69; special counsel to U.S. president Richard Nixon, 1969–73; lay minister, president and founder of Prison Fellowship, 1975—.

Charles Colson grew up in Boston, Massachusetts, during the Great Depression. His father worked as a bookkeeper at a meatpacking plant while attending law school at night. In 1949, the younger Colson attended Brown University where he led an active life as a fraternity member, class officer, and commandant of Brown's ROTC unit. After graduation in 1953, Colson joined the U.S. Marine Corps where he attained the rank of captain before the end of his two-year tour of duty.

In 1955, he became assistant to the assistant secretary of the Navy and from 1956–61, administrative assistant to U.S. senator Leverett Saltonstall (R–Mass.). Colson was not even thirty years old when he successfully managed Saltonstall's reelection to the senate in 1960. During his service to Saltonstall, Colson completed a law degree at George Washington University (1959). He then joined the law firm of Gadsby and Hannah in 1961, where he became a senior partner by 1969.

Colson's life took an abrupt turn in 1969 when Richard M. Nixon asked him to join the White House staff as special counsel to the president. Colson's reputation as a hardnosed political operator quickly made him one of the most infamous members of an administration that was filled with scandalous characters. When the Watergate scandal began to unfold, Colson's primary mission was to protect the president at all costs. For that misplaced loyalty, he paid a devastating price, for as Nixon came increasingly under attack, so did Colson. It was a time of personal and spiritual crisis for Colson that resulted in his committing his life to Christ in the summer of 1973.

Colson's conversion to evangelical Christianity became a media event. Skeptics thought he was only attempting to dodge responsibility for his part in the Watergate affair. Many of those same skeptics were dumbfounded in 1974 when Colson pleaded guilty for passing libelous information to the press regarding antiwar activist Daniel Ellsburg, a crime for which Colson had not even been charged. The admission led to a seven-month incarceration at Maxwell Federal Prison It was during his confinement that Colson caught a vision for a new project that would thoroughly dominate his life.

After his release in January 1975, Colson formulated the plan that would lead to the establishment of Prison Fellowship Ministries, an organization designed to lead prisoners to Christ and to help them grow in their faith. With the assistance of friends and the royalties from his book, *Born Again*, Colson launched Prison Fellowship in 1976. Fifteen years after its creation, Prison Fellowship had grown to a network of 40,000 Christian volunteers from churches all across America and thousands more in forty other countries.

In addition to introducing prisoners to Christ, Prison Fellowship seeks to equip them to become responsible and productive citizens upon their release.

Services to the families of prisoners also exist in the form of seminars on marriage and gifts to prisoners' children at Christmas. Prison Fellowship is also active in criminal justice reform efforts, restoration for crime victims, and restitution to communities through inmate work projects.

The success of Prison Fellowship has made Charles Colson a much-admired figure in contemporary evangelical circles. Although his earlier books were more autobiographical (*Born Again* in 1975, *Life Sentence* in 1979), several later books offered a pungent criticism of contemporary American culture (*Presenting Belief in an Age of Unbelief*, 1986 and *Kingdoms in Conflict*, 1987). In the mid–1990s, Colson collaborated with Richard John Neuhaus, the editor of the journal *First Things*, to produce the document "Evangelicals and Catholics Together," a statement of ecumenical solidarity and religious social justice. The document, with six accompanying essays, was published in 1995 by Word Publishing. Assisted by contributors around the world and the proceeds from the 1993 Templeton Prize, Colson, the "hatchetman" turned lay minister, continues to promote the worthy agenda of Prison Fellowship.

*Bibliography*

A. *Born Again* (Old Tappan, N.J.: Chosen, 1976); *Life Sentence* (Minneapolis, Minn.: Grason, 1979); *Presenting Belief in an Age of Unbelief* (Wheaton, Ill.: Victor, 1986); *Kingdoms in Conflict* (New York: Morrow, 1987); *Evangelicals and Catholics Together* (Dallas: Word, 1995).

B. *CANR* 54:88–91; Andrea Sachs, "Colson Wins Templeton Prize," *ABA Journal* 79 (May 1993): 38–39; Stella Wiseman, *Charles Colson and the Story of Prison Fellowship* (London: Marshall Pickering, 1995).

**CRAWFORD, PERCY B.** (20 October 1902, Minnedosa, Manitoba–31 October 1960, Trenton, NJ). *Education*: Bible Institute of Los Angeles (BIOLA); UCLA; B.A., Wheaton College, 1929; Th.B., Westminster Theological Seminary, 1932; M.A., University of Pennsylvania, 1932; D.D., Bob Jones University, 1940. *Career*: Youth minister; religious broadcaster; college educator and administrator.

An often neglected, yet highly significant figure in the history of twentieth-century American evangelicalism, Percy Crawford was a pioneer in the development of parachurch youth ministries, as well as the use of modern mass media to promote revivalism.

Crawford was born in Canada and converted to the Christian faith in the Church of the Open Door in Los Angeles in 1923. After studying at BIOLA and UCLA, Crawford moved on to Wheaton College where he obtained his bachelor's degree. While at Wheaton, Crawford resolved to enter the Presbyterian ministry and later enrolled in Westminster Seminary in Philadelphia. During his second year of theological studies, he became focused on "reaching youth with the truth." Translating his vision into action, Crawford initiated the Young People's Church of the Air radio broadcasts over Philadelphia station

WIT in 1931. Assisted by his wife, Ruth, Crawford became one of the best-known ministers to youth in the United States. He was constantly in demand as a speaker and revival leader at youth rallies throughout the country in the 1930s and 1940s.

Although not formally associated with Youth for Christ (YFC), Crawford's work became the model and inspiration for YFC founders *Torrey M. Johnson and Jack Wyrtzen. During World War II, Crawford often spoke at YFC rallies, including the first anniversary of the Chicagoland Youth for Christ gathering in 1944, which drew some 70,000 attendees. By this time, the Young People's Church of the Air was broadcast by the Mutual and American networks on 450 stations. With the exception of *Charles E. Fuller, Crawford was responsible for the most listened to religious radio program in America. Anxious to take advantage of newer technology, Crawford developed one of the first coast-to-coast religious television broadcasts in 1950.

In addition to his work as a youth evangelist and broadcaster, Crawford organized and operated three Pinebrook Bible Camps, which were headquartered at Stroudsburg, Pennsylvania, as well as King's College in Briarcliff Manor, New York. Crawford was still making numerous speaking appearances at churches around the country when he died after suffering a heart attack in 1960.

*Bibliography*

A. *The Art of Fishing for Men* (Philadelphia: n.p., 1935).

B. *DCA* 326; *New York Times* [obituary] (1 November 1960): 40; *PTR* 68–69; Robert Bahr, *Man with a Vision: The Story of Percy Crawford* (Chicago: Moody, 1987).

**CROSBY (VAN ALSTYNE), FANNY** (24 March 1820, Putnam County, NY– 12 February 1915, Bridgeport, CT). *Education*: New York School for the Blind. *Career*: Teacher, 1848–58; hymn writer, 1844–1915.

The writer of some of the best-known evangelical hymns of the nineteenth century was blind from the age of six weeks because of the blunder of a physician. Yet Fanny Crosby, who wrote an amazing 9,000 hymns in her long life, never asked for pity or displayed remorse over her circumstances. Rather, she praised God for her great gift and thought that her blindness actually made her a better songwriter.

Crosby was born to a family of venerable ancestry in Putnam County, New York. In addition to her blindness, she suffered the death of her father when she was less than one year old. This necessitated the move of the Crosby family to North Salem, New York, then (in 1828) to Ridgefield, Connecticut, where Crosby grew up. More than compensating for her disability, Crosby developed her memory in phenomenal fashion, memorizing the first four books of the Old and New Testaments by the time she was ten years old. Crosby's family was devoutly Christian, and she was imparted a deep appreciation for religious faith at an early age. She also loved to learn and was especially attracted to the study of literature and poetry.

Beginning in 1835, she studied formally at the New York School for the Blind. Thirteen years later she became a teacher at the school, a career that she pursued until she married Alexander Van Alstyne, a musician who was also blind, in 1858. Her love for the Christian Scriptures and poetry and her deep faith in God translated into creative compositions. Her first publication, *The Blind Girl and Other Poems*, appeared in 1844. The hymns began to surface at the same time; by the end of the Civil War Crosby was writing them at a rapid pace. Among Crosby's works are some of the best loved hymns in American evangelicalism: "All the Way My Savior Leads Me," "Blessed Assurance," "I Am Thine, O Lord," "Jesus, Keep Me Near the Cross," "Praise Him, Praise Him," "Rescue the Perishing," "Redeemed, How I Love to Proclaim It," "Tell Me the Story of Jesus," and "To God Be the Glory." More than writing compelling hymns, however, Crosby succeeded in creating an entire genre of religious music; the rhyme and diction of her hymns continue to resonate in contemporary evangelical songs.

As her lyrics became known and loved by her generation, Crosby enjoyed a measure of fame largely unmatched by any other American woman in the nineteenth century. The greatest musicians—among them Howard Doane, George Stebbins, and Ira Sankey—clamored to add notes to her inspiring words. Her poetry was admired by such luminaries as Queen Victoria, John Quincy Adams, Henry Clay, John Tyler, James Polk, Stephen Douglas, William Seward, William Cullen Bryant, Jefferson Davis, Horace Greeley, and Grover Cleveland, among others. Yet through it all she remained humble. Seeing her talent and accompanying fame as a way to preach the gospel, she traveled regularly on speaking tours. Never permitting her blindness to become an obstacle, she usually made her journeys alone and even contemplated becoming a missionary to Africa for a time. At the unlikely age of sixty, she began a ministry among the poor in New York City's Bowery district.

Crosby never became wealthy from her prodigious creative output. She accepted only about $2 for each of her compositions, and she and her husband lived frugally in southern Connecticut. "Mrs. Crosby," as she was known to the public, continued to pen lyrics right up to her death. Her last hymn, "In the Morn of Zion's Glory," written to comfort a neighbor family who had lost a young child, was completed on 11 February 1915. One day later, at age ninety-four, Crosby died. Yet her amazing musical legacy lives on in thousands of churches across America where on any given Sunday a hymn written by Fanny Crosby can be heard.

*Bibliography*

A. *Memories of Eighty Years* (Boston, Mass.: J. H. Earle, 1900); *Fanny Crosby's Life-Story, By Herself* (New York: Every Where, 1903).

B. *DARB* 131–32; *DCA* 329; *RLA* 116; Bernard Ruffin, *Fanny Crosby* (Westwood, N.J.: Barbour, 1976); Ethel Barrett, *Fanny Crosby* (Ventura, Calif.: Regal, 1984).

**CROUCH, ANDRAE** (1 July 1942, Los Angeles, CA—). *Education*: San Fernando Valley Junior College; Life Bible College (CA). *Career*: Gospel singer and songwriter.

One of the major figures in contemporary Christian music, Andrae Crouch was born in Los Angeles, California, during World War II. The son of a Holiness minister, Crouch displayed an early aptitude for music, and began to play piano and sing in the church choir at a young age. He found that performing helped him to overcome a lifelong stuttering problem.

Crouch began his professional musical career by forming the Crouch Trio with his twin sister Sandra and a brother. By the early sixties this group had evolved into the Church of God in Christ Singers (COGICS). Besides Crouch and his sister, many participants in the COGICS went on to have successful musical careers of their own, including Billy Preston, Blinky Williams, Gloria Jones, Frankie Spring, and Edna Wright. In the late 1960s, Crouch formed the Disciples, a group that became a prominent force not only in black gospel music, but also in the nascent ''contemporary Christian'' sound.

Skillfully combining a talent for songwriting with an ability to synthesize rhythm and blues, jazz, and popular arrangements, Crouch has toured the world many times with his musical ministry. Of his more than 300 gospel songs, the best known are: ''My Tribute,'' ''Through It All,'' ''Soon and Very Soon,'' and ''The Blood Will Never Lose Its Power.'' In the 1980s, Crouch became one of the first gospel ''crossover'' artists to enjoy a substantial amount of success in the larger nonreligious American musical market when his music for the film ''The Color Purple'' received an Oscar nomination. Several of his most popular songs are now included in recent editions of various denominational hymnals.

*Bibliography*

A. *Through It All* (Waco, Tex.: Word, 1974).

B. *DPCM* 230; *EAAR* 214–15.

# D

**DEHAAN, MARTIN R.** (23 March 1891, Zeeland, MI–13 December 1965, Grand Rapids, MI). *Education*: Hope College, 1909–10; B.A., M.D., University of Illinois, 1914; B.D., Western Theological Seminary, 1925. *Career*: Medical doctor, 1914–22; pastor, 1925–38; religious broadcaster, 1938–64.

One of the most popular religious radio broadcasts in American evangelicalism was started by Martin DeHaan in the late 1930s. DeHaan, the son of first generation Dutch immigrants, grew up in western Michigan and decided to become a medical doctor after a year at Hope College in Holland, Michigan. After graduating from the College of Medicine at the University of Illinois in 1914, DeHaan was licensed to practice medicine and, with his new wife, settled down to become a small town doctor in Byron's Corner, Michigan.

In 1921, DeHaan's life took a most unexpected turn when he almost died after experiencing a severe allergic reaction to some medicine. While recovering in the hospital, DeHaan professed faith in Christ and decided to give up medicine in favor of the ministry. After graduating from Western Theological Seminary in 1925, he became pastor of the Calvin Reformed Church in Grand Rapids. DeHaan's thirteen-year pastoral career was a rocky one. He had been raised in the Reformed tradition, yet while at seminary he became a premillennialist through his study of the *Scofield Reference Bible*. His studies also persuaded him that there was no scriptural justification for infant baptism. Both of these new views placed him at odds with traditional Reformed doctrines. In accord with his new beliefs, DeHaan withdrew from the Reformed Church in America in 1929 and founded an independent fundamentalist assembly. DeHaan pastored his Calvary Undenominational Church for nine years before disagreements with church members and a heart attack caused him to resign in 1938.

Upon the suggestion of a friend, DeHaan began to teach a Bible study class over a Detroit radio station. The program attracted many listeners. In 1941, DeHaan moved his radio ministry to Grand Rapids as the "Radio Bible Class." Slowly but steadily the ministry became a national enterprise until eventually it was heard on several hundred radio stations around the world. The "Radio Bible Class" was just that, as DeHaan distributed the radio Bible lessons to his listeners via the mail. These Bible lessons became known as *Our Daily Bread*, one of the most used devotional booklets in post–World War II American evangelicalism.

For twenty-five years, DeHaan's voice was heard throughout the world as the host and teacher of the "Radio Bible Class." During periods of ill health, DeHaan was relieved by his son Richard, who succeeded him at the helm of the "Radio Bible Class" upon Martin's death in 1965. In the 1980s, Richard DeHaan extended the family ministry into television with the highly rated "Day of Discovery" program.

*Bibliography*

A. *Daniel the Prophet* (Grand Rapids, Mich.: Zondervan, 1947); *Our Daily Bread: 366 Devotional Meditations* (Grand Rapids, Mich.: Zondervan, 1959).

B. *DCA* 347; *PTR* 79–80; *RLA* 128; James Adair, *M. R. DeHaan: The Man and His Ministry* (Grand Rapids, Mich.: Zondervan, 1969).

**DOBSON, JAMES C., JR.** (21 April 1936, Shreveport, LA—). *Education*: B.S., Pasadena College, 1958; M.A., Ph.D., University of Southern California, 1962, 1967. *Career*: Public school teacher and counselor, 1960–64; psychologist, 1964–66; professor, School of Medicine, University of Southern California, 1966–83; founder and president, Focus on the Family, 1977—.

Prominent in late twentieth-century American evangelicalism, Dobson was born in Louisiana, but was raised in several small towns across Oklahoma and Texas. The only child of a Church of the Nazarene pastor, Dobson was highly influenced by his fundamentalist parents. He attended Pasadena College, a Nazarene institution, to pursue interests in education and psychology and then received master's and doctoral degrees from the University of Southern California. After a short career in California public schools, Dobson joined the faculty of the USC medical school in 1966.

Dobson came to prominence with his book *Dare to Discipline* in 1970. Intended as a conservative Christian alternative to the "permissive" child rearing philosophy popularized by Benjamin Spock, *Dare to Discipline* combined Dobson's experience as a psychologist with biblical principles to emphasize consistent use of discipline, including corporal punishment, in parenting. The book was particularly popular among evangelical Christians who blamed a host of societal evils at the end of the 1960s on parental permissiveness. Dobson's book led to a series of workshops on parenting, a video series, and a radio program entitled "Focus on the Family."

The approach taken in *Dare to Discipline* was not well received by everyone. Skeptical psychologists accused Dobson of offering his readers authoritarian and simplistic answers to difficult behavioral problems. On the other hand, some evangelicals voiced suspicion of a methodology that was somewhat sympathetic to that of behavioralists like B. F. Skinner. It was clear however, that Dobson had touched a nerve in the American evangelical community.

In 1977, Dobson founded the organization Focus on the Family in Pomona, California. By that time, his prominence as a radio commentator led to an appointment to a national task force on children and the family by President *Jimmy Carter. Additional books like *The Strong-Willed Child* (1978) and *Straight Talk to Men and Their Wives* (1980) built upon and expanded themes explored in Dobson's first book. In 1994, *Dare to Discipline*, which had sold more than 2 million copies, was reissued as *The New Dare to Discipline*.

By the mid–1990s, Focus on the Family, now headquartered in Colorado Springs, Colorado, was a formidable force in evangelical circles. Reaching 5 million listeners on 2,500 radio stations and controlling a $101 million budget related to sixty-two different ministries, Dobson was increasingly seen as an ascendant figure in the religious right. He was also more explicitly political, speaking out stridently against abortion, pornography, and homosexuality. Through the establishment of a national Family Research Council and thirty-five state Family Councils, which are officially independent from Focus on the Family, Dobson promoted a conservative "family values" political agenda that was highly attractive to the one-third of all Republicans who identified themselves as evangelical Christians. In the 1996 presidential campaign, Dobson's threats to lead his constituency out of the GOP over a perceived softening concerning the Republican Party's antiabortion stand was taken very seriously by GOP leaders. Increasingly, the various Family Research Councils have shown a willingness to mount legal challenges to laws that mandate the separation of church and state in the public sphere.

Respected by many, although feared by some, Dobson remained one of the more influential evangelical commentators in the late 1990s.

*Bibliography*

A. *Dare to Discipline* (Wheaton, Ill.: Tyndale House, 1970); *The Strong-Willed Child* (Eastbourne: Kingsway, 1978).

B. *PTR* 81–82; *TDCB* 124–25; Rodney Clapp, "Meet James Dobson," *CT* 26:9 (7 May 1982): 14–15; Tim Stafford, "His Father's Son," *CT* 32:7 (22 April 1988): 16–22; Dale D. Buss, "Focusing on the Family With James Dobson," *The American Enterprise* 6:6 (November-December 1995): 43–47.

# E

**ELLIOT, ELISABETH HOWARD** (21 December 1926, Brussels, Belgium—). *Education*: B.A., Wheaton College, 1948; Prairie Bible Institute. Career: Missionary to Ecuador, 1952–63; adjunct professor, Gordon-Conwell Theological Seminary, 1974–80; writer-in-residence, Gordon College, 1981—; radio commentator, 1988—.

Drawing from a wealth of personal experiences as a foreign missionary and twice-widowed mother, Elisabeth Elliot is a powerful inspirational author. She was born in Brussels, Belgium, where her father was a missionary, in 1926. By the age of twelve, Elliot began to believe that she should follow the example of her parents and become a missionary. This conviction deepened during her years at Wheaton College where she met and fell in love with the dynamic Jim Elliot, who shared a similar calling.

After graduating from Wheaton College in 1948, Elisabeth prepared in earnest to serve as a missionary. Four years later, after an intensive study of the Spanish language, Elisabeth joined Jim in a ministry to the Quichua people in Ecuador. Together they worked on translating the New Testament into the native Quichuan language. Their long relationship blossomed into marriage on 8 October 1953; less than two years later the Elliots' only child, Valerie, was born.

For years Jim had prayed about taking the Christian gospel to the Auca Indians, a primitive and ruthless tribe in the jungles of Ecuador. Working with pilot Nate Saint and fellow missionaries Ed McCully, Pete Fleming, and Roger Youderian, Jim finally achieved contact with the Aucas on 6 January 1956. All the excitement and hope of this initial contact tragically evaporated two days later when Aucan warriors turned on the missionaries and brutally murdered them.

Jim Elliot's death led Elisabeth to continue the mission efforts among the Aucas. In 1958, Elisabeth entered the village of the Aucas—the first white woman to do so—and lived and ministered among them for five years. She also became the chronicler of her late husband and his associates through such books as *Through the Gates of Splendor* (1957), *Shadow of the Almighty* (1958), and *The Journals of Jim Elliot* (1979). Her own work among the Aucas was detailed in *The Savage My Kinsman* (1961).

Returning to the United States in 1963, Elliot met and married her second husband, Addison Leitch, a professor at Gordon-Conwell Theological Seminary, on 1 January 1969. However, her domestic bliss was shattered in 1973 when Leitch died of cancer. In the 1960s and early 1970s, Elliot channelled her grief into several books that reflected upon the faithfulness of Christ in the face of life's storms: *No Graven Image* (1966), *Who Shall Ascend?* (1968), *The Liberty of Obedience* (1968), and *A Slow and Certain Light* (1973). The largely auto-biographical *These Strange Ashes* was published in 1975. In actuality, however, all of Elliot's books contain substantial reflections on her own life.

After Leitch's death, Elliot taught at Gordon-Conwell, toured as a Christian speaker, and continued to write. In 1977, she married E. Lars Gren. Since then, Elliot's books have dwelt on the themes of suffering, the family, womanhood, marriage, and discipline. In the late 1980s, Elliot began hosting "Gateway to Joy," a daily radio program sponsored by Back to the Bible Ministries of Lincoln, Nebraska. "Gateway to Joy" was aimed at an evangelical female audience and dealt with such issues as motherhood, femininity, and marriage.

*Bibliography*

A. *Through the Gates of Splendor* (New York: Harper, 1957); *Shadow of the Almighty* (New York: Harper, 1958); *The Savage My Kinsman* (New York: Harper, 1961); *These Strange Ashes* (San Francisco: Harper & Row, 1975).

B. *CANR* 6: 160; *PTR* 84; *TDCB* 132.

# F

**FALWELL, JERRY** (11 August 1933, Lynchburg, VA—). *Education*: B.A., Baptist Bible College (Springfield, MO), 1956. *Career*: Independent Baptist pastor, 1956—; founder and president, Moral Majority, 1979–89.

With the exception of *Billy Graham, no American evangelical received more attention from the press in the late 1970s and 1980s than Jerry Falwell. Born to a fundamentalist mother and a non-Christian, alcoholic, businessman father, Falwell developed early religious attitudes that were decidedly schizophrenic. As a young man he drifted away from the Christian faith only to return in his late teens. After receiving a theological education at Baptist Bible College in Springfield, Missouri, he became the new pastor of a splinter group of the Park Avenue Baptist Church in Lynchburg in 1956. Rechristened the "Thomas Road Baptist Church," the congregation enjoyed spectacular growth increasing from a initial group of thirty-five in 1957 to 10,000 in 1970 and 15,000 in 1978.

Crucial to Falwell's success as a pastor was his use of the media. After starting Thomas Road Baptist Church, he initiated a daily radio ministry entitled "Deep Things of God." This was followed by a television broadcast of the weekly Sunday service. By 1966, the televised service was syndicated throughout the country as "The Old-Time Gospel Hour." The similarity to *Charles E. Fuller's "Old Fashioned Revival Hour" radio program in the 1940s was intentional, as Fuller's use of the media to spread the gospel greatly influenced Falwell's own approach.

By the mid–1970s, membership numbers at Thomas Road Baptist brought Falwell prominence in evangelical circles. Yet he found greater fame through his growing social activism. Heretofore this activism was unthinkable for a separatist fundamentalist like Falwell, who in the 1960s placed preaching the gospel above all social causes. However, by the 1970s, Falwell resolved that national crises like the breakdown of the family, legalization of abortion, and the proliferation of pornography necessitated a more active response by Christians in the political arena. Passivity, not activism, threatened to destroy the lifestyle of American evangelicals. Thus, Falwell emerged from the 1970s as a key leader of a "new fundamentalism" that eschewed separatism for highly organized political confrontation. The key vehicle to translate this activist philosophy into action was the Moral Majority, formed by Falwell in 1979.

As the pivotal figure in the Moral Majority, Falwell was both glorified and vilified by the American public. Many evangelicals believed it was high time for Christians to "reclaim America for God." These people found the message of the Moral Majority particularly compelling. The national media, on the other hand, were at a loss on how to regard Falwell and his organization. Others, while somewhat sympathetic to Moral Majority's concerns, looked askance at a highly mobilized religious organization that threatened to overturn the time-honored institutionalized American separation between church and state. To these people there was something fearfully un-American about a Baptist pastor like Falwell leading the fundamentalist charge to the political battlefield. Finally, to complete the ring of opposition to Falwell's new activism, there were the traditional separatists who viewed his change of heart as something akin to apostasy—a repudiation of the proper priority of preaching the gospel to win souls. As Billy Graham did in the late 1950s, Falwell in the early 1980s found himself under a withering attack at the hands of his fundamentalist soulmates who believed he had departed from his proper calling.

For Falwell, the criticism, particularly from his co-fundamentalists, was taxing. Especially vexing to Falwell was the inability of the Moral Majority to implement its socially conservative agenda even with the Reagan administration and the Republican legislators in office. It was probably this fact more than anything else that led Falwell to dissolve the Moral Majority in 1989. Another factor contributing to Falwell's retreat from the public eye was his ill-fated attempt to bring order to the scandal-ridden PTL ministry of Jim and Tammy Faye Bakker in 1987. Originally asked by the Bakkers to save their ministry, Falwell soon found himself attacked in the media by the Bakkers and their supporters for "stealing" the PTL corporation. In retaliation, Falwell blew the whistle on Jim Bakker's homosexual activities and further financial abuses before withdrawing to the sanctuary of Lynchburg.

Although Falwell has maintained a much lower public profile in the 1990s, he remains a powerful force in contemporary evangelicalism. In the American tradition of dynamic evangelical preachers, Falwell has built an empire with a large megachurch, a worldwide media presence, and Liberty University, an accredited institution of higher education. As if to confirm his commitment to the "new fundamentalism," however, Falwell occasionally stepped into the national spotlight as with his highly publicized attacks on President Bill Clinton in the mid–1990s.

*Bibliography*

A. *Strength for the Journey* (New York: Simon and Schuster, 1987); *Falwell, an Autobiography* (Lynchburg, Va.: Liberty House, 1997).

B. *DCA* 427–28; *PTR* 93–99; *RLA* 146–47; *TDCB* 138; *TSAPR* 133–41; Gerald Strober and Ruth Tomczak, *Jerry Falwell: Aflame for God* (Nashville: Thomas Nelson, 1979).

**FULLER, CHARLES E.** (25 April 1887, Redlands, CA–18 March 1968, Los Angeles, CA). *Education*: B.S., Pomona College, 1910; B.D., Bible Institute of Los Angeles, 1921. *Career*: Businessman, 1911–19; pastor, 1925–33; radio and television evangelist; 1933–68; co-founder of Fuller Theological Seminary, 1947.

Charles Fuller was born to a prosperous southern California orange grove owner in 1887. Although raised by devout Methodists, Fuller displayed little interest in religious matters as a youth. After securing a degree in chemistry from Pomona College in 1910, he seemed content to take up the business interests of his father. A year after college, Fuller married his high school sweetheart, Grace Payton, and appeared settled in a comfortable lifestyle.

Fuller's interest in spiritual matters did not blossom until he was converted under the preaching of Paul Rader, pastor of Chicago's Moody Church, in 1916. At Placentia Presbyterian Church, Fuller began to teach an adult Sunday School class, and, feeling unfulfilled in his various business endeavors, entered the Bible Institute of Los Angeles (BIOLA) in 1919 to receive training for the pastorate. Under the tutelage of BIOLA's dean, *Reuben A. Torrey, Fuller developed a religious perspective that was strongly weighted toward fundamentalism and dispensationalism. Fuller then dabbled in volunteer religious work in the Los Angeles area for several years until his fundamentalist views forced him and many of his Sunday school class to split from Placentia Presbyterian in 1925. After obtaining ordination from a group of churches associated with the Baptist Bible Union, Fuller became pastor of the class, which renamed itself Calvary Church.

Convinced that God had given him an evangelistic mandate, Fuller held revival meetings all down the western U.S. coast. He also used radio to spread the gospel. By 1930, he was regularly broadcasting Calvary's Sunday services as well as a Bible study program over southern California stations. When his congregation grew uneasy with the amount of time that Fuller spent on his radio evangelism, he resigned his pastorate in 1933 and formed the nonprofit Gospel Broadcasting Association (GBA) to support his radio and itinerant evangelistic efforts.

Fuller's business acumen enabled him to piece together a patchwork of local and regional radio networks in the 1930s, over which he broadcast a series of inspirational programs. Early on he developed the format of a revival service in front of a live studio audience, a format that served him well for the remainder of his ministerial career. Fuller took this radio show to a national audience when he became part of the Mutual Broadcasting System in 1937. His program was an immediate success. Renamed ''The Old Fashioned Revival Hour,'' it was carried on 456 Mutual stations by 1942 and attracted an audience of over 10 million listeners worldwide.

In a period of prolonged national anxiety, Fuller offered his listeners a simple, yet comforting, Christian gospel (despite his strongly fundamentalist proclivities) that was delivered in a folksy style. The participation in the program of Fuller's wife, Grace, was also instrumental in creating a family-like atmosphere. The studied informality of ''The Old Fashioned Revival Hour'' became a regular presence in millions of American homes throughout the late 1930s and 1940s.

Ironically, even as the new medium of television was beginning to impact his radio ministry in a negative fashion in the late 1940s, Fuller conceived his greatest enduring legacy to modern American evangelicalism: the creation of Fuller Theological Seminary. As early as 1939, Fuller spoke of starting a ''Christ-centered, Spirit-directed training school'' for ministers. In 1942, the Fuller Evangelistic Association, building on a fund started by his father, prepared actively for the formation of such a school. Five years later, on property purchased in Pasadena and under the leadership of *Harold John Ockenga, Fuller Seminary opened its doors. Led by an impressive cast of evangelical scholars such as *Carl F. H. Henry and *Edward John Carnell, the new seminary's intellectually respectable ''neoevangelicalism'' seemed at odds with Charles Fuller's simple brand of premillennial fundamentalism. And, although Fuller supported the work of his seminary both personally and financially, he remained quietly ambivalent about its theological stance. In large part, it was the assur-

ances of Fuller's theologian son Dan that calmed the elder Fuller's fears and
encouraged him to stay the course.

When Fuller died in 1968, his important role as a major figure in the development of post–World War II neoevangelicalism was not fully appreciated. Yet
his organizational skill, his masterful use of the radio medium, his vision for
Christian higher education, and his willingness to moderate the more divisive
aspects of his own fundamentalist background made him a significant force in
the development of the modern American evangelical ethos.

*Bibliography*

B. *DARB* 191–92; *DCA* 460; *MTC* 160–64; *PTR* 105–9; *RLA* 163–64; *TDCB* 146–47;
Wilbur M. Smith, *A Voice for God: The Life of Charles E. Fuller* (Boston: W. A.
Wilde, 1949); Daniel P. Fuller, *Give the Winds a Mighty Voice: The Story of Charles
E. Fuller* (Waco, Tex.: Word, 1972).

# G

**GAITHER, WILLIAM J. (BILL)** (28 March 1936, Alexandria, IN—) and
**GLORIA** (4 March 1942, Battle Creek, MI—). *Education* (Bill): B.A., Anderson College (IN), 1959; M.A, Ball State University, 1961; (Gloria): B.A., Anderson College (IN), 1963. *Career* (Bill): High school teacher, 1959–65;
composer/songwriter/performer, 1965—; (Gloria): High school teacher, 1963–
65; songwriter/ performer/ author, 1965—.

It is difficult to conceive of any personalities more significant in the genre of
late twentieth-century American evangelical music than the husband and wife
team of Bill and Gloria Gaither. After publishing some of the best-known gospel
songs in the evangelical subculture, the Gaithers' place in history is secure.

This promise was hardly suggested when Bill, a high school English teacher
from Alexandria, Indiana, published his first song, "He Touched Me," in 1963.
Only one year before, Bill had married Gloria Sickal, a substitute French instructor who started her teaching career in Alexandria the same day as Bill. On
weekends, the Gaithers, with Bill's brother Danny, dabbled in Bill's lifelong
love and hobby: singing in various churches in the Alexandria area as a gospel
trio. Although they sang many of the church standards, the Gaithers also performed several songs that Bill wrote and arranged; among them was "He
Touched Me." This was a breakthrough hit and an instant favorite with Christian
vocalists around the country.

By the mid–1960s, the Gaithers embarked on a highly successful performing
career that was fueled by songs written by Bill, often with assistance from
Gloria. Among them were titles that became staples in evangelical congrega-

tions: "I Believe in a Hill Called Mt. Calvary" (1968), "The Old Rugged Cross Made the Difference" (1970), "Something Beautiful" (1971), "Get All Excited" (1972), "Let's Just Praise the Lord" (1972), "Because He Lives" (1974), "I Just Feel Like Something Good Is Going to Happen" (1974), "I Lost It All to Find Everything" (1976), and "It Is Finished" (1976).

The Gaithers' success as songwriters has been credited to their ability to write theologically sound and understandable lyrics. On the stage, their accessible style made them favorites as well. With the success came awards, among them honorary doctorates, several Dove Awards for Songwriter of the Year, and induction into the Gospel Music Association Hall of Fame.

While raising their three children in the 1960s and 1970s, the Bill Gaither Trio turned down many requests to perform publicly. The original trio consisted of Bill, Gloria, and Danny, with occasional assistance from Bill's sister, Mary Ann. In the 1980s, Bill formed the New Gaither Vocal Band with three other male singers (Gary McSpadden, Larnell Harris, and Mike English) in an effort to replicate the male quartet sound he loved as a child and to experiment with various contemporary styles and arrangements. In the 1990s, Bill honored the musical genre that nourished him by producing a series of musical videos that present gospel performers of yesteryear.

Always a creative partner, Gloria has authored five books in addition to her musical contributions. These books are: *Make Warm Noises* (1971), *Rainbows Live at Easter* (1974), *Because He Lives* (1977), *Decisions: A Christian's Approach to Making Right Choices* (1982), and *Fully Alive* (1984). She also coauthored a fifth book with James Dobson's wife, Shirley, entitled *Let's Make a Memory* (1983).

Criticized by some for secularizing traditional gospel music, the Gaithers now represent the establishment, with several of their best known songs included in various denominational hymnals. Within the contemporary gospel music scene the respect given the Gaithers by their peers is undeniable.

*Bibliography*

A. (Gloria) *Because He Lives* (Old Tappan, N.J.: Fleming H. Revell, 1977); (Bill) *I Almost Missed the Sunset: My Perspectives on Life and Music* (Nashville: Thomas Nelson, 1992).

B. *PTR* 111–12; *RLA* 166; *TSAPR* 155–62.

**GORDON, (A)DONIRAM (J)UDSON** (19 April 1836, New Hampton, NH–2 February 1895, Boston, MA). *Education*: B.A., Brown University, 1860; B.D., Newton Theological Seminary, 1863. *Career*: Baptist pastor, 1863–95; chairman, American Baptist Missionary Union, 1888–95; founder, Boston Missionary Training School, 1889.

A. J. Gordon was born to a large New England family deeply devoted to the Calvinistic tradition, Gordon received his name from the famous Baptist missionary to Burma. As a young man, he worked in his father's mill, but at the age of fourteen Gordon was converted to Christianity and decided to enter the ministry.

After preparatory training at New London Academy (1853–57), Gordon went on to study at Brown University and Newton Theological Seminary. Immediately after graduating from Newton, he married Maria Hale and became pastor of the Baptist Church in Jamaica Plain, a Boston suburb. Gordon served there for six years until he moved to the Clarendon Street Baptist Church, Boston, where he was pastor for the remainder of his life.

Clarendon Street, considered the most prominent Baptist church in Boston, was a congregation of considerable affluence. Gordon was repelled, however, by what he believed were his parishioners' attachments to respectability, complacency, and "heathen thought." Immediately he set about changing the atmosphere of Clarendon through what Gordon termed "scriptural simplicity." He abolished the use of paid musicians and the renting of pews, turned away from polished rhetorical preaching, and emphasized seasons of prayer and works of charity. Gradually, Clarendon Street changed from what Gordon felt was a secular assembly to one that demonstrated genuine spiritual life.

For Gordon this transformation was consummated through a series of revival meetings held in Boston by *Dwight L. Moody in 1877. Moody's Boston meetings also marked the beginning of a friendship between Gordon and the Chicago evangelist. In the mid–1870s Gordon began attending Moody's summer conferences in nearby Northfield, Massachusetts, and it was through these conferences that Gordon was introduced to the Keswick higher life teachings, divine healing doctrines, and premillennialist dispensational eschatology that dominated his mature theological thought.

Although Gordon wrote several books on Christian theology, the most prominent of which was *The Ministry of the Spirit* (1894), he was primarily a person of action not reflection. Inspired by Moody's example, Gordon founded the Boston Industrial Temporary Home as a ministry to unemployed men. In 1878, he founded and edited until his death a journal entitled *The Watchword*, which emphasized biblical prophecy and the imminence of Christ's return.

His premillennialist dispensational world-view fueled a growing devotion to missions in his last years, evidenced by his participation in the American Baptist Missionary Union (ABMU). As chairman of the ABMU, Gordon guided the missionary activities of his denomination from 1888 until his death. In addition, he took on the editing duties of ABMU's *Missionary Review of the World*. However, Gordon's greatest gift to missions was his founding of the Boston Missionary Training School in 1889. This school was the antecedent of what became Gordon College and Gordon-Conwell Theological Seminary in the twentieth century.

As a pastor, supporter of missions, and religious activist, Gordon was a prime example of the reforming strain of nineteenth-century evangelicalism. Through his devotion to the Spirit-filled life, divine healing, and premillennial dispensationalism, he also evidenced what would be called fundamentalism in the next century. Thus, Gordon is a crucial figure in the transformation of American evangelicalism at the end of the nineteenth century.

*Bibliography*

A. *Grace and Glory* (Chicago: Fleming H. Revell, 1880); *The Twofold Life* (Chicago: Fleming H. Revell, 1882); *The Ministry of the Spirit* (Philadelphia: American Baptist Publication Society, 1894).

B. *DARB* 208–9; *DCA* 487–88; *RLA* 177–78; C. A. Russell, "Adoniram Judson Gordon: Nineteenth-Century Fundamentalist," *American Baptist Quarterly* 4 (March 1983): 61–89; Ernest Gordon, *Adoniram Judson Gordon: A Biography* (New York: Fleming H. Revell, 1896).

**GRAHAM, WILLIAM FRANKLIN (BILLY)** (7 November 1918, Charlotte, NC—). *Education*: Bob Jones College; B.D., Florida Bible College, 1940; B.A., Wheaton College, 1943. *Career*: Pastor, 1943–45; staff evangelist, Youth For Christ, 1945–47; president, Northwestern Bible College, 1947–51; evangelist and president, Billy Graham Evangelistic Association, 1950—.

If any one person personifies the modern American evangelical subculture with all its diversity, it is Billy Graham. He was born to a modest Presbyterian farming family outside Charlotte, North Carolina. While in high school, Graham committed his life to Christ, and after some internal struggle, he decided to enter the ministry. Spending just one semester at Bob Jones College, then in Cleveland, Tennessee, he transferred to Florida Bible College, outside Tampa, where he graduated in 1940. Ordained by the Southern Baptist Convention, Graham continued his education at Wheaton College. At Wheaton, he met and married Ruth Bell, the daughter of missionary-pastor L. Nelson Bell, in 1943. Upon graduation, Graham briefly served as the pastor of Western Springs Baptist Church in Illinois. The experience convinced him that his calling was as an evangelist.

In 1945, Graham became a travelling evangelist for *Torrey M. Johnson's Youth For Christ. Speaking at meetings held throughout America and Britain, Graham gained valuable insight into the workings of itinerant revivalism and also established friendships with Cliff Barrows and George Beverly Shea, people who would one day figure prominently in his own organization.

At the urging of William Bell Riley, Graham accepted the presidency of Northwestern Bible College in Minneapolis, Minnesota, in 1947. All the while, however, his heart was in evangelism. The watershed moment for Graham's ministry occurred in Los Angeles in 1949 when newspaper magnate William Randolph Hearst ordered his papers to "puff Graham." The subsequent publicity energized the revival meetings and catapulted Graham onto the national stage.

In 1950, Graham formed the Billy Graham Evangelistic Association (BGEA). Assisted by Barrows, music leader Shea, and other staff evangelists, Graham led scores of "crusades" that made him a household name throughout America by the mid–1950s. Especially crucial in his efforts was his use of the media: the radio program "Hour of Decision" (1950); feature films (beginning in 1951); a syndicated newspaper column, "My Answer" (1952); a series of books (the first, *Peace With God*, was published in 1953); the televising of his crusades (beginning in 1957); and *Decision* magazine (1958).

Many mainline Protestants looked askance at the fiery young evangelist who spoke against the evils of communism and frequently punctuated his preaching with the phrase, "The Bible says. . . ." However, Graham was well received when he spoke at Union Theological Seminary in 1954, and then enjoyed extraordinary success at a sixteen-week campaign in London immediately afterward. The London crusade squarely placed Graham on a track to become a bona fide "evangelist to the world," as many revival campaigns all over the globe followed.

By the late 1950s, Graham was clearly departing from the doctrinaire narrowness of his own fundamentalist upbringing. He insisted on racially integrated services in his southern homeland and alienated fundamentalists by entering into cooperative efforts with many Protestant and Catholic churches to promote his crusades. His friendship with Dwight Eisenhower also established Graham as an unofficial chaplain to U.S. presidents, a role that has carried a measure of liability given its political overtones.

Although he consistently challenged his hearers to recognize their sinful state and to repent and receive Jesus as savior, Graham seemed to offer America a reassuring presence during the 1960s and 1970s. Year after year he was voted one of the most admired people in America. His books were consistent best sellers, and efforts to penetrate the Communist countries of Eastern Europe and Asia with the gospel finally bore fruit by the early 1980s.

As Graham was winding down his ministry in the late 1990s and turning more of his preaching duties over to his son, Franklin, it is significant to note that he has preached to more people than any other person (over 110 million; countless others through radio and television). Decisions for Christ at his crusades have been estimated at over 2 million.

Although Graham has often lamented his own lack of advanced theological training, he has been important in the institutionalization of contemporary America evangelicalism. He has done this through his support for the creation and consolidation of Fuller Theological Seminary (1947), the establishment of *Christianity Today* magazine as the leading evangelical periodical in the world (1956), and his sponsorship of key international evangelistic conferences in Berlin (1966) and Lausanne (1974).

*Bibliography*

A. *Peace With God* (Garden City, N.Y.: Doubleday, 1953); *World Aflame* (Garden City, N.Y.: Doubleday, 1965); *Angels: God's Secret Agents* (Garden City, N.Y.: Doubleday, 1975); *Just as I am: The Autobiography of Billy Graham* (San Francisco: HarperSanFrancisco, 1997).

B. *DCA* 491–92; *MTC* 174–81; *PTR* 117–21; *TDCB* 157; *TSAPR* 179–86; William C. Martin, *A Prophet with Honor: The Billy Graham Story* (New York: William Morrow, 1991).

**GRANT, AMY** (25 November 1960, Augusta, GA—). *Education*: Furman University, Vanderbilt University. *Career*: Singer, songwriter, 1976—

Amy Grant is one of the first avowedly Christian music performers to win sizable popularity in the musical mainstream. The youngest of four daughters, she was born in Augusta, Georgia, in 1960, to a prominent physician. She grew up in Nashville, where her family attended a local Churches of Christ congregation. As a youth, she taught herself how to play guitar and, with no formal musical training, enjoyed composing her own songs.

At the age of fifteen, while working part time at a recording studio, she put together a tape of her songs as a gift to her parents. By accident an official from Word Records heard the tape and invited her to record an album. Released in 1976, the album entitled *Amy Grant* was an immediate favorite in Christian music circles.

During the late 1970s and early 1980s, Grant sought to complete her education, attending Furman University and then Vanderbilt. She also recorded two albums, *My Father's Eyes* (1977) and *Never Alone* (1978). In addition, her concerts were recorded as two live albums in 1979 and 1980. Grant's breakthrough album was *Age to Age*, released in 1983. With the popularity of *Age to Age*, Grant decided to forego the remainder of her college education and become a full-time musical performer. At about the same time, she married Gary Chapman, a guitarist-songwriter whom she met in 1979.

After *Age to Age*, Grant decided to reach out to a larger audience. This effort was accomplished through her next two albums, *Straight Ahead* (1984) and *Unguarded* (1985). The fact that *Unguarded* seemed to be less overtly "religious" in its content made Grant the first contemporary Christian performer to cross over into the popular market in a serious fashion.

In her effort to reach a larger, generally un-Christian audience, Grant was criticized amidst her success. Many of her traditional fans did not know what to make of the newer music, which seemed deliberately to broach less obviously religious themes. On the other hand, the secular press seemed somewhat baffled by the frequent faith claims of the young, vivacious, and attractive singer. This image was further muddled when "The Next Time I Fall," a duet with Peter Cetera, lead singer for the pop group Chicago, topped the singles charts in 1988.

Grant's 1988 album *Lead Me On* reflected the conflict in her life. Unlike *Unguarded*, the dominant mood of *Lead Me On* was somber. It did not sell well and represented the first real professional setback in Grant's career. She appeared to be back on track with *Heart in Motion* (1991), an album that even more than *Unguarded* was a deliberate effort to crack the secular market. The lead single from the album, "Baby, Baby," was inspired, said Grant, by her infant daughter, Millie. However, the single's accompanying video on MTV again exposed her to criticism from traditionalists when it showed her singing rather flirtatiously to an actor who was not her husband. However, *Heart to Heart* was nominated for several Grammy awards and won Grant many more listeners outside the evangelical subculture.

At the end of the 1990s, Grant retained the ambivalent image that she developed throughout her career. On the one hand, she enjoyed a degree of popularity heretofore unknown among evangelical musical performers. On the other hand, she continued to resist the efforts of her traditional Christian fans to categorize her music and her ministry. In her struggle to reconcile her persona as a popular cultural icon with that of a bona fide evangelical witness, Grant personified a dominant conflict within American evangelicalism at the end of the twentieth century.

*Bibliography*

B. Jeanne M. Lesinski, "Amy Grant," in *Contemporary Musicians: Profiles of the People in Music*, vol. 7, edited by Michael L. LaBlanc (Detroit: Gale: 1992), 83–85. Carol Leggett, *Amy Grant* (New York: Pocket Books, 1987); Bob Millard, *Amy Grant: The Life of a Pop Star* (New York: St. Martin's, 1996).

# H

**HENRY, CARL (F)ERDINAND (H)OWARD** (22 January 1913, New York, NY—). *Education*: B.A., M.A., Wheaton College, 1938, 1940; Th.D., Northern Baptist Theological Seminary, 1942; Ph.D., Boston University, 1949. *Career*: Newspaper reporter, editor, 1929–35; professor of theology, 1940–55; 1968–74; editor, *Christianity Today*, 1955–68; lecturer-at-large, World Vision International, 1974–87; lecturer-at-large, Prison Fellowship Ministries, 1990—.

Perhaps the most significant theologian in the early "neoevangelical" movement, Carl F. H. Henry was born to German immigrant parents just before the outbreak of World War I. Raised on Long Island, Henry became interested in journalism, and by the age of nineteen, he edited a weekly newspaper in New York's Nassau County. After his conversion to Christianity, Henry attended Wheaton College, obtaining his bachelor's and master's degrees (1938 and 1940). Bent on pursuing an academic career in theology, he completed doctoral studies at Northern Baptist Theological Seminary (1942) and later at Boston University (1949). He was ordained in the Northern Baptist Convention in 1941, and from 1940 until 1947, he taught theology and philosophy of religion at Northern Baptist Seminary. In 1947, he accepted the call of *Harold John Ockenga to become the first professor of theology at the new Fuller Theological Seminary in Pasadena, California.

Henry took a prolonged sabbatical from his teaching duties in 1955 to become the first editor of *Christianity Today*, a publication conceived by *Billy Graham and L. Nelson Bell and financed by Sun Oil magnate *J. Howard Pew as an evangelical alternative to the *Christian Century*. Under Henry's guidance, *Christianity Today* became the leading journalistic mouthpiece for neoevangelicalism and lent the movement intellectual respectability.

Faced with long hours away from his family, conflicts with Pew and Bell over editorial issues, and criticism from the fundamentalist wing of evangelicalism, Henry resigned the reins of *Christianity Today* in 1968. After a year of studies at Cambridge University, Henry became professor of theology at Eastern Baptist Seminary (1969–74) and visiting professor at Trinity Evangelical Divinity School (1974). After 1974, he served stints as lecturer-at-large for World Vision International (1974–87) and Prison Fellowship Ministries (1990—).

From the beginning of his academic career, Henry aspired to lead Protestant fundamentalism to a greater intellectual and social engagement with the larger American culture. As such, with Ockenga and Graham, he is one of the most significant leaders of the "new evangelicalism" of the post–World War II era. In fact, Henry's book *The Uneasy Conscience of Modern Fundamentalism* (1947) is often seen as a kind of "neoevangelical manifesto" marking the nascent movement's break with separatist fundamentalists.

Henry also demonstrated his leadership of the neoevangelical movement through his presidency of the Evangelical Theological Society (1967–70) and the American Theological Society (1979–80), as well as his organizing role in the Berlin (1966) and Lausanne (1974) World Conferences on Evangelism. Henry's many books, the most famous of which is the six-volume *God, Revelation, and Authority* (1976–83), consistently reiterate the themes of biblical theism, objective revelation in propositional form, the authority and inerrancy of the Scriptures, and the rational apologetic defense of Christianity. Paradoxically, Henry has been attacked throughout his career by separatist fundamentalists for urging a more united evangelical witness, while being criticized by liberal evangelicals for his insistence on biblical inerrancy. Despite this carping, the historical significance of the person *Time* magazine once called in 1977 "the leading theologian" of American evangelicalism is incontestable.

*Bibliography*

A. *The Uneasy Conscience of Modern Fundamentalism* (Grand Rapids, Mich.: Eerdmans, 1947); *God, Revelation, and Authority*, 6 vols. (Waco, Tex.: Word, 1976–83); *Confessions of a Theologian* (Waco, Tex.: Word, 1986).

B. *BT* 518–38; *DCA* 520–21; *HET* 260–75; *RLA* 202; *TDCB* 175–76; Bob E. Patterson, *Carl F. H. Henry* (Waco, Tex.: Word, 1983).

**HESTENES, ROBERTA L.** (5 August 1939, Huntington, CA—). *Education*: Whittier College; B.A., University of California, Santa Barbara, 1963, M.Div., D.Min., Fuller Theological Seminary. *Career*: Director of adult education,

1967–74; professor, 1975–87; board of directors, World Vision International, 1980—; president, Eastern College (PA), 1987–96; pastor, 1997—.

In a conservative evangelical subculture that tends to restrict the role of women, Roberta Hestenes is both pioneer and iconoclast. Born to teens who conceived her out of wedlock, Hestenes suffered at the hands of an alcoholic father and a bitter, argumentative mother. She decided to become a lawyer, and attended Whittier College in the late 1950s. Hestenes was led to Christianity by the faculty sponsor of Whittier's Lutheran student group. She matured in her faith largely through the use of Navigator ministry materials, an evangelical Quaker church, and a college Bible study.

Few could match Hestenes's dynamism. She enjoyed discipling young people and felt a strong call to full-time Christian service. By the time she reached her junior year at Whittier, Hestenes met her future husband, John, at an InterVarsity Christian Fellowship training conference. John was intent on becoming a missionary in Latin America. The two married in 1960 and took classes at Fuller Seminary shortly thereafter.

By the early 1960s however, their goal of missionary service had faded. To that end, the Hesteneses withdrew from Fuller and returned to UC Santa Barbara, where John attended graduate school and Roberta finished her undergraduate degree. With the added responsibility of children, John decided to eschew the mission field altogether while Roberta struggled with God's calling on her life. That struggle inched toward resolution when the Hesteneses moved to Seattle, Washington, in the mid–1960s and Roberta fell under the influence of Robert Munger, the pastor of United Presbyterian Church. Munger's perception of women in ministry had been shaped by Henrietta Mears, the long-time director of Christian education at First Presbyterian Church of Hollywood, California. Munger was willing to let Hestenes teach at United Presbyterian. Eventually her work led to a full-time job as director of adult education.

Convinced that she would need official credentials to continue in the ministry, Hestenes re-entered Fuller Seminary in 1974. As she studied for her master's and doctoral degrees, she also taught communications at the seminary. Winning a reputation as an excellent teacher, Hestenes invented a new major called "Christian Formation and Discipleship." Small group Bible studies became her speciality, and she taught and wrote extensively on the subject. In the midst of her duties at Fuller, Hestenes was also ordained in the Presbyterian Church, U.S.A. and pastored part time.

During the late 1970s, Hestenes began to think of herself as an "evangelical Christian feminist," motivated by love not anger, who believed that the Scriptures, properly interpreted and applied, taught the full partnership of women and men in the church, the family, and society. This growing conviction led her to plumb the depths of her service to Christ more deeply. In 1980 she joined the board of directors of World Vision International, a parachurch relief agency. By the mid–1980s she realized her service at Fuller was at an end. Consequently, when Eastern College, a small Baptist school in Pennsylvania, approached her about becoming its president in 1987, she accepted. As the first woman president of a Coalition of Christian Colleges school, Hestenes again broke the mold. Hestenes held the presidency of Eastern College until 1996 when she moved back to California to become senior pastor of Solano Beach Presbyterian Church.

Slowed temporarily by a heart attack in 1995, Hestenes remained a highly evangelical feminist as the century drew to a close. As moderator of the Ordination and Human Sexuality Committee of the Presbyterian Church, U.S.A., she spearheaded passage of the 1996 policy permitting the ordination of gays who remain celibate. In addition, she participated in the PBS series, "Genesis: A Living Conversation," in 1996.

*Bibliography*

A. *Women and the Ministries of Christ* (Pasadena, Calif.: Fuller Theological Seminary, 1979); *Using the Bible in Groups* (Philadelphia: Westminster, 1984).

B. "Woman at the Helm: A Christian College Pioneer," *CT* 32:4 (4 March 1988): 34; Tim Stafford, "Roberta Hestenes: Taking Charge," *CT* 33:4 (3 March 1989): 17–22.

**HODGE, CHARLES** (27 December 1797, Philadelphia, PA–19 June 1878, Princeton, NJ). *Education*: B.A., College of New Jersey (Princeton), 1815; B.D., Princeton Theological Seminary, 1819. *Career*: Seminary professor, 1820–78.

Few nineteenth-century personalities have exerted a greater influence on contemporary American evangelicalism than Charles Hodge. He was raised by his mother after his surgeon father died of yellow fever in 1797. Despite financial hardship, Hodge was afforded an exemplary education, attending both Princeton College and Seminary. His Princeton experience was decisive. Under the influence of seminary president and theologian, Archibald Alexander, Hodge was converted to Christian faith (1815) and set on his career path of Presbyterian theologian and professor (1820).

Troubled by theological trends in Europe that ran counter to traditional Calvinistic theology, Hodge left his teaching post and traveled to Germany in the late 1820s where he studied the pietism associated with Halle, post-Kantian philosophy, and the theology of Friedrich Schleiermacher. His European experience served to affirm Hodge's traditional Presbyterian faith all the more strongly, and he returned to Princeton in 1828 to take up a teaching career that directly affected over 2,000 students in a fifty-year period.

Hodge's theology was a synthesis of conservative Calvinism tempered by a warm piety and undergirded by the Scottish Common Sense philosophy he inherited from Alexander. Living in an age when theological ideas greatly influenced the larger American culture, Hodge became a towering figure. Not only through his professorship, but through his long tenure as editor of the *Biblical Repertory* (1825–72; later renamed the *Princeton Review*), Hodge stoutly and eloquently defended traditional "Old School Calvinism" against a host of countervailing theological trends that appeared throughout the mid–nineteenth century.

A survey of Hodge's controversial writings provides a revealing outline of the intellectual struggles that traditional American evangelicalism faced. Against the Arminianizing tendencies of Charles Finney's revivalism, Hodge proposed an alternative based on subdued religious experience and objective Calvinistic theology. Against the corrosive biblical criticism of the European theologians, Hodge defended a verbally inspired and authoritative Bible. Faced with the modifications of traditional Calvinism offered by the "New Haven School" of Nathaniel Taylor, Hodge asserted all the more strongly his belief in total depravity, human inability apart from the grace of God, and the substitutionary death of Christ. Even near the end of his life, in *What Is Darwinism?* (1874), Hodge attacked the theory of natural selection as incongruent with the notion of divine design.

Within the narrower confines of the (Northern) Presbyterian Church, USA and Princeton Seminary, Hodge's influence was dominant. After the schism of 1837, he defended the Old School perspective against the revivalists, and although opposed to the institution of slavery, Hodge regularly attacked the abolitionist wing of the New School Presbyterians. He wrote an influential lay theology book for the American Sunday School Union in 1841 and served as moderator for the Old School General Assembly in 1846. As a biblical theologian, he wrote commentaries on the books of Romans (1836), Ephesians (1856), 2 Corinthians (1857) and 1 Corinthians (1859). Because of the prestige of Princeton as the leading conservative seminary in mid–nineteenth century America, Hodge's theology had an impact on many students who were not aligned with the Reformed and Presbyterian denominations, thus preserving a transdenominational core of theological conservativism within American evangelicalism.

Of all his many works, Hodge's most enduring was his three-volume *Systematic Theology* (1872–73), which was based on decades of lectures as gleaned from his studies of the Scriptures, Calvin, and seventeenth-century Reformed theologians like Francois Turretini. The basic premise of the book—that theology is an inductive science in which theologians gather facts from the Bible to construct an objective system of truth—clearly reflects its philosophical common sense underpinnings.

Hodge influenced countless theologians, although none more prominent than his son, Archibald Alexander Hodge (who succeeded his father as professor of theology at Princeton from 1878–86), and especially *Benjamin Breckinridge Warfield, who became the elder Hodge's real intellectual successor in the defense of conservative Presbyterianism in the late nineteenth century. Charles Hodge's role as theological conservator within the evangelicalism of his day is perhaps best summed up by his statement that a new idea never originated in Princeton Seminary.

*Bibliography*

A. *Constitutional History of the Presbyterian Church in the U.S.*, 2 vols. (Philadelphia: W. S. Martien, 1839–40); *Systematic Theology*, 3 vols. (New York: Scribners, 1872–73); *What Is Darwinism?* (New York: Scribner, Armstrong, 1874).

B. *DARB* 245–46; *DCA* 537–38; A. A. Hodge, *The Life of Charles Hodge: Professor in the Theological Seminary, Princeton, N.J.* (New York: Scribners, 1880).

**HYBELS, WILLIAM (BILL)** (12 December 1951, Kalamazoo, MI—). *Education*: Dordt College; B.A., Trinity College (IL), 1975. *Career*: Pastor, 1975—.

If the measure of pastoral success in late twentieth-century American evangelicalism is building a large "megachurch," then few can exceed the feat of Bill Hybels, the senior pastor of Willow Creek Community Church in South Barrington, Illinois. Hybels grew up in Kalamazoo, Michigan, the son of a produce executive. With an idealism that belied his comfortable upper middle-class upbringing, Hybels decided to enter the ministry after experiencing a religious conversion as a high school student. Entering Trinity College, an Evangelical Free Church school in Deerfield, Illinois, in the early 1970s, he studied theology while leading the "Son City" youth ministry of South Park Church, Park Ridge, Illinois.

In 1972, Hybels met Gilbert Bilezikian, a Franco-Armenian biblical studies professor from Wheaton College, who became his theological mentor. After moving to America and receiving advanced religious training, Bilezikian attempted to put his convictions about the local church—that it should be the dynamic, loving, new community of God's people that would penetrate the culture—into practice. At Trinity College, the person who most thoroughly absorbed Bilezikian's ideas was Hybels.

With three like-minded friends, Hybels spent six weeks in 1975 conducting door-to-door surveys in the Chicago area to find out what people wanted in a church. Those surveyed wanted a church that was relevant to their lives. Hybels and his cohorts set about building a congregation that would defer to the customer except where it conflicted with Scripture. Some years later, Hybels's original assembly of 150 blossomed into the behemoth of Willow Creek.

At Willow Creek, Hybels's strategy was to translate the traditional concept of Christian community into a contemporary idiom while retaining biblical essentials. Thus, Willow Creek instituted a bifurcated approach to "doing church." Weekend services are aimed at seekers, unchurched people who reject traditional forms of worship as either boring or irrelevant. The seeker services use music, drama, dance, and multimedia presentations to present a highly moralistic and inspirational message. The message is designed to lead the seekers to Christ, but without trappings of conventional evangelical Protestantism such as theological language, symbols, and hymns. The service is to be entertaining but purposeful. Hybels's use of marketing jargon like "customers" and "user value" recalls the teachings of Peter Drucker, a leading management theorist who stands as a second major influence upon Hybels's "Christian research and development."

The reaction of the evangelical community to Hybels and Willow Creek has been twofold. On the one hand, critics accuse Hybels of compromising the gospel through the use of modern cultural devices. On the other hand, emulators try to match Willow Creek's success through imitation. The Willow Creek Association, which numbered more than 2,200 churches from seventy denominations in the mid–1990s, was formed to provide support to other seeker-sensitive congregations.

Hybels insists that Willow Creek, although independent, is a conservative, nonfundamentalist, evangelical assembly that bases its actions on an infallible Bible. In this sense, it is truly the medium, not the message, that distinguishes the seeker services. Living with his wife, Lynne, on a modest salary, Hybels consciously deemphasizes his role at Willow Creek. Calling itself a genuine "community church," Willow Creek has eschewed broadcasting its services. Hence, Hybels has been able to avoid the pitfalls associated with the personality cult of televangelism. Instead, the senior pastor spends a good deal of his time delegating his authority to the church's 260 full and part-time employees, while traveling frequently to speak at Willow Creek's many sister congregations.

*Bibliography*

A. *Honest to God?: Becoming an Authentic Christian* (Grand Rapids, Mich.: Zondervan, 1990); *Becoming a Contagious Christian* (Grand Rapids, Mich.: Zondervan, 1994).

B. *Contemporary Authors*, edited by Susan M. Trosky (Detroit: Gale, 1989), 126:191; Michael G. Maudlin and Edward Gilbreath, "Selling Out the House of God?" *CT* 38:8 (18 July 1994): 21–25; Katrina Burger, "JesusChrist.com: Willow Creek Runs its Church Like a Business," *Forbes* 159:9 (5 May 1997): 76–81; Lynne Hybels, *Rediscovering Church: The Story and Vision of Willow Creek Community Church* (Grand Rapids, Mich.: Zondervan, 1995).

# J

**JOHNSON, TORREY M.** (15 March 1909, Chicago, IL—). *Education*: B.S., Wheaton College, 1930; B.D., Northern Baptist Theological Seminary, 1936. *Career*: Pastor, 1930–52; 1967–82; seminary professor, 1936–40; radio evangelist, 1941–43; founder and president, Youth For Christ, 1945–48; itinerant evangelist, 1953–67.

One of the most important pioneers in evangelical youth revivalism, Torrey Johnson was born and raised in suburban Chicago. His parents were first-generation Americans from Norway and members of the Evangelical Free

Church with its close ties to independent evangelical institutions like Moody Bible Institute. Johnson was named after *Reuben A. Torrey and was influenced as a youth by the preaching of Paul Rader, pastor of Moody Church in Chicago.

Despite the strong faith of his parents, Johnson experienced a spiritually unsettled adolescence. He was sent to Wheaton College by his parents in the late 1920s, only to drop out after two years. He briefly pursued a premedical degree at Northwestern University and contemplated becoming a missionary to Africa. By 1929, however, he was back at Wheaton in a more settled frame of mind, and he graduated a year later.

As a twenty-one-year-old college graduate, Johnson accepted a call to become pastor of Messiah Baptist Church in Chicago and was ordained to the Baptist ministry. This pastorate lasted but twelve months, after which Johnson spent two years touring the rural upper Midwest as an itinerant evangelist. In 1933, he organized the Midwest Bible Church on Chicago's northwest side. Johnson remained with Midwest during a period of substantial growth until 1952. While a pastor, Johnson also attended Northern Baptist Theological Seminary, graduated with a bachelor's degree, and came within an uncompleted thesis of receiving his doctorate in the early 1940s. During his student years at Northern Baptist, Johnson taught several introductory courses, particularly Greek.

A major factor in the growth of Johnson's church was his use of radio to broadcast the services. The style and format of these services emulated the pioneering efforts of *Percy B. Crawford and Jack Wyrtzen. In 1941, Johnson developed a program entitled "Chapel Hour," and four years later came "Songs in the Night." The latter broadcast synthesized a traditional preaching service with the contemporary music and thematic styles attractive to young people. Through the success of these programs, Johnson was persuaded that the thrust of his ministry should be aimed at the youth of Chicago.

During the summer of 1944, Johnson and his brother-in-law, Bob Cook, entered youth evangelism through their organization of the Chicagoland Youth for Christ rallies. The climax of the summer was a meeting that drew 28,000 people to Chicago Stadium. The success of these youth gatherings and the favorable press that accompanied them brought inquiries about how similar rallies might be started around the country. The youth rallies led directly to the formation of Youth For Christ (YFC) at Winona Lake, Indiana, in 1945. Besides Johnson as its first president, YFC hired *Billy Graham as one of its staff evangelists.

By 1948, Johnson left the presidency of YFC to Cook, in favor of his pastorate at Midwest Bible Church. In 1953, he became a full-time itinerant evangelist. Johnson remained a travelling preacher until 1968 when he became pastor of the Bibletown Community Church and president of Bibletown Bible Conferences and Concerts in Boca Raton, Florida. In the 1990s, Johnson remains active, taking on the issue of adequate and affordable housing for retirees. Through a continuing life of service he represents a vital link to the energetic formative days of contemporary American evangelicalism.

*Bibliography*

A. *Reaching Youth for Christ* (Chicago: Moody, 1944).

B. *MTC* 282–87; *PTR* 165; Mel Larson, *Young Man on Fire: The Story of Torrey Johnson and Youth For Christ* (Chicago: Youth Publications, 1945); *The Youth For Christ Movement and Its Pioneers*, edited by Joel A. Carpenter (New York: Garland, 1988).

# K

**KENNEDY, (D)ENNIS JAMES** (3 November 1930, Augusta, GA—). *Education*: B.A., University of Tampa, 1958; B.D., Columbia Theological Seminary, 1958; Th.M., University of Chicago, 1969; D.D., Trinity Evangelical Divinity School, 1969; Ph.D., New York University, 1979. *Career*: Dance instructor, 1952–58; pastor, 1959—.

If the imperative of evangelicalism is to lead souls to faith in the savior Jesus Christ, then one of the most influential individuals in the contemporary American evangelical subculture is D. James Kennedy. Born in Georgia to a glass salesman in 1930, Kennedy was raised in Chicago until his family moved to Tampa, Florida, when he was in his midteens. His parents were Methodists, although Kennedy remembers little contact with the church during his youth. Enrolling at the University of Tampa to pursue an English major and music minor, Kennedy was a lackadaisical student and quickly dropped out of college for six years to work as a dance instructor. During this period, he met his future wife, Anne Lewis, in 1956.

Kennedy became a Christian in 1955 when he happened to tune to Donald Grey Barnhouse's radio program, "The Bible Study Hour." After returning to the University of Tampa to finish his bachelor's degree, Kennedy earned a divinity degree from Columbia Theological Seminary, a Presbyterian seminary in Georgia.

Kennedy's only pastorate has been at Coral Ridge Presbyterian Church in Fort Lauderdale, Florida. When he arrived at the church in 1959, it had only seventeen members and met in the cafeteria of an elementary school. Within three years, Kennedy developed a systematic program to train his laity in the basics of sharing the Christian gospel through personal witnessing. The program, which Kennedy called "Evangelism Explosion," resulted in the immediate growth of Coral Ridge, making it the fastest growing Presbyterian church in America for fifteen years in a row. Since increasing the membership of a church is one of the surest ways to attract attention in the evangelical subculture, Kennedy and "Evangelism Explosion" quickly became objects of great interest throughout conservative Protestantism. Used by many Presbyterian churches,

"Evangelism Explosion" was also adopted by other denominations, and by the 1990s, had expanded its activities all over the world.

In 1978, Kennedy assented to the televising of Coral Ridge's worship services. Yet, in keeping with the more formal worship of Presbyterianism and wishing to avoid the televised excesses of other media evangelists, Kennedy has always sought to keep his weekly "The Coral Ridge Hour" a minimalist production. With the exception of a few feature interludes and one twenty-second appeal for funds, the program is primarily a rebroadcast of the live service. In the 1990s Kennedy expanded his presence on the radio through a daily discussion program entitled "Truths That Transform" and a daily three-minute topical feature, "The Kennedy Commentary." As with his sermons on "The Coral Ridge Hour," Kennedy's later programs aimed at a more sophisticated and educated audience within evangelicalism than did many televangelistic offerings.

Like *James C. Dobson Jr., Kennedy attracted widespread media attention outside religious circles relatively late in his career. The attention came when, like Dobson, Kennedy spoke out more stridently about controversial social issues like gay rights, church-state separation, abortion, and education. In his direct-mail appeals, Kennedy routinely waved the red flag of "secular humanism," an ill-defined but highly volatile issue that resonated throughout the evangelical subculture.

Kennedy had all the credentials and opportunities to be a major player in contemporary American evangelicalism. He occupied the pulpit of a large (7,000 member) church; he administered a widely used program of evangelism that had transdenominational significance; he became a respected voice within the evangelical media; and he evidenced staunch support of "Christian education" through his founding of Westminster Academy, a K-12 school in Fort Lauderdale (1971), and Knox Theological Seminary, which opened campuses in Fort Lauderdale in 1990 and Colorado Springs, Colorado, in 1993.

*Bibliography*

A. *Evangelism Explosion* (Wheaton, Ill.: Tyndale, 1970); *Delighting God* (Ann Arbor, Mich.: Vine, 1993); *Foundations for Your Faith* (Grand Rapids, Mich.: Fleming H. Revell, 1994).

B. *PTR* 172–74; Russell Chandler, *The Kennedy Explosion* (London: Coverdale, 1971); Herbert L. Williams, *D. James Kennedy: The Man and His Ministry* (Nashville: Thomas Nelson, 1990).

**KING, MARTIN LUTHER, JR.** (15 January 1929, Atlanta, GA–4 April 1968, Memphis, TN). *Education*: B.A., Morehouse College, 1948; B.D., Crozer Theological Seminary; Ph.D., Boston University, 1955. *Career*: Pastor, 1954–60; president, Southern Christian Leadership Conference, 1960–68.

Martin Luther King Jr. was born in Atlanta, Georgia, in 1929. His father was pastor of the Ebenezer Baptist Church and a leader in the local black community. Although acquainted with racial injustice, the younger King enjoyed a fairly comfortable upbringing. Completing high school early, King enrolled at Morehouse College, where he graduated in 1948. As a youth, King decided to follow the example of his father and pursue a pastoral career. He was ordained and studied theology at Crozer Theological Seminary in Chester, Pennsylvania. Under Crozer's liberal evangelical faculty, King discovered the thought of social reformers like Walter Rauschenbusch and Mohandas Gandhi. His interest in ethics led him to Boston University, where he received a Ph.D. in 1955.

In Boston, King met Coretta Scott, and they were married in 1953. The next year King became the pastor of Dexter Avenue Baptist Church in Montgomery, Alabama. As one of the chief architects of the 1955–56 black boycott of the city bus system that followed Rosa Parks's act of defiance, King was catapulted into national prominence.

In 1957 the young pastor helped to form the Southern Christian Leadership Conference (SCLC) to coordinate the growing civil rights movement in the South. King was elected the SCLC's first president and set out to promote the cause of civil rights throughout the nation. Although a part-time endeavor at first, the work of the SCLC quickly consumed his time, and in 1960 King resigned from the pastorate to devote himself totally to the organization.

In the early 1960s, King was involved in nearly all the major confrontations between blacks and white segregationists in the South. Arriving in Birmingham, Alabama, in 1963 to lead the protest over segregated public facilities, King was arrested when he refused to obey a court order to cease leading the protests. This apparent setback gave King the opportunity to write his "Letter from Birmingham Jail," a powerful indictment of racial injustice that attracted more sympathizers to his cause.

After the Birmingham confrontation, President John Kennedy began to call for new civil rights legislation on public housing, desegregation of public facilities, and employment. King's stature rose even higher when he joined with over 250,000 others in August 1963 for the "March on Washington." His "I Have a Dream" speech, replete with biblical imagery and delivered in the rhetorical style of black evangelical preaching, has become one of the most memorable utterances of the twentieth century.

In 1964 King received the Nobel Peace Prize, a clear sign that he had been embraced not only by American blacks but by the white liberal establishment as well. Not all in that establishment honored King, of course. Among the most powerful of his detractors was J. Edgar Hoover, the head of the FBI, who wiretapped King's conversations and built a massive file for the purpose of defaming King publicly.

Early in 1965, King led protests in Selma, Alabama, over voting rights for blacks. Although a King-led march from Montgomery to Selma was turned back by police on 9 March 1965, the Johnson administration threw its support behind the black protesters, and before the end of the year, the Voting Rights Act of 1965 was signed by Lyndon Johnson, with King in attendance.

Despite King's prominence, the civil rights movement began to fracture in

1966. Radicals like Stokely Carmichael and Malcolm X called for more extreme measures to "liberate" black Americans from what they saw as an irredeemable white establishment. By late 1966, King realized that the Vietnam War was undermining the Johnson administration's "War on Poverty," which he saw as essential to the cause of civil rights. When King spoke out against the war however, he alienated himself from the Johnson administration and further divided the broad coalition that had supported him until that time.

Increasingly obsessed with plans to promote antipoverty legislation for a wider variety of ethnic groups in America, King traveled to Memphis, Tennessee, in March and April 1968 to support striking sanitation workers. On the evening of 4 April 1968, he was shot and killed by an assassin. James Earl Ray confessed to the murder in March 1969, but allegations of conspiracy followed. Although criminal investigators repeatedly stated their conviction that Ray acted alone when he assassinated King, the government reopened the case for review in the late 1990s.

It is difficult to assess King's place within the American evangelical subculture, partly because of the ambivalent relationship that black evangelicals have had over the years with the larger white evangelical community. Although the groups share many beliefs, their unique histories have institutionalized a number of crucial differences between them. There is also the theology of King himself, which was highly influenced by nonevangelicals like Reinhold Niebuhr, Rauschenbusch, and even Gandhi. Still, there is no denying that in many important ways, King was shaped by a religious ethos that was characteristically evangelical, even if the evangelicalism was transmuted to meet the unique challenges of civil rights.

*Bibliography*

A. *A Testament of Hope: The Essential Writings and Speeches*, edited by James Washington (San Francisco: HarperSanFrancisco, 1991).

B. *DARB* 290–91; *DCA* 615–16; *EAAR* 428–31; *TSARP* 217–25; Coretta Scott King, *My Life with Martin Luther King, Jr.* (New York: Holt, Rinehart and Winston, 1969); David L. Lewis, *King: A Critical Biography* (New York: Praeger, 1970); David J. Garrow, *Bearing the Cross: Martin Luther King, Jr., and the Southern Christian Leadership Conference, 1955–1968* (New York: William Morrow, 1986).

**KUHLMAN, KATHRYN** (9 May 1907, Concordia, MO–20 February 1976, Tulsa, OK). *Education*: Simpson Bible Institute (WA); Lighthouse of International Foursquare Evangelism (CA). *Career*: Itinerant preacher, 1923–47; healing evangelist, 1947–76.

Kathryn Kuhlman was born on a farm in central Missouri in 1907. Just one generation away from German immigrant status, her parents were fairly well-to-do. Shuffled between Baptist and Methodist churches as a youth, Kuhlman eventually settled in the former and experienced a religious conversion at age fourteen. Two years later she left home to begin an itinerant evangelistic ministry.

Kuhlman's older sister married evangelist Everett B. Parrott, and beginning in 1923, the Parrotts and Kuhlman began working with Charles S. Price, an influential healing revivalist. Price appealed to his audiences to receive the "higher life" available through the baptism of the Holy Spirit. Although she never credited Price with bequeathing this pattern of ministry to her, Kuhlman came to emphasize the same concepts.

At the age of twenty-one, Kuhlman struck out on her own as an independent itinerant. With the assistance of Helen Gulliford, a former pianist of Price, Kuhlman held revival meetings throughout Pacific northwest. After a successful campaign in Denver, Colorado, Kuhlman established the Kuhlman Revival Tabernacle in 1934. It immediately became one of the fastest growing evangelical assemblies in the West. By the mid-1930s, Kuhlman's services were broadcast live by a local Denver radio station.

Kuhlman was one of the best-known woman revivalists in America when scandal struck. The scandal involved a love relationship that had developed between Kuhlman and a Texas evangelist named Burroughs A. Waltrip. In 1938, one year after preaching at the Tabernacle, Waltrip divorced his wife and abandoned his two children to marry Kuhlman. The shock waves were severe. Gulliford resigned from Kuhlman's employment immediately, and the Denver congregation quickly dwindled to nothing. Kuhlman tried to carry on. However, the scandal preceded her everywhere and effectively stymied her ministry.

Kuhlman's situation began to improve in 1944. Early that year she received what she believed to be the baptism of the Holy Spirit. A few days later, Kuhlman left Waltrip and started her ministry over in Franklin, Pennsylvania. Establishing the Gospel Revival Tabernacle, Kuhlman duplicated her earlier success. Many services were broadcast by radio, and Kuhlman set aside special times for healing at the end of each session. Still, chary about the propriety of healing services, Kuhlman determined that she would not indulge in the sensationalism that was obvious in most healing revivals.

Her own healing ministry began in 1947 when people began to claim deliverance from various infirmities. In her services there were no healing lines, individualized prayers for the sick, or special touch from the evangelist. Kuhlman simply credited the results to the power of the Holy Spirit.

For the next twenty-five years, Kuhlman's fame grew in an astonishing fashion. Her mild demeanor set her apart from the flamboyant histrionics of many of her contemporaries. Also crucial to her success were the liaisons she established with young revivalists like *Oral Roberts and Rex Humbard. Roberts was an especially ardent supporter of Kuhlman, and the two of them probably did more than anyone else to legitimize the charismatic revival within American evangelicalism in the 1950s and 1960s.

From 1950 until 1966, Kuhlman held weekly "miracle services" in Pittsburgh that were broadcast by radio. Even as she established the Kathryn Kuhlman

Foundation in 1957 to manage her ministry, Kuhlman's operation remained spartan and well-managed, rarely soliciting funds outside of the miracle services until her later years.

Kuhlman's first book, *I Believe in Miracles*, was published in 1962 and sold millions of copies. In 1965 she relocated her ministry to Los Angeles. A venture into television beginning in 1967 was extremely popular. In nine years, Kuhlman taped 500 half-hour programs that were carried on sixty stations around the country. The high cost of a television ministry forced Kuhlman to travel incessantly and exacerbated a chronic heart condition. Despite the workload, several more books were written in the late 1960s and early 1970s as well.

The last couple years of her life were an unfortunate denouement on a fifty-year ministry. Legal conflicts alienated friends and crippled the foundation charged with carrying on Kuhlman's work. After experiencing complications associated with heart surgery, Kuhlman suffered a heart attack and died on 20 February 1976.

Kuhlman's healing ministry could trace its lineage to the Pentecostal pioneers of the early twentieth century: Price, *Aimee Semple McPherson, *Maria B. Woodworth-Etter, and others. Yet its uniqueness was the manner in which Kuhlman was able to distance herself from the Pentecostal healing establishment led by *William M. Branham and others. As an ecumenical healing revivalist (as many as 60 percent of the participants in her services were Roman Catholics), Kuhlman stands as one of the most significant woman evangelicals of this century.

*Bibliography*

A. *I Believe in Miracles* (New York: Pyramid, 1962); *Nothing Is Impossible with God* (Englewood Cliffs, N.J.: Prentice-Hall, 1974).

B. *ACSL* 145–46; *DARB* 298–99; *DCA* 622–23; *PTR* 179–83; *TSARP* 225–33; Allen Spraggett, *Kathryn Kuhlman: The Woman Who Believes in Miracles* (New York: World, 1970); Wayne E. Warner, *Kathryn Kuhlman: The Woman Behind the Miracles* (Ann Arbor, Mich.: Servant Publications, 1993).

# L

**LADD, GEORGE ELDON** (31 July 1911, Alberta, Canada–5 October 1982, Pasadena, CA). *Education*: B.Th., Gordon College, 1933; B.D., Gordon Divinity School, 1941; Boston University; Ph.D., Harvard, 1949. *Career*: Pastor, 1933–49; professor, Fuller Theological Seminary, 1950–80.

One of the most significant evangelical theologians of the last half of the twentieth century, George Eldon Ladd was born in Canada, but was raised in New Hampshire. He was converted to evangelical Christianity in 1929 under the ministry of a graduate of Moody Bible Institute who was preaching at the small Methodist church that Ladd attended. Not long after his conversion he resolved to become a preacher, and to prepare himself properly, he commuted to Gordon College while serving as a student pastor in Gilford, New Hampshire. In 1933, Ladd graduated from Gordon with a bachelor of theology degree. The same year he was ordained to the ministry by the Northern Baptist Convention and also was married.

While at Gordon, Ladd was attracted to the academic vocation, although he wanted to combine any future teaching career with one in a pastoral ministry. Thus, even while he was pursuing advanced degrees at Gordon, Boston University, and Harvard, Ladd was laboring in pastorates such as the First Baptist Church of Montpelier, Vermont (1936–42), and Blaney Memorial Church in Boston (1943–49).

In 1950 Ladd joined the faculty of Fuller Theological Seminary. His research specialty was New Testament theology, and he taught the subject at Fuller for thirty years until his retirement in 1980. Although a passionate and enthusiastic instructor, Ladd made a greater contribution to modern evangelicalism through his written series of theological investigations that moved the post–World War II subculture beyond the dispensationalism that had held a straitjacket on the movement since the turn of the century.

Beginning with his book *Crucial Questions About the Kingdom of God* (1952) and continuing through such efforts as *Jesus and the Kingdom* (1964), *The New Testament and Criticism* (1967), and his magnum opus, *A Theology of the New Testament* (1974), Ladd combined a deep love for the Scriptures with a judicious appropriation of historical-critical methodology. Having no axes to grind with the dispensationalists, Ladd nevertheless painstakingly analyzed their biblical hermeneutic and found it incongruent with an honest reading of New Testament theology. No friend of biblical liberals, however, Ladd was even more severe with scholars like Rudolf Bultmann who sought to "demythologize" what Ladd believed was valid salvation history.

Although Ladd repeatedly challenged dispensationalism, he readily acknowledged the importance of eschatology as the fulcrum in shaping the theology of the New Testament writers. His "already/not yet" view that the Kingdom of God, although ultimately futuristic, has already broken into present history through the Christian faith remains very influential in evangelical circles. This view is seen in its most extravagant sense in the "power religion" teachings of *John Wimber and C. Peter Wagner. More in the theological mainstream, Ladd championed "historical premillennialism" as a viable alternative to dispensationalism in the evangelical community. In that way, he helped to mitigate the social pessimism that held sway over many evangelicals for several generations.

*Bibliography*

A. *Crucial Questions About the Kingdom of God* (Grand Rapids, Mich.: Eerdmans, 1952); *The Blessed Hope* (Grand Rapids, Mich.: Eerdmans, 1956); *A Theology of the New Testament* (Grand Rapids, Mich.: Eerdmans, 1974).

B. *BT* 480–95; *DCA* 626–27; David Allan Hubbard, "Biographical Sketch and Appreciation," in *Unity and Diversity in New Testament Theology: Essays in Honor of George E. Ladd*, edited by Robert A. Guelich (Grand Rapids, Mich.: Eerdmans, 1978), pp. xi-xv.

**LETOURNEAU, ROBERT G.** (30 November 1881, Richford, VT–1 June 1969, Longview, TX). *Education*: Marginal. *Career*: Foundry worker, 1902–17; mechanic, 1917–29; industrialist/inventor, 1929–66.

Robert G. LeTourneau found personal success in spite of the dire circumstances he experienced as a youth. Born in Vermont as the fourth of eight children, he was characterized as a troublesome student because of a short attention span. He ran away from home at age thirteen, but ended his frustrating school experience just one year later to work in an iron foundry. Although given a good Christian example by his parents, LeTourneau resisted personalizing his faith until the age of seventeen when he prayed to receive Christ as his personal savior. The next year LeTourneau headed west after the foundry where he worked burned down.

After enduring the shock of the 1906 San Francisco earthquake, LeTourneau settled in Stockton, California, where he eloped with sixteen-year-old Evelyn Peterson, learned the skills of a mechanic, and built a successful automobile dealership. Still, LeTourneau learned well the lesson that being a Christian did not guarantee him favorable circumstances in this life. While living in Stockton, he endured a broken neck, a fire in his repair shop, the death of his infant son from influenza, and bankruptcy from the ineptness of a business partner. Instead of discouragement however, the multifold trials only seemed to deepen his faith in the providence of God.

As a young married couple, the LeTourneaus became deeply involved in the missionary efforts of the Christian and Missionary Alliance Church. LeTourneau dedicated himself to serving God first and running his business second. This became the philosophy that guided the rest of his life. As his new company began to expand in the 1920s, LeTourneau toured the country as a lay witness who was never unwilling to share his faith in Christ with others. In time LeTourneau enjoyed a good deal of business success. Mechanically inclined, he was responsible for either inventing or perfecting most of the heavy earthmoving equipment in use today. Modern offshore oil rigs were also the product of the fertile mind of LeTourneau.

Yet from his early teens until his death in 1969, LeTourneau's priority was his Christian faith. He traveled hundreds of thousands of miles to speak to countless groups about it, maintained a chapel program within his company, gave in abundance to foreign missions, and, ironically for an eighth grade dropout, handsomely endowed LeTourneau College in Longview, Texas, an undergraduate institution that continued to flourish in the late 1990s.

Clearly, LeTourneau's importance to American evangelicalism was not his example alone, for there were other outstanding evangelical businessmen in the twentieth century. Rather, LeTourneau's significance was his "ultraism," his willingness to devote totally his life and his company to Christ without reservation. In its Christ-like example did LeTourneau's life shine like a beacon that illuminated thousands of lives that might never have been touched by a more formalized version of evangelicalism.

*Bibliography*

A. *Mover of Men and Mountains: The Autobiography of R. G. LeTourneau* (Englewood Cliffs, N.J.: Prentice-Hall, 1960).

B. *DCA* 644; *MTC* 344–49; Albert W. Lorimer, *God Runs My Business: The Story of R. G. LeTourneau* (New York: Fleming H. Revell, 1941).

**LINDSELL, HAROLD** (22 December 1913, New York, NY–15 January 1998, Lake Forest, CA). *Education*: B.S., Wheaton College, 1938; M.A., University of California, Berkeley, 1939; Harvard University, 1939–40; Ph.D., New York University, 1942; D.D., Fuller Theological Seminary, 1964. *Career*: Professor, 1942–64, 1983–89; dean and vice-president, Fuller Theological Seminary, 1951–64; associate editor (1964–67), editor (1968–72), editor and publisher (1972–78), *Christianity Today*.

Born in New York City to Presbyterian parents, Harold Lindsell was raised as a fundamentalist. By the time he attended Wheaton College in the late 1930s, Lindsell was an advocate of inerrancy in the tradition of *Benjamin Breckinridge Warfield and *J. Gresham Machen. At Wheaton, Lindsell befriended *Carl F. H. Henry. The careers of these two major figures in American evangelicalism would move in an odd tandem for the next thirty years. The stimulating intellectual environment of Wheaton convinced Lindsell to lay aside a planned business career in order to pursue one in academics. Upon graduation, Lindsell became an itinerant graduate student traveling to Berkeley, Harvard, and back to his native New York to earn advanced studies in history. Along the way he preached at local churches as he was able.

In 1942 Lindsell joined the faculty of Columbia Bible College in South Carolina. At Columbia, Lindsell, persuaded by the Baptist insistence on adult baptism and decentralized ecclesiology, converted from Presbyterianism to the Baptist faith. In 1944 he was ordained by a local Southern Baptist church. The same year, Lindsell followed Henry to Northern Baptist Seminary in Chicago where Lindsell became professor of missions and church history. Three years later Lindsell accepted the call of *Harold John Ockenga to join the original faculty of Fuller Theological Seminary.

Although not as acute a thinker as Henry or *Edward John Carnell, Lindsell became an indispensable member of the fledgling institution. Not only did he teach, but Lindsell also took on the administrative duties of the seminary. First as registrar (1947–50), then as dean of the faculty (1951–61), and, finally, as vice-president (1961–64), Lindsell served as a superb manager. More than anyone, he was responsible for securing Fuller's accreditation by the Association of American Theological Schools in the late 1950s.

By the early 1960s however, Lindsell expressed his unhappiness with Fuller. More of a separatist fundamentalist than his colleagues, Lindsell was alarmed by the elevation of David A. Hubbard to the presidency of the seminary in 1963, an act that symbolized to Lindsell Fuller's retreat from its conservative theological roots. In Lindsell's mind evangelicalism was a rudderless faith without the firm anchor of an inerrant Bible, and Hubbard was no inerrantist. But Lindsell was also weary from years of struggle with Fuller's tangled administrative affairs. Thus, he was grateful to accept an employment offer by Carl Henry in 1964. At the behest of *Billy Graham, Henry had served as editor of *Christianity Today* since 1956 and was desperate for assistance in his publishing efforts. Joining the editorial board in 1964, Lindsell provided that aid for three years. In 1968, Lindsell succeeded Henry as chief editor of *Christianity Today*.

Lindsell's ten-year term as editor was characterized by a conservative editorial stance. The chief issue addressed was biblical inerrancy. As it turned out, Lindsell's turn at *Christianity Today*'s helm coincided with an uproar in several evangelical denominations over the issue of theological liberalism. Tremors were strongest in the Lutheran Church, Missouri Synod and the Southern Baptist Convention (SBC). In the case of the SBC, Lindsell contributed to the turmoil, first, through a provocative editorial, "Whither Southern Baptists," in a 1970 issue of *Christianity Today* and then through his two books, *The Battle for the Bible* (1976) and *The Bible in the Balance* (1979).

Lindsell brought the issue of inerrancy squarely before the American evangelical community. His unequivocal assertion was that inerrancy was indispensable to evangelicalism. Some evangelicals disagreed, although in often nuanced ways. Others, like Henry, concurred with Lindsell on the theological rationale of inerrancy, but took issue with the divisive manner in which Lindsell framed the issue. By the time he left *Christianity Today* in 1978, the conflagration Lindsell ignited was still burning brightly.

Except for the six years (1983–89) that Lindsell spent serving as professor of apologetics at the Simon Greenleaf School of Law, the years prior to his death in 1998 were uncharacteristically quiet. Still, his career suggested that a strain of combative fundamentalism still flowed through the veins of "neoevangelicalism" well into the late twentieth century.

*Bibliography*

A. *The Battle for the Bible* (Grand Rapids, Mich.: Zondervan, 1976); *The Bible in the Balance* (Grand Rapids, Mich.: Zondervan, 1979).

B. *CANR* 5: 330; David E. Kucharsky with Heather L. Johnson, "CT Editor Emeritus Lindsell [obituary]," *CT* 42:3 (2 March 1998): 67.

**LINDSEY, HAL** (? 1930, Houston, TX—). *Education*: University of Houston; Th.M., Dallas Theological Seminary, 1962. *Career*: Sailor, U.S. Coast Guard;

tugboat captain; staff member, Campus Crusade for Christ, 1962–72; campus minister, UCLA, 1972–78; author, lecturer, and radio commentator, 1969—.

Born in Houston, Texas, Hal Lindsey grew up as an agnostic. In the early 1950s, he left college after two years to enlist in the U.S. Coast Guard during the Korean War. After the war he worked as a tugboat captain on the Mississippi River. A host of personal crises, culminating with the breakup of his first marriage and thoughts of suicide, led him to the Christian faith.

As a new Christian, Lindsey was convinced that Christianity had relevance for modern life only after he was introduced to biblical prophecy in 1956. Deciding to pursue a ministerial career, Lindsey enrolled at Dallas Theological Seminary, where he graduated in 1962. With his second wife, Lindsey became a student minister for Campus Crusade for Christ. For nearly ten years the Lindseys labored in such hotbeds of student rebellion as Berkeley and San Francisco State. Working with students forced Lindsey to translate the formalized theology he learned at seminary into a more contemporary idiom. Chafing under the hierarchical command structure of Campus Crusade president *Bill Bright, the Lindseys left the organization in 1972 to establish their own ministry on the campus of UCLA.

In 1969 Lindsey hired freelance writer Carole C. Carlson to help him organize his sermon notes into a book that was published in 1970 under the title *The Late Great Planet Earth*. Since the book was distributed almost exclusively by religious bookstores, it did not appear originally on the *New York Times* Best Seller List, and so its phenomenal sales figures were not appreciated for quite some time after its original publication. *The Late Great Planet Earth* quickly established Lindsey as the preeminent speaker on eschatology in modern American evangelicalism. *The Late Great Planet Earth* purports to follow a biblical scheme of prophecy. In reality, however, the book is a popularized reconstruction of the dispensational premillennialism that has dominated the world-view of American fundamentalism since the nineteenth century.

At a time when many Americans gravitated to a more fundamentalist variety of Christianity, *The Late Great Planet Earth* was an easily digestible theological lesson. Because it glibly connected every major event of the early 1970s, from Arab oil embargoes to Communist alliances, with biblical prophecy, the book also generated a great aura of relevance. Despite charges that Lindsey was forcing on the Scriptures prophetic claims that many passages never intended to suggest, *The Late Great Planet Earth* has sold tens of millions of copies.

In the 1970s and 1980s Lindsey published several more books that elaborated on the themes suggested in his first. *Satan Is Alive and Well on Planet Earth* (1972), which was also written with Carlson, insisted that the increase of Satan's influence in the present world is a primary sign that the end of human history is near. Other major works by Lindsey during this period were *There's a New World Coming* (1973), *The Liberation of Planet Earth* (1974), *The Terminal Generation* (1976), *The 1980's: Countdown to Armageddon* (1980), *The Rapture: Truth or Consequences* (1983), and *Combat Faith* (1986). All of these books were boilerplate efforts that examined the traditional dispensationist viewpoint from every angle imaginable.

In the early 1970s Lindsey established Hal Lindsey Ministries, a charitable foundation that supports various student ministries. For over twenty years, he hosted several weekly talk shows on Christian radio. Lindsey's success as an author and lecturer illustrates both the genius and the dangers inherent in the modern evangelical subculture. In one sense, Lindsey stands in the line of the frontier farmer-preachers who, armed with only a Bible, validated their ministry by the power of their sermonic deliveries rather than by their theological sophistication. On the other hand, Lindsey faces a possible indictment of giving his audience a reconstruction of the Scriptures that was built on the clouds of his own imagination. Undeniably, however, the wide distribution of his books guaranteed Lindsey one of the largest audiences of any later twentieth-century evangelical spokesperson.

*Bibliography*

A. (with C. C. Carlson) *The Late Great Planet Earth* (Grand Rapids, Mich.: Zondervan, 1970); (with C. C. Carlson) *Satan Is Alive and Well on Planet Earth* (New York: Bantam, 1972).

B. *PTR* 205–8; *TSAPR* 247–55; Paul Boyer, *When Time Shall Be No More: Prophecy Belief in Modern American Culture* (Cambridge, Mass.: Belknap Press of Harvard University Press, 1992).

# M

**McDOWELL, JOSLIN D. (JOSH)** (17 August 1939, Union City, MI—). *Education*: Kellogg College; B.A., Wheaton College, 1962; M.Th., Talbot Theological Seminary, 1966. *Career*: Welder and airplane mechanic, Air National Guard, 1957–58; evangelist, Campus Crusade for Christ, 1964—.

Josh McDowell was born on a farm just outside Battle Creek, Michigan, in 1939. He was one of three children, the younger son of a hard working, yet alcoholic and physically abusive, dairy farmer. As a boy, McDowell uneasily mixed a measure of admiration and repulsion for his father, who constantly disrupted the family home life even while instilling a strong work ethic in his son.

Raised with little consideration for personal religious faith, McDowell was an energetic youth who sought to escape his family circumstances through sports and academics. After graduating from high school in 1957, he enlisted in the Air National Guard where he worked as a welder and an aircraft mechanic. A head injury cost McDowell an appointment to the U.S. Air Force Academy, and he returned to Michigan to attend Kellogg College, a junior college near the family farm. He decided to become a lawyer and to pursue a political career.

At Kellogg College, McDowell resolved to perform a historical study that would refute Christianity as a meaningless fable. Instead of disproving the veracity of the Christian record, however, McDowell found himself persuaded and converted by it. In his characteristically exacting fashion, McDowell traced his acceptance of Christ as savior to 8:30 P.M., on 19 December 1959.

By 1960 McDowell began to believe that God might be calling him into the ministry. Although he still entertained thoughts about a legal career, McDowell transferred to Wheaton College and graduated from there in 1962. During his senior year at Wheaton, McDowell made a number of acquaintances who confirmed his conviction to enter the ministry. These people included *Torrey M. Johnson, the founder of Youth for Christ, and *Bill Bright, the founder and president of Campus Crusade for Christ. Both men were impressed with McDowell's intelligence and dedication and arranged opportunities for him to minister with youth and to grow in his faith.

From Illinois, McDowell set out for UCLA, but ended up at Talbot Theological Seminary in LaMirada, California. Even before he graduated from Talbot, McDowell joined Campus Crusade as a full-time staff member in 1964, a position he still holds. Throughout the late 1960s, McDowell worked on the campus of the University of British Columbia where he evangelized and discipled students. He also proved to be an able administrator and was given the responsibility of organizing many special Crusade conferences. After working in Canada for several years, McDowell was transferred to South America where he ministered among the Marxist students of the University of LaPlata in Buenos Aires, Argentina. The brash McDowell took on the dangerous challenge with enthusiasm and honed his evangelistic talents in a crucible of radical disbelief. McDowell was particularly adept in reaching out to students within the context of their own culture. He tried to lead them to Christ through both a concerned and intellectually convincing witness.

In the early 1970s, McDowell was an itinerant university minister for Campus Crusade. His quick wit and challenging manner made him a favorite speaker at many universities and colleges across America. The year 1972 marked the publication of *Evidence That Demands a Verdict*, a weighty apologetic tome compiled from McDowell's own investigations into the historicity of the Christian faith and supplemented with additional research from Campus Crusade staff members. Within a short period of time *Evidence* became one of the most widely read books among evangelical college students, along with the works of C.S. Lewis, *Hal Lindsey, and *Francis A. Schaeffer. More books followed in the 1970s and 1980s. Among the major efforts were *More Than a Carpenter* (1977), *More Evidence That Demands a Verdict* (1979), and *The Resurrection Factor* (1981). In the late 1980s and into the 1990s, McDowell shifted his ministry emphasis somewhat from apologetics to "family life" concerns like marriage, teen sexuality, and the impact of secular culture on the quality of contemporary American life.

In the 1980s, McDowell formed his own ministry, first in Southern California, then outside Dallas, Texas, where he lived with his wife and their four children. He remained a salaried employee of Campus Crusade and received no royalties for his many books. By the early 1990s it was estimated that McDowell had spoken to more than 7 million people on over 800 university and college campuses in 60 countries.

*Bibliography*

A. *Evidence That Demands a Verdict* (San Bernardino, Calif.: Here's Life Publishers, 1972); *More Than a Carpenter* (Minneapolis, Minn.: World Wide, 1977).

B. Joe Musser, *Josh: Excitement of the Unexpected* (San Bernardino, Calif.: Here's Life Publishers, 1981).

**MACHEN, (J)OHN GRESHAM** (28 July 1881, Baltimore, MD–1 January 1937, Bismarck, ND). *Education*: B.A., Johns Hopkins, 1901; Ph.M., Princeton University, 1904; B.D., Princeton Theological Seminary, 1905; Ph.D., Marburg University, 1906. *Career*: professor of New Testament and theology, 1906–37; Presbyterian minister, 1914–37.

J. Gresham Machen was born into a wealthy Baltimore family. From his lawyer father he acquired a lifelong interest in classical literature. The greater influence in Machen's life however, came from his mother who taught him all the Presbyterian creeds in the Old School tradition. Acquiring an uncommonly broad education for such a religiously conservative youth, Machen attended Johns Hopkins University where he majored in the classics. After an additional year of graduate study at Hopkins, Machen moved toward clerical studies in the Presbyterian Church. In 1903, he enrolled simultaneously in Princeton University, where he earned a master of philosophy degree in 1904, and Princeton Seminary, where he took a bachelor of divinity degree in 1905. While at the seminary, Machen came under the influence of *Benjamin Breckinridge Warfield, who at the time was perhaps the best-known theologian in American Presbyterianism. In addition to Warfield, Machen was greatly influenced by Princeton's William Park Armstrong, the seminary's professor of New Testament. Encouraged by Armstrong, Machen spent a year in Germany studying at the universities of Göttingen and Marburg from 1905–6. The experience was definitive for Machen, who sampled the theological liberalism of the Germany academy and found it wanting. He returned to Princeton Seminary in 1906 to take up the position of instructor in New Testament studies, more confirmed in his Old School Presbyterianism than ever before.

Although he was ordained into the (Northern) Presbyterian Church in the U.S.A. in 1914, Machen's lifelong field of ministry was essentially the classroom. His academic interest was Pauline studies, and his first major book, *The*

*Origin of Paul's Religion* (1921), was a carefully researched rejoinder to the German critics who had argued that the Apostle Paul founded a radically different variety of Christianity discontinuous with the simple preaching of Jesus of Nazareth.

By the early 1920s, Machen was regarded as the most significant apologist of conservative Presbyterianism and seen as the theological successor to the great Warfield. Machen's reputation as a defender of orthodoxy grew beyond Presbyterianism with the publication of his *Christianity and Liberalism* (1923). In this work, Machen argued forcefully that historical Christianity and modern liberalism were two entirely distinct religions. In a time of growing polarization within American evangelicalism, Machen's logic led him into the thicket of denominational combat within the Northern Presbyterian fold. Although Machen disliked being characterized as a fundamentalist, he was increasingly regarded as the movement's theological champion and spokesperson. Unfortunately for Machen, the Northern Presbyterian denomination became an increasingly inhospitable place for a conservative evangelical. A substantial reorganization of Princeton Seminary in the late 1920s undermined Machen's own position to the extent that he felt compelled to leave Princeton and establish Westminster Theological Seminary in Philadelphia in 1929. Assisted by a core group of like-minded professors, Machen's intent was to preserve the Old School tradition through Westminster. Momentous for the later course of American evangelicalism was the fact that several key seminarians followed Machen to Westminster like *Harold John Ockenga, Carl McIntire, and, later, *Francis A. Schaeffer.

After the formation of Westminster, a hardening of Machen's own conservative proclivities was obvious. Although in 1930 he produced another work of erudite New Testament scholarship, *The Virgin Birth of Christ*, the remainder of Machen's life was dominated by ecclesiastical controversy. Especially wary of what he regarded as theological liberalism on the mission field, Machen led other Presbyterian conservatives in the formation of the Independent Board for Presbyterian Missions in 1933. This act outraged liberals and moderates alike in the Northern Presbyterian church and led to Machen's trial by the General Assembly and dismissal from the denominational ministry in 1935. After an unsuccessful appeal of the assembly's verdict in 1936, Machen formed a new denomination, the Presbyterian Church of America (later the Orthodox Presbyterian Church). Characterized as a sectarian by his opponents, Machen labored hard to win support for his new denomination. It was during just such a campaign that he contracted pneumonia and died on 1 January 1937.

Paradoxically, Machen helped give birth to the two major strains of the modern evangelical subculture: separatist fundamentalism and the more inclusive neoevangelicalism that has guided the movement since World War II. Although his own revulsion to theological liberalism led him to ecclesiastical separatism, his cosmopolitan attitude toward culture and education provided a model for his later disciples to follow.

*Bibliography*

A. *The Origin of Paul's Religion* (New York: Macmillan, 1921); *Christianity and Liberalism* (New York: Macmillan, 1923).

B. *ACSL* 163–65; *DARB* 337–38; *DCA* 689–90; *HET* 129–43; George M. Marsden, "Understanding J. Gresham Machen," *Princeton Seminary Bulletin*, n.s. 11:1 (1990): 46–60; D. G. Hart, *Defending the Faith: J. Gresham Machen and the Crisis of Conservative Protestantism in Modern America* (Baltimore, Md.: The Johns Hopkins University Press, 1994).

**McPHERSON, AIMEE SEMPLE** (9 October 1890, Ingersoll, Ontario, Canada–27 September 1944, Oakland, CA). *Education*: High school. *Career*: Evangelist, 1908–44; founder, International Church of the Foursquare Gospel, 1927.

Aimee Semple McPherson was born as Aimee Kennedy into a successful farming family in Ontario, Canada, in 1890. Her father was an active Methodist, but her mother, Minnie, was an even more enthusiastic member of the Salvation Army. As a youngster, Aimee was deeply impressed by the Army's raucous worship. With a natural bent toward the theatrical, she was a skillful speaker and toyed with the idea of becoming an actress.

As an adolescent, Aimee grew skeptical of her mother's faith and joined her father's Methodist church. During the winter of 1907, however, she attended a Pentecostal revival meeting and experienced the baptism of the Holy Spirit, which rekindled her religious fervor. Within a year, she also married Robert Semple, an itinerant evangelist. The Semples traveled throughout Ontario and the upper American Midwest as revivalists from 1908–10. Robert was the major preacher, while Aimee gave testimonies and other assistance. In 1909 she was ordained at a Full Gospel Assembly in Chicago.

The Semples journeyed to Hong Kong to serve on the mission field in 1910. The experience was a disaster for Aimee, mitigated only by the birth of her daughter, Roberta. Aimee was ill for the better part of a year; then Robert contracted typhoid and died. Only with the financial assistance of her mother were Aimee and her baby able to return home.

In early 1912, Aimee married Harold McPherson, and one year later gave birth to her son, Rolf. Aimee's marriage to Harold was unpleasant, and she chafed under the restricting roles of housewife and mother. Believing she must again take up the call of evangelism, Aimee left Harold and went to live with her parents in 1915. Although the McPhersons reconciled briefly, they were divorced in 1918.

Aimee began to hold revival meetings in Ontario by 1920. She developed a penchant for dramatic preaching, and wore a "gospel uniform" that resembled the dress of a nurse. With the final departure of Harold McPherson from her life, Aimee relied heavily on the astute business talents of her mother. Using Salvation Army pioneer Evangeline Booth as a model, Aimee developed a distinctive persona as an independent Pentecostal revivalist.

The years 1918–23 were spent crisscrossing America. Hundreds of revival meetings and publicity generated by her periodical, the *Bridal Call*, helped McPherson to develop a sizable following by the early 1920s. On 1 January 1923, she opened Angelus Temple, a 5,000-seat worship facility located in Santa Monica, California. Financed by donations totalling $1.5 million, the Temple became McPherson's headquarters and the center of activities for her estimated 50,000 followers.

McPherson was an innovator in the mingling of popular entertainment with traditional worship. Hollywood props were used to illustrate sermons; music was performed by a brass band, an orchestra, and a robed choir. McPherson donned costumes to act out her sermons. Radio was also used aggressively to promote the gospel. McPherson was something of a pioneer in this area, too, as she started broadcasting in 1923 on the Angelus Temple's station KFSG, the first American radio station owned and operated by a religious institution. McPherson was the first woman to gain a Federal Communication Commission license to broadcast and was the first woman to deliver a sermon over the airwaves.

Without intending it, McPherson organized a denomination, the International Church of the Foursquare Gospel (ICFG), around her Angelus Temple. The notion of "Foursquare Gospel," said McPherson, came to her in a vision of Christ's fourfold role as savior, baptizer, physician, and king. To this newly institutionalized church was added a Bible college, the Lighthouse of International Foursquare Evangelism.

A firm believer in the miraculous work of the Holy Spirit, McPherson dedicated one Angelus Temple service per week to prayer and healing. Despite a good deal of sensationalism associated with her ministry, however, McPherson used the ICFG facilities to minister extensively to the local indigent population. Free medical care, clothing, shelter, and over 1.5 million meals were provided to the poor of Los Angeles during the 1930s.

From the mid–1920s onward, McPherson's life was increasingly characterized by bizarre behavior and personal problems. After a mysterious six-week disappearance in 1926 during which she was feared drowned, McPherson was found wandering in the Arizona desert. Police eventually charged her with perpetrating a public hoax in order to cover up a sex scandal, but the charges were dropped after McPherson mounted a highly publicized legal defense of her actions.

In 1931, McPherson entered into another unhappy marriage, which lasted just four years. Throughout this period she struggled with alcoholism and the pain of estrangement from her mother and daughter. Despite these many problems, the ICFG continued to grow, as did the membership of Angelus Temple. McPherson remained popular with her flock and toured the country making plans for her denomination's expansion across America.

At the time of her death from an accidental overdose of sleeping pills in September 1944, the ICFG was poised to begin broadcasting the Angelus Temple's services on television—what would have been another innovation. After the death of McPherson, the ICFG continued to grow under the leadership of Rolf McPherson until his retirement in 1988.

As a forerunner of evangelical feminism, McPherson was a bold innovator and synthesizer of popular culture and traditional Pentecostalism. Struggling against societal prejudice, she became one of a handful of successful female entrepreneurs in contemporary evangelicalism.

*Bibliography*

A. *This Is That: Personal Experiences, Sermons, and Writings* (Los Angeles: Bridal Call Publishing, 1919); *The Story of My Life* (Waco, Tex.: Word, 1973).

B. *ACSL* 168–70; *DARB* 335–36; *DCA* 696–97; *DPCM* 568–71; *PTR* 221–25; *TSAPR* 263–70; Edith L. Blumhofer, *Aimee Semple McPherson: Everybody's Sister* (Grand Rapids, Mich.: Eerdmans, 1993).

**McQUILKIN, ROBERT C., JR.** (16 February 1886, Philadelphia, PA–15 July 1952, Asheville, NC). *Education*: B.A., University of Pennsylvania, 1917. *Career*: Clerk and estimator, 1902–11; associate editor, *Sunday School Times*, 1912–17; Bible conference teacher and organizer, 1913–23; president, Columbia Bible College (SC), 1923–52.

Through his role as conference organizer and college president, Robert McQuilkin was a key figure in the institutionalization of the "higher" or "victorious" life movement in twentieth-century American evangelicalism. McQuilkin was born in Philadelphia and joined the United Presbyterian Church after undergoing a conversion experience as a young man. His original career objective was to become a successful businessman, and from 1902–11, he worked as a clerk and estimator.

While attending a missionary conference in 1911, McQuilkin came into contact with the teachings of the Keswick circle and experienced what he believed was the freedom over the power of sin through the action of the Holy Spirit. The power of this experience transformed McQuilkin into an enthusiastic advocate of what was known in the United States as the victorious life movement. His involvement with the victorious life movement brought McQuilkin into contact with *Charles G. Trumbull, the influential editor of the *Sunday School Times*. Trumbull took McQuilkin under his tutelage and made him the associate editor of his paper from 1912–17. Concurrent with his association with the *Sunday School Times*, McQuilkin married Marguerite Lambie in 1912.

His own experience convinced McQuilkin of the value of the victorious life movement, and beginning in 1913, he organized a series of conferences that were held consecutively at Oxford, Pennsylvania (1913), Princeton, New Jersey (1914–18), Stonybrook, New York (1919–22), and Keswick Grove, New Jersey (1923). In addition to organizing the conferences, McQuilkin also taught at them. In order to extend his education, he attended the University of Pennsylvania, graduating from there in 1917.

McQuilkin was a strong supporter of missions and planned to go to the African mission field in 1917—a scheme that was foiled by America's entry into the First World War. Despite this setback, McQuilkin put his significant administrative abilities to good use, becoming director of the Latin American Mission and the Mexican Indian Mission. In addition, his victorious life conferences supported many missionaries all around the world.

By the early 1920s, McQuilkin developed a keen interest in higher education. Suspending his annual victorious life conferences in 1923, McQuilkin was instrumental in the establishment of Columbia Bible College (CBC) in Columbia, South Carolina. He was named the first president of CBC, a position he held until his death in 1952. During his years as a college administrator, he led in the founding of Ben Lippen Bible Conference center in Asheville, North Carolina (1928), and the Ben Lippen School (1940). Deeply concerned with ensuring the quality of education offered by independent Bible colleges, McQuilkin helped to found the Evangelical Teacher Training Association, an organization he headed for its first ten years of existence (1931–41).

Throughout his manifold duties, McQuilkin remained a much-traveled speaker and author. Among his significant literary works were *Victorious Life Studies* (1918), *The Baptism of the Spirit: Shall We Seek It?* (1935), *The Lord Is My Shepherd (1938),* and *Victory in Christ* (1939). A long-time member of the Presbyterian Church in the U.S.A., McQuilkin joined the more conservative fellowship of Independent Evangelical Churches just one year before his death.

*Bibliography*

A. *Victorious Life Studies* (Philadelphia: Christian Life Literature Fund, 1918); *The Life of Victory and the Baptism of the Holy Spirit* (Chicago: Moody, 1953).

B. *DCA* 697–98; *RLA* 310; *TDCB* 250; Marguerite McQuilkin, *Always in Triumph: The Life of Robert C. McQuilkin* (Columbia, S.C.: Bible College Bookstore, 1956).

**MAIER, WALTER A.** (4 October 1893, Boston, MA–11 January 1950, St. Louis, MO). *Education*: Concordia Collegiate Institute; B.A., Boston University, 1913; B.D., Concordia Theological Seminary, 1916; M.A., Ph.D., Harvard University, 1920, 1929. *Career*: Executive secretary, Walther League, 1920–22; editor, *Walther League Messenger*, 1920–45; professor of Old Testament, Concordia Theological Seminary, 1922–44; radio host, "The Lutheran Hour," 1930–31; 1935–50.

An important pioneer in the American evangelical use of the mass media, Walter Maier was born in Boston, Massachusetts, the son of German immigrants, in 1893. He grew up in the highly conservative Lutheran Church, Missouri Synod. Maier enjoyed a comprehensive education that he resolved to put to service for Christ as a Lutheran minister. By 1920, Maier had earned degrees at Boston University, Concordia Seminary, and Harvard University. In addition, he was ordained to the ministry, made assistant pastor of his home church, and admitted to the doctoral program at Harvard in Semitic studies.

During World War I, Maier served as a U.S. Army chaplain to German prisoners of war, and in 1920, he became the first executive secretary of the Walther League, the Missouri Synod's youth program. As head of the program, he expanded the Walther League's role in overseas missions and also took up duties as editor of the *Walther League Messenger*, a responsibility he held until 1945.

In 1922, Maier moved to the Concordia Theological Seminary where he became professor of Old Testament studies. At a time when fundamentalism was on the ascendancy in America, some Missouri Synod officials looked askance at Maier's graduate work at Harvard, that citadel of theological liberalism. Yet Maier proved to be an excellent addition to the faculty at Concordia and was a particular favorite with the students. In 1924, Maier married schoolteacher Hulda Eickhoff, and in 1929, he received his doctorate in Semitics.

Early on it was apparent that Maier's gifts were in the area of communications. He was a perceptive writer and editor and a powerful speaker. Just two years into his service at Concordia Seminary (1924), Maier was able to convince the Walther League to support a new communicative venture: the financing of the school's radio station, KFUO. In the midst of his other duties, Maier prepared and presented two weekly religious programs for the station. The response to the programming was overwhelmingly positive, and by 1927, KFUO expanded its broadcasting schedule dramatically.

Through his editorial columns in the *Messenger* and his radio commentaries, Maier became a prominent personality in conservative evangelicalism. Although he criticized theological liberalism and the crass consumerism of the 1920s, Maier was quite moderate in many of his social stances. This set him apart from the more strident voices in the fundamentalist community.

Despite the onset of the Great Depression, Maier wanted to move forward with his broadcasting initiative. On 2 October 1930, through an arrangement with CBS, Maier hosted "The Lutheran Hour" for the first time. Public response to the "Hour" was extremely favorable. Still, financial support was scarce, and "The Lutheran Hour" was forced to discontinue its broadcasting schedule from 1932–35 until permanent underwriting was secured from General Motors.

The second series of "The Lutheran Hour," which commenced in 1935, established Maier's signature format: his introduction by announcer R. W. Janetzke, some attention to current events, a sermon, an invitation for the listener to receive Christ as savior, and intercessory prayer. It was this simple style, along with the concern that permeated Maier's broadcasts, that were seen as his strengths.

Despite his immense popularity, Maier handled much of the workload of "The Lutheran Hour" by himself. Finally, in the mid–1940s he reluctantly began to divest himself of some of his other duties, principally his editorship of the *Messenger* and his teaching load at Concordia Seminary. In 1949, "The Lutheran Hour" was televised for the first time, and Maier was characteristically optimistic about the prospects of spreading the gospel through television. The future of "The Lutheran Hour," however, would not include Maier, who died of a heart attack in 1950.

At the time of his death, Maier was probably the most popular radio preacher in America. Through the style and content of his messages, he set a high standard that has not always been emulated by other evangelicals. In addition to his groundbreaking activities on radio, Maier also helped his denomination move closer to the American mainstream by publicizing its key doctrines to a mass audience.

*Bibliography*

A. *The Best of Walter A. Maier*, edited by Paul L. Maier (St. Louis: Concordia Publishing, 1980).

B. *DCA* 699–700; *PTR* 214–15; *RLA* 287; *TSAPR* 270–77; Paul L. Maier, *A Man Spoke, A World Listened: The Story of Walter Maier and the Lutheran Hour* (New York: McGraw-Hill, 1963).

**MARSDEN, GEORGE M.** (25 February 1939, Middletown, PA—). *Education*: B.A., Haverford College, 1959; M.A., Yale University, 1961; B.D., Westminster Theological Seminary, 1963; Ph.D., Yale University, 1965. *Career*: History professor, Calvin College, Duke University, and the University of Notre Dame; author, 1965—.

George Marsden's greatest fame as a historian comes from his work on American fundamentalism. But his keen understanding of the phenomenon comes in part from his own formative immersion in it. By the time Marsden was born in Middletown, Pennsylvania, his father Robert Marsden had followed *J. Gresham Machen out of Princeton Seminary into Westminster Seminary and the Orthodox Presbyterian Church (OPC). Because the elder Marsden served as both missionary secretary for the OPC and chief executive officer at Westminster, the turbulent waves of Presbyterian ecclesiastical politics were regularly breaking over the Marsden home.

At the age of sixteen, Marsden entered Haverford College. Early on he decided to pursue an academic career in the field of history, and graduated with the bachelor's degree in that subject in 1959. The Haverford experience was both stimulating and disturbing for Marsden. Religious shibboleths inherited from his fundamentalist upbringing had been shaken severely. To repair the breach, Marsden headed to Westminster Seminary where he studied apologetics under his father's colleague, Cornelius Van Til. After a year, with his doubts only somewhat settled, Marsden moved on to Yale to work on a graduate degree in American studies. The unexpected death of his father made for a particularly depressing first winter in New Haven, Connecticut. Marsden found his gloom lifted only after he had a significant experience of spiritual renewal while serving as a church camp counselor in the summer of 1961.

With a fresh sense of God's calling, Marsden returned to Westminster to finish his divinity degree in 1963, then headed back to Yale where he earned his doctorate under the tutelage of Sydney Ahlstrom in 1965. His dissertation topic was the New School Presbyterianism of the early nineteenth century. The subject served as a catalyst that led him to his later examinations of fundamentalism.

As he finished his studies at Yale, Marsden secured a teaching job at Calvin College in Grand Rapids, Michigan. The sturdy Dutch Reformed tradition of Calvin opened up new intellectual vistas for Marsden. With fellow scholars like C. T. McIntire and Nicholas Wolterstorff, Marsden saw ways that he could integrate his Christian faith and intellect in service to Christ and His Church. Not only did Marsden remain at Calvin College for nearly a quarter of a century, but he also joined the Christian Reformed Church, a denomination that reflected the integrative approach to faith and learning.

In 1980, Marsden produced his first major work, *Fundamentalism and American Culture*. In this book Marsden asserted persuasively that twentieth-century American fundamentalism was a complex religious, social, political, and intellectual phenomenon that was shaped by the resistance of nineteenth-century evangelicalism to various modernist trends in the larger culture. Marsden's book demolished the facile stereotypes of fundamentalism characterizing investigations of the movement since the 1920s. In the process, it encouraged a new flowering of evangelical history.

Some seven years later Marsden authored *Reforming Fundamentalism: Fuller Seminary and the New Evangelicalism* (1987). It is appropriate to see *Reforming Fundamentalism* as the final installment in a series that began with Marsden's dissertation and continued with *Fundamentalism and American Culture*. There is a symmetry in this triad of works as the triumphal reform-minded evangelicalism of Charles Finney returns from its exile on the cultural periphery of America as the "new evangelicalism" typified by the Fuller Seminary faculty of *Harold John Ockenga, *Carl F. H. Henry, and *Edward John Carnell. Yet, there is also a certain pathos in *Reforming Fundamentalism* as the great Fuller objective, to return evangelicalism to the center of American religious life, ultimately falls short of its goal.

In the late 1980s, with his reputation as a preeminent historical scholar growing, Marsden left Calvin College for a brief sojourn at Duke University before moving on to Notre Dame. During this period of professional flux, he authored *The Soul of the American University: From Protestant Established to Established Nonbelief* (1994). This work asserted Marsden's conviction that the religious faith that had so contributed to the building of American higher education had been systematically driven out of most colleges and universities in the twentieth century. In a postscript to *The Soul of the American University*, Marsden suggested that American higher education needed to be more open to explicit expressions of religious faith. This notion, which unleashed a wide ranging debate in the academy, was expanded in his book *The Outrageous Idea of Christian Scholarship* (1997).

Marsden stood preeminent among late twentieth-century evangelical historians. His fame rested, not only on his groundbreaking studies in American fundamentalism, but also on his attempts to bring the issue of religious faith into the town square of the secular academy.

*Bibliography*

A. *Fundamentalism and American Culture* (Oxford: Oxford University Press, 1980); *The Soul of the American University: From Protestant Established to Established Nonbelief* (New York: Oxford University Press, 1994); *The Outrageous Idea of Christian Scholarship* (New York: Oxford University Press, 1997).

B. *CANR* 12:296–97; Maxie B. Burch, *The Evangelical Historians: The Historiography of George Marsden, Nathan Hatch and Mark Noll* (Lanham, Md.: University Press of America, 1996).

**MARSHALL, SARAH CATHERINE WOOD** (27 September 1914, Johnson City, TN–18 March 1983, Boynton Beach, FL). *Education*: B.A., Agnes Scott College (GA), 1936. *Career*: Author, 1949–83.

As an inspirational author, Catherine Marshall spoke effectively to the hopes and fears of ordinary people. This she did through her biographical works about her first husband, Peter, but also through deep reflective pieces on her own tumultuous life.

Marshall was born in the mountains of eastern Tennessee in 1914, the daughter of a Presbyterian minister. A shy child, she grew up in Canton, Mississippi, and Keyser, West Virginia. As a student at Agnes Scott College in Decatur, Georgia, Catherine met her dynamic future husband, Peter Marshall, a Scotsman who was serving as pastor of Westminster Presbyterian Church in Atlanta. The couple married on 4 November 1936, and eleven months later Peter assumed the influential pastorate of New York Avenue Church in Washington, D.C.

Peter quickly became one of the most popular ministers in the District of Columbia. In the midst of great demands placed upon their personal lives, the Marshalls enjoyed a measure of happiness highlighted by the birth of their only child in 1940. Still, the expectations of parishioners took their toll on Catherine, and she contracted tuberculosis in March 1943. Her health broken, Catherine remained bedridden for over two years. The silver lining of a difficult period, however, was a heightened feeling of the presence of God in her life.

No sooner had Catherine's health returned when the Marshalls faced another crisis in the form of a heart attack that Peter suffered in 1946. Peter recovered and went on to enjoy the most fruitful phase of his ministry as chaplain of the U.S. Senate. But he suffered another heart attack and died on 25 January 1949.

Facing an uncertain future, Catherine was approached by the Fleming H. Revell Company to produce an edited book of her husband's sermons. Somewhat hesitantly, Marshall put together what became *Mr. Jones, Meet the Master*. Unexpectedly, this book became a runaway best seller in 1950. Even more popular was Marshall's next book, *A Man Called Peter*, a warm account of her husband's life that was published in 1951. With two very popular books to her credit, Marshall became something of a celebrity. Awarded the 1953 "Woman of the Year" award in literature by the Women's Press Club, Marshall wrote many more articles and oversaw the transformation of *A Man Called Peter* into a well-received movie in 1955. In 1957, she published her own life's story under the title, *To Live Again*.

The unexpected professional success that Marshall experienced did little to ease the deep sense of loneliness and unfulfillment that she experienced. These feelings did not pass until Marshall married Leonard LeSourd, the executive editor of *Guideposts* magazine on 14 November 1959. Marshall and LeSourd proved to be a prodigious literary team, spiriting nearly a dozen works into print. With two friends, they started Chosen Books, a small Christian publishing house that published several significant titles. All the while, the couple was moving in new spiritual dimensions, establishing a prayer ministry called "The Intercessors" in 1980.

Marshall died on 18 March 1983 of a chronic lung ailment. She did not live to enjoy the measure of posthumous renown that came to her when her novel *Christy* was made a network television show on CBS in the 1990s.

*Bibliography*

A. *Mr. Jones, Meet the Master* (Westwood, N.J.: Fleming H. Revell, 1950); *A Man Called Peter* (Westwood, N.J.: Fleming H. Revell, 1951); *To Live Again* (Westwood, N.J.: Fleming H. Revell, 1957); *Christy* (New York: McGraw-Hill, 1967).

B. *CANR* 57:344–46; *DCA* 709–10; *TDCB* 239; *TSAPR* 283–92; Paul Boyer, "Minister's Wife, Widow, Reluctant Feminist: Catherine Marshall in the 1950s," *American Quarterly* 30 (Winter 1978): 703–21.

**MOODY, DWIGHT LYMAN** (5 February 1837, E. Northfield, MA–22 December 1899, E. Northfield, MA). *Education*: Minimal. *Career*: Shoe salesman, 1854–60; pastor and evangelist, 1860–99.

Dwight L. Moody was not only the most successful Protestant evangelist of the late nineteenth century, he also was a significant progenitor of both the Keswick "higher life" movement and fundamentalism in America. Moody was born just outside Boston, Massachusetts, in 1837. His father, who was a mason, died when Moody was very young, leaving him and his six siblings in the care of his devoutly Unitarian mother in whose church Moody was baptized and raised. His family suffered through great financial uncertainties, which prompted Moody to cut short his formal education. Traveling to Boston to live with an uncle, he became a shoe clerk. He was also converted to evangelical Christianity through the ministry of a Congregationalist Sunday school teacher in Boston.

In 1856, Moody moved to Chicago, where he became a successful shoe salesman and a member of Plymouth Congregational Church. Early on Moody exhibited significant evangelistic skills. Just two years after joining Plymouth church, he led a Sunday school class on the north side of Chicago that grew to about 1,500 attendees. Moody particularly enjoyed working with youth and was an early and enthusiastic supporter of the YMCA, becoming its national president in 1865.

Convinced of his ministerial calling, Moody gave up the shoe business in 1860 in order to become a full-time evangelist. Despite lacking formal ordination, Moody organized the nondenominational Illinois Street Church in 1863. The congregation grew to a respectable size, but Moody gave up the pastorate of Illinois Street after the church was destroyed in the Chicago Fire of 1871.

In the early 1870s, Moody entered into a new phase in his ministerial career. Teaming with the music evangelist Ira D. Sankey, whom Moody met at a YMCA meeting, the pastor-turned-revivalist set off for a preaching tour of the British Isles in 1873. For a memorable two-year period, Moody and Sankey saw many decisions made for Christ under their British ministry. While they left America as virtual unknowns, they returned in 1875 as international celebrities. During the last quarter of the nineteenth century there was no better known nor more effective urban revivalist than Moody. Among his successful revivals from 1875–79 were campaigns in Brooklyn, Philadelphia, New York City, Chicago, and Boston.

By the late 1870s, Moody was able to parlay his considerable fame into numerous ministries. In 1879, he founded Northfield Seminary for girls and, two years later, the Mount Herman School for boys. As early as 1880, Moody held summer conferences on the Northfield campus that attracted some of the most prominent names in the American evangelical community. By 1886, the Student Volunteer Movement emerged from the Northfield conference as a powerful missionary force. In the same year, Moody established one of the first Bible schools in America, the Chicago Evangelization Society. This was the forerunner of Moody Bible Institute. Concerned about a dearth of inexpensive Christian literature, Moody created the Colportage Association in 1895.

As sizable as his influence was both through his revival campaigns and his extended network of ministry, Moody also exerted a great deal of influence on early twentieth-century evangelicalism by his support of the higher life movement and his advocacy of dispensational premillennialism. In similar fashion, Moody left his imprint on evangelicalism through the many young ministers who were directly influenced by the content and style of his revivalistic approach. Among these ministers were several who would directly shape the course of American religious history in the new century: *J. Wilbur Chapman, *Reuben A. Torrey, *A. J. Gordon, and *Lewis Sperry Chafer. Thus, in many different ways, Moody was the most influential American evangelical of his age.

*Bibliography*

A. *The Way to God* (Chicago: Fleming H. Revell, 1884); *Prevailing Prayer* (Chicago: Fleming H. Revell, 1885); *A Treasury of Dwight L. Moody* (Grand Rapids, Mich.: Eerdmans, 1949).

B. *DARB* 371–72; *DCA* 768–69; *MTC* 140–47; *RLA* 322–23; William R. Moody, *The Life of Dwight L. Moody* (New York: Fleming H. Revell, 1900); James Findlay,

*Dwight L. Moody: American Evangelist, 1837–1899* (Chicago: University of Chicago Press, 1969).

**MULLINS, (E)DGAR (Y)OUNG** (5 January 1860, Franklin County, MS–23 November 1928, Louisville, KY). *Education*: A.B., Texas A&M, 1879; B.D., Southern Baptist Theological Seminary, 1885; Johns Hopkins University, 1891–92. *Career*: Telegraph operator, 1876–79; pastor, 1885–99; associate secretary, Southern Baptist Foreign Mission Board, 1895–96; president and professor of theology, Southern Baptist Theological Seminary, 1899–1928.

Through his denominational statesmanship, his administration of Southern Baptist Theological Seminary, and his several theological works, E. Y. Mullins may be among the most influential Southern Baptists of the twentieth century. Although his family hailed from Mississippi, Mullins was raised in central Texas. His father was a college graduate and a Baptist preacher who established a school and a church in Corsicana, Texas. Learning was highly valued in the Mullins household, and the firm expectation was that all the Mullins children would attend college.

Working as a telegraph operator to assist his family, Mullins was a member of the first class to enter Texas A&M in 1876. A serious young man, Mullins planned a career as a lawyer. Those plans were changed, however, when he was converted to the Christian faith at a revival meeting in Dallas. Shortly after his conversion, Mullins decided to enter the ministry and enrolled at the Southern Baptist Theological Seminary in 1881. At Southern, Mullins demonstrated his considerable leadership abilities as manager of the dormitory, a highly responsible position that he held until his graduation in 1885.

Ill health forced Mullins to abandon his plan for a missionary career in Brazil. Consequently, he accepted a pastorate in Harrodsburg, Kentucky (1885–88), where he met and married his wife, Isla May Hawley. During his next pastorate in Baltimore (1888–95), Mullins studied briefly at the Johns Hopkins University. He resigned his pastorate to work for a few months (1895) for the Foreign Mission Board of the Southern Baptist Convention, and then resumed his pastoral career at the Baptist Church in Newton Centre, Massachusetts.

In the midst of theological and financial upheaval, Southern Baptist Theological Seminary elected Mullins as its president in 1899. Under Mullins's leadership, Southern not only stabilized, but flourished. The school added students and faculty, increased its endowment substantially, and became one of the preeminent educational institutions in Southern Baptist life, not only through the classroom, but also through the theological journal *Review and Expositor*.

Mullins's more durable legacy was his influence upon many Baptist ministers and educators as a professor of theology. Although a firm believer in the infallibility of the Bible, Mullins was somewhat open to the newer historical criticism that placed a greater emphasis on the role of human experience in the authorship of the Scriptures and the expression of Christian faith. Mullins's particular formulation of these theological notions is found in his doctrine of ''soul competency,'' a conviction that the Holy Spirit renders the believer ''competent'' to interpret the Bible and to apply its teachings in matters of faith and practice. Despite a grueling administrative schedule and little formalized advanced theological training, Mullins authored several significant works on theology and Baptist beliefs such as *Why Is Christianity True?* (1905), *The Axioms of Religion* (1908), *Baptist Beliefs* (1912), and *The Christian Religion in Its Doctrinal Expression* (1917).

In an age when Southern Baptists were very much a culturally and geographically isolated people, Mullins was remarkably nonprovincial. He was asked by the organizers of the Federal Council of Churches to help bring the Southern Baptist Convention (SBC) into the new organization. Although Mullins failed in that endeavor, he did succeed in getting the SBC to join the new Baptist World Alliance in 1907. When many American evangelical denominations were wracked by theological controversies over fundamentalism in the 1920s, Mullins was instrumental in steering the SBC through the tumult intact. As president of the SBC from 1921–25, he also contributed significantly to the creation of the ''Baptist Faith and Message'' (1925), the first confession of faith ever adopted by Southern Baptists.

Mullins is the best representative of the theologically moderate leadership that helped to make the SBC the largest American evangelical denomination by the end of the twentieth century. The fact that his activities and theological writings influenced an audience beyond the Baptist fold only enhances his stature as a significant figure in twentieth-century evangelicalism.

*Bibliography*

A. *Why Is Christianity True?* (Philadelphia: American Baptist Publication Society, 1905); *The Axioms of Religion* (Philadelphia: American Baptist Publication Society, 1908); *Baptist Beliefs* (Louisville, Ky.: Baptist World Publishing, 1912); *The Christian Faith in Its Doctrinal Expression* (Nashville: Broadman, 1917).

B. *BT* 330–50; *DARB* 383; *DCA* 783; *HET* 54–66; *RLA* 332; Isla M. Mullins, *Edgar Young Mullins: An Intimate Biography* (Nashville: Sunday School Board of the SBC, 1929); William E. Ellis, *''A Man of Books and a Man of the People'': E. Y. Mullins and the Crisis of Moderate Southern Baptist Leadership* (Macon, Ga.: Mercer University Press, 1985).

# O

**OCKENGA, HAROLD JOHN** (6 July 1905, Chicago, IL—8 February 1985, Hamilton, MA). *Education*: A.B., Taylor University, 1927; Princeton Theological Seminary, 1927–29; Th.B., Westminster Theological Seminary, 1930; Ph.D., University of Pittsburgh, 1939. *Career*: Pastor, 1930–69; president, Fuller

Theological Seminary, 1947–54, 1959–63; president, Gordon-Conwell Seminary, 1969–79.

One of the founders of the post–World War II "neoevangelical" movement, Harold John Ockenga was born on the west side of Chicago in 1905. Because of the concern of his devoutly religious mother, Ockenga was raised in an odd amalgam of Methodism and Presbyterianism. Over the course of his life, both denominational traditions would impact Ockenga substantially. His first religious home was Wesleyan Methodism where he became a Christian at the age of eighteen. The Wesleyan influence was deepened immensely in Ockenga's life through his college days at Taylor University, a Holiness college in Upland, Indiana. At Taylor, Ockenga was thoroughly involved in numerous extracurricular activities, the most important of which were religious. By the time he graduated in 1927, he had resolved to enter the pastorate.

Through his admittance to Princeton Theological Seminary in 1927, Ockenga made a commitment to enter the Presbyterian ministry. Soon after his arrival at Princeton, Ockenga became part of the circle of students attracted to *J. Gresham Machen, the chief apologist of conservative Northern Presbyterians. When Machen left Princeton to establish Westminster Theological Seminary in 1929, Ockenga followed his mentor to complete his ministerial studies in 1929–30.

Ockenga began his pastoral career in 1930. Successively he served as assistant pastor under Clarence E. Macartney at First Presbyterian Church of Pittsburgh, Pennsylvania (1930–31); pastor of the Point Breeze Presbyterian Church of Pittsburgh (1931–36); and pastor of the Park Street Congregational Church of Boston, Massachusetts (1936–69). Possessed of superior organizational and oratory talents, Ockenga became one of the best-known evangelical pastors in America during his long ministry at Park Street Church.

In part because of his own diverse background in American evangelicalism, Ockenga sought to moderate the extreme separatism that had characterized fundamentalism since the early part of the twentieth century. To that end, he helped to found the National Association of Evangelicals (NAE) and served as its first president (1942–44). In 1947, Ockenga answered the call of *Charles E. Fuller to become president of Fuller Theological Seminary, an institution envisioned as the leading higher educational center of the new or neoevangelicalism.

Ockenga served two terms as president of Fuller, 1947–54 and 1959–63. He provided the fledgling school with able leadership, despite commuting between Park Street Church and California the entire time. Ockenga was also an early supporter of the ministry of *Billy Graham, introducing him to New England through a January 1950 evangelistic campaign. The Graham-Ockenga friendship led to their mutual support of the magazine *Christianity Today*, which started publication in 1956 under the editorship of *Carl F. H. Henry, one of Ockenga's faculty members at Fuller.

Tiring of the endless commuting between coasts and unwilling to relinquish his Boston pastorate, Ockenga resigned from Fuller in 1963. He served as pastor of Park Street Church for six more years and then became president of Gordon College and Divinity School in 1969. He was a major force behind the merger that resulted in the creation of Gordon-Conwell Theological Seminary and served as chief administrator of that institution from 1970–79.

Despite his conviction that evangelicalism should play a larger religious role in contemporary American society, Ockenga remained a theological conservative throughout his entire academic career. This is seen most vividly in his support of *Harold Lindsell's book *Battle for the Bible* (1976), a work that stridently defended inerrancy as the most characteristic aspect of evangelicalism.

*Bibliography*

A. *These Religious Affections* (Grand Rapids, Mich.: Zondervan, 1937); *Our Evangelical Faith* (New York: Fleming H. Revell, 1946); *Faithful in Jesus Christ* (New York: Fleming H. Revell, 1948).

B. *DCA* 837; *RLA* 345; *TDCB* 282; Harold Lindsell, *Park Street Prophet: A Life of Harold John Ockenga* (Wheaton, Ill.: Van Kampen, 1951); John Marion Adams, "The Making of a Neo-evangelical Statesman: The Case of Harold John Ockenga" (Ph.D. diss., Baylor University, 1994).

# P

**PACKER, (J)AMES (I)NNELL** (22 July 1926, Gloucester, England—). *Education*: B.A. (classics), B.A. (theology), M.A., D.Phil., Oxford University, 1948, 1950, 1952, 1954. *Career*: Seminary professor, 1948–50, 1955–61; Anglican curate, 1953–55; librarian, 1961–63; director, Latimer House, Oxford, 1963–70; principal, Tyndale Hall, 1970–79; professor, Regent College, 1979—.

Although he never lived in the United States, J. I. Packer had a powerful influence on late twentieth-century evangelicalism through his advocacy of conservative theology and Puritan spirituality. Packer was born the son of a railway worker in Gloucester, England, in 1926. A nominal Anglican as a youth, he came to faith through the Oxford Inter-Collegiate Christian Union and was strengthened in his new faith through a study of the Puritan theologians, John Owen and Richard Baxter.

After the completion of a bachelor's degree in classical studies, Packer taught at the Anglican Theological Seminary near London where he began to sense a call to a teaching ministry. Returning to Oxford, Packer took a bachelor's degree in theology (1950), a master's in philosophy (1952), and a doctorate in philosophy (1954). Even while serving as an Anglican clergyman and teacher in the late 1950s, Packer was pursuing scholarly research in Puritan studies.

A great turning point in Packer's career occurred in 1958 with the publication of his first book, *"Fundamentalism" and the Word of God*. The clarity and accessibility of his writing made Packer a well-known figure in evangelicalism on both sides of the Atlantic. His next book, *Evangelism and the Sovereignty of God* (1961), was a powerful defense of Calvinistic evangelicalism that further strengthened his reputation as a scholar in the conservative tradition.

The 1960s were a controversial time for the irenic Packer. In 1966–67, Packer, along with John R. W. Stott, resisted the efforts of their fellow evangelical Martyn Lloyd-Jones to separate from the Anglican establishment as an apostate body. As a younger man Packer sat under the ministry of Lloyd-Jones, the prominent preacher of Westminster Chapel, and Packer's subsequent estrangement with his religious mentor caused the former no little distress. The other major controversy to overtake Packer in the 1960s was a proposed union between English Methodists and Anglicans, which he opposed. It was not Packer's opposition to the union proposal that raised the ire of his fellow Free Church evangelicals, but rather the impression that in his opposition, Packer was making common cause with the dreaded Anglo-Catholic faction of the Church of England.

In 1973, Packer published his best-selling book, *Knowing God*, which was a synthesis of Calvinistic theology and Puritan spirituality. The book brought Packer renown as a truly international figure in the modern evangelical movement. He stolidly took on the mantle of leadership commensurate with that prominence by assuming a primary role in the International Council of Biblical Inerrancy beginning in 1978 and extending into the mid–1980s. He also relocated himself and his family to Vancouver, British Columbia, in 1979 to become professor of historical and systematic theology at Regent College.

Packer holds a unique role in the contemporary evangelical subculture. He is not only a thorough and exacting theologian in the conservative, Reformed tradition, but he is also a profound writer in the area of Puritan spirituality. To that end, Packer is an excellent model of what the best of late twentieth-century evangelicalism can represent.

*Bibliography*

A. *"Fundamentalism" and the Word of God* (Leicester, Eng.: InterVarsity, 1958); *Evangelism and the Sovereignty of God* (Downers Grove, Ill.: InterVarsity, 1961); *Knowing God* (Downers Grove, Ill.: InterVarsity, 1973).

B. *HET* 379–87; *TDCB* 288; *Doing Theology for the People of God: Studies in Honor of J. I. Packer*, edited by Donald Lewis and Alister McGrath (Downers Grove, Ill.: InterVarsity, 1996); Alister McGrath, *J. I. Packer: A Biography* (Grand Rapids, Mich.: Baker, 1997).

**PARHAM, CHARLES FOX** (4 June 1873, Muscatine, IA–29 January 1929, Baxter Springs, KS). *Education*: Southwestern Kansas College, 1890–93. *Career*: Methodist preacher, 1892–94; independent evangelist, 1894–1929.

A founder of the modern American Pentecostal movement, Parham grew up in rural Kansas. His early years were spent in the Methodist Episcopal Church. He became a Christian through a Methodist revival meeting in 1886, and shortly thereafter became a Sunday school teacher and a licensed preacher, also in the Methodist church. While at college he contracted rheumatic fever and was given up for dead by doctors. Parham recovered, however, and, believing himself cured by prayer, committed himself to a ministerial career.

After two years of preaching on a Methodist circuit, Parham abruptly left that church for an independent revivalist ministry. Increasingly preoccupied with faith healing, Parham and his wife, Sarah, opened ''Beth-el,'' a healing home in Topeka, Kansas, in 1898. Beth-el was reserved for those who would rely on ''God alone'' for their healing. During this time Parham built a sizable following and started publishing a periodical called the *Apostolic Faith*.

While Parham was on an evangelistic trip in 1900, the control of his ministry fell into the hands of others. Moving across town, Parham started over, opening a new healing center. At this new location, Parham and his small band of disciples began to pray for insight about how to interpret passages of the New Testament, like Acts 2, which refer to the baptism of the Holy Spirit. By the end of 1900, Parham's followers were convinced that the coming of the Holy Spirit in a Christian believer's life was always marked by speaking in tongues. On 1 January 1901, Parham and the students prayed over one Agnes Ozman and were amazed when she began to speak in what they interpreted to be Chinese, a language Ozman had never learned. In Pentecostal history, Ozman is designated as the first person in modern times to receive the gift of speaking in tongues as an answer to prayer for the baptism of the Holy Spirit. During the next few days, Parham and about one-half of his thirty-four students were likewise baptized by the Spirit.

Energized by what he felt was a sign from God, Parham began to travel widely throughout Kansas, Oklahoma, and Texas, preaching his message about tongues and the Holy Spirit. In 1905, he opened a Bible school in Houston, Texas, where his convictions made a deep impression upon *William J. Seymour, a black Holiness minister. Consequently, Seymour took Parham's teachings to Los Angeles, where a significant ''Pentecostal revival'' broke out at the Azusa Street mission church.

Convinced that the widespread evidence of speaking in tongues was a sign that the Christian church was entering the last days before Christ's return, Parham worked assiduously during 1906–7 to consolidate his personal control over the ''latter rain'' revival. By 1907, however, Parham's efforts had failed. Not only did he fail to win over the followers of deceased healing revivalist John Alexander Dowie in Zion City, Illinois, but Parham also lost any influence he had over the Azusa Street revival that followed the leadership of Seymour.

The final and fatal blow to Parham's ambitions came in 1907 when he was arrested in San Antonio, Texas, on a charge of sodomy. Although the authorities eventually dropped all charges against Parham, the mere scent of scandal caused many of his followers to distance themselves from him. In 1911, Parham settled in Baxter Springs, Kansas, where he consolidated his remaining core group of disciples into the Apostolic Faith Church. By the time he died in 1929, Parham was virtually unknown to a younger generation of Pentecostals who were making the latter rain movement a worldwide phenomenon.

*Bibliography*

A. *A Voice Crying in the Wilderness* (Baxter Springs, Kans.: Apostolic Faith Bible College, 1910).

B. *ACSL* 216–18; *DARB* 417–18; *DCA* 865; *DPCM* 660–61; Sarah E. Parham, *The Life of Charles F. Parham, Founder of the Apostolic Faith Movement* (Joplin, Mo.: Hunter Printing Company, 1930); James R. Goff Jr., *Fields White Unto Harvest: Charles F. Parham and the Missionary Origins of Pentecostalism* (Fayetteville, Ark.: University of Arkansas Press, 1988).

**PEALE, NORMAN VINCENT** (31 May 1898, Bowersville, OH–24 December 1993, Pawling, NY). *Education*: B.A., Ohio Wesleyan, 1920; B.S.T., M.A., Boston University, 1924. *Career*: Pastor, author, 1924–84.

One of the most influential religious figures in post–World War II America, Peale was born in Ohio just before the beginning of the twentieth century. He was the son of a physician turned Methodist minister. Peale originally set out to become a journalist, but quickly gave up that profession in favor of the ministry. He was ordained in the Methodist Episcopal Church in 1922, and studied theology at Boston University while pastoring a small church in Berkeley, Rhode Island.

A charismatic speaker and effective pastor, Peale was successful in attracting large numbers of people to every church in which he pastored. This was true in the Methodist congregations he served in Brooklyn (1924–27) and Syracuse, New York (1927–32), as well as the Reformed Church in which he spent most of his ministerial career, Marble Collegiate Church in New York City (1932–84).

Peale became most famous for promoting a pragmatic and therapeutic blend of positive thinking and psychiatry through his many books. Among his written works were *The Art of Living* (1937), *You Can Win* (1939), *A Guide to Confident Living* (1948), and *The Art of Real Happiness* (1950). Peale's most famous book, however, and the one that made him nationally known was *The Power of Positive Thinking* (1952). This book, which stayed on the *New York Times* best-seller list for about three years, led to a syndicated newspaper column entitled "Confident Living" and a larger audience for his radio program, "The Art of Living" (started by Peale in 1933).

In the mid–1940s, Peale started *Guideposts* magazine as a small, inspirational pamphlet designed to bring encouragement to its readers. After some early years of struggle, *Guideposts* attracted a sizable number of subscribers and eventually achieved a circulation of more than 1 million. Along with stories written by

Peale, *Guideposts* featured inspirational testimonies from people who had over-come adversity through a positive attitude and faith in God.

By the 1960s Peale was one of the best known pastors and authors in America. He was profiled in many popular magazines, and in 1953, *Life* named him one of the twelve great living American preachers. Although criticized for diluting the "hard truths" of the Christian gospel in a sugar coating of universal affir-mation, Peale's message comported well with America's post–World War II emphasis on self-help and personal well-being. The concentration on success and positive thinking can be seen subtly in much of modern American evan-gelicalism, although it appears most prominently in the teachings and sermons of Robert Schuller, as well as Pentecostal sects like the Word of Faith move-ment. By the time Peale died in 1993, many religious historians believed that he personified the overall character of modern American religion perhaps better than any other individual.

*Bibliography*

A. *A Guide to Confident Living* (New York: Macmillan, 1948); *The Power of Positive Thinking* (New York: Prentice-Hall, 1952); *The True Joy of Positive Living: An Au-tobiography* (New York: Morrow, 1984).

B. *DCA* 877–78; *PTR* 256–60; *RLA* 358; *TSAPR* 326–34; Carol George, *God's Salesman: Norman Vincent Peale and the Power of Positive Thinking* (New York: Oxford Uni-versity Press, 1993).

**PEW, (J)OHN HOWARD** (27 January 1882, Bradford, PA–27 November 1971, Ardmore, PA). *Education*: B.S., Grove City College (PA), 1900; Mas-sachusetts Institute of Technology. *Career*: Petroleum engineer, 1901–6; busi-ness executive and philanthropist, 1906–47; board of directors, Sun Oil Company, 1906–71.

J. Howard Pew was a wealthy businessman who helped to make the late twentieth-century revival of American evangelicalism possible through his gen-erous philanthropy. Pew was the second of five children born to Joseph Newton Pew, the founder of the Sun Oil Company. The younger Pew attended a series of private schools, culminating with Grove City College, a nondenominational Christian school. After an abortive year of graduate studies at the Massachusetts Institute of Technology, Pew joined the family business as a development en-gineer and remained with Sun Oil until his death in 1971.

Because of both his ability and family connections, Pew rose rapidly in the ranks at Sun Oil. He was part of a research team that discovered a profitable way to manufacture a high-grade lubricating oil (1903) and a petroleum-based asphalt (1904). In 1906, Pew became a vice-president and director of the com-pany, and in 1912, he ascended to the position of president upon the death of his father. Under Pew's leadership, Sun Oil became a huge multinational cor-poration with over 28,000 employees by 1971. A pioneer in innovation within the petroleum industry, Sun Oil contributed to such important discoveries as high-octane gasoline, synthetic rubber, and new methods of ship building.

Pew was a political and religious conservative. A lifelong Presbyterian, he served as president of the board of trustees of the General Assembly of the Presbyterian Church (U.S.A.) for three decades. He was also an elder in his local Presbyterian church in Ardmore, Pennsylvania. As early as World War II, conservative Protestant leaders regularly approached Pew for both his counsel and his financial support. Two of Pew's most prominent friends were the Presbyterian clergyman and missionary L. Nelson Bell and Bell's son-in-law, *Billy Graham.

Largely because of Pew's backing, Graham was able to start the periodical, *Christianity Today*, in 1956 as a conservative, evangelical alternative to the more liberal *Christian Century*. Pew and Graham were pleased to secure the services of *Carl F. H. Henry as *Christianity Today's* first editor. After some years, however, Henry began to chafe under the unremitting conservatism of Pew, and the theologian-editor gave up his duties at the magazine in 1967.

A consistent supporter of many evangelical causes, Pew, with his brothers and sisters, established the Glenmede Trust Company in 1956 to coordinate their sizable philanthropic interests. After Pew's death in 1971, a part of the Glenmede Company became the J. Howard Pew Freedom Trust, which continues to fund many evangelical projects to this day.

*Bibliography*

B. *DCA* 894–95; *TDCB* 299–300; Mary Sennholz, *Faith and Freedom: The Journal of a Great American, J. Howard Pew* (Grove City, Pa.: Grove City College, 1975).

**PRICE, EUGENIA** (22 June 1916, Charleston, WV–28 May 1996, Brunswick, GA). *Education*: Ohio State University, 1932–35; Northwestern University Dental School, 1935–37. *Career*: Radio script writer, 1939–46, 1950–56; producer, 1945–56; freelance writer and lecturer, 1949–96.

One of the best-selling inspirational authors of the twentieth century, Eugenia Price was raised a Methodist. By the time she graduated from high school she was no longer involved with the church, and while attending Ohio State University in the early 1930s, Price became a committed atheist. As a young adult she had some difficulty in choosing a profession. She dropped out of Ohio State in order to attend Northwestern's dental school. After just two years of dentistry studies, Price left Northwestern with the intent of studying philosophy at the University of Chicago. These plans were interrupted, in turn, when she began to write commercially for radio. From 1939–46, Price wrote radio scripts for the National Broadcasting Company and Procter and Gamble. Her success in the radio medium led Price to establish her own production company, which she operated from 1945–49.

Success in Price's professional life, however, could not compensate for the personal emptiness that she felt for much of the 1940s. Through the guidance of Episcopal minister Samuel Shoemaker, Price experienced a dramatic conversion to Christianity in 1949. Her new-found faith led to a transformation of her professional life. From 1950–56 she wrote, produced, and directed the radio show "Unshackled" for the Pacific Garden Mission. Even more momentously, Price settled in Chicago in the 1950s and began to write the inspirational books for which she is best known.

Price's first book was entitled, *Discoveries Made from Living My New Life* (1953). This was followed by a description of her conversion to Christianity, *The Burden Is Light! The Autobiography of a Transformed Pagan Who Took God at His Word* (1955). By the 1960s, Price was well known in evangelical circles for the inspirational theme that ran through all her early works. In 1965, however, Lippincott published Price's book, *The Beloved Invader*, a novel set in St. Simon's Island, Georgia (where Price had moved in the early 1960s). This was the first installment of what proved to be a very popular "St. Simon trilogy." In 1969 and 1971, respectively, the trilogy was completed with the publication of *New Moon Rising* and *Lighthouse*. The St. Simon trilogy established Price as a popular writer of Christian fiction. Although she occasionally returned to inspirational and autobiographical works, the trilogy marked a new emphasis on novels. During the 1980s, Price wrote the "Savannah quartet": *Savannah* (1983), *To See Your Face Again* (1985), *Before the Darkness Falls* (1987), and *Stranger in Savannah* (1989).

By the time of her death in 1996, Price saw more than 40 million copies of her books sold in eighteen different languages. Even her historical novels, which were fictional by design, testified to the existence of a personal God who interceded in everyday life in extraordinary ways.

*Bibliography*

A. *Discoveries Made from Living My New Life* (Grand Rapids, Mich.: Zondervan, 1953); *The Beloved Invader* (New York: Lippincott, 1965); *New Moon Rising* (New York: Lippincott, 1969); *Lighthouse* (New York: Lippincott, 1971); *Savannah* (New York: Doubleday, 1983); *To See Your Face Again* (New York: Doubleday, 1985); *Before the Darkness Falls* (New York: Doubleday, 1987); *Stranger in Savannah* (New York: Doubleday, 1989).

B. *CANR* 18: 370–71; *MTC* 131–33; *RLA* 375.

# R

**REVELL, FLEMING H., JR.** (11 December 1849, Chicago, IL–11 October 1931, Yonkers, NY). *Education*: Marginal. *Career*: Publisher, 1869–1929.

Fleming Revell was one of the most influential publishers of evangelical literature in American history. Born in Chicago around the middle of the nineteenth century, he was the only son of two poor, first-generation English immigrants. Revell left school at the age of nine to support his family. While he was still a young man, his sister Emma married *Dwight L. Moody. The up and coming evangelist came to exert a tremendous influence over Revell as his pastor, counselor, and, later, client.

After touring England in 1867, Moody started a monthly Sunday school publication, *Everybody's Paper*, the editorship of which he turned over to Revell in 1869. One year later, Revell started his own publishing company, which was destroyed by the Chicago fire of 1871. Starting over again, Revell enjoyed tremendous initial success as the official publisher of Moody's sermons. As a member of Moody's inner circle, Revell persuaded many of the evangelist's colleagues to allow the Fleming H. Revell Company to publish their sermons and works. The first book to be published under the Revell imprint was *Grace and Truth under Twelve Different Aspects* by W. P. Mackay (1872). The biggest selling and most influential book published by Revell was *Jesus Is Coming* by William Blackstone (1878). This strongly premillennial work sold more than 840,000 copies over fifty years and several editions.

In 1905, Revell moved his business to New York City, where it remained for forty-five years. By this time the Revell Company was truly a worldwide operation with offices in Toronto, London, and Edinburgh. Revell was a shrewd businessman and built his company through careful attention to the needs of the American evangelical public. Not only did the Revell Company sell books, pamphlets, and tracts, but it also carried maps, banners, and a wide range of Sunday school literature. Revell carefully cultivated the important contacts he made through Moody and also developed close personal relationships with many of the early American fundamentalist leaders at the beginning of the twentieth century.

A Presbyterian, Revell assumed a significant place in American evangelicalism in his own right. He was a trustee of Moody's Northfield school and of Wheaton College, a director of New York Life Insurance Company and the New York YMCA, and treasurer of the American Mission to Lepers. In 1929, with the Great Depression already underway, Revell retired, leaving the presidency of his company to his son. Two years later, the elder Revell died after complications stemming from a fractured pelvis.

*Bibliography*

B. *DCA* 1009; *RLA* 389; ''Revell: Seventy-Five Years of Religious Book Publishing,'' *Publishers Weekly* (9 December 1944): 2232–36; Allan Fisher, *Fleming H. Revell Company: The First 125 Years, 1870–1995* (Grand Rapids, Mich.: Fleming H. Revell, 1995).

**ROBERTS, (GRANVILLE) ORAL** (24 January 1918, Pontotoc County, OK—). *Education*: Phillips University. *Career*: Pastor, 1941–47; Pentecostal and Methodist revivalist and faith healer, 1935–41; 1947—; founder and president, Oral Roberts University, 1965—.

During the twentieth century, when Pentecostalism became one of the mightiest forces within Christianity, Oral Roberts attained the lofty status of Pentecostalism's best-known representative. Roberts was born into the household of a Pentecostal evangelist in rural Oklahoma. As a youth, he struggled with the strict upbringing of his parents and the stuttering that afflicted him. Resentful of his homelife, Roberts moved away from his parents to attend school in another town. His independence lasted barely a year when he was stricken by tuberculosis and forced to return home in 1935. After five months in a sickbed, Roberts attended a faith healing revival in Ada, Oklahoma, where he believed that God healed him of the tuberculosis and his stuttering.

Soon, Roberts began to assist in his father's evangelistic ministry. By 1938, Roberts was a prominent personality in the growing Pentecostal movement. He believed that he received the baptism of the Holy Spirit; he met and married his wife, Evelyn; and he wrote for the denominational newspaper, the *Pentecostal Holiness Advocate*. With his apprenticeship over, Roberts started his own ministry, first as a pastor, then as an itinerant.

From 1941 to 1946, Roberts served a succession of churches in North Carolina, Oklahoma, and Georgia as pastor. Increasingly restless of his settled life, Roberts returned to Oklahoma in 1946, where he assumed the pastorate of a church in Enid and started attending classes at Phillips University. Within a year of his return to Oklahoma, Roberts "heard" the voice of God telling him to institute a faith healing ministry. Immediately, he added weekly healing services to the ministry of his church. The response was so overwhelmingly positive that Roberts quickly resigned his pastorate to take up full-time evangelism and healing.

From 1947 until 1960, Roberts was the most prominent individual in the post–World War II Pentecostal and charismatic revival. This position was attained through hard work, innovation, and careful planning. Establishing his own evangelistic association in Tulsa in 1947, Roberts purchased a tent in 1948 and travelled throughout the United States conducting healing services. Typically, after a sermon, Roberts would commence the healing service through touch and prayer. Despite criticism from the press, Roberts attracted an unprecedented following for a healing evangelist. In addition to his itinerant ministry, he continued to write books (his first effort was published in 1938) and was one of the first Christian ministers to utilize television (1954).

A large part of Roberts's success in the 1950s can be attributed to his willingness to broaden the appeal of his ministry beyond sectarian Pentecostalism. In 1952, Roberts lent his support to *Demos Shakarian in the efforts to start the Full Gospel Business Men's Fellowship International (FGBMFI). The FGBMFI was clearly an ecumenical effort that signaled the eclipse of denominational Pentecostalism by a larger and more amorphous charismatic movement. His activities in the charismatic movement brought Roberts criticism from the Pentecostal establishment, which suggested he was altering his theology to enhance his popularity. Roberts denied this, claiming a change of emphasis, not theology. Still, it is evident in retrospect that Roberts was moving toward mainstream evangelicalism by the late 1950s.

This move toward the mainstream became obvious by the 1960s. The first signpost was the establishment of Oral Roberts University (ORU), which opened in 1965. Originally seen as yet another Bible college, ORU became, through the considerable efforts of Roberts, a respected institution of higher learning. The second sign of Roberts's swing toward the mainstream was his participation in the Berlin World Congress on Evangelism in 1966. At the Congress, Roberts was well received and developed significant friendships with many non-Pentecostal evangelicals like *Billy Graham. The final and most controversial sign of Roberts's changing focus was his decision to unite with Tulsa's Boston Avenue (United) Methodist Church in 1968. The change in church membership was a clear sign that Roberts was aiming to influence an audience larger than that of sectarian Pentecostalism.

In the 1970s and 1980s, Roberts's ministry continued to grow, although more through his use of television and mass mailing than revivalism. Indeed, Roberts became so preoccupied with raising funds for ORU and his projected "City of Faith," that he ended his weekly television series in 1967 and his crusades in 1968 in favor of prime-time TV specials. With the change in methodology came a change in emphasis. Now Roberts emphasized evangelism and the attainment of personal success through "seed faith" rather than the more traditional beliefs of Pentecostalism. Much more than the criticism Roberts received for these changes, he was rocked by a series of family crises in the 1970s and 1980s: the death of his daughter and son-in-law in 1977; the divorce and remarriage of son Richard the heir apparent to Oral Roberts's ministry, in 1979–80; the suicide of son Ron in 1982; and the birth and death of Roberts's namesake grandson in 1984.

By the late 1980s Roberts had won back a good deal of his core support among his old Pentecostal constituency as his pioneering efforts as a healing revivalist were better appreciated. However, this did not keep Roberts from being pilloried by a skeptical secular press that derided Roberts's frequent claims to hear the audible voice of God, not to mention his "encounter" with a 900-foot tall Jesus in 1980 and his belief that God would "take him home [to Heaven]" if supporters did not come through with needed funds for the "City of Faith" in 1987. Despite these criticisms, Roberts's pivotal role in bringing traditional Pentecostal beliefs to a wider ecumenical audience and his pioneering use of the mass media have secured his status as one of the most significant members of the twentieth-century American evangelical subculture.

*Bibliography*

A. *My Twenty Years of Miracle Ministry* (Tulsa, Okla.: The Author, 1967); *The Miracle of Seed Faith* (Charlotte, N.C.: Commission Press, 1970); *The Call: An Autobiography* (Garden City, N.Y.: Doubleday, 1972).

B. *DCA* 1020; *DPCM* 759–60; *PTR* 282–86; *RLA* 395–96; *TSAPR* 342–49; David E. Harrell Jr., *Oral Roberts: An American Life* (Bloomington, Ind.: Indiana University Press, 1985).

**ROBERTSON, MARION GORDON (PAT)** (22 March 1930, Lexington, VA—). *Education*: B.A., Washington and Lee University, 1950; University of London; J.D., Yale Law School, 1955; M.Div., New York Theological Seminary, 1959. *Career*: U.S. Marine Corps, 1950–52; Baptist minister, 1961–87; 1988—; television host, "The 700 Club," 1968–87; 1988—; founder and president, Christian Broadcasting Network, 1961—; founder and chancellor, Regent (formerly CBN) University, 1978—; founder, Christian Coalition, 1989.

Few figures in American evangelical history have had a greater impact on the late twentieth-century subculture than Pat Robertson. Scion of a Virginian family that included two U.S. presidents, Robertson's father was a U.S. senator in the 1940s and 1950s. Robertson enjoyed a privileged upbringing and, despite little effort, graduated with honors from Washington and Lee University in 1950. After a tour of duty in the Marines, Robertson gravitated toward the political career path of his father. To that end, he studied economics briefly at the University of London and returned to the United States where he attended Yale Law School. While at Yale, Robertson met and married Adelia "Dede" Elmer in 1954, and the first of four children was born shortly thereafter.

Raised with only a nominal religious upbringing, Robertson moved to New York City in the mid–1950s, but was disillusioned when he failed to pass that state's bar examination. Disillusionment turned to thoughts of suicide as Robertson suffered through a dismal year of employment with W. R. Grace & Company from 1955–56. The great turning point came in 1956 when Robertson was led to personal faith in Christ by evangelist Cornelius Vanderbreggen. Almost immediately, Robertson gave up his business career and enrolled in New York Theological Seminary. While studying for the ministry, Robertson was asked by Harald Bredesen, a prominent figure in the burgeoning charismatic revival, to join him as associate pastor at the First Reformed Church in Mount Vernon, New York. During his three-year apprenticeship with Bredesen, Robertson was definitively influenced by the charismatic movement with its emphases on the baptism and miraculous gifts of the Holy Spirit.

Robertson graduated from seminary in 1959 and, after a brief ministry in the slums of Brooklyn, returned to Virginia where he purchased a defunct UHF television station in Portsmouth. Presciently seeing the tremendous promise of television as a tool for evangelistic ministry, Robertson began broadcasting religious programming on 1 October 1961, the same year he was ordained as a

Southern Baptist minister. His earliest efforts were plagued by a chronic shortage of money, a shortage that persisted until Robertson developed that idea of "faith partners," the commitment of 700 people who would pledge ten dollars a month to keep the station operating. From this notion eventually came "The 700 Club," a religious talk and news program with Robertson as its host. As his Christian Broadcasting Network (CBN) began to enjoy solvency, Robertson added Jim and Tammy Faye Bakker to his staff in 1965.

In the 1970s, Robertson began broadcasting via satellite and made "The 700 Club" a nationally syndicated program in 1972. Slowly but surely, Robertson became a prominent individual in the evangelical subculture, both as a leader in the ecumenical charismatic movement and as a religious broadcaster. With the success of CBN, Robertson was able to start a "Christian university" in the form of CBN (later Regent) University in 1978. By the late 1980s, Regent was an established institution of higher education with several professional schools.

Sharing the conviction of many evangelicals that "secular humanism" threatened to lead America into moral decay, Robertson started to dabble in national politics by the early 1980s. He joined with several other prominent evangelical ministers in organizing a "Washington for Jesus" rally that drew an estimated 200,000 people to the nation's capital in 1980. In 1986, Robertson announced he would make himself a candidate for the U.S. presidency if 3 million people would commit to support his efforts financially and through prayer. When this goal was met, Robertson ran for the Republican nomination in 1988. Although he experienced some early success, Robertson eventually lost the nomination to George Bush. Returning to CBN and Regent University, he founded the Christian Coalition, an effort to organize Christians politically at the local and state levels. After establishing the Christian Coalition, Robertson turned its leadership over to Ralph Reed, one of his associates.

In many ways Robertson epitomized the late twentieth-century evangelical activist. Through a canny use of the mass media and an ecumenical approach, he successfully led discontented evangelicals to involvement in the educational and political sectors of American culture. That effort was received with suspicion by some nonevangelicals, but it remained one of the most tangible efforts to achieve cohesion within the widely diverse evangelical subculture.

*Bibliography*

A. *Shout it from the Housetops!* (South Plainfield, N.J: Logos, 1972); *Answers to 200 of Life's Most Probing Questions* (Nashville: Thomas Nelson, 1984); *America's Date with Destiny* (Nashville: Thomas Nelson, 1986).

B. *DCA* 1021–22; *DPCM* 761–62; *PTR* 288–92; *TSAPR* 349–56; David E. Harrell Jr., *Pat Robertson: A Personal, Religious, and Political Portrait* (San Franciso: Harper & Row, 1987); Robert Boston, *The Most Dangerous Man in America?: Pat Robertson and the Rise of the Christian Coalition* (Amherst, N.Y.: Prometheus, 1996).

# S

**SCHAEFFER, FRANCIS A.** (30 January 1912, Germantown, PA–15 May 1984, Rochester, MN). *Education*: B.A., Hampden-Sydney College, 1935; B.D., Faith Theological Seminary, 1938. *Career*: Presbyterian pastor, 1938–48; missionary, Independent Board for Presbyterian Foreign Missions, 1948–55; founder, L'Abri Fellowship, 1955; author and lecturer, 1968–84.

For one who expanded the intellectual horizons of so many evangelicals in the last half of the twentieth century, Francis Schaeffer emerged from a very conservative religious background. Schaeffer was nurtured in a solidly Presbyterian tradition and attended Westminster Theological Seminary in 1935 after graduating from Hampden-Sydney College. Studying under *J. Gresham Machen and Cornelius Van Til, Schaeffer was one of several Westminster students to split with Machen over premillennialism. Those, like Schaeffer, who favored a premillennial interpretation of Christ's second coming, left Westminster and formed Faith Theological Seminary and the Bible Presbyterian Church under the leadership of Carl McIntire. Schaeffer graduated from Faith Seminary in 1938 and was the first pastor ordained by the Bible Presbyterian Church.

About the time Schaeffer started his seminary studies he married Edith Seville, the daughter of a missionary, who became his life-long partner in ministry. The Schaeffers spent roughly ten years (1938–48) in Presbyterian pastorates in Pennsylvania and Missouri before heading to Europe as missionaries in 1948. Appalled by the intellectual and spiritual disillusionment of post–World War II Switzerland, the Schaeffers labored seven years for the Independent Board for Presbyterian Foreign Missions. In 1955, they cut their ties with the Board and formed their own independent mission that they named "L'Abri ["shelter"] Fellowship."

Almost by word-of-mouth, Schaeffer and L'Abri became famous among college-aged Christians and spiritual "seekers" in the 1960s. Schaeffer developed a detailed critique of modern culture that sought to turn individuals toward a distinctly biblical worldview. Hundreds of people visited L'Abri over three decades to hear the teachings of Schaeffer and to experience the hospitality of Edith.

By the mid–1960s, Schaeffer had a sizable following and was profiled by religious and secular publications. His growing fame led to invitations by evangelical student groups in Europe, Britain, and America to deliver lectures on contemporary culture and biblical faith. In 1968 these lectures took book form in his first published works, *The God Who Is There* and *Escape from Reason*. The basic theme of Schaeffer's critique was that modern culture, from Hegel onward, had abandoned the biblical notion that truth is absolute in favor of a synthetic, relative, and distinctly "postmodern" interpretation. Schaeffer's survey, which included analyses of many major philosophers, authors, artists, and other prominent intellectuals, contained a comprehensiveness that was foreign to most American evangelicals. As his books were devoured by intellectually hungry young evangelicals, Schaeffer was revered as a kind of guru by his followers, a role that the former pastor accentuated by his appearance, which included shoulder-length hair and knickers.

By the 1970s, the Schaeffers left the administration of L'Abri in the hands of their daughters and sons-in-law and took up a full-time ministry of lecturing and book writing. Significant written efforts in the 1970s and 1980s included such titles as *How Should We Then Live?* (1976), *A Christian Manifesto* (1981), and *The Great Evangelical Disaster* (1984). With the aid of C. Everett Koop (later U.S. surgeon general) and his son Franky, Schaeffer made *How Should We Then Live?* into a very influential film series in the late 1970s.

Although Schaeffer's popularity was undeniable among many evangelicals, the scholarly community questioned the superficiality of his historical and philosophical analysis of modern intellectual culture. Some evangelicals were also troubled by Schaeffer's commitment to political conservatism, his uncompromising stance against abortion, and his unequivocal support of divisive doctrines like biblical inerrancy. All these distinctives received increasing emphasis in Schaeffer's later writings, which struck an increasingly bellicose stance.

Rather than characterizing Schaeffer as an academician, which he was not and never claimed to be, it is probably more appropriate to view him as both prophet and popularizer. Clearly, his overall critique of modern culture struck a nerve in the evangelical subculture, even if his analysis lacked the imprimatur of the academy. Even more significant, Schaeffer was instrumental in popularizing and legitimizing the life of the mind for many twentieth-century evangelicals. To that end Schaeffer served a prominent role in the neoevangelical effort to surmount the obscurantism of its forebears.

*Bibliography*

A. *Complete Works*, 5 vols. (Wheaton, Ill.: Crossway Press, 1982).

B. *DCA* 1050–51; *HET* 245–59; *RLA* 410–11; Edith Schaeffer, *The Tapestry: The Life and Times of Francis and Edith Schaeffer* (Waco, Tex.: Word Books, 1981); Louis Parkhurst Jr., *Francis Schaeffer: The Man and His Message* (Wheaton, Ill.: Tyndale, 1986); Michael S. Hamilton, "The Dissatisfaction of Francis Schaeffer," *CT* 41:3 (3 March 1997): 22–30.

**SCOFIELD, (C)YRUS (I)NGERSON** (19 August 1843, Lenawee County, MI– 24 July 1921, Douglaston, Long Island, NY). *Education*: Self-taught; legal apprentice, St. Louis, MO, 1866–69. *Career*: Confederate army soldier, 1861–65; lawyer, 1869–71; 1873–79; Kansas state legislator, 1871–73; U.S. attorney, Kansas district, 1873; superintendent, St. Louis YMCA, 1880–82; pastor, 1880– 1901; religious educator, conference speaker, and author, 1901–21.

C. I. Scofield was born to Episcopalian parents in rural Michigan in the early 1840s. As a child, Cyrus and his family moved to Tennessee where he remained until the Civil War erupted in 1860. During the war Scofield distinguished himself as a member of the cavalry in the Confederate army. After the conclusion of the war, Scofield moved to St. Louis where he married Leontine Cerre, the youngest daughter of a prominent Roman Catholic family. The Scofields had three children, born within the period 1867–72. Through an apprenticeship to a St. Louis lawyer (1866–69), Scofield resumed his formal education. Moving with his young family to Atchison, Kansas, Scofield passed the state bar exam and joined a local law firm.

For a brief period in the early 1870s, Scofield gave every promise of a stellar career in law and politics. From 1871 to 1873, he served in the Kansas legislature, and in 1873, he was appointed U.S. attorney for the district. After only seven months on the job, however, Scofield resigned his appointment under the unsubstantiated charges that he had accepted bribes not to prosecute a case.

The devastating reversal of professional fortune apparently started Scofield on the road to alcohol abuse. Family troubles multiplied, and a return to St. Louis did not improve the situation. In 1879, Scofield separated from his wife, who moved back to Kansas with the children. Now broken personally as well as professionally, Scofield was led to saving faith in Christ by a business acquaintance by the end of 1879. Shortly thereafter, he joined the Compton Avenue Presbyterian Church, which was under the pastorship of James Brookes.

That Scofield should fall under the influence of Brookes was a monumental event. By the 1880s, Brookes was one of the most influential evangelicals in America and a proponent of dispensational premillennialism. Brookes's dispensational interpretation of the Scriptures left an indelible impression on Scofield.

A second definitive influence upon Scofield was *Dwight L. Moody. Shortly after his conversion, Scofield assisted in a St. Louis revival campaign led by Moody, and the two became life-long friends. Through the discipling of Brookes and the leadership of Moody, Scofield dedicated himself to full-time Christian service. From 1880–82, he became acting superintendent of the St. Louis YMCA, while serving the Pilgrim Congregational Church in a pastoral function.

In 1882, Scofield traveled to Dallas, Texas, where he assumed the pastorate of a small Congregationalist mission church. By the 1890s, Scofield was introduced to a larger audience through his Bible correspondence series and his book, *Rightly Dividing the Word of Truth* (1888), a work that established him as the leading defender of dispensational premillennialism. In addition, the membership of his church in Dallas had multiplied many times over, reaching 800 by the mid–1890s. After securing a divorce from his first wife in 1882, Scofield married a member of the Dallas congregation a year later.

In 1895, Scofield assumed the pastorate of Moody's home church in East Northfield, Massachusetts. For nearly a decade, Scofield was a significant member of Moody's inner circle. Not only did he pastor Moody's former church, but Scofield also played an important role in the administration of the Northfield

Bible School and the two preparatory schools established by Moody. Particularly after Moody's death in 1899, Scofield became a popular teacher on the "Bible prophecy circuit."

By the beginning of the twentieth century, Scofield started to compile a Bible annotated with a series of explanatory outlines. With the assistance of several co-editors, the fruit of his labors was published by Oxford University Press in 1909: the *Scofield Reference Bible* (SRB). It was Scofield's greatest contribution to contemporary evangelicalism. In the twentieth century, millions of evangelicals came to theological maturity under the tutelage of "Scofield's Notes."

Although he returned to his Dallas church in 1903, Scofield's popularity as a conference speaker and his affinity for theological education led him back to the Northeast by 1910. With the assistance of *Lewis Sperry Chafer, Scofield helped to establish the New York Night School of the Bible (1911; later, Scofield School of the Bible) and the Philadelphia Bible Institute (1914). Most of Scofield's last decade of life, however, was taken up by the Bible prophecy circuit and revisions to both the King James Bible (1911) and his own SRB (1917). Plagued by progressively declining health for years, Scofield was forced to end virtually all of his professional activities after a major physical breakdown in 1918. Three years later, he died of advanced cardiovascular disease.

Scofield was the most prominent early spokesperson for dispensational premillennialism in America. Although he personally had little to do with the burgeoning fundamentalist movement, it was usually his reference Bible that the conservative evangelicals brandished as they rode off to do battle with the forces of modernism throughout the twentieth century. To many souls, "Scofield's Notes" were virtually synonymous with Scripture.

*Bibliography*

A. *Rightly Dividing the Word of Truth* (n. p., 1888); (general editor) *Scofield Reference Bible* (New York: Oxford University Press, 1909).

B. *DARB* 477–78; *DCA* 1057–58; *TDCB* 341; *TSAPR* 371–81; Charles G. Trumbull, *The Life Story of C. I. Scofield* (New York: Oxford University Press, 1920).

**SEYMOUR, WILLIAM J.** (2 May 1870, Centerville, LA–28 September 1922, Los Angeles, CA). *Education*: Marginal. *Career*: Waiter, 1895–1900; Holiness and Pentecostal preacher, 1900–1922.

A pioneer of the American Pentecostal movement, William Seymour was born the son of emancipated slaves in southern Louisiana. As a young man with almost no formal schooling, Seymour traveled to Indianapolis where he supported himself by waiting tables in a hotel restaurant. Around 1900, Seymour moved to Cincinnati. Through his affiliation with the Methodist Episcopal church, he was introduced to the Holiness movement and was exposed to his first interracial church services.

While in Cincinnati, Seymour joined the Evening Light Saints, a Holiness group associated with the Church of God Reformation Movement. The Saints placed special emphasis of the cardinal Holiness conviction that sanctification was a distinct experience for the Christian subsequent to salvation. Although he felt called to the ministry, Seymour rejected the call until he was blinded in his left eye by smallpox. After receiving ordination from the Saints, Seymour settled in Houston, Texas, around 1902. Over the next three years, Seymour pastored a black Holiness church and made significant contacts with such white Holiness leaders as Charles Price Jones and *Charles Fox Parham.

Around the beginning of 1906, Seymour accepted the call of a small Holiness congregation in Los Angeles. Taking up that pastorate with great enthusiasm, Seymour began to teach that speaking in tongues should be synonymous with the baptism of the Holy Spirit and a part of every Christian's religious experience. On 9 April 1906, a black man in Seymour's church began to speak in tongues, and soon virtually the entire group was following suit. Curious crowds of blacks and whites began to frequent the church services, and by 12 April, the first white attendee spoke in tongues. Growing throngs of visitors forced a relocation of Seymour's church to 312 Azusa Street, known later as "the Azusa Mission."

Participants in the Azusa Street Revival not only spoke in tongues, but also claimed prophetic utterances that they believed were miraculous signs of Christ's imminent second coming. In the most famous such proclamation, a man claimed on 17 April 1906 that Los Angeles would be destroyed unless it turned to God. The next day a devastating earthquake struck San Francisco; its effects were plainly felt as far south as Los Angeles. Now, fueled with an additional apocalyptic fervor, the Azusa assembly swelled to over 1,000. In addition, Pentecostal missionaries began to leave southern California for the four corners of the globe to testify of God's mighty works at Azusa. Heavily publicized by the *Los Angeles Times* and other newspapers, the revival drew an increasing stream of people, both black and white, from all over the United States.

In the beginning, Seymour was clearly the leader of the Azusa revival. He delegated authority to twelve overseers, ordained ministers, and commissioned missionaries. He also began publishing a newspaper, the *Apostolic Faith*, in September 1906. Within one year, the circulation of Seymour's paper reached 40,000 issues. With the notable exception of Parham, who was uncomfortable with the mixing of races at Azusa, many other prominent Holiness preachers, like G. B. Cashwell and C. H. Mason, made the pilgrimage to Los Angeles to preach and pray alongside Seymour.

The flames of revival at Azusa burned brightly until 1908. At that time, Seymour's controversial marriage to a coworker caused a schism in the congregation. Disapproving of Seymour's action, Azusa's mission secretary resigned her post, moved to Portland, Oregon, and with a purloined mailing list, began publishing the *Apostolic Faith* without Seymour. Without possession of the mailing list, Seymour lost control of the newspaper, and his authority over the burgeoning Pentecostal revival began to slip. Other rivals to Seymour, such as William H. Durham, came to Azusa and began to teach doctrines at variance

with Seymour's own. The combined effect of all these challenges was to atten-
uate Seymour's role in the movement he had helped to start.

Although Seymour retained control of the Azusa Street Mission as its pastor
until his death from a heart attack in 1922, his significant contributions to the
larger American Pentecostal movement were largely minimized by his contemporaries. Only recently have historians rediscovered the full measure of Seymour's essential contribution to the "third force" in twentieth-century
Christianity.

*Bibliography*

B. *DARB* 487; *DCA* 1078; *DPCM* 778–81; *EAAR* 685–86; *TSAPR* 381–87; James Tinney,
    "William J. Seymour: Father of Modern-Day Pentecostalism," in *Black Apostles*,
    edited by Randall Burkett and Richard Newman (Boston: G. K. Hall, 1978), pp. 213–
    25.

**SHAKARIAN, DEMOS** (21 July 1913, Downey, CA—). *Education*: Marginal.
*Career*: Dairy farmer/businessman; founder, Full Gospel Business Men's Fellowship International, 1951—.

Demos Shakarian's family emigrated to the United States in 1906. The Shak-
arians were members of the Armenian Pentecostal Church and were among those
who escaped genocide at the hands of the Turks in the early part of the twentieth
century. Demos was born in southern California in 1913 and as a young man
assisted in the operation of the family dairy farm. He was raised in the shadow
of the early American Pentecostal movement that was emanating from Azusa
Street in Los Angeles. Shakarian became a Christian at a young age and believed
that he received the baptism of the Holy Spirit at age thirteen.

A pious and increasingly prosperous layman, Shakarian forged strong ties
with a number of prominent Pentecostal evangelists in the 1940s and 1950s. A
friendship was formed with Charles S. Price after Price miraculously healed
Shakarian's sister following an automobile accident. In 1951, Shakarian supported *Oral Roberts's Los Angeles revival campaign. At that time Roberts
learned of Shakarian's vision to start a Christian testimonial group among lay
businessmen. Roberts became an enthusiastic supporter, attending the first meeting of what became known as the Full Gospel Business Men's Fellowship International (FGBMFI) in a Los Angeles cafeteria in 1951.

Despite Shakarian's best efforts, the FGBMFI foundered for over a year,
finding little support among the business community of southern California.
Shakarian's intent was to establish local chapters of pious Christian laypeople
who would share their faith through planned luncheons, guest speakers, and
testimonials. Besides sharing Christ, a major focus of the FGBMFI was to present the "fullness" of the Gospel message, namely essential Pentecostal doctrines
like the baptism of the Holy Spirit, miraculous divine healing, and speaking in
tongues.

With Shakarian's determination and organizing talents and the strong support of high-profile Pentecostal leaders like Roberts, the FGBMFI began to catch on, eventually establishing chapters in nearly ninety countries. In many ways, the distinctly informal and interdenominational structure of the FGBMFI made it the perfect conduit for the growing charismatic revival that gathered steam in Protestant and Roman Catholic circles after World War II.

Logging many thousands of travel miles to assist local chapter leaders, Shakarian led the FGBMFI until suffering a severe stroke in 1984. Even in his advanced years, he continued to serve in an advisory role to the FGBMFI and received numerous honors and forms of recognition for his significant role in mobilizing a crucial segment of the American evangelical community in the last half of the twentieth century.

*Bibliography*

A. *The Happiest People on Earth* (Old Tappan, N.J.: Chosen, 1975).

B. *DCA* 1078–79; *DPCM* 781–82; *RLA* 418–19; Brian Bird, ''The Legacy of Demos Shakarian,'' *Charisma* 11:11 (June 1986): 20–30.

**SIMPSON, (A)LBERT (B)ENJAMIN** (15 December 1843, Bayview, Prince Edward Island, Canada–29 October 1919, Nyack, NY). *Education*: B.A., Knox College (Toronto), 1865. *Career*: Presbyterian pastor, 1865–81; author/editor/hymn writer, 1882–1919; founder, Christian and Missionary Alliance, 1897.

A. B. Simpson was the fourth child of fervently religious Scottish Covenanter Presbyterian parents. In their native Scotland, the Covenanters were characterized by an opposition to governmental control of the church and by strict adherence to the Westminster Confession. At the age of fourteen, Simpson had a conversion experience, and after graduating from Knox College in Toronto, he dedicated himself to the ministry.

From 1865 until 1882, Simpson served several Presbyterian churches as pastor: Knox Presbyterian in Hamilton, Ontario (1865–73); Chestnut Presbyterian in Louisville, Kentucky (1873–79); and Thirteenth Street Presbyterian in New York City (1879–82). Simpson's spiritual life was transformed in 1874 after he read William Boardman's *The Higher Christian Life*. That same year, he experienced what he believed to be the baptism of the Holy Spirit and thereafter became a leading advocate of the ''higher life'' movement within American evangelicalism.

By the early 1880s, Simpson's explorations into the deeper Christian life led him to resign his Presbyterian pastorate and to establish an independent ministry. He started to edit a religious periodical in 1882 and formed a congregation of like-minded believers who incorporated themselves into the ''Gospel Tabernacle'' in 1883. Soon the Gospel Tabernacle formed its own missionary society, opened a ''Home for Faith and Physical Healing,'' and founded the New York Missionary Training College (now Nyack College and Alliance Theological Seminary).

The heart of Simpson's theological convictions was summarized in ''the Fourfold Gospel," which emphasized Christ's essential roles as "Saviour, Sanctifier, Healer, and Coming King." This emphasis was clearly expounded through the regular services of the Gospel Tabernacle and was given substance by Simpson's sizable personal commitment to evangelism, the higher Christian life, and missions.

In 1887, Simpson started the "Christian Alliance," an ecumenical effort to involve believers in benevolence activities related to evangelism, and the "Evangelical Missionary Alliance," a group supporting foreign missions. Ten years later, the two alliances combined their efforts to establish a new denomination, the Christian and Missionary Alliance (CMA).

Simpson was a pioneer in the Bible college movement. As American evangelicals moved into the twentieth century, his example in founding the New York Missionary Training College was emulated many times over. Simpson was also a prodigious and influential author, producing such works as *The Gospel of Healing* (1885), *Christ in the Bible* (26 vols., 1888–1929), *The Holy Spirit* (2 vols., 1895), and *The Four-Fold Gospel* (1888). Possessing a keen appreciation of the power of music as a significant part of Christian ministry, Simpson also wrote many hymns, some of which have become well-known among evangelicals like "Jesus Only," "Yesterday, Today, Forever," and "What Will You Do With Jesus?"

The last twenty years of Simpson's life were preoccupied with the organization and consolidation of the CMA. Simpson wanted the CMA to act as a bridge in American evangelicalism through which Christians could be introduced to the fullness of the fourfold gospel. Simpson and the CMA did serve that important role, although it greatly grieved Simpson when the Holiness and deeper life movements began to divide over the use of the "sign gifts" of the Holy Spirit in the Pentecostal revival of the early twentieth century. Although Simpson believed in a baptism of the Holy Spirit subsequent to conversion, he concluded that speaking in tongues was not an essential mark of the baptism. By taking this stand, Simpson established himself and the CMA as characteristic representatives of the American Holiness movement in the twentieth century.

*Bibliography*

A. *The Gospel of Healing* (New York: Alliance, 1885); *The Four-Fold Gospel* (New York: Word, Work and World, 1888); *Christ in the Bible*, 26 vols. (New York: Word, Work and World, 1888–1929); *The Holy Spirit*, 2 vols. (New York: Christian Alliance, 1895).

B. *ACSL* 260–61; *DCA* 1087; *TDCB* 349–50; A. E. Thompson, *The Life of A. B. Simpson* (Brooklyn, N.Y.: Christian Alliance, 1920).

**SUNDAY, WILLIAM ASHLEY (BILLY)** (19 November 1862, Ames, IA–6 November 1935, Chicago, IL). *Education*: Evanston Academy. *Career*: Professional baseball player, 1883–91; assistant secretary, religion department, Chicago YMCA, 1891–93; administrative assistant to J. Wilbur Chapman, 1893–95; revivalist, 1895–1935.

Billy Sunday, probably the best known American revivalist at the beginning of the twentieth century, was born to a poor farming family in rural Iowa. Sunday's father died while serving in the Union army, less than two months after Sunday's birth. In 1874, after years of struggle, Sunday's mother was forced to place Sunday and one of his two older brothers in an orphanage. Because of his difficult homelife, Sunday received only a rudimentary formal education and little religious training.

By the late 1870s, Sunday was on his own, taking odd jobs to support himself. He was a fine athlete, however, and after distinguishing himself on a number of local Iowa baseball teams, he signed a professional contract with the Chicago White Stockings in 1883. In his eight-year career he also played with Pittsburgh and Philadelphia. Less than three years after moving to Chicago, Sunday converted to Christianity at the city's Pacific Garden Rescue Mission. Some claimed that Sunday embraced Christianity to impress Nell Thompson, the pious daughter of a prominent Chicago businessman. If this was the reason, then Sunday succeeded in his aim, for Thompson and Sunday married in 1888.

But further change was brewing in Sunday's life. In 1891 he left baseball to work for the Chicago YMCA. At the ''Y,'' Sunday distributed tracts, arranged prayer meetings, kept the office in order, and taught classes. Through his religious work, Sunday met *J. Wilbur Chapman, a prominent Presbyterian revivalist of the 1890s. Seeing a good deal of promise in Sunday, Chapman taught him the intricacies of organized evangelism. Serving as an advance man for Chapman, Sunday was responsible for handling the myriad details that had to be dealt with prior to Chapman's arrival in any given city. In addition to learning about revivalism, Sunday also built a network of clerical contacts around the Midwest that served him well at a later time.

Following a three-year stint with Chapman, Sunday set out on his own. After leading his first revival in Garner, Iowa, in 1896, Sunday had his evangelistic organization (which for many years consisted of only himself and his wife) off and running. Laboring in small towns as an itinerant preacher, Sunday was licensed by the Presbyterian church in 1898 and ordained to the ministry in 1903. Even more crucially, he developed a flamboyant homiletic style that made him famous. Utilizing every manner of theatrics and even acrobatics drawn from his athletic career, Sunday carved out a niche for himself in the annals of American evangelicalism.

As Sunday's fame grew, he held revival campaigns in larger cities, and by 1910, he was a national celebrity. Building upon the knowledge gleaned from Chapman, Sunday, with the assistance of song leader Homer Rodeheaver, refined the art of revivalism to a science. During World War I, Sunday was America's most popular preacher. Although he never associated himself with the nascent fundamentalist movement within American Protestantism, Sunday employed a rhetoric that suggested one in sympathy with the cause of the evangelical conservatives. Unabashedly patriotic, Sunday preached intensely moralistic sermons, challenging his hearers to "walk the sawdust trail" or come forward to make a decision for Christ. Yet Sunday defied simplistic characterization. He favored women's rights, reached out to black Americans, and campaigned long and hard for the passage of Prohibition at the end of the war. Among his friends, Sunday counted the irascible H. L. Mencken, certainly no friend of fundamentalism.

Although he probably preached to more people and counted more conversions in his services than any other revivalist up to that time, Sunday's career began a long period of decline in the 1920s. His credibility was questioned after a number of books that he claimed to author were revealed to have been written by ghostwriters. There was also the growing perception that Sunday had unduly prospered through his revivals. The man from modest means was listed as a millionaire by Dun and Bradstreet in 1920.

At a time when much of America was becoming more urbanized and sophisticated, Sunday was increasingly seen as the most prominent representative of an evangelistic style—loud, forceful, simplistic—that had seen its best days pass away. For the last fifteen years of his life, he continued to hold revivals, but primarily in the South and rural Midwest. He suffered one heart attack in 1933 and another, fatal one in 1935. Although he left behind a mixed legacy, it is incontestable that Sunday stood in a long line of prominent revivalists who changed the fabric of American religious and social life.

*Bibliography*

A. *Wonderful, and Other Sermons* (Grand Rapids, Mich.: Zondervan, 1940).

B. *DARB* 530–31; *DCA* 1145–46; *PTR* 338–40; *TSAPR* 410–17; Homer Rodeheaver, *Twenty Years with Billy Sunday* (Nashville: Cokesbury, 1936); William G. McLoughlin, *Billy Sunday Was His Real Name* (Chicago: University of Chicago Press, 1955); Lyle Dorsett, *Billy Sunday and the Redemption of Urban America* (Grand Rapids, Mich.: Eerdmans, 1991).

# T

**TORREY, REUBEN A.** (28 January 1856, Hoboken, NJ–26 October 1928, Biltmore, NC). *Education*: A.B., Yale University, 1875; B.D., Yale Divinity School, 1878; Universities of Leipzig and Erlangen (Germany), 1882–83. *Career*: Congregationalist pastor, 1878–1882, 1883–89, 1894–1906, 1915–24; superintendent, Chicago Training Institute (later Moody Bible Institute), 1889–

1908; revivalist, 1902–1911; dean, Bible Institute of Los Angeles (BIOLA), 1912–24.

Reuben A. Torrey was an important transitional figure between nineteenth-century American evangelicalism and twentieth-century fundamentalism. Torrey was raised in the Congregationalist faith and educated in New York and at Yale University and Divinity School in Connecticut. Upon receiving his divinity degree in 1878, he was ordained as a Congregationalist pastor and served a church in Garretsville, Ohio. After pastoring for four years, Torrey studied at the Universities of Leipzig and Erlangen during 1882–83. At the conclusion of this brief international sojourn, Torrey returned to the pastorate. From 1883 to 1889, he ministered to two congregations in Minneapolis, Minnesota.

By 1889, his friendship with *Dwight L. Moody led Torrey to Chicago. When he became the superintendent of the Chicago Training Institute (1889) and the pastor of Chicago Avenue Church (1894), Torrey seemed the heir apparent to Moody's expansive ministry. Clearly, Torrey's activities as a pastor, evangelist, and educator established him as, arguably, Moody's most significant successor.

For the first dozen years of the twentieth century, in addition to his regular duties, Torrey preached to more than 15 million people in the United States, Canada, Great Britain, Germany, France, Australia, New Zealand, India, China, and Japan as part of a worldwide revival ministry. It was a common pattern throughout Torrey's professional life to combine pastoral duties with an administrative position at an institute of Christian higher education. Torrey took on these dual roles in Chicago from 1894 to 1906 and duplicated the pattern in Los Angeles when he became dean of BIOLA (1912–24) and pastor of the Church of the Open Door (1915–24). In 1924 Torrey became an itinerant evangelist and guest lecturer at Moody Bible Institute, roles he maintained until his death in 1928.

A good deal of Torrey's prominence in American evangelicalism issued from his indefatigable nature. In addition to his demanding schedule as a pastor, evangelist, and educational administrator, Torrey authored or edited forty books and countless pamphlets dealing with significant doctrines of the Christian faith. He also served as the primary editor for the journals of Moody Bible Institute (*The Institute Tie*) and BIOLA (*The King's Business*). Although he wrote important works that defended the inerrancy of Scripture, championed the "higher life," and evidenced a dispensational premillennial world-view, Torrey's best remembered literary endeavor is his involvement in the publication of *The Fundamentals* series (1910–15). As the third editor of the project, Torrey was responsible for completing this wide-ranging and highly influential set of booklets.

In the later years of his life, Torrey was a leading figure in the militantly antimodernist faction of American evangelicalism. This leadership role was evidenced by his involvement in the founding of the World's Christian Fundamentals Association (WCFA) after World War I. He was also responsible for establishing the influence of evangelicalism in southern California during the first quarter of the twentieth century through his work at BIOLA and the Church of the Open Door, institutions that contributed to the religious development of such significant twentieth-century evangelicals as *Charles Fuller and *Dawson Trotman.

*Bibliography*

A. *How to Succeed in the Christian Life* (Chicago: Moody, 1900); *The Person and Work of the Holy Spirit* (New York: Fleming H. Revell, 1910); *Fundamental Doctrines of the Christian Faith* (New York: Fleming H. Revell, 1918).

B. *DARB* 556–58; *DCA* 1180–81; *RLA* 477; *TDCB* 391; Robert Harkness, *Reuben Archer Torrey: The Man, His Message* (Chicago: Bible Institute Colportage Association, 1929); Roger Martin, *R. A. Torrey: Apostle of Certainty* (Murfreesboro, Tenn.: Sword of the Lord Publishers, 1976).

**TROTMAN, DAWSON** (25 March 1906, Bisbee, AZ–18 June 1956, Schroon Lake, NY). *Education*: Los Angeles Baptist Theological Seminary, 1928; Bible Institute of Los Angeles, 1929. *Career*: Minister and conference organizer, 1928–33; founder and president, Navigators, 1933–56.

Dawson Trotman was born in Arizona, but grew up in California. As a youth he was not much interested in religion, but became a Christian at the age of twenty while attending Lomita Presbyterian Church. Gregarious and goal-driven, Trotman immediately immersed himself in the various discipleship ministries offered by his church. Foremost among these ministries was the Fishermen Club, an organization that Trotman eventually came to lead. By the early 1930s, Trotman had dedicated himself to the career of an evangelist. Working primarily with youth, the centerpiece of his discipleship regiment was the memorization of Scripture.

In 1933, Trotman began discipling sailors in Long Beach through a home Bible study. He and his like-minded ministerial friends started calling themselves "Navigators." Throughout the mid– and late 1930s the Navigators developed into a full-fledged organization involving several hundred people. During World War II, over 1,000 Navigators led discipleship ministries on U.S. naval ships and stations. The Navigators were legally incorporated in 1944 with Trotman as their first president. After the war, the Navigators made a concerted effort to expand their efforts to American college campuses. With their emphasis on routinized spirituality—Bible memorization, prayer, personal evangelism, and conservative lifestyle, the Navigators became an influential force within the growing evangelical parachurch movement. Trotman personified all the emphases of the Navigators through his leadership in the organization.

In 1951, Trotman was asked to join *Billy Graham's revival crusade as a consultant. Graham had long been concerned with the lack of success many evangelists had in "follow up"—that is, keeping new converts growing in their faith. Impressed with the Navigators' technique, Graham asked Trotman to develop what became known as ''B Rations,'' a systematic devotional approach to assist new Christians in keeping faithful. The ''B Rations'' have long served as the core of the Billy Graham Evangelical Association's method of ''follow up.''

Trotman's friendship with Graham opened many doors for the Navigators. The organization grew sufficiently to open a large campus in Colorado Springs, Colorado, in 1953. Despite having a wife and children, Trotman continued to travel extensively as a popular evangelist and speaker for the Navigators until he drowned while attempting to rescue a swimmer at Schroon Lake in upstate New York in June 1956.

*Bibliography*

A. *Introductory Bible Study* (Colorado Springs, Colo.: NavPress, 1951); *Follow-up: Conserving the Fruits of Evangelism* (Colorado Springs, Colo.: The Navigators, 1952).

B. *DCA* 1186; *MTC* 165–68; *TDCB* 394; Betty Skinner, *Daws: The Story of Dawson Trotman* (Grand Rapids, Mich.: Zondervan, 1974).

**TRUMBULL, CHARLES G.** (20 January 1872, Hartford, CT–13 January 1941, Pasadena, CA). *Education*: A.B., Yale University, 1893. *Career*: Assistant editor, *Sunday School Times*, 1893–1903; editor, *Sunday School Times*, 1903–41; Bible conference teacher and organizer, 1910–24.

Along with his friend and associate, *Robert C. McQuilkin Jr., Charles Trumbull was the best-known exponent of the American ''higher'' or ''victorious life'' movement at the beginning of the twentieth century. Much more than McQuilkin, however, Trumbull served as the chief publicist for the movement through his editorship of the highly influential *Sunday School Times*.

For the Trumbull clan, the *Sunday School Times* was something akin to a family business. Charles's father, Henry, became editor of the periodical in 1875 and held the position until his death in 1903. Ten years earlier, upon the graduation of Charles from Yale, the son went to work for the father as assistant editor. A staunch supporter of the Sunday school movement in nineteenth-century American evangelicalism, Henry imparted a similar passion to Charles and also an appreciation of the power of the printed word to achieve the ends of religious education. After Henry's death, Charles assumed the editorship of the *Sunday School Times*, a post he would occupy for nearly forty years. A thorough-going journalist, the younger Trumbull also wrote religious articles for the *Toronto Globe*, the *Philadelphia Evening Public Ledger*, and a host of other newspapers.

Raised in the Congregationalist church, Trumbull found his entire religious orientation changed in 1910 when he was exposed to the victorious life teachings of the Keswick movement. Foremost among these teachings was that the Christian believers filled with the Holy Spirit could have victory over sin and power for service. For the rest of his life, Trumbull labored to advance the victorious life doctrines, both through the organization of conferences all around the United States and, more significantly, through the *Sunday School Times*.

By the late 1920s and 1930s, Trumbull was a significant leader of American fundamentalism. With McQuilkin, Trumbull was responsible for institutionalizing the victorious life movement in America with the establishment of a permanent conference center at Keswick Grove, New Jersey, in 1924. Despite his many accomplishments in journalism and religious education, Trumbull is best remembered for his role in popularizing the victorious life doctrines and integrating them into ''mainstream'' American evangelicalism.

*Bibliography*

A. *Men Who Dared: Studies in Old Testament Manhood* (New York: YMCA, 1907); *Taking Men Alive* (London: Religious Tract Society, 1907); *Victory in Christ* (Philadelphia: Sunday School Times, 1959.

B. *DCA* 1186–87; *TDCB* 396; Philip E. Howard, *Charles Gallaudet Trumbull, Apostle of the Victorious Life* (Philadelphia: Sunday School Times, 1944).

# W

**WALLIS, JAMES (JIM)** (4 June 1948, Redford Township, MI—). *Education*: B.S., Michigan State University, 1970; Trinity Evangelical Divinity School. *Career*: Editor, *Sojourners*, 1971—; pastor, 1975—.

While it is true that late twentieth-century American evangelicals tended to be overwhelmingly conservative in their approach to social issues, exceptions to the rule exist. In the case of evangelicalism, the small but vocal left was represented well by Jim Wallis, editor of *Sojourners* magazine and pastor of Sojourners Fellowship.

Wallis was born and raised in suburban Detroit, Michigan. His parents were members of a conservative Plymouth Brethren congregation, and Wallis grew up in an unremarkable fashion. As he came to maturity in the mid–1960s, however, Wallis was changed by the social dislocations that were erupting all around him. At age thirteen, he dropped out of the Boy Scouts just short of attaining Eagle Scout rank, quit organized sports, and grew his hair long. Wallis expressed rebellion against all authority figures, including the religious ones that had previously held sway over his life.

The years 1967–68 left a particularly indelible mark on Wallis's soul. The riots that engulfed Detroit in the summer of 1967 brought Wallis face-to-face with the reality of racism in America. Additionally, the assassinations of *Martin Luther King Jr. and Robert F. Kennedy in 1968 deepened the hopelessness that Wallis felt about the problems facing mid–twentieth-century America. Wallis came to believe that traditional evangelical Christian responses to difficult social problems were particularly inadequate.

While attending college at Michigan State, Wallis became an active leader in the student protests against the Vietnam War. Yet, unlike many of his generation, Wallis turned back to the New Testament for hope. There he found a Jesus who was an outspoken advocate for the poor, the outcasts, and the dispossessed. In the Sermon on the Mount, Wallis discovered a bold mandate for social activism. Unlike the conservative and inert Christianity of traditional American evangelicalism, the gospel that Wallis discovered for the first time was a prophetic one that reverberated with truth and justice. This was a gospel that Wallis could embrace, but one that would put him at odds with most of the evangelical community.

Captured by a new sense of purpose, Wallis attended Trinity Evangelical Divinity School from 1970 to 1972 to learn more about the Bible. While at Trinity, he found a handful of like-minded people who were interested in recovering the prophetic tradition and applying it to the problems of modern America. Despite resistance from Trinity's administration and many of their fellow students, Wallis and his associates developed a philosophy of radical Christian discipleship. Their ideas crystallized into a publication called the *Post-American*, which was published for the first time in the summer of 1971.

By 1975, Wallis and twenty others relocated to Washington, D.C. The community adopted the name Sojourners Fellowship. The *Post-American*, which was circulating tens of thousands of issues by the mid–1970s, was renamed *Sojourners*. Through the mouthpiece of *Sojourners*, Wallis consistently articulated a Christian perspective on such issues as poverty, racism, human rights, world hunger, population growth, and nuclear proliferation that was on the liberal side of the political spectrum. For his efforts, Wallis won the disdain of such politically conservative evangelicals as *Jerry Falwell, who once likened Wallis to Adolf Hitler.

Many years after beginning a venture that originated in a burst of youthful idealism, Wallis remained committed to the cause. Practicing an ascetic personal lifestyle that includes writing, travel, and speaking engagements, Wallis continued to exert a benevolent pastoral leadership over the Sojourners Fellowship. In addition to the editorial opportunities afforded him by *Sojourners* magazine, Wallis has produced several book-length manifestos that articulate his social philosophy. Among these books are *Agenda for Biblical People* (1976), *The Call to Conversion* (1981), and *The Soul of Politics* (1994).

*Bibliography*

A. *Agenda for Biblical People* (San Francisco: Harper & Row, 1976); *Revive Us Again: A Sojourners Story* (Nashville: Abingdon, 1983); *The Soul of Politics* (New York: New Press, 1994).

B. *CANR* 50: 451–52; *TSAPR* 431–36; Richard Quebedeaux, *The Young Evangelicals* (New York: Harper & Row, 1974).

**WARFIELD, BENJAMIN BRECKINRIDGE** (5 November 1851, Grasmere, KY–16 February 1921, Princeton, NJ). *Education*: B.A., College of New Jersey (Princeton), 1871; B.D., Princeton Theological Seminary, 1876; University of Leipzig. *Career*: Pastor, 1877–78; seminary professor, 1878–1921.

Possibly the most significant of conservative Reformed theologians from Princeton Seminary, Warfield was born just outside Lexington, Kentucky, in 1851. His mother's family was politically prominent and Warfield's father was a well-to-do gentleman farmer who served as a Union officer in the Civil War. Warfield was raised on the family estate, privately tutored, and possessed of a keen interest in mathematics and science as a boy.

Warfield's entrance into the College of New Jersey (later Princeton University) in 1868 coincided with the arrival of the college's new president, James McCosh, from Ireland. McCosh was a conservative Presbyterian and an exponent of Scottish Common Sense philosophy. So favorably impressed with McCosh was Warfield that he began to think seriously about entering the ministry. After a year-long tour of Europe and work on the family farm, Warfield entered Princeton Seminary in 1873. At the seminary, Warfield was particularly influenced by an aging, but still active, *Charles Hodge. Warfield's later theological achievements were largely an extension of the earlier efforts of his great mentor, Hodge.

After graduating from Princeton Seminary in 1876, Warfield was married, then spent a year studying at Leipzig in Germany. While in Europe, Warfield's wife was seriously traumatized and rendered a semi-invalid for the rest of her life. Largely because of this, Warfield adopted the persona of a scholarly recluse. Eschewing Hodge's career of a church statesman, Warfield rarely ventured far from his ailing wife's side.

Briefly serving as a supply minister at Baltimore's First Presbyterian Church (1877–78), Warfield began his long teaching career at Western Seminary in Allegheny, Pennsylvania, in 1878. Nine years later, upon the death of Archibald Alexander Hodge, Warfield moved to Princeton where he became professor of didactic and polemic theology. Over the course of thirty-four years, Warfield taught more than 2,700 students and influenced thousands more through his many books and essays and his editorship of the *Princeton Review* (1890–1903).

Warfield was the most widely known confessional Calvinist scholar of his era. In an age when theological liberalism was in ascendancy, Warfield championed an authoritative, inerrant Bible, and a strict Calvinistic theology. Warfield was the most effective evangelical apologist of the late nineteenth century, and he used logic, the great patristic writers, and the Reformation theologians to rebut liberalism with a measure of clarity and force. Warfield's most durable legacy to modern American evangelicalism was his concept of Scriptural inerrancy. First put before the public in his 1881 article, "Inspiration" (with A. A.

Hodge), Warfield argued that the Christian Scriptures in the original autographs were absolutely without error. He also maintained that God providentially preserved the veracity of the Bible through the ages so as to render copyist errors as incidental.

The cornerstone of Warfield's theology and his apologetic methodology was Calvinism. He viewed Calvinism as the purest form of Christianity and consistently followed the great French Reformation scholar in a thoroughly Augustinian view of God, sin, and salvation through Christ. Despite Warfield's own reclusive tendencies, his Calvinistic interpretation of Christianity demanded that the believer contest the faith on a worldwide stage that was the panoramic arena of God's redemptive activity. Warfield's strict Calvinism led him to spar not only with theological liberalism, but also with those groups that he labelled collectively as "perfectionism" (i.e., the Finneyites, the Higher Life movement, and the Oneida community). A key to understanding Warfield's apologetics was his strict adherence to Scottish Common Sense realism, which supposed that non-Christian naturalists could be persuaded to embrace the truths of faith through an inductive examination of the facts. Warfield was intrigued, dumbfounded, and ultimately unconvinced by the school of Dutch Calvinists led by Abraham Kuyper who argued that rationalistic apologetics were much less persuasive in the modern era.

Warfield continues to exert a sizable influence on American evangelicalism. Most of his works remain in print, and his concept of inerrancy is embraced by the most conservative of the subculture. Yet Warfield himself was no fundamentalist. His low view of dispensationalism, his confessional Calvinism, and his willingness to accept nonnaturalistic evolution placed Warfield at odds with the growing fundamentalist movement of his later life. In their selective appropriation of Warfield's theology, some modern fundamentalists do the Princetonian a great disservice and trivialize the sublime sophistication of his thinking.

*Bibliography*

A. *Works*, 10 vols., edited by Ethelbert Warfield (New York: Oxford University Press, 1927–32).

B. *DARB* 581–83; *DCA* 1234–35; *HET* 26–39; Mark A. Noll, *The Princeton Theology 1812–1921* (Grand Rapids, Mich.: Baker, 1983); W. Andrew Hoffecker, "Benjamin B. Warfield," in *Reformed Theology in America*, edited by David F. Wells (Grand Rapids, Mich.: Baker, 1989), pp. 65–91.

**WILLARD, FRANCES** (28 September 1839, Churchville, NY–18 February 1898, New York, NY). *Education*: Milwaukee Female College; A.B., Northwestern Female College (Evanston, IL), 1859. *Career*: Teacher, 1860–67; author, 1864–93; college administrator, 1871–74; president, Woman's Christian Temperance Union, 1879–98.

Perhaps the most prominent evangelical feminist in America before 1900, Frances Willard was New England–born who greatly prized education. In the

1820s, Willard's family devoted themselves to evangelical Christianity after coming under the influence of Charles G. Finney's revivals in western New York. In order to participate in the abolitionist cause and to attend Finney's college, the Willards moved to Oberlin, Ohio, for a time in the 1840s before settling in Wisconsin.

An avid reader who loved the outdoors, Willard resolved to acquire a college education and become a teacher. While attending college, she experienced a religious conversion and joined the Methodist Episcopal church. Settling first in Evanston, Illinois, for a time, Willard later taught school from 1860 to 1867 in Pittsburgh, Pennsylvania, and Lima, New York. After returning from a two-year tour of Europe, she actively participated in the temperance movement. By 1879, Willard was elected president of the Woman's Christian Temperance Union (WCTU), a position she retained until her death in 1898. Willard was responsible for making the WCTU a much more activist organization than it had been previously. With Willard at its helm, the WCTU vigorously supported the cause of women's suffrage and helped to organize the Prohibition Party in 1882. Working for no salary for a number of years, Willard largely gave up the teaching profession to become a full-time activist and temperance crusader.

A staunch advocate of ''home protection,'' Willard viewed the consumption of alcohol as the greatest threat to American society in the late nineteenth century. As both public speaker and author, she toured America, Britain, and Europe throughout the 1880s and 1890s. Endorsing a ''do everything'' policy to stop the manufacture, sale, and use of alcoholic beverages, Willard believed that the temperance movement's best weapon in the cause would be to win the vote for women. Her efforts made the WCTU the largest and most influential women's organization in America before the twentieth century.

*Bibliography*

A. *Woman and Temperance* (Hartford, Conn.: Park Publishing, 1883); *Woman in the Pulpit* (Boston: D. Lothrop, 1888); *Glimpses of Fifty Years* (Boston: G. M. Smith, 1889).

B. *DARB* 607–8; *DCA* 1256–57; *RLA* 504–5; Anna A. Gordon, *The Beautiful Life of Frances E. Willard* (Chicago: Woman's Temperance Publishing, 1898); Ruth Bordin, *Frances Willard: A Biography* (Chapel Hill, N.C.: University of North Carolina Press, 1986).

**WIMBER, JOHN** (25 February 1934, Peoria, IL–17 November 1997, Santa Ana, CA). *Education*: Fuller Theological Seminary. *Career*: Professional musician, 1952–71; pastor, 1970–75, 1977–94; staff member and instructor, School of World Mission, Fuller Theological Seminary, 1971–85; founder and international director, Association of Vineyard Churches, 1977–97.

Perhaps the most dynamic force in late twentieth-century American evangelicalism was ''third-wave Christianity,'' that is, Pentecostalism and all its various permutations. It is difficult to imagine a more prominent practitioner of this third-wave than John Wimber. Born in Illinois during the Great Depression,

Wimber moved to California with his mother after his father left the family. An early interest in music developed into a career even before Wimber married at age twenty-two.

As a young man, Wimber grew up ignorant of conventional religion. It was not until he had a dramatic "mystical" experience in 1963 that Wimber had any awareness of things spiritual. Ironically, his conversion experience occurred in the midst of Wimber's greatest commercial success as a musician, while he was working as a keyboard player for the Righteous Brothers. Slowly, the Christian faith tightened its grip on Wimber's life. By 1970, he was ordained by the California Yearly Meeting of Friends (Quakers). At the same time, he gave up the life of a professional musician to serve as co-pastor (1970–75) of the Yorba Linda Friends Church.

In 1971, while studying at Fuller Seminary's School of World Mission, Wimber met the school's director, C. Peter Wagner. Wagner promptly hired Wimber to serve on the staff of the school as a church growth consultant. By the mid–1970s, Wimber had grown restless with his own spiritual life, which seemed to be devoid of dynamism and power. Increasingly intrigued by the world Pentecostal movement, which was a topic of interest for Wagner and the School of World Mission, Wimber adopted a more charismatic approach to his faith that was contingent upon a vivid awareness of the supernatural and the modern deployment of spiritual "sign gifts." This new emphasis did not go over well with Wimber's Yorba Linda congregation, and he and forty others left in 1977 to form what eventually was known as the Anaheim Vineyard. With additional ties to Calvary Chapel in Costa Mesa, California, the Anaheim Vineyard grew to several thousand members by the early 1980s.

Wimber became internationally known in the world Pentecostal movement after he began to advocate "power religion." For Wimber, power religion meant the revelation of God to an individual or group through spiritual gifts or other supernatural phenomena. Through the publication of two key books, *Power Evangelism* (1986) and *Power Healing* (1987), Wimber's teachings were the catalyst that fueled the expansion of the Vineyard movement from one congregation in Anaheim to over 700 in the United States and abroad by 1998.

Despite his unpretentious demeanor, Wimber was a controversial figure in late twentieth-century evangelicalism. His emphasis on an extravagant form of worship that claimed to result in the routine answering of prayers, healing of diseases, and even raising of the dead offended many. Yet even as his own failing health slowed him in the early 1990s, Wimber was the clear patriarch of hundreds of like-minded Vineyard churches all around the world.

*Bibliography*

A. (with Kevin Springer) *Power Evangelism* (San Francisco: Harper & Row Publishers, 1986); (with Kevin Springer) *Power Healing* (San Franciso: Harper & Row, 1987).

B. *DPCM* 889; *TDCB* 428; Tim Stafford, "Testing the Wine from John Wimber's Vineyard," *CT* 30:11 (8 August 1986): 17–22; Donald Kammer, "The Perplexing Power of John Wimber's Power Encounters," *Churchman* 106:1 (1992): 45–64; "John Wimber [obituary]," *Daily Telegraph* [London] (25 November 1997): 25.

**WOODWORTH-ETTER, MARIA B.** (22 July 1844, Lisbon, OH–16 September 1924, Indianapolis, IN). *Education*: Marginal. *Career*: Housewife, 1862–80; preacher and healing revivalist, 1880–1924.

The dynamic revival ministry of Maria Woodworth-Etter was not only significant in its own right, but it formed a model for later female evangelists like *Aimee Semple McPherson and *Kathryn Kuhlman. Some details of her life are sketchy. However, it is clear that Woodworth-Etter was born as Maria Underwood into a large rural Ohio family in 1844. Her father died when Maria was twelve years old, and as one of eight children, she quit school to help support her family financially. At age thirteen, she experienced a powerful religious conversion during a revival meeting held in the local Disciples of Christ congregation.

Shortly after her conversion, Maria was baptized and felt a strong call to become a minister. The fulfillment of this calling was delayed for years as Maria married P. H. Woodworth and settled down to give birth to six children. Maria's first marriage was filled with hardship and tragedy. Five of her six children died from various illnesses, and her husband was unfaithful to her. The couple divorced in 1891.

After renewing her spiritual commitment in a Friends revival service in 1879, Woodworth-Etter began to preach. Aligning herself first with the United Brethren and then the Churches of God (Winebrenner) in 1884, she experienced considerable success in her local revival meetings and dedicated herself to the life of a full-time itinerant minister. By 1885, Woodworth-Etter's services attracted thousands of attendees and drew the notice of even the *New York Times*. Scenes reminiscent of the old-time frontier revivals were common, with not only conversions, but also healings, trances, and visions often reported.

Woodworth-Etter was a transitional figure between the established denominations of late nineteenth-century American evangelicalism that utilized spiritual gifts on an informal and occasional basis and the separate Pentecostal groups that formed in the twentieth century. An ecumenist who opened her services to people of all faiths, Woodworth-Etter also insisted that her meetings be racially integrated, even in the South. Increasingly, Woodworth-Etter adopted the vocabulary of the Pentecostals, urging her hearers to seek both conversion and a subsequent baptism of the Holy Spirit.

As a successful and independent female revivalist, Woodworth-Etter modeled a lifestyle that comported well with the growing women's rights movement. In the midst of her busy schedule, she married Samuel Etter in 1902, but her deepest attachment was to her calling as a revivalist. She remained faithful to that calling without hesitation, preaching revival services almost up to her death in 1924.

*Bibliography*

A. *Life and Experience of Maria B. Woodworth* (Dayton, Ohio: The Author, 1885); *Signs and Wonders Wrought in the Ministry for Forty Years* (Indianapolis, Ind.: The Author, 1916).

B. *DARB* 625–26; *DCA* 1270–71; *DPCM* 900–901; *RLA* 512; Wayne B. Warner, *The Woman Evangelist: The Life and Times of Maria B. Woodworth-Etter* (Metuchen, N.J.: Scarecrow, 1986).

# Index

Main entries for biographical profiles are cited in **boldface**

## ABOUT THE AUTHORS

**ROBERT H. KRAPOHL** is University Librarian at Trinity International University. He has contributed articles to *Popular Religious Magazines of the United States* (Greenwood, 1995) and the *American National Biography* (1998).

**CHARLES H. LIPPY** is the Leroy A. Martin Distinguished Professor of Religious Studies at the University of Tennessee. He is the author of a number of previous books including *Modern American Popular Religion* (Greenwood, 1996), *Being Religious, American Style* (Greenwood, 1994), *Twentieth-Century Shapers of American Popular Religion* (Greenwood, 1989), *Religious Periodicals of the United States* (Greenwood, 1986) and co-editor of *Popular Religious Magazines of the United States* (Greenwood, 1995).